Why Is There No Labor Party in the United States?

PRINCETON STUDIES IN AMERICAN POLITICS

HISTORICAL, INTERNATIONAL, AND
COMPARATIVE PERSPECTIVES

Series Editors

Ira Katznelson, Martin Shefter, and Theda Skocpol

A list of titles in this series appears at the back of the book.

Why Is There No Labor Party in the United States?

Robin Archer

PRINCETON UNIVERSITY PRESS

PRINCETON AND OXFORD

Published by Princeton University Press, 41 William Street, Princeton,
New Jersey 08540

In the United Kingdom: Princeton University Press, 3 Market Place, Woodstock,
Oxfordshire OX20 1SY

Library of Congress Cataloging-in-Publication Data

Archer, Robin.
  Why is there no labor party in the United States? / Robin Archer.
    p. cm.—(Princeton studies in American politics)
  Includes bibliographical references and index.
  ISBN 978-0-691-12701-9 (hardcover : alk.paper)
  1. Labor unions—United States—Political activity—History.   2. Labor unions—Australia—
Political activity—History.   3. Political sociology.   I. Title.
  HD6510.A73 2007
  322′.20973—dc22   2007020626

British Library Cataloging-in-Publication Data is available

This book has been composed in Goudy Typeface

Printed on acid-free paper. ∞

press.princeton.edu

Printed in the United States of America

10   9   8   7   6   5   4   3   2

To my Pa

Richard Douglas Archer

Contents

List of Figures

List of Tables

Notes and sources for the tables can be found in the appendix, p. 245.

List of Abbreviations

AFL	American Federation of Labor
AF	*American Federationist*
APA	American Protective Association
ARU	American Railway Union
ASL	Australian Socialist League
ASU	Amalgamated Shearers' Union of Australasia
AWU	Australian Workers' Union
AW	*Australian Workman*
CIO	Congress of Industrial Organizations
CN	*Coming Nation*
CSJ	*Coast Seamen's Journal*
CT	*Chicago Times*
FOTLU	Federation of Organized Trades and Labor Unions
ICTUC	Intercolonial Trades Union Congress (from 1889: Intercolonial Trades and Labor Union Congress)
IWA	International Workingmen's Association
LEL	Labor Electoral League
LFM	*Locomotive Firemen's Magazine*
ML	Mitchell Library, Sydney
MP	Member of Parliament
NLT	*National Labor Tribune*
NSW	New South Wales
NYT	*New York Times*
QSU	Queensland Shearers' Union
QLU	Queensland Labourers' Union
RT	*Railway Times*
SLP	Socialist Labor Party
SMH	*Sydney Morning Herald*
THC	Trades Hall Council
TLA	*Trades and Labour Advocate*
TLC	Trades and Labour Council
ULP	United Labor Party
UMW	United Mine Workers of America
UMWJ	*United Mine Workers' Journal*

Acknowledgments

COMPARATIVE HISTORICAL ANALYSIS requires scholars to immerse themselves in a vast array of primary and secondary sources about the politics, society, and culture of different countries or cases. This process of gathering evidence and testing arguments is, in some ways, quite a solitary task. Yet it is dependent, of course, on the earlier efforts of numerous scholars, and it would scarcely be possible without the help of a great many institutions and people.

Much of this book was written while I was the Fellow in Politics at Corpus Christi College, Oxford. I am very grateful to the college, and my colleagues there, for providing me with sabbatical leave, the time to think, and a marvelous working environment. I am also grateful to University College, Oxford, and especially to Ngaire Woods, with whom I shared the teaching of a generation of politics students, as well as to my new home at the LSE, with its rich tradition of engagement with the labor movement and social reform. In addition, I would like to thank the Arts and Humanities Research Board of England and Wales for funding teaching replacement under its research leave scheme, and the Beit and Mellon Funds at Oxford University for providing financial support.

Long periods in both the United States and Australia have been indispensable, and a number of universities have made this possible by welcoming me as a Visiting Fellow. The Department of Political Science at Columbia University has twice offered an invaluable base from which to conduct research and debate my ideas. The Department of History at Princeton University provided me with a stimulating, generous and collegial environment in which to work. And the Departments of Industrial Relations and Government at Sydney University graciously provided a similar base in Australia. In addition, some of the ideas in this book, especially those about religion, were initially developed during periods at the Jawaharlal Nehru University and Delhi University in India. I am particularly grateful to Ira Katznelson at Columbia, Robert Darnton and Sean Wilentz at Princeton, Russell Lansbury at Sydney, and Rajeev Bhargava and Neera Chandhoke in India for making these stays possible.

I have also had a great deal of assistance from some fine libraries and archives. Along with the libraries of Columbia, Princeton, and Sydney Universities, these have included the New York Public Library, the Bancroft Library at Berkeley, the Library of the University of New South Wales, the Melbourne University Archives, and the Library of Rhodes House at Oxford University, as well as the Tamiment Institute at New York University, with its excellent labor history collections, and the Mitchell Library in Sydney, with its irreplaceable holdings on Australian history.

Acknowledgments are also due to a number of publishers. Some of Chapter 4 first appeared in "Unions, Courts, and Parties" in *Politics and Society*, vol 26, no 3, September 1998, an earlier version of Chapter 5 appeared in "Can Repression Help to Create Labor Parties?" in *Studies in American Political Development*, vol 15, no 2, Fall 2001, and part of Chapter 6 appeared in "American Liberalism and Labour Politics" in *Labour History*, no. 92, May, 2007.

I have been particularly fortunate to benefit from the comments and expertise of many colleagues and friends. Michael Freeden, Gary Gerstle, Jim Hagan, Vicky Hattam, Seth Moglen, Richard Oestreicher, Sanjay Seth, and Kim Voss read and commented on various chapters, and I have had helpful discussions about particular points with many other people, including Judy Brett, Alan Brinkley, Rick Halpern, Richard Jensen, Ross McKibbin, Greg Patmore, Michael Quinlan, Bruce Scates, Adam Steinhouse, and Charles Tilly. I have also benefited from feedback in seminars at various universities and institutes in the United States, Australia, Britain, Germany, Austria, and India, and I would like to thank all those who helped arrange these discussions as well as those who participated in them.

In addition, Daniel Rodgers has been particularly generous in sharing his deep understanding of American political culture, Gary Marks brought an expert eye to the entire manuscript, and Chuck Myers patiently shepherded the book to publication. I would especially like to thank Ira Katznelson. He has taken an enduring interest in this project from the outset and has been a wonderful help throughout.

Completing a project like this would be difficult without friends and loved ones, and no one has been more intimately involved with it than Elisabeth Koegler. She has lived and breathed the issues that lie at the heart of this book for more than a decade, amidst all the obligations of her own highly demanding work. Elisabeth has helped make this work possible in some very fundamental ways, and she has been an absolutely rock-solid source of encouragement and support.

I am also very grateful to my parents. On one memorable occasion, they both spent the day with me in the Mitchell Library helping estimate the number of sheep shearers in particular electoral districts and the social composition of nineteenth-century police forces. My Ma, in particular, has been a tremendous help in finalizing the text. She has spent countless hours reading through the entire manuscript and saved me from numerous errors, omissions, and missing references. For this, and for so much else, I cannot thank her enough.

I have acknowledged my father in everything that I have published. These have not been casual or formal acknowledgments. For my father has read and commented on each and every piece. He read every chapter of this book too.

And he was always ready to help in numerous other ways—from finding a rare out-of-print volume, to tracking down the records of a long-forgotten parliamentary debate. I am very sad that he is not here to see this book in print.

My father was an eminent aeronautical engineer. He greatly enjoyed his field of teaching and research, but he also had an extraordinary breadth of knowledge about history, politics, and much else besides. He believed in the importance of learning and teaching, in the value of understanding different times and places, and in the craftsmanship of mental and manual work. He has always been a very special source of encouragement for me. But his contribution is far deeper than anything I can say or write.

Introduction

LABOR-BASED POLITICAL PARTIES have been an important electoral force in every advanced capitalist country. Every one, that is, except the United States. Elsewhere, these parties were established in the late nineteenth or early twentieth centuries, and, ever since then, there has been a great debate about why the American experience was different.

The late nineteenth century was also a critical period in the United States. Indeed, in the early 1890s, amid a wave of social and political unrest, the American union movement came close to establishing a labor party. At its annual convention in 1894, the American Federation of Labor debated a "Political Programme" that sought to commit the unions to independent political action. The Programme had been referred back to the Federation's affiliates by the previous year's convention, and many delegates were mandated to vote in favor of it. In fact, some unionists had already begun to build party organizations in a number of key cities and states. But AFL President Samuel Gompers and his allies were strongly opposed to the Programme, and with the help of some procedural machinations, they prevailed on the Federation to reject any foray into party politics. However, it was more than just procedural machinations that produced this result. For just one year later, delegates voted overwhelmingly for a resolution that declared that "party politics whether democratic, republican, socialistic, prohibition, or any other, should have no place in the convention of the A.F. of L."[1] Moreover, subsequent conventions repeatedly confirmed the AFL's opposition to any form of partisan political action (whether through the establishment of a labor party or through involvement in one of the existing parties). In spite of the efforts of a substantial minority of unionists, the rejection of labor party politics became firmly entrenched.

The failure to establish a labor party had fundamental and wide-ranging consequences, not only for the political development of the United States, but also for its subsequent social and economic development. If a labor party had been established, it is highly likely that business interests would have had less influence over public policy, that income and wealth would have been more equally distributed, that trade unions would have been stronger, and that a more comprehensive welfare state would have developed. This last point can be made with particular confidence. After more than two decades of comparative research, it is now widely accepted that there is an important causal link between the influence wielded by labor-based parties, and the extent, type, and timing of welfare state development. Indeed, this "working-class power resources" or "social democratic" model of welfare state development has become a kind of orthodoxy. Like all orthodoxies, it has its challengers, and its supporters accept the need for various revisions and modifications. But even after all due weight has been given to a range of additional factors, there is good evidence that the political influence of organized labor is a key part of the explanation for some of the most important variations in social and economic policy.[2]

The failure to establish a labor party also lies at the heart of a wider debate about "American Exceptionalism," and it provides an important vantage point from which to assess what, if anything, is distinctive about American politics and society. Some scholars now rail at the very mention of this debate, but there can be little doubt about its longstanding centrality in American intellectual life, or about its enduring influence over broader popular perceptions of the United States. Understanding what, if anything, is distinctive about American politics and society, and the nature of its institutional and ideological traditions, is, of course, a matter of great interest to Americans. But it need hardly be said that it is also of far more than local significance. Given the power the United States has to influence the rest of the world, the task of understanding the forces that shape its development is a matter of global importance.

In this book, I want to address a series of nested questions. At the center of the book is the title question about why there is no labor party in the United States. But the book also addresses both a more specific and a more general question. The more specific question concerns the decision that the American Federation of Labor took at its crucial convention in 1894, as well as the failure of various state-level initiatives at that time. The more general question concerns the longstanding effort to identify distinctive characteristics of American politics and society, and to offer an account of their origins and effects. Some of these questions will be familiar. But the approach to them will be novel, and it will, I hope, produce some unexpected answers.

The standard explanations for why there is no labor party rely on comparison with Europe. They point to various characteristics of the United States, like its high standard of living, its well-entrenched democracy, and its culture of liberal individualism. Explanations based on factors like these have become a kind of received wisdom, and they frequently appear in public commentaries, college textbooks, and scholarly debates.

But are they correct? In this book, I want to take a fresh look at these explanations. I propose to reassess them, and develop a new explanation, not by comparing the New World with the Old, but rather by pursuing a "most similar" comparison of one New World country with another. In particular, I propose to compare the United States with Australia. Many of the conventional explanations look much weaker when the United States is compared with Australia. For Australia had most of the same New World characteristics as the United States, and yet it produced one of the earliest and most electorally powerful labor parties in the world.

Comparison with Australia is especially appealing because Australian unions established their party in the early 1890s, just when American unions came closest to establishing a party of their own. In each case, discussions about the establishment of a labor party took place against a similar backdrop of events. In the early 1890s, both countries suffered from the worst depression of the nineteenth century, and a series of major industrial confrontations took place in which governments sided with employers and left the unions completely defeated. But in each case, the response of the union movement was different. After some initial vacillation, the American Federation of Labor rejected any form of party political involvement, and opted to remain committed to "pure-and-simple" unionism. The Australian unions, on the other hand, put aside their longstanding apolitical traditions and decided to launch a party.

In order to clear the way for the systematic comparison that I envisage, I will begin by addressing a number of preliminary issues. First, I will clarify what I mean by a "labor-based party." Second, I will outline the comparative explanatory strategy I propose to pursue. Third, I will consider a number of possible objections to my approach. Fourth, I will provide a brief account of the history of the labor movement in the United States and Australia in the late nineteenth century. Fifth, I will consider whether unionists in these countries were aware of each other's activities. And finally, I will offer a short guide to the topics discussed in the chapters that follow.

LABOR-BASED PARTIES

The question about why there is no labor-based party in the United States needs to be distinguished from a number of related questions with which it is often confused. These include, most famously, the question about why there is no socialist party in the United States. But they also include questions about why there was not a more class-conscious labor movement, and why there was not a revolutionary labor-based party. In the extensive literature on these questions, the distinctions between them have often become blurred. I will frequently draw on the insights and causal hypotheses that emerge from this literature, but my focus will remain on the question about why there is no labor-based party. After all, it is only in this respect that the experience of the United States is distinctive. There were other advanced capitalist countries that did not establish a socialist party, or that did not have a very class-conscious labor movement, and there were many countries without significant revolutionary parties.

The labor-based parties that emerged in the late nineteenth and early twentieth centuries took different forms in different countries. Some were social democratic parties (like in Germany), some were socialist parties (like in France), and some were labor parties (like in Britain). But all of these parties saw themselves, and were seen by others, as members of a common political family. Indeed, they established an international organization—the Second International—that formalized and institutionalized this family relationship. And ever since they emerged, they have been regularly treated this way in numerous academic studies, newspaper commentaries, and public debates. What all these parties had in common was the uniquely privileged position they attributed to workers. Parties can be defined and categorized in terms of their ideology and identity, their organizational structures, and the social groups they represent. Labor-based parties attributed a uniquely privileged position to workers in all three of these respects, and it was this combination of characteristics that set them apart. In some cases, this privileged position was an informal and de facto one. More often, it was codified and formally entrenched.

The ideological pronouncements of labor-based parties made the pursuit of workers' interests the central focus of their objectives, and the symbols they adopted made their self-image as the party of workers the centerpiece of their identity. In most cases, their ideology was a form of socialism. But this was not invariably so. In Britain and Australia, labor-based parties were initially established without a socialist objective, and in France, Italy, and Spain, anarchist currents were influential (Bartolini, 2000, 66–87). Labor-based parties were distinctive because of their labor-based ideology, not because of the radicalism, socialism, or leftism of that ideology. The organizational structure of labor-based parties gave a uniquely privileged place to trade unions. This manifested itself through the interpenetration of party and union organizations and the cross-linkages between them. These cross-linkages usually took the form of interlocking organizational ties, although they were occasionally more informal and contingent (Bartolini, 2000, 241–262). In some cases, the party was predominant; in some cases, the unions; and in some cases, neither. But in all cases, labor-based parties were distinctive because of the central importance attributed to their organizational ties with unions, and the priority these were given over relationships with other organized social groups.[3] Workers were also the most important source of support for labor-based parties. Lack of polling data before the second half of the twentieth century makes it difficult to be precise, but there is a great deal of evidence that the predominance of working-class support was a common feature of these parties (Geary, 1981, 94–97). Labor-based parties might also appeal to other social groups (like small farmers or middle-class intellectuals), but workers remained the single most important group they represented.

The kind of labor-based party that was most likely to emerge in the United States was a labor party. This was the kind of labor-based party that emerged in all the other English-speaking countries. And although some socialists persisted with other models, this was the kind of party that the main proponents of labor-based party politics sought to establish in the United States in the late nineteenth century. It is thus also the kind of party with which I will be principally concerned.

Labor parties were established as the political wings of union movements. Unlike both social democratic and socialist parties, where Marxism and other socialist or revolutionary doctrines had an important influence, they were initially motivated more by pragmatic objectives than doctrinal ones. But labor parties themselves could take a number of more specific forms. In both the United States and Australia, the kind of labor party that union leaders sought to establish in the early 1890s was a labor-populist party, in which unions aimed to build an alliance with small farmers. In the United States, the main proponents of labor party politics sought to achieve their goal by building on and remolding the People's parties that had recently been formed by farmers' organizations. The attempt in 1894 to turn the People's party in Chicago into a vehicle for labor party politics was meant to provide a model of how this could be done.

This attempt highlights the fact that there were two ways in which a labor party might have emerged. It might have emerged as the result of a national decision by the American Federation of Labor. But it might also have emerged as a result of the successful establishment of a model party in one or more key states: a model that was then emulated and spread to others. It will be important to keep both these possibilities in mind. In order to do this, I will have to pay careful attention, not only to the national decisions of the union movement, but also to the decisions of union leaders in states like Illinois.

The claim that there was no labor-based party in the United States requires some qualification. After all, a number of socialist and labor parties did appear in the late nineteenth and early twentieth centuries. But these organizations never attained the significance that labor-based parties attained in the rest of the advanced capitalist world. All statements about party systems require some criteria against which to determine the significance of individual parties. Just as we can meaningfully characterize the United States as having a two-party system, despite the existence of numerous minor parties, so, too, the claim that there has not been a labor-based party captures an important truth. This claim is really shorthand for the claim that there has not been an enduring electorally viable labor-based party. The most important labor parties—the United Labor parties in 1886, the labor-populist parties in 1894, and the farmer-labor parties after the First World War—were briefly able to garner significant electoral support, but they were not able to endure. The most important socialist parties—the Socialist Labor party in the late nineteenth century, and the Socialist party in the early twentieth—were enduring organizations, but despite a handful of local successes, they were not electorally significant. In other advanced capitalist countries, labor-based parties almost always became one of the main contenders for government office: backed by the support of between a third and a half of the electorate (Sassoon, 1996, 42–43). Even where they did not command this level of support, they always developed into important political actors. At the very least, they acquired "coalition" or "blackmail" potential (Sartori, 1976). Socialist parties in the United States met none of these criteria.

But what about the Democratic party? A third-party insurgency was not the only way in which a labor-based party might have emerged in the United States. In principle, such a party might also have resulted from an attempt to change the nature of one of the two main established parties. An early national move to align the unions with the Democratic party began in 1906 (Greene, 1998, and Sarasohn, 1989). But the most important move in this direction occurred during the New Deal, when, following the rise of the Congress of Industrial Organizations (the CIO), much of the union movement set aside its rejection of partisan politics. It is sometimes said that the resulting realignment turned the Democrats into a quasi-social democratic party. But while workers and their unions did become an important part of the New Deal coalition, they did not acquire a uniquely privileged position within the Democratic party.[4] In terms of ideology and identity, New Deal liberalism was built around an eclectic mix of messages and measures, in which working-class interests had to jostle for position with the interests of other social and economic groups. In terms of organizational structure, unions and their Political Action Committees had to compete with the continuing importance of urban machines associated with ethnic and religious organizations, as well as with deeply entrenched southern conservative power brokers. In terms of party support, workers became one of at least four important electoral bases: taking their place alongside various ethno-religious groups, southern whites, and African-Americans. The Democratic party may have developed a quasi-social democratic tincture, but it did not become a labor-based party. The fact remains that the United States has never had an enduring electorally significant party of that sort.

Explaining by Comparing

A century or more of debate has thrown up a great many factors that may potentially help explain why there is no labor party in the United States. How are we to decide which, if any, of these factors really did have a significant effect? Natural scientists deal with this kind of problem by conducting experiments to control for the effects of different potential agents. Experiments enable them to isolate the effect of one agent by holding the others constant. But the application of this method is rarely possible for those seeking to explain social outcomes. We cannot just go back to 1894 and run that year again with, say, a new electoral system, or a different set of cultural values. Social scientists and historians have to rely instead on the comparison of cases that have actually occurred in the "laboratory" of history.

One way to try to control for the effects of different factors under these circumstances is to undertake the comparison of closely matched or "most similar" cases. This method of comparison attempts to approximate some of the advantages of experimental control by making the best possible use of the real-world cases that history has provided. It does this by comparing cases that have been carefully selected to ensure that, while they differ with respect to the outcome to be explained, they are as similar as possible in other respects. The aim is to control for as many potential explanatory factors as possible in order to identify the critical factor (or small cluster of factors) that differentiates the cases, and that might thus have helped cause the outcome in question.[5]

A most-similar comparison of the United States and Australia lies at the heart of this book. The basic justification for undertaking this comparison is methodological. It rests on the claim that systematic comparison with Australia makes it possible to use the most-similar method to maximum effect.

But comparison between the United States and Australia is not the only comparison that plays an important role in the book. One reason for this is that comparison with Europe, though it is perhaps less clearly visible, appears in the background throughout. Studies based on this conventional comparison provide most of the principle initial explanatory hypotheses that I will be seeking to test and reassess. Additional hypotheses suggested by comparison with Australia will also be examined, but it is the conventional comparison with Europe that underpins the study by providing its starting point. Thus, the two-country comparison that lies at the heart of this work does not stand on its own. Rather it self-consciously builds on over a century of scholarship and comparative effort.

There is also a more explicit sense in which the book rests on the comparison of multiple cases. For I will regularly supplement the principle intercountry comparison with the comparison of intracountry cases. Some of these are intertemporal comparisons, such as the comparison of labor party experiments in the United States in 1894 and 1886. Others are comparisons of territorial units within the United States and Australia. In this respect, I pay particular attention to the case of Illinois, but I also consider other states, especially in the industrialized Northeast and Midwest. Within Australia, I pay particular attention to the case of New South Wales, but I also make use of the cases of Victoria, Queensland, South Australia, and other states.

The choice of comparative methods invariably involves trade-offs.[6] The best we can hope to ensure is that these trade-offs are reasonable, given the question at hand. In addition to the possibility of exercising "semi-experimental" control, the close comparison of a small number of similar cases offers some other significant advantages. This kind of comparison makes it possible to pay careful attention to detail, complexity, and the timing of developments. It helps avoid the inaccurate or trivial conclusions that can result from conceptual "stretching" or the retreat into high levels of abstraction. And it facilitates the examination of interaction effects at critical conjunctures. Furthermore—and this is especially significant—it makes it possible to complement the search for correlation with the search for causal mechanisms.

However, this kind of comparison also has some well-known limits. It may, for example, provide insufficient cases to test all the potential explanatory factors. Here, the mix of comparisons on which my argument rests, and, in particular, the ability to make use of supplementary temporal and territorial cases, helps compensate for this. Intracountry cases provide good material for additional comparisons, because they share most of the characteristics of the main country cases of which they are a part. They also make it possible to increase the number of cases without incurring the prohibitive costs of time and effort that would be required to fully characterize a number of completely new countries. Another well-known limitation of the comparison of a small number of cases concerns the difficulty of generalizing findings to other cases. Here, I will be primarily concerned with explaining developments in the United States, rather than with formulating a general theory of the emergence of labor-based party politics. Nevertheless, the fact that the book builds on the outcome of earlier comparisons with European countries goes some way towards addressing this problem.

Overall, the comparison I propose to pursue seems to offer a reasonable way of negotiating the trade-offs involved in choosing between different methods. It not only allows me to take full advantage of the most-similar method. It also enables me to take advantage of the close analysis that the comparison of a small number of cases makes possible, while retaining at least some of the advantages that come from the comparison of a larger number of cases.

In each chapter, I will consider one or more of the main potential explanatory factors. First, I will consider the extent to which each factor was present in the United States and Australia. Then, I will consider its effects. I aim to offer a nuanced and authoritative causal account (underpinned by carefully documented archival and secondary research), while at the same time retaining a clear analytical and explanatory focus.

In order to assess the extent to which each factor was present in the two countries, I need to bring together a great deal of information about the economic, social, political, and cultural characteristics of the United States and Australia in the late nineteenth century. Though simple in concept, in practice this is a difficult and labor-intensive task. So much so that one practitioner has warned that "no sane person would attempt it" (Fredrickson, 1997, 11). Undertaking this task, however, makes it possible to do two things.

First, it enables me to check whether the explanation in question rests on an accurate characterization of the United States. It may seem unnecessarily pedantic to insist on this, and I will not dwell on this point in every chapter.

But, as we will see, a number of conventional explanations rely on unduly simplistic, partial, or otherwise misleading characterizations. Indeed, some rely on characterizations that are incompatible with each other.

Second, and most importantly, it enables me to cast doubt on the significance of a great many potential explanatory factors by demonstrating that these factors were present in both the United States and Australia. Indeed, as we will see, many of the best known and most widely accepted explanations appeal to factors of this sort. It is possible that one or more of these factors may still retain some explanatory significance because of their interaction with other factors, and I will need to bear this in mind when considering their effects.[7] But provisionally at least, though only provisionally, I can set them to one side.

In order to assess the effects of each of the main potential explanatory factors, I need to identify whether or not there is a plausible causal mechanism that links the factor in question to the failure to establish a labor party.

A causal mechanism consists of a chain of causes and effects that connects a given explanatory factor to a given outcome, and accounts for how the causal impact of the factor is exerted. Identifying a plausible causal mechanism involves (a) breaking down the relationship between the factor and the outcome into a series of component relationships with one or more intermediate factors, and (b) showing that each of the factors in this series—both the initial explanatory factor and the various intermediate factors—have well-known or widely accepted effects, which, when taken together, help generate the outcome. As its name suggests, the concept of a causal mechanism is based on an analogy. It appeals to the idea that we should be able to specify the metaphorical cogs and levers that connect causes to outcomes.[8]

I will typically attempt to identify these "cogs and levers" by considering the way in which each potential explanatory factor altered the opportunities and constraints facing labor leaders or workers. I will try to offer a more fine-grained account of the causes and effects at work, by showing how various factors both shaped the interests and identities of key individuals and groups, and generated incentives that altered their choices and actions.

Comparison with Australia helps identify plausible causal mechanisms in the United States. Sometimes it contributes to establishing the plausibility of an already identified causal mechanism. Sometimes it points to a more plausible alternative. And sometimes it draws attention to the importance of particular intervening factors. But comparison with Australia is not, of course, the only way to identify plausible causal mechanisms, and where a potential explanatory factor is absent, it is less likely to help.

Where a factor is common to the United States and Australia, examining its effects helps determine whether the earlier provisional finding that it is not causally significant should be confirmed. A simple most-similar comparison of the extent to which a factor is present can cast doubt on its causal significance.

But only after the additional examination of its effects is it warranted to reach the stronger conclusion that it can be ruled out. Comparison with Australia not only helps confirm that many factors can indeed be ruled out. It also helps show that some of these factors had effects in the United States that were quite different from those that are usually ascribed to them. In this way, it challenges some of the most entrenched conventional wisdom about American political development, and provides a vantage point that has the potential to alter the way we view the United States as a whole.

Where a factor differentiates the United States from Australia, examining its effects helps determine whether it really is causally significant, for correlation alone is insufficient to establish causation. Even if a potential explanatory factor is a distinctive characteristic of the United States, it can only be causally significant if there is a plausible causal mechanism linking it to the outcome we are seeking to explain. This stipulation enables us to distinguish between spurious or coincidental associations and real causal effects. Although comparison with Australia (supplemented by the comparison of various time-periods and states) does a better job of controlling for the effects of potential explanatory factors than comparison with Europe, it still leaves us with a number of contending explanations. There is no reason we should expect to find a mono-causal explanation. But we still need to determine which of the remaining factors really did have a significant effect. This is a problem that faces almost every attempt to use the most-similar method. Some countries, time-periods, or states are more similar than others. However, when dealing with the explanation of complex social phenomena, no cases are so similar that they enable us to rule out all bar one of the potentially relevant factors. The effort to identify plausible causal mechanisms helps surmount this problem. It enables us not only to confirm whether common factors can be excluded, but also to test which of the remaining factors really are causally significant, and to rule out those that are not.

Some Possible Objections

There are, of course, a number of possible objections to the project I propose to pursue. In this section, I want to try to preempt some of those that are most likely to be raised. Two concern comparison with Australia, one concerns the temporal focus, and another two concern the nature of the project itself.

The first objection concerns the political status of Australia. According to this objection, comparison with Australia is inappropriate, because, in the late nineteenth century, each Australian state was still a British colony. As a result, it might be thought that Australia is unable to provide a separate case with which to test explanations that derive from comparison between Europe and the United States. There is no doubt that the Australian colonies were not fully sovereign, legally independent states in the late nineteenth century. But, for my purposes, this is much less important than it might at first seem. For although the Australian states were still colonies, they were *self-governing* colonies. Not wanting a repeat of the Boston Tea Party, the British authorities in the mid-nineteenth century had sought to retain Australian loyalty (and minimize their own costs) by accepting demands for a form of self-government within the British Empire. Each colony had its own independently elected parliament and government, which not only controlled taxation, tariffs, and almost all other aspects of domestic economic and social policy, but also controlled immigration and its own police and military forces.[9] So the Australian colonies were sufficiently independent political units to make comparison with them meaningful. And this was particularly true with respect to the matters of most concern to the labor movement. In any case, when unionists established labor parties in Australia, they were certainly not emulating or importing a British institution. For the British labor party did not yet exist.[10]

The second objection concerns the choice of Australia as a most-similar case. According to this objection, while Australia may indeed provide a similar case for comparison with the United States, there are other even more similar cases on which we should focus on instead. In particular, it might be thought better to compare the United States with Canada. The establishment of a stable labor-based party in Canada in 1932 was a somewhat belated development, and it did not become one of the two main national parties.[11] Nevertheless, like other advanced capitalist countries, Canada did establish a labor-based party, and so it is eligible to be considered as a possible most-similar case. Canada undoubtedly shares some important underlying similarities with the United States, and comparison between the two has been fruitfully pursued in a number of studies, most notably those of Seymour Martin Lipset.[12]

For my purposes, however, the Australian case has two important advantages. The first stems from the fact that it not only shared many underlying similarities with the United States, but also shared many important proximate similarities because of the common circumstances that unions experienced in the two countries in the early 1890s. In part, this was simply because Australian unionists and their American counterparts were deciding whether or not to establish a labor party around the same time. The second advantage stems from the fact that Canadian unions were not independent organizations. Most were actually branches of unions in the United States, and the Canadian Trades and Labour Congress consisted almost entirely of Canadian locals of the unions that constituted the American Federation of Labor. As a result, the decisions Canadian unionists reached were heavily influenced by the decisions of their American counterparts: the very decisions we are trying to explain. Like the decisions of unionists in Illinois or other American states, the decisions of Canadian unionists can provide additional explanatory lever-age (King et al., 1994, 222). But the organizational independence of the Aus-tralian union movement makes Australia a better principal case around which to build a most-similar comparison.

The third objection concerns the decision to focus on the late nineteenth century, and especially on the early 1890s. The economic and social turmoil of the early 1890s, and the loosening of political ties that accompanied it, provided the proponents of labor party politics with particularly propitious circumstances. However, others have pointed to the importance of different periods. Some have focused on the period around 1886 (Fink, 1983, and Voss, 1993), and some on the period after 1906 (Greene, 1998, and Sarasohn, 1989), while others have focused on the New Deal realignment of the 1930s, or the decade leading up to it or just after it (Brody, 1983, and Lichtenstein, 1989). Much can be learned from these periods, and I, too, will discuss them at points. But the 1890s are especially worthy of attention for at least three reasons. This was when the American union movement as a whole gave the question of whether to establish a labor party its most sustained and serious at-tention. This was when it came closest to actually establishing such a party. And this was when the rejection of this option became firmly entrenched as settled official policy.

The fourth objection I want to consider concerns the "Why no labor party?" question itself. Proponents of this objection argue that questions that seek to explain an absence or a non-occurrence are not proper questions for historical inquiry. They complain that, instead of calling for the explanation of what actually happened, this kind of question focuses on the failure of peo-ple to act in accordance with certain theoretical predictions or presumed norms. This objection has been made in various ways. Some complain of "negative questions" and an "epistemology of absence." Others complain of "presumed norms of historical development," "deviations from an expected trajectory," and "a priori" or "essentialist" assumptions.[13] There are a number of ways to respond to this objection, but the most powerful response is a very simple one. In asking why there is no labor party in the United States I am not trying to explain an "absence" or a "non-occurrence." Rather, I am trying to explain something that *did* happen. I am trying to explain a decision that American labor leaders made in 1894, and reaffirmed repeatedly thereafter: a decision not to establish a labor party.

The objection to comparing the experience of the United States against pre-sumed international norms is often associated with a fifth objection that con-cerns the "American Exceptionalism" debate as a whole. This objection has now itself become a kind of norm, with various authors noting that the debate about American exceptionalism is in "ill repute," declaring themselves to be "against exceptionalism" and arguing that "the first thing" that comparative studies must avoid are "the ideas of norms and its corollary, exceptions."[14] It is easy to see why many writers are wary of the American exceptionalism paradigm. It can seem uncomfortably close to a misleading and self-congratulatory rhetorical posture, which often comes to the fore in American public life. The ritual incantations of politicians and journalists whenever a new president is inaugurated provide a typical example. These commentators invariably speak in awed tones about the peaceful transfer of power that is taking place, and the genius of the American system that allows it, seemingly oblivious to the fact that there are other countries that have managed this trick for generations. Some have even managed it without assassinations and civil wars.

I am sympathetic to the spirit of this objection. I, too, will reject the claim that the United States is exceptional in a great many of the ways that it is usually thought to be. Indeed, a recognition of just how similar the United States was to at least one other country lies at the heart of my entire approach. But there is no escaping the fact that some aspects of American political development have been exceptional. And the question that I am addressing—a question that lies at the heart of the traditional debate about American exceptionalism—concerns one such aspect. As the critics point out, it is wrong to assume the existence of international norms as a matter of pre-empirical commitment. But it is just as wrong to make a pre-empirical assumption that there cannot be any such norms. As a matter of fact, labor-based parties were established in all of the other advanced capitalist countries in the late nineteenth and early twentieth centuries. So, in this respect, there is an international norm, and the experience of the United States is exceptional.[15] The exceptionalism with which I will be concerned is simply a matter of observed empirical fact. It is a fact that calls for explanation.

HISTORICAL OVERVIEW

Since not all readers will be familiar with both of the two main countries that I will be comparing, I want to provide a brief overview of the development of the labor movement in each.

The United States

The labor movement first emerged in the United States in the 1820s and 1830s after some sporadic earlier activity. However, it was not until the 1850s and 1860s that stable unions were established. The printers were the first to form a durable national union organization. They were followed by other groups of skilled craft workers, especially after a revival of union activity that took place during and after the Civil War.

In the 1830s, and again in the 1860s, these unions formed Trades Assemblies or Trades and Labor Councils to coordinate their activities in major towns and cities. But it was only after the depression of 1873 to 1878 that city-based Trades Assemblies began to have a continuous existence. A number of short-lived national union organizations were also founded. But in 1881, craft unions laid the basis for a more enduring organization when they met to establish the Federation of Organized Trades and Labor Unions of the United States and Canada. This body was the direct predecessor of the American Federation of Labor, and it was relaunched with that name in 1886.

In the late nineteenth century, unskilled and semi-skilled workers also began to organize unions, especially in the mining and railroad industries. The repeated bursts of industrial action on the railroads were particularly significant because this industry lay at the heart of the American economy. The growth of organization among unskilled and semi-skilled workers was connected to the sudden rise and fall of the Knights of Labor, which organized local assemblies open to all workers. However, these were not, strictly speaking, union organizations since, with a few exceptions, non-employees could also join. The Knights, which had begun as a small secret society in 1869, experienced rapid growth in the mid-1880s. At its high point in 1886, the Knights claimed 703,000 members (up from 104,000 the previous year). But its loss of membership was just as precipitate, and within a few years it had lost most of its influence.

The rise and fall of the Knights of Labor was closely associated with the "Great Upheaval," which came to a head in 1886. In that year, there was a wave of industrial unrest (following an earlier victory for the Knights against a railroad magnate), the newly relaunched American Federation of Labor began a national campaign for an eight-hour workday, and there was an upsurge in political repression (especially following the Haymarket bombing in Chicago). In the wake of these events, United Labor parties were formed to contest elections in many cities and states, but despite some impressive results, these parties did not survive long.

In the early 1890s, a number of developments combined to produce a new and unprecedented period of social conflict. Industrywide unions of coal miners and railroad workers were established. A series of major strikes took place, in which governments deployed military forces to intervene on behalf of the employers, and in which the unions were completely defeated. Populist farmers established People's parties, which made gains in a number of states and appealed directly for the support of organized labor. And the economy sank into the worst depression of the nineteenth century.

It was in this context that the AFL came close to establishing a labor party. The 1893 AFL Convention voted to consider a "Political Programme." The Programme was modeled on the recently adopted program of the British Independent Labour party, and it called on the unions to establish the capacity for independent political action. The Programme was referred back to the AFL's constituents, who were asked to instruct their delegates on whether or not to vote in favor of its final adoption at the following year's convention. Many unions had long been opposed to the establishment of a labor party, but a marked change in attitude began to appear.

The favorable reception the Programme was receiving gave a boost to those unionists who supported the idea of forming an alliance with small farmers, and saw the People's parties as providing a vehicle that offered the best hope for establishing a new labor-based party. The supporters of this labor-populist strategy were especially strong in Chicago. First there, and then in a number of other cities and states, they sponsored conferences that saw the People's party adopt most of the policy planks set out in the AFL's putative Programme, and then began to put their plan into practice.

As the AFL's 1894 convention approached, it seemed that a majority of delegates may have been mandated to support the Political Programme. However, AFL President Gompers and his allies remained firmly opposed to it, and using a series of arguments and procedural maneuvers, they managed to prevail. Supporters of the Programme retaliated by replacing Gompers as president. But at its 1895 convention, the AFL reconfirmed its position of opposition to the establishment of a labor party, and re-elected Gompers as president. Thereafter, both the position and the president became firmly entrenched.

With the AFL's position decided, the People's party fell under the control of its more conservative wing. The party then dropped most of labor's demands, and placed its main emphasis on the demand for the free coinage of silver, which was offered as an all-purpose panacea. These free-silver populists then merged with the Democratic party, and in the elections of 1896, a major electoral realignment occurred, which enabled the Republican party to dominate national politics for most of the period until the New Deal.

Australia

The first unions were formed in Australia in the 1830s and 1840s, but it was only after the turmoil of the gold rushes in the early 1850s that stable union organizations began to emerge. These were craft unions formed by skilled workers, and a number of them, especially in the building trades, had important early successes with the achievement of an eight-hour workday.

Largely as a result of cooperation in the eight-hours movement, unions began to establish Trades and Labour Councils (TLCs) to coordinate their activities in each of the colonial capitals, beginning with the Melbourne Trades Hall Council in 1856, and the Sydney TLC in 1871. From 1879, the unions also began to coordinate their affairs on an Australia-wide basis at meetings of the Intercolonial Trades Union Congress. However, it was the TLCs that remained the main focus for cooperation.

In the 1870s, and even more so in the 1880s, the union movement expanded beyond its original craft base to include large numbers of unskilled and semi-skilled workers. This "new unionism" grew rapidly on the water-front, on the railways, in mining, and in the pastoral industry. The formation of the Amalgamated Shearers' Union (ASU) in 1886 was a particularly important development because of the pivotal role that the export of wool played in the Australian economy.

In the early 1890s, just before the onset of the same great depression that afflicted the United States, these unions became involved in a series of full-scale showdowns with employers. The first of these, the so-called "Maritime strike," had two immediate sources: the attempt by ship owners to force the Marine Officers' Association to disaffiliate from the Melbourne Trades Hall Council, and the attempt by shearers to establish a closed shop. The dispute spread throughout the economy as miners refused to supply coal to the ship owners, and waterside workers refused to handle non-union wool. The strike lasted for two months and was followed by further struggles in the mining and pastoral industries. In each case, governments sided with employers and deployed armed forces—and in each case the unions were defeated.

It was against this background that labor parties were formed in a number of colonies. Although they had occasionally experimented with the election of individual candidates, most unions had long been opposed to the idea of entering the electoral arena. This now began to change. The first labor party was established in NSW. In early 1890, before the Maritime strike had started, the NSW TLC had drawn up a plan to run candidates in the general election that was due the following year. However, most affiliates remained unenthusiastic about the plan, and it was only in 1891, after the defeat of the Maritime strike, that they agreed to establish a labor party. Similar proposals were being formulated in Queensland and South Australia, and the 1891 Intercolonial Trades Union Congress endorsed all these initiatives and called on other colonies to emulate them.

In its first electoral test in 1891, the new NSW Labor party—the Labor Electoral League—won 22 percent of the votes and 25 percent of the seats, leaving it holding the balance of power between the established parliamentary groupings of Free Traders and Protectionists. However, the party was soon dogged by defections and divisions. This experience led it to adopt a stricter system of party discipline, which a number of its parliamentarians refused to accept. In the 1894 elections, the party's vote was reduced to 16 percent, and it won only 11 percent of the available seats, but the more disciplined party structure ultimately proved a more solid base on which to build support. In 1895, the party regained the balance of power, and in 1904 it became the official opposition.

Labor parties also began to build support in other colonies, and, after its establishment in 1901, in the new federal parliament. By 1899, the Queensland Labor party was able to form a minority government—the world's first labor government—although it only lasted for six days. In 1904, and again in

1908–1909, Labor was able to form longer-lasting minority governments in the federal parliament, and the success of the party forced its two main opponents to merge. By 1910, both federally and in NSW, the Labor party was able to win power with a majority in its own right.

Mutual Awareness

Developments in the United States and Australia did not take place in complete isolation from each other. The labor press covered news of developments in other countries, and labor leaders referred to these developments to an extent that readers may now find surprising. In both the United States and Australia, news of developments in Europe, and especially Britain, received particular attention. But labor leaders in these two countries were also aware of each other's major developments.

Australian labor leaders learned about developments in the United States through reports of major American industrial and political conflicts in the Australian labor and daily press, by reading American labor journals, and in some cases through individual travel and contacts. When, in far outback New South Wales, a leader of the Broken Hill Miners' strike obliquely urged fellow unionists to take direct action against strikebreakers by acting "how strikers acted in America," he clearly felt able to assume that his audience was aware of recent confrontations there.[16]

Given the size and growing importance of the United States, not just economically but also as a political and ideological model, it is not surprising that Australian unionists followed developments there with interest. Many Australians looked at the United States as another English-speaking settler society that offered an image of their own future. The influence of developments in the American labor movement was part of a wider cultural influence of the United States as a whole. Indeed, in certain respects, the influence of these developments rivaled that of developments in Britain.

The very name of the Australian Labor Party provides some evidence of this influence. In Australia, the word *labor* is spelled "labour" with a "u" as in Britain. But, to this day, in the name of the Australian Labor Party, it is spelled without one, as in the United States. The exact reason for this is unclear, and the spelling varied in the early years of the party's existence. But it seems to have reflected the influence of American experiments in the minds of some of the party's main backers.[17]

Labor leaders in the United States were also able to follow developments in Australia through reports in the labor press, and, again, in some cases through individual contacts. But the influence of Australian developments on the labor movement in the United States was not as broad or deep as the influence of American developments in Australia. Outside the Pacific Coast, it was largely limited to leaders, activists, and intellectuals. In the minds of these leaders, Australia was notable because it was seen as a similar society in which the labor movement was unusually strong, well-developed, and advanced. AFL President Gompers, for example, claimed that he sometimes read the Melbourne papers in order to follow the success of the movement for an eight-hour workday. He told the 1892 AFL convention that "comparatively speaking" unions in Australia are "the most extensive, general, and perfected." And during the debate over the Political Programme in 1894, he published a letter from the President of the Melbourne Trades and Labour Council that gave details of the number of labor members in the various Australian parliaments.[18]

The most detailed source of information about the Australian labor movement in the early 1890s was the *Coast Seamen's Journal*. This highly professional and well-edited publication was the official organ of the Sailors' Union of the Pacific. Once a month it published "Our Australian Letter", which often appeared on its front cover, while on other weeks it frequently carried a lengthy column of "Australian News." The letter, which was written by the Secretary of the Seamen's Union in Sydney, provided detailed information about the latest industrial and political developments affecting the Australian labor movement. The amount of information about Australia in this journal was quite exceptional. However, the journal certainly circulated beyond San Francisco and the Pacific coast. It must have been read in the Chicago head-quarters of the National Seamen's Union, and from there, it presumably reached others in Chicago—a city that was at the center of labor reform movements and labor party experiments.

The 1893 World's Fair in Chicago provided another conduit through which information about the Australian labor movement reached labor leaders in the United States. The commissioners who organized the NSW exhibit published a number of accompanying pamphlets, including one on "Social, Industrial, Political and Co-operative Associations." A wide range of American labor leaders attended the "World Labor Congress" that took place under the auspices of the Fair, and at which they discussed a number of "profoundly stimulating" reports on labor movements in Europe and the Antipodes. Henry Demarest Lloyd, the Chicago-based intellectual who helped organize these meetings, and who was at the center of the effort to establish a labor party, was certainly aware of the emergence of the Australian Labor party, which he specifically alluded to in some influential speeches. In March 1893, he began a sustained investigation of developments in Australia and New Zealand, and by 1894 he had come to see the Antipodes as providing a model for the United States.[19]

By the early twentieth century, Australia came to be seen, in both the United States and Europe, as something of a social laboratory. The consolidation of the Labor party, the introduction of arbitration courts, and the beginnings of a welfare state seemed to place Australia in the advanced guard of an international movement for social reform. And a number of social scientists and labor-oriented intellectuals studied developments there and published their findings. This interest waned after the First World War, although occasional articles continued to be published. In the mid-twentieth century, the best-known scholars of American exceptionalism were certainly aware of the importance of testing their arguments against the Australian case, and the significance of the case is sometimes briefly acknowledged in more recent comparative treatments of the American labor movement. However, despite its methodological advantages, there has never been an attempt to offer a systematic comparison of the development of labor politics in the two countries.[20]

CHAPTER SUMMARY

Each of the chapters that follow considers one or more of the main factors that may potentially help explain why there is no labor party in the United States. As Table 0.1 shows, these factors can be grouped into three loosely defined categories. However, these categories should not have too much importance ascribed to them, for many of the factors could easily be placed in more than one category. The arguments in each chapter build on those that precede it. But the chapters have also been written so that each can be read as a relatively self-contained whole by those principally interested in one particular aspect of social and political development.

TABLE 0.1.
Potential Explanatory Factors

Economic and Social Factors	Prosperity
	Union Organization
	Farmers
	Race
	Immigration
Political Factors	Early Suffrage
	Electoral System
	Federalism
	Presidentialism
	Courts
	Repression
	Party System
Ideas and Values	Social Egalitarianism
	Individual Freedom
	Religion
	Socialism

Chapter 1 considers the economic interests of workers. First, it examines the argument that the level of prosperity in the United States ensured that economic grievances were insufficient to support the establishment of a labor party. Second, it examines the impact of different types of union organization, paying special attention to the weakness of "new" unions that organized large numbers of unskilled and semi-skilled workers. And third, it examines whether it was possible for unions to facilitate a labor-populist alliance between workers and small farmers. In the process, the chapter also aims to provide important background information about workers and their organizations.

Chapter 2 considers questions of race and immigration. It examines the argument that racial consciousness and racial conflict reduced the viability of class-based movements. In particular, it examines the claim that anti-black and anti-Chinese sentiments generated divisions between workers that hindered the establishment of a labor party, both directly (by weakening its electoral viability) and indirectly (by making it more difficult to organize mass industrywide unions). The chapter also considers the conflicts and changing attitudes that accompanied the growth of immigration from southern and eastern Europe in the late nineteenth century. It examines the claim that the racialization of hostility towards these immigrants strengthened intraclass divisions between skilled and unskilled workers and further undermined the prospects for the establishment of a labor party.

Chapter 3 considers some basic institutional features of the American political system. First, it examines the argument that the early removal of property qualifications and the introduction of manhood suffrage for whites removed the kind of class-based political grievance that a labor party needed in order to mobilize support. Second, it examines the argument that the electoral system reinforced the position of the two main existing parties and made it extremely difficult for any third party to gain legislative seats. Third, it examines the argument that federalism hampered the emergence of a labor party by dispersing political authority among different political units and by multiplying the number of elections the party would have to contest. And fourth, it examines the argument that presidentialism, and the two-party reinforcing effects of presidential elections, generated incentives that undermined the independent political strategy many labor leaders hoped to pursue.

Chapter 4 considers the role of the courts. In the late nineteenth century, unions in the United States experienced a wave of intense judicial hostility. The chapter examines the argument that this led unions to conclude that it was either futile or foolish to engage in electoral politics. According to this argument, unions reached this conclusion because judicial review gave the courts the final say on the political decisions that mattered most to them, and because the courts were largely immune to external political influence. The chapter also summarizes the evolution of labor law and traces the development of union attitudes to politics. It highlights the fact that these attitudes varied along more than one dimension.

Chapter 5 considers police and military intervention, as well as the overall impact of repression. There are two conventional theses that see repression as having had an important impact. According to the soft repression thesis, there was so little repression in the United States that unions did not have sufficient incentive to engage in political action, while according to the hard repression thesis, there was so much repression that unions were cowed into adopting an apolitical stance. This chapter examines which, if either, of these arguments is right. The chapter also discusses the development of police and military forces, and provides an account of the main strikes that unions experienced in the early 1890s.

Chapter 6 considers liberal ideas and the weakness of feudal traditions. First, it examines the argument that the prevalence of the idea of social egalitarianism—an egalitarianism, not of economic resources, but of social status—minimized or eliminated the status-based grievances and class consciousness that might otherwise have made it possible to build support for a labor party. Second, it examines the argument that the prevalence of the idea of individual freedom delegitimized the interventionist political goals of the labor movement, and underpinned a sense of American identity that was inimical to these goals. The chapter considers both how labor leaders interpreted these ideas, and whether their interpretations were likely to seem plausible to ordinary workers. In assessing the plausibility of these interpretations, it considers the social behavior of capitalists and other elites, the involvement of the state in economic development, the "mateship" ethos, the influence of the "New Liberalism," and the growth of industrial concentrations and monopolies.

Chapter 7 considers religion. It examines the extent of religious involvement, the nature of religious beliefs and practices (including the level of support for different denominations and the strength of evangelicalism and revivalism), the attitudes of the Protestant and Catholic clergy, and the response of labor leaders to these attitudes. The chapter pays special attention to the relationship between religion and the party system. It examines the political salience of religious sectarianism in the late nineteenth century, and considers conflicts over temperance, education, and organized anti-Catholicism. In particular, it examines the argument that religious sectarianism fostered intense Democratic and Republican loyalties among ordinary workers, and that this led labor leaders to fear that union organization would be severely disrupted if they entered the electoral arena.

Chapter 8 considers left-wing factions and their reform ideologies. It examines the influence of socialists, anarchists, populists, proponents of Henry George's single tax, "nationalist" followers of Edward Bellamy, cooperative colonists, Knights of Labor, and "pure and simple" unionists. The chapter looks at the level of support for each of these schools of thought among labor leaders and activists, and considers the impact that tensions between them had on labor party experiments. The chapter also pays special attention to the influence of Marxian socialism, and the extent of factional conflict between those who were influenced by it. It examines the argument that this conflict led many labor leaders to fear that the establishment of a labor party would produce an outbreak of socialist sectarianism that could destroy the unions themselves.

The conclusion draws together the main findings of the book. It emphasizes that these findings rule out many of the best-known conventional explanations for the fate of labor party politics, and it suggests that some of the factors to which these explanations appeal had effects that were very different from those that are usually attributed to them. It then sets out which factors really do help explain why there is no labor party in the United States, and examines the interaction between them. Finally, it considers the consequences of these findings for the wider debate about the character of American politics and society.

CHAPTER 1

Workers

THE STANDARD ACCOUNT of the rise of labor politics is an economic one. According to this account, labor parties emerged in the late nineteenth and early twentieth centuries because of the development of industrial capitalism. This had produced a class of workers who both shared significant economic interests and grievances, and had the capacity to force their grievances to be addressed. Since the United States was certainly a prime example of the growth of industrial capitalism, some writers have focused on more specific features of the American economy, and the class relations to which it gave rise, in order to try to explain why no labor party was established there. In this chapter, I want to consider two well-known versions of this kind of explanation. The first concerns the effects of economic prosperity. The second concerns the effects of different types of union organization. I will then turn to a third question that arises specifically in the context of comparison with Australia. This concerns the capacity of unions to facilitate an alliance between workers and small farmers.

PROSPERITY

One of the most frequently cited explanations for why there is no labor party in the United States rests on the claim that the economic grievances of American workers were simply not sufficiently great. According to this explanation, the enormous capacity of the American economy to generate wealth produced a society in which enough workers were sufficiently prosperous to stymie any effort to mobilize them electorally in pursuit of their economic interests. This argument is one of the great hardy perennials of the literature on American exceptionalism.

The best-known version of the argument appears in the work of Werner Sombart (1976 [1906]). Sombart gathers evidence (in Section II, Chapter 1–4) to show that the standard of living of workers in the United States was two or three times higher than it was in Germany in the late nineteenth century. In what is by far the largest and most empirically detailed section of his book, he draws on data about wages, the cost of living, and the expenditure of workers to make his case. Given the effort he puts into establishing this, Sombart's discussion of its effect (in Section II, Chapter 5) is surprisingly perfunctory. Indeed, he proposes to "leave it to specialists in dietetics . . . to uncover the connections that exist between the anti-Socialist mentality of the American worker and his predominantly meat-and-pudding diet" (Sombart, 1976, 105). Nevertheless, he claims that, given the "comfortable circumstances" of the American worker, "any dissatisfaction with the 'existing social order' finds difficulty in establishing itself," and famously goes on to conclude (I hesitate to quote the passage yet again) that in the United States "all Socialist utopias came to nothing on roast beef and apple pie" (Sombart, 1976, 105–6). Unlike Sombart, I am not principally concerned with the weakness of American *socialism*. But the question with which I am concerned—the question about why there is no *labor party*—must also address the claims of this prosperity thesis.

More recent studies have suggested some qualifications to Sombart's conclusions about relative living standards in the United States and Europe. Brown and Browne (1968, 157–74) confirm that, in the United States, average real wages were about twice as high as those in Germany, but also suggest (with qualifications) that it was only after 1900 that they drew ahead of those in Britain. Shergold (1982, 207–30) finds that average real wages *were* higher in the United States than they were in Britain, but emphasizes that wage differentials were also much higher. While skilled workers in Pittsburgh received real wages that were 50 to 100 percent greater than those of their counterparts in Birmingham or Sheffield, unskilled workers in Pittsburgh received real wages that were little different from those of their British counterparts. The comparison of living standards in different countries is fraught with difficulties (Zamagni, 1989). Nevertheless, there is little doubt that the average American worker earned higher real wages than the average European worker even in countries, like Germany and Britain, that were the most heavily industrialized.

The trouble for the prosperity thesis is that this was also true of Australia. Indeed, in the second half of the nineteenth century, Australia was the most prosperous country in the world—more prosperous even than the United States. The depression of the 1890s, which was especially severe and long in Australia, eventually changed this. But it was only at the turn of the century, after the full effects of the depression had been felt, that GDP per capita in the United States came to exceed that in Australia (see Table 1.1). This nineteenth-century prosperity fed through into the living standards of workers. Indeed, according to the conventional interpretation, Australia was a "workingman's paradise" during the long boom of the 1860s, 1870s, and 1880s. The conventional interpretation is based on the writings of contemporary observers and the pioneering statistical work of Coghlan and Mulhall.[1] It has been challenged, however, by a revisionist interpretation that emphasizes the insecure nature of much of the available employment (Lee and Fahey, 1986), and various highly unsatisfactory aspects of the quality of life (Fitzgerald, 1987). The revisionist studies correctly point out that life was harsh for many people. But this was not peculiar to Australia, and subsequent studies by economic historians support the claim that, compared

TABLE 1.1.
GDP Per Capita in the United States and Australia (in U.S. Dollars at 1985 U.S. Prices)

	1870	1880	1890	1900	1910
United States	2,254	2,929	3,115	3,757	4,559
Australia	3,123	3,772	3,923	3,532	4,586

Notes and source: see appendix

with other countries in the late nineteenth century, the standard of living in Australia was unusually high. These studies have used various measures of income, consumption, health, and wealth to capture differences between the standard of living in Australia and other countries. But they are in general agreement that in 1891 "Australia was clearly the most prosperous country in the world" (Thomas, 1995, 24). There is some debate about how much better off Australians were compared with people in Britain and the United States, but the basic fact that they were better off now seems well established.[2]

Moreover, there is no doubt that, in terms of real wages (the measure of living standards we have been considering in the case of the United States), Australian workers, both skilled and unskilled, had one of the highest standards of living in the world (Allen, 1994, 118–122). Figures 1.1 and 1.2 show real wages for building laborers and average annual earnings for manufacturing workers in three English-speaking countries. The figures confirm that, during the 1880s, real wages in Australia were substantially higher than they were in either the United States or Britain. While Australian laborers retained this lead until well into the twentieth century, Australian manufacturing workers lost it to their American counterparts by the end of the 1890s. An alternative real wage series developed by Williamson (1995, 178–80) suggests that unskilled urban laborers in the United States caught up with their Australian counterparts a little earlier, in the mid-1880s, and that they pulled ahead in the late 1890s.[3] Whichever series is used, though, it is clear that, at the beginning of the 1890s, Australian workers received real wages that were either similar to, or higher than, those in the United States, and that in both countries real wages were substantially higher than in Britain or any other European country. These conclusions are supported by the observations of visitors from Europe and the United States, like Metin (1977 [1901], 181–2) and Clark (1906, 51), who were forming their impressions at the same time as Sombart, as well as by occasional pieces of firsthand evidence from workers themselves. James H. Kelly traveled to the United States after many years working in Australia as a laborer in the mines and on the railroads. In 1891, he sent a letter to the Sydney *Bulletin*, setting out the wages and conditions that he had found for comparable work in the United States "for the benefit of

1896 Manchester
pence per day

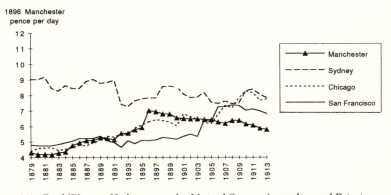

Figure 1.1. Real Wages of Laborers in the United States, Australia, and Britain
Source: Robert C. Allen, "Real Incomes in the English-Speaking World, 1879–1913," in George Grantham and Mary MacKinnon, eds., *Labour Market Evolution,* Routledge, 1994, figure 6.4, p. 120.

1896 Manchester £

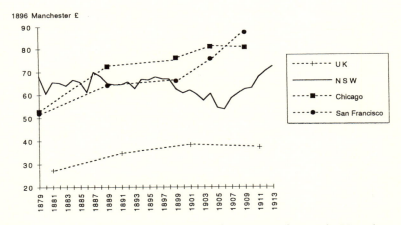

Figure 1.2. Average Annual Earnings of Manufacturing Workers in the United States, Australia, and Britain
Source: Robert C. Allen, "Real Incomes in the English-Speaking World, 1879–1913," in George Grantham and Mary MacKinnon, eds., *Labour Market Evolution,* Routledge, 1994, figure 6.5, p. 120.

my co-workers in Australia." He concluded that "for the labouring man this place is, in my opinion, a long way behind Australia."[4]

What about roast beef and apple pie? According to Sombart, the average American worker ate about twice as many eggs, three times as much flour, and four times as much sugar as his German counterpart.[5] This he put down to "a substantial indulgence in pies and puddings" (Sombart, 1976, 97–98). But

TABLE 1.2.
Annual Per Capita Consumption of Foods (in Pounds)

	NSW (Australia)		United States	
	1891	1901	1889	1899
Meat	291.5	297.2	—	142.8
Beef	176.7	166.5	—	67.8
Flour	260.0	238.2	223.9	222.2
Sugar	93.5	107.8	52.6	61.0
Potatoes	206.5	197.7	176.0	187.2

Notes and sources: see appendix

look at Table 1.2. There are no Australian figures for eggs. But with even more flour, and much more sugar being consumed in Australia, indulgence there seemed to know no bounds. As for beef, Americans ate about three times as much meat as Germans (Sombart, 1976, 97–98). But Australians ate twice as much again. This was not just a product of the consumption patterns of the wealthy. "High and low, rich and poor, all eat meat to an incredible extent" noted one keen observer (Twopeny, 1883, 63–64).[6] Reporting on the 1891 census, the NSW government statistician calculated that people in NSW consumed more energy in the form of food than anyone else in the world. Indeed, he added in a slightly worried tone, the average person ate more than twice what was necessary in order to do an average day's work (Coghlan, 1892, 841–43). With more beef and pies than was good for them, Australian workers set about forming a labor party.

In both the United States and Australia, labor leaders acknowledged that wages and living standards in their country were superior to those elsewhere in the world. The labor press in both countries was full of details of wages, working conditions, and labor struggles in Britain and other European countries. This often took the form of short one-line accounts, or paragraph summaries drawn from the labor press overseas. But it could also involve detailed discussion of the prevailing conditions in a particular industry.[7] Moreover, when explicit comparisons were made between working conditions in the United States and Australia, contributors to the labor press typically recognized that workers in each had some of the highest standards of wages and working conditions in the world. But they usually concurred that those in Australia were the highest.[8]

However, these labor leaders and journalists railed at the suggestion that, because of this relative prosperity, workers had no cause to feel aggrieved. "It was enough to make men's blood boil," said one prominent Australian union leader, adding that politicians who spoke of Australia as "the paradise of workingmen were traitors and charlatans."[9] Indeed, in both the United States and Australia, a number of union leaders viewed the prosperity that workers had achieved in their countries as a spur to organization and protest. According to an article in the *American Federationist*, "slaves and the lowest classes of workmen have not at first desired better conditions because their environments robbed them of the energy and ambition necessary to initiate and carry on a reform movement." The *Australian Workman* agreed. Commenting on the "underfed condition of the European masses," it argued that "had they been, like our people, full of meat, they would have . . . risen up in their strength and overwhelmed . . . their oppressors."[10]

Comments like these draw attention to another problem with prosperity-based explanations for the political quiescence of the American labor movement, because they force us to consider the causal mechanism that is implicit in these explanations. The effect that a given level of prosperity has on the labor movement is not only a function of actual living standards. It is also a function of the perceptions that workers have about the standards against which their circumstances should be judged. These perceptions are in turn a function of expectations that are derived from a number of comparative reference points. Sombart simply assumed that, for workers in the United States, the level of prosperity in Europe played the central role in generating these expectations.[11] But in order to properly assess the extent of the dissatisfaction that workers felt, we also need to examine other comparative reference points that might have influenced their expectations. In each case, we need to consider whether there was a gap between workers' expectations and the actual standard of living they experienced. For it was the size of this gap, rather than the standard of living itself, that determined the level of economic discontent.

Of course, conditions in Europe may have provided *one* of the comparative reference points that influenced workers' expectations, especially in the case of recent immigrants, and, given the higher living standards of the New World, this kind of comparison may indeed have dampened the dissatisfaction of these workers. However, in the early 1890s, immigrants comprised about 32 percent of the population of Australia, but only about 15 percent of the population of the United States (U.S. Census Office, 1894b, lxxix, and Vamplew, 1987, 8–9). This suggests that the dampening effect of comparison with Europe should have had less impact in the United States, and hence that the level of dissatisfaction in the United States should have been greater than in Australia.

In any case, for most workers—especially for the native-born—expectations generated within the United States would have been more important than those resulting from comparison with Europe. At least three such internal comparative reference points could have produced a large gap between the actual standard of living that workers experienced and their expectations.

First, workers may have been discontented because of the gap between their standard of living and that of those who were richer than them. Data about the average standard of living tell us nothing about the distribution of wealth, and an inequitable distribution could have been a source of grievance. The distribution of wealth was quite unequal in Australia, but it was still more un-equal in the United States (and in Britain). So this comparative reference point would have produced greater discontent in the United States than in Australia (Snooks, 1995). However, some argue that distributional discontent resulted less from differences between workers and the rich than from differ-ences among workers themselves. But the gap between high-paid and low-paid workers in Australia was also substantially less than it was in the United States (or Britain), and while this gap was getting even smaller in Australia, it was growing even larger in the United States (Pope and Withers, 1994, 258, and Markey, 1988, 46). So this, too, suggests there was greater cause for dis-content in the United States than in Australia.

Second, workers could have been discontented because of the gap between their actual standard of living and the still greater prosperity promised by the America of myth—that is, they could have been discontented because of the gap between the real and the ideal America. The ideal America took a num-ber of forms. For many labor leaders, the ideal America was a society in which each individual was able to develop all their human capacities to the full and take a full part in the life of the community. An article in the *American Feder-ation* typified this approach. It argued that "The labor question is, above all things, a moral one. The material advances for which the trade union strives are essential, in order that the wage worker may have some opportunity to de-velop his moral and intellectual attributes. He must have a fair standard of liv-ing in order to become a worthy participant of a high civilization."[12] But the ideal America could also take a more purely material and acquisitive form. In this form, it promised that everyone could get rich and become a Carnegie. Similar ideals were also present in Australia. There, too, labor leaders often emphasized that further material improvement was not an end in itself, but a prerequisite for mental and moral development.[13] And there, too, there was a widespread belief in the promise of individual material success (Davison, 1979, 11 and 13, and Fitzgerald, 1987, 103). A thorough comparison of the extent to which workers in each society partook of these ideals, would be a major task in its own right. However, there seems little doubt that their influ-ence was at least as great in the United States as in Australia, and hence that the gap between the real and the ideal, and the discontent it generated, was also at least as great.

Third, inter-temporal comparison could have made workers discontented. Discussions of inter-temporal comparison have usually revolved around the issue of social mobility, and this has typically been thought to dampen rather than foster discontent.[14] There is controversy over the extent of social mobility in both the United States and Australia during the second half of the nineteenth century. However, it seems likely that both at times offered workers greater prospects for improving their position than they would have had in Europe.[15] But I do not propose to dwell on this discussion here, because the evidence from the early 1890s suggests that workers in both countries were far more concerned about a very different inter-temporal comparison. The focus of their concern was the gap that was emerging between the prosperity of the past and the conditions of the present. Workers feared that the gains they had achieved, and which they had come to expect, were being taken from them. Labor leaders gave voice to these fears in no uncertain terms. The *Australian Workman* viewed employers' actions in the early 1890s as an "Outrageous Attempt to Degrade Australian Labour," and "to force . . . wages down to the degrading European level." American union leaders agreed. According to the Carpenters leader and AFL Vice President, P. J. McGuire, the depression was threatening "to bring American labor to the pauperized condition of the workers of foreign lands."[16]

It is easy to see why "degradation" rather than upward mobility was the focus of workers' concerns. The early 1890s saw the worst depression of the nineteenth century: worse than any that had been experienced in living memory. In Chicago, for example, unemployment in large firms reached 40 percent, and those who were lucky enough to retain employment typically received wage cuts of 10 to 20 percent.[17] When the depression of the 1890s struck, the expectations generated by the prosperity of earlier decades (augmented, as always, by the promise of still greater prosperity) tended to exacerbate workers' grievances rather than dampen them. Inter-temporal comparison thus increased the incentive for workers to mobilize in order to defend what they had come to expect as rightfully theirs (Calhoun, 1988). Looked at from this perspective, the prosperity prior to the depression of the 1890s might be thought to explain the political mobilization of Australian workers, but it is a poor explanation for the failure of American workers to adopt a similar course of action. In fact, Australian unions decided to establish a labor party in late 1890 and early 1891, just before the depression struck, while their American counterparts decided against a similar initiative in late 1894, even though they were then experiencing the full force of the depression.

So, in order to assess the level of discontent workers felt about their standard of living, we need to consider a number of comparative reference points that might have given rise to a gap between the conditions workers actually experienced and their expectations. For some workers, conditions in Europe may indeed have been a relevant reference point. For most, internal reference points, like the three we have been considering, were probably more important. However, for all four of these reference points, the conclusion is the same. Each leads to the conclusion that discontent about living standards in the United States was likely to be at least as great, and probably greater, than it was in Australia. Since the level of discontent in Australia was sufficient to facilitate the political mobilization of labor, we need to look beyond the standard of living to explain the different attitude to politics that was adopted by the labor movement in the United States.

SKILLED AND UNSKILLED WORKERS

In the 1890s, the United States (along with Britain and Germany) was one of the three most industrialized countries in the world. It had a large industrial working class and a number of huge enterprises that employed hundreds or even thousands of unskilled and semi-skilled workers. The union movement, however, was still dominated by a "closed" model of craft unionism that had its roots in an earlier artisanal form of production. In other countries—notably Britain, which had a long tradition of craft unionism similar to that in the United States—a "new unionism" emerged in the late 1880s, which organized unskilled and semi-skilled workers into large "open" industrial or general unions. However, similar unions found it difficult to establish themselves in the United States. Both the Knights of Labor and the American Railway Union briefly managed to organize hundreds of thousands of unskilled workers. But neither was able to survive for long. Indeed, only a handful of industrial unions managed to survive and flourish. The most important of these was the coal miners' union, although during the AFL's debate in 1894, its survival was also far from assured.

A number of writers have connected the absence of a labor party in the United States to the weakness of this "new unionism." I will sometimes refer to their argument as the "new unionism thesis." The proponents of this thesis draw on the British case, where the rise of the Independent Labour Party was closely connected with the rise of the new unionism (Pelling, 1965 and 1992). They argue that the new, more inclusive, unions had both the motivation and the resources to engage in independent political activity.[18] The new unions had the motivation to engage in political activity because, unlike "closed" craft unions, they could not hope to control the supply of particular skills, and consequently they had a greater need for political intervention in order to achieve their goals and redress their grievances. They had the motivation to engage in *independent* political activity because their inclusive recruitment strategy, and the mass mobilization on which they relied for industrial power, fostered a consciousness of class that encouraged members to see politics in class terms. The new unions also had the resources to engage in independent political activity because their large memberships could potentially be translated into large numbers of votes, which could in turn be translated into legislative seats.

Does comparison with Australia support this argument about the connection between the new unionism and the formation of labor parties? Like its

British and American counterparts, the Australian union movement was rooted in the craft tradition of union organization. The oldest unions—some dating back to the 1830s and 1840s—were organizations of skilled tradesmen in the building, metal working, engineering, and printing industries. According to the standard account of Australian labor history, unions began to expand beyond this original craft base, first in the 1870s, and then, much more quickly, from the middle of the 1880s, when large numbers of unskilled and semi-skilled workers began to join union organizations. This Australian version of the "new unionism" grew rapidly on the waterfront, on the railways, in metal and coal mining, and in the pastoral industry. The first to act were the coal miners, who established a districtwide organization in the fields north of Sydney in 1870. They were followed by wharf laborers and seamen a few years later. But the paradigm examples of the new unionism are usually thought to be found in the Amalgamated Miners' Association (which brought together a number of local metal mining unions in 1882) and the Amalgamated Shearers' Union (which did the same for shearers in 1886). The formation of the shearers' union was particularly important because of the pivotal role that the export of wool played in the Australian economy.[19]

This standard account hides a number of complications. In principle, a new union had at least five characteristics. First, it recruited all those within an industry irrespective of skill. Second, it adopted a policy of low membership fees in order to enable poorly paid unskilled workers to join. Third, it held the funds it acquired for strike relief, rather than for extensive benefit schemes. Fourth, it was unable to control the labor market by monopolizing certain skills. And so, fifth, it relied instead on mobilizing a mass membership. In fact, there was not always a clear-cut dichotomy between the new unions and older craft unions, and few if any of the new unions had all of these characteristics.

Few of the Australian new unions were fully industrywide organizations. Most made some provision for strike pay, as indeed did most craft unions. But many of the new unions also offered benefit schemes to their members. And to support these schemes, the new unions had to levy relatively high union dues and membership entrance fees, although their dues were usually only about half the cost of those levied by some of the older craft unions.[20]

Nevertheless, in some key respects, the new unions in Australia *were* clearly different from traditional craft unions. First, their membership was largely composed of unskilled or semi-skilled workers. Second, they found it difficult to control access to the labor market, or otherwise limit the supply of workers who could do their jobs. And third, they relied on the mobilization of a mass membership. The presence of a significant body of unionists in organizations that shared these characteristics distinguished the Australian union movement from its American counterpart in the early 1890s.

How strong were unions in the United States and Australia at the time when decisions about whether or not to establish a labor party were being taken? In mid-1891, about 21 percent of wage-earners in NSW were union members, and of these about two-thirds were affiliated with the Trades and Labour Council (Markey, 1988, 140 and 318–19, and Docherty, 1973, 184–93). But this represents a membership peak that was followed by sharp losses in the wake of the strike defeats and severe depression of the early 1890s. By 1894, the seamen's union retained only a fifth of its peak membership in NSW, and by 1897 the shearers retained perhaps a third (Docherty, 1973, 183, and Markey, 1988, 141, 162, and 164). There are no satisfactory Australia-wide figures. Later government estimates suggest that about 6 percent of wage-earners in Australia were union members in 1891 (Turner, 1965, 5–6 and 249–50). The peak figure that year may have been more than twice this, but by the mid-1890s an estimate of 5 to 6 percent (similar to that for the mid-1880s) is probably reasonable.[21] American estimates present similar problems. By late 1894, after a surge in membership had collapsed, following strike defeats and the onset of depression, perhaps 3 percent of wage-earners in the United States were union members, and of these, about three-fifths were affiliated with the AFL.[22] However, in states like Illinois, union membership density was significantly higher. In Chicago, it may have been about 14 percent at the end of 1894, down from perhaps 30 percent a year earlier.[23]

What proportion of these unionists belonged to the new unions? The limitations of the available data make it difficult to provide a comprehensive answer to this question. But the contrast between the two countries is quite clear. While the seven largest unions in NSW were new unions, the seven largest unions in the United States were traditional craft unions. In NSW, 63 percent of all unionists belonged to new unions in the maritime, rail, mining, or pastoral industries. Not all of them were affiliated with the TLC, but those that were comprised 61 percent of its affiliated membership.[24] In the United States, by contrast, about 10 percent of all unionists belonged to new unions at the end of 1894. Those who were affiliated to the AFL comprised about 15 percent of its affiliated membership, and their representatives controlled about 20 percent of the votes at the AFL's 1894 Convention.[25]

As we will see in later chapters (especially Chapters 4 and 5), these differences came about for a number of reasons. But they were certainly compounded by the different organizing strategies that union leaders adopted. Among Australian union leaders, a commitment to craft traditions came to be supplemented, and at times displaced, by a commitment to the new unionism. In the United States, many senior union leaders rejected a similar shift.

These different organizing strategies were already evident before the great strikes of the early 1890s. They were especially evident in NSW and Queensland. In NSW, despite the fact that its leaders were principally drawn from traditional craft unions, the TLC and its Organising Committee became increasingly involved in the organization of unskilled urban workers in the second half of the 1880s. Sometimes this involved the TLC itself establishing new unions. More often, it involved supporting others who were doing so (Nairn, 1967, 157 and 166, Markey, 1988, 153 and 157, and Markey, 1994, 23). In the late 1880s, meetings of the Australia-wide Intercolonial Trades and Labor Congresses also began to emphasize the importance of organizing the unskilled, and of joining all unionists—skilled and unskilled—in a single federation of labor. A carpenters' delegate from Queensland who proposed a resolution to this effect, called for "a system resembling the Knights of Labor in America" (ICTUC, 1888, 37).[26] Then, during the London dock strike in 1889, a sympathetic stance towards the new unionism was adopted almost universally, albeit vicariously, when Australian union leaders and other prominent citizens organized mass rallies and raised the then enormous sum of 30,000 pounds for the striking dockers. The London dock workers' union was the internationally recognized paradigm example of the new unionism, and by enabling the dockers to remain on strike, this contribution of financial solidarity was instrumental in securing their victory (Donovan, 1972).[27]

Prior to the strikes of the early 1890s, AFL leaders were probably more conscious about their rejection of the new unionism than their Australian counterparts were about their embrace of it. British models of union organization also had a major impact in the United States. However, it was not the "new unionism" of the dock workers, but the older "new model" trade unionism that British craftsmen had established in the 1850s and 1860s (Webb, 1920, 181, 204, and 217–24, and Pelling, 1992, 40) that was embraced and promoted by the key leaders of the AFL. In the late 1870s and early 1880s, Samuel Gompers and Adolph Strasser had based their successful reorganization of the Cigar Makers' Union on a version of this model. Thereafter, the Cigar Makers' Union was frequently held up as the model that all American unions should follow. Strasser argued that a system of high dues and benefits was "*the secret* of the growth and power of trade unions in England" (Kaufman, 1986, 71). Gompers argued that without such a system unions could not long survive, and told the 1887 AFL convention that "I can scarcely find language strong enough in which to impress this fact upon your minds" (AFL, 1887, 10). Speaking to the American Social Science Association in 1891 about "opposing methods in organizing toilers," Gompers called for the preservation of "trade lines" and "the autonomy of each trade." He described the promise of "an 'Ideal' (some would say Idealistic) organization" of inclusive "mixed unions" as a "siren song" (Kaufman and Albert, 1989, 99–100). Institutional interests also led AFL leaders to reject more inclusive organizing strategies. Indeed, one of the main reasons why the AFL had been founded was to defend craft-based trade unions against the more inclusive aspirations of the Knights of Labor.

In the wake of the strike defeats of the early 1890s, these differences between the organizing strategies adopted by union leaders in the United States and Australia became even sharper.

In Australia, union leaders noticed the relative ease with which employers had been able to replace strikers, and drew the lesson that future success depended on the establishment of more inclusive unions and a serious effort to recruit the mass of unskilled workers. They also concluded that it was necessary to establish a strong central federation to coordinate any industrial action.[28] The shearers' leader, W. G. Spence, told his union's 1891 annual conference that unions "have been too conservative, too narrow and exclusive . . . High entrance fees have also seriously militated against our success. . . . the chief aim should be to gather as many of the workers as possible into the ranks, instead of raising barricades with a view to keeping them out."[29] Spence had already been committed to a more inclusive form of unionism. But it was not just him. There was widespread consensus among labor leaders that unions had to rid themselves of high entrance fees and the "scourge" of craft sectionalism if they were to prevail in future industrial confrontations (TLC, 1891, 11). "Too much stress can not be placed on the necessity for low entrance fees," wrote the Labour Defence Committee (1890, 18) which had coordinated the strike in Sydney, and its conclusions were broadly endorsed by the leaders of the NSW TLC and the Intercolonial Trades and Labor Union Congress, as well as by prominent labor journalists.[30] Moreover, a number of the new unions acted on these recommendations. The wharf laborers, the trolley and draymen, and the shearers reduced or abolished their entrance fees, as well as some other financial impediments to membership.[31]

In the United States, the response of Gompers and many other AFL leaders was the exact opposite. In his first articles for the *American Federationist* after his return to the presidency in 1896, Gompers redoubled his emphasis on the necessity of high fees, elaborate benefit schemes, and trade-based organization. He argued that "the history of the labor movement points to no one thing more clearly than this fact, that it is the manifest duty of the workers to organize in the unions of their trade and pay high dues into their unions." He observed that unionists who paid low dues suffered from the worst wages and conditions (although he did not consider the possibility that it may have been because of these conditions that they paid low dues). He even went so far as to suggest that "it is better that the worker remain unorganized than to organize on mere enthusiasm."[32] Not all union leaders agreed with this position. In a thoughtful post-mortem on the Pullman strike, the *United Mine Workers' Journal* commended the American Railway Union for attempting to organize all railroad workers. It argued that the prevalence of the craft-based "aristocratic" model of union organization was one of the principle reasons why the union movement had been unable to protect the Pullman workers.[33] But the influence of this kind of response was constrained because it was not in harmony with the dominant response of the AFL. The craft ethos of the AFL was sufficiently powerful that even a natural ally like the Seamen's Union balked at embracing the new unionism, and instead insisted on characterizing itself as representing the "seafaring craft."[34]

In the wake of the strike defeats of the early 1890s, the commitment of many Australian union leaders to the "new unionism" became a more conscious one. Indeed, a number of them embraced the term explicitly in order to describe their organizations, or those they were trying to build.[35] In the United States, by contrast, the term became highly politicized. It was embraced by some of Gompers's most bitter opponents, who sought to use the kudos associated with the London dock strike to discredit him and his AFL allies. In the process, the term acquired a distorted meaning and a narrow sectarian flavor.[36]

THE EFFECT OF THE NEW UNIONISM

Did the strength or weakness of the new unionism affect the prospects for labor politics in the way that the new unionism thesis suggests? Comparison of the United States and Australia in the early 1890s certainly supports the claim that there was a correlation between the proportion of members in new unions and the propensity to establish a labor party. With more than 60 percent of its unionists in new unions, the NSW TLC set about establishing a labor party. With 15 or 20 percent of its unionists in new unions, the AFL did not. Comparison *within* Australia also provides evidence of this correlation. In Victoria, the new unions were less influential than in NSW, and urban craft unions remained dominant in the early 1890s. The union movement in Victoria did establish a labor party, but they were slower to do so than their New South Wales counterparts, and the party they established was little more than a wing of the liberal party until the 1900s.[37] Moreover, in both Australia and the United States, contemporaries typically saw a tendency towards political action as an integral part of the new unionism.[38]

But how did individual new unions and their craft-based counterparts actually behave? Do the decisions of individual unions provide evidence that supports the new unionism thesis, and the causal mechanism the thesis proposes?

In Australia, there was no simple one-to-one correspondence between whether a union included or excluded the unskilled and semi-skilled, and whether it favored or opposed the establishment of a labor party. Moreover, as we will see in Chapter 5, the defeat of the Maritime strike had a significant effect on attitudes towards politics throughout the union movement. Nevertheless, it is possible to identify a number of important ways in which the growth of the new unionism fostered the establishment of a labor party. Some of these influences were felt before the Maritime strike, and had an effect on the initial decision to establish the party. Others were felt after the party's initial success, and had an effect on its subsequent consolidation.

Before the strike, the rise of the new unionism affected the prospects for labor party politics both directly and indirectly. Directly, the growth of the new unions in the second half of the 1880s coincided with a growing interest in the possibility of competing in elections. The clearest evidence of this emerged at the most rarefied level of union representation: in the Australia-wide Intercolonial Trades and Labor Union Congress. Beginning in 1884, these congresses regularly passed resolutions calling for the direct representation of labor in parliament.[39] These resolutions had no immediate consequences since it was the TLCs, and not the congresses, that were in a position to initiate such an experiment. But they provide evidence of growing support among some senior labor leaders for the principle that labor should seek independent representation. Some new unionists embraced these ideas wholeheartedly (Harris, 1966, 15–17). Others, like W. G. Spence—the most important new union leader in the late 1880s—were interested but more cautious (Merritt, 1986, 180).

However, the most important effects of the new unionism before the Maritime strike were indirect. First, the new unions encouraged the development of class consciousness. One manifestation of this among union leaders was the growing support for plans to establish a classwide union organization: a plan that was being promoted by new unionists like Spence (Gollan, 1960, 94 and 106–9). Another was the growing support for direct parliamentary representation. But greater class consciousness was also transmitted to a much broader group of unionists and workers, both through the more inclusive practices of the new unions themselves, and through the influence of intellectuals and labor papers associated with these unions. The growth of this common class identity both strengthened the rationale for establishing a labor party and increased the probability that such a party would receive electoral support.

Second, the organizational strategies adopted by the new unions to pursue their industrial goals had a number of consequences, which although unforeseen by many unionists at the time, would eventually predispose the union movement to undertake political action. The new unions often relied on mass mobilization in order to have leverage in industrial disputes. Maritime workers arranged for support from coal miners in a dispute over shipping,[40] and shearers sought an alliance with maritime workers in order to be able to stop non-union wool getting to overseas markets (Merritt, 1973, 601–3). But the new unions discovered that, in spite of these alliances, their members could still easily be replaced. Just as the new unionism thesis suggests, they responded to the ensuing defeat by attempting to bolster their position by translating the support of their mass membership into political influence. Because of their size and importance, the new unions drew the union movement as a whole into the Maritime strike. The involvement of other union leaders in the dispute, and their experience of its defeat, led them, too, to look more favorably on the possibility of independent political action.

The new unions also played a critical role in consolidating the labor party after the initial decision had been taken to establish it. At election time, they mobilized core blocks of voters in a number of constituencies. The wharf laborers, the shearers, the metal miners, and, in a more ambiguous and independent way, the coal miners, all did this. So, too, did the railway workers, despite their ongoing reluctance to engage in industrial mobilization. In addition, after the party's initial success, it was these unions that provided the party with much of the organizational infrastructure it needed to ride out various difficulties and reversals. The shearers' union was especially important. By providing logistical support, finance, organizers, and a newspaper, it gave the fledgling party essential organizational ballast.[41]

So, although the causal mechanisms were not always direct, and were sometimes complex, the Australian experience broadly supports the new unionism thesis. The new unions (and the intellectuals that supported them) fostered the establishment of a labor party in a number of ways. They pursued policies that strengthened class consciousness in the late 1880s. They were at the center of the industrial struggles of the early 1890s that cemented union support for the formation of a labor party. And they provided the organizational base that enabled the fledgling labor party to sustain itself after the first flush of success.

In the United States, there was also no simple one-to-one correspondence between whether a union was more or less inclusive and whether or not it favored independent labor politics. A number of craft unions supported independent political action during the AFL's 1894 debate, and there was a range of different factors that could help generate this support. These included the experience of a catastrophic defeat (in the case of the iron and steel workers), depression-induced unemployment and a consequent membership collapse (in the case of the carpenters), and the influence of socialist activists (in the case of the boot and shoe makers).[42]

Nevertheless, it was "new" inclusive unions that provided the most important bases of support for independent labor politics in the early 1890s. The two most important industrial unions in the early 1890s were the United Mine Workers and the American Railway Union. Both adopted a favorable attitude towards independent political action, even before the strikes that each undertook in 1894. As with the new unions in Australia, the huge industrial disputes in which these unions were involved relied on the mass mobilization of workers. And as in Australia, the outcome of these disputes strongly reinforced the disposition of these unions to engage in independent labor politics. Indeed, compared with their Australian counterparts, these unions responded by placing even more emphasis—or, rather, more singular emphasis—on the possibility of redemption through political action.[43]

The attitude of these unions was part of a more general pattern. Voting records show that the unions within the AFL that were open to unskilled and semi-skilled workers were far more likely to support independent political activity than were the more closed craft unions that dominated the union movement in the United States (Marks, 1989, 206–7 and 235–38). Late nineteenth-century data on the success and failure of strikes reinforce this picture. On the railroads, for example, strikes by skilled engineers and firemen were almost twice as likely to succeed as those by unskilled switchmen and yardmen (Edwards, 1981, 121 and 272), and strikebreakers, who were more likely to be used against unskilled workers, had a powerful effect on the likelihood of success. Where they were used, only 28 percent of strikes were wholly or partially successful for the unions. Where they were not used, 73 percent were wholly or partially successful (Rosenbloom, 1998, 185–86). This suggests that open or inclusive unions were embracing independent labor politics, at least in part, in response to the different incentives they faced.

Both the overt behavior of industrial unions in the United States, as well as the different incentives that skilled and unskilled unionists faced, provide support for the new unionism thesis, and the causal mechanism the thesis proposes. Overall, therefore, comparison of union organization in the United States and Australia supports the claim that unions open to unskilled and semi-skilled workers were more likely than craft unions to foster support for independent political action, and thus, that the weakness of the new unionism in the United States does indeed help explain why no labor party was established there.

WORKERS AND FARMERS

However, the new unionism in Australia also raises a further issue. As in other countries, the impetus to form inclusive new unions was strong in the mining, maritime, and railroad industries. But in Australia, this impetus was also present in the pastoral industry. Through the organization of the shearers' union, the pastoral industry became one of the most important bases for the new unionism and for labor party politics. As we have seen, the shearers' union—which amalgamated with the smaller shed-hands' union to form the Australian Workers' Union (AWU)—played an important role in the establishment of the Labor party. It was able to do this, not only because it was the leading proponent and most important example of the new unionism, but also because it was able to forge an alliance between rural workers and small farmers (or "selectors") which brought a significant section of the rural population under the influence of the labor movement.

At the beginning of the 1890s, Australia was even more urbanized than the United States. As Table 1.3 shows, close to a third of the population of the United States lived in towns of 5,000 or more. But close to half of the Australian population lived in towns of this size. Not only that, but in

TABLE 1.3.
Urban and Rural Population, as a Percentage of the Total Population, by Size of
Urban Settlement

Population	United States	Illinois	Australia	NSW
>100,000	15.4	28.7	34.5	34.3
>5,000	31.5		46.8	45.1
>1,000	39.1		56.7	61.9
Rural	60.9		43.3	38.1

Notes and sources: see appendix

NSW—which in this respect was typical of Australia—more than a third of the population lived in just one city. Some American states had a similar population structure. Illinois, for example, with 28 percent of the population living in Chicago, was also dominated by one large city. However, despite their urbanization, both countries still had large rural populations, and this was so both in the longest settled areas of Australia, and in the industrialized states of the American Northeast and Midwest. Approximately two-fifths of the population of Australia, and approximately three-fifths of the population of the United States, lived either on farms or in towns of less than 1,000. These rural populations were politically important both because of their size and because of the ideological significance of the yeoman ideal.[44]

In the United States, the importance of the rural population helps explain why the kind of independent labor politics being most seriously considered in the late 1890s was a labor-populist alliance, in which workers would join with farmers to build a People's party. This is what the main leaders who were urging the labor movement to embrace independent labor politics were hoping to achieve. Socialists like Thomas J. Morgan, the principle proponent of the political program within the AFL, New Liberals like Henry Demarest Lloyd, and leaders of the main industrial unions like Eugene Debs of the American Railway Union, and John McBride of the United Mine Workers, were all pursuing this goal.

In Australia, it was just such an alliance that provided support for the NSW Labor party. And it was the new unions in the pastoral industry that underwrote the success of this alliance. Indeed, a number of leading unionists—especially in the shearers' union—saw the People's party, as well as earlier American efforts to construct an alliance between farmers' organizations and the Knights of Labor, as models for the party they were seeking to build in Australia. Arthur Rae, the Wagga shearers' leader and a member of parliament, made this argument explicitly and gave it pride of place at the head of his electoral manifesto.[45]

TABLE 1.4.
Geographical Distribution of Labor Party Seats in the New South Wales Parliament
(Number of Seats, by Year)

	1891	1894	1895	1898	1901	1904	1907
Rural	13	5	5	8	11	13	14
Urban	16	5	7	5	10	6	10
Mining	6	5	7	7	4	6	8
Total	35	15	19	20	25	25	32

Notes and sources: see appendix

The shearers' union was well placed to foster a labor-populist alliance, because it exercised an influence over the two largest sections of the rural population. The majority of its members were itinerant workers. But the union also
organized large numbers of shearer-selectors: small farmers who did seasonal
work as shearers in order to supplement their income. It is likely that at least
35 percent of the shearing workforce were selectors or their sons. Selectors
were also a larger proportion of the shearing workforce in the older regions of
settlement than they were further inland. These shearer-selectors often played
an important organizational role because their land gave them a permanent
rural base the whole year round. In NSW, five of the seven branches of the
shearers' union were dominated by selectors.[46]
   In short, the shearers' union not only brought a number of rural workers
into a largely urban union movement, but it also forged an alliance between
workers and some small farmers. The electoral significance of this composite
constituency of workers and selectors can be seen in Table 1.4. However, se-
lector support was not a prerequisite for the successful establishment of a labor
party. The labor-populist alliance was most important in NSW and Queensland, where the pastoral industry was concentrated, and the influence of the
shearers' union was strongest.[47] By contrast, in Victoria and South Australia,
agricultural small-holding was more developed. South Australia, in particular,
had come closest to the yeoman ideal of establishing a large class of small independent farmers. In Victoria, as we have seen, the party (and the new
unionism) was weak. But in South Australia, the Labor party quickly established itself as an important force, in spite of minimal small-holder support
(Murphy, 1975, 241 and 244, and Merritt, 1986, 276–77). Moreover, even in
NSW, while the labor-populist alliance did play a vital role in enabling the
Labor party to gain a parliamentary majority in the early twentieth century, it
was not essential to the unions' original goal of establishing a third force in
parliament. As Table 1.4 suggests, the party could still have established its
presence with support from urban and mining areas alone. Nevertheless, the

fact remains that small farmers provided some Australian labor parties with an important base of support in their formative years.

Does comparison with this Australian experience help to illuminate the fortunes of labor-populism in the United States? Any comparison must start by noting that, in the course of the nineteenth century, vast tracks of land were "opened up"—that is, seized from the indigenous inhabitants—as settlers pushed further inland from the original urban centers founded on the east coasts of their respective continents. In both countries, attempts were made to regulate this process through legislation, which had, as its primary aim, the establishment of a class of independent yeoman farmers. In the United States, the Homestead Act of 1862 provided free land to settlers so long as they built a dwelling on the land and lived there. Similar Selection Acts were passed by various Australian parliaments between 1860 and 1862: though these usually required settlers (or "selectors") to make some payment.[48]

However, according to the conventional interpretation of Australian history, it was clear by the end of the 1880s that the United States had been more successful than Australia in establishing a class of small-holding farmers. Within Australia, some colonies (like Victoria and South Australia) had been more successful than others (like NSW and Queensland), but, overall, the wealthy "squatters" who had established vast sheep stations in the first half of the nineteenth century retained control of the best land (McNaughton, 1955, 115–22, and Clark, 1955, 126–54).

There is little doubt that small-holders were more numerous in the United States, and that agriculture was stronger and more diversified. But the class composition of the rural population in Australia was more similar to that in the United States than is usually realized. In 1891, census takers in NSW found that about 45 percent of the workforce on farms and pastoral stations were wage earners, and that tenants operated 18 percent of rural holdings. In 1890, their counterparts in the United States found that 36 percent of the agricultural workforce were hired laborers (although in 1880 and again in 1900 this figure was 43 percent), and that 26 percent of farms were operated by tenants. This was not just a result of the organization of agriculture in the South. In Illinois, 35 percent of the (male) farm workforce were paid laborers, and 34 percent of all farms were operated by tenants.[49]

There are some major problems with this census data. First, the distinctions between various occupational categories are often unclear. Second, by forcing each individual into a single category, the data fail to capture the multiple occupational tasks in which many individuals were engaged. And third, because of the seasonal nature of so much agricultural employment, the census data in both countries are unable to provide reliable estimates for the number of individuals employed in tasks like shearing and harvesting, many of whom worked on their own small holdings at other times. These problems serve to highlight another important similarity between the United States and Australia. In both countries, many small farmers occupied multiple class locations, and as a result, their overall class interests were ambiguous.[50]

Given these similarities, what were the conditions that enabled a labor-populist alliance to take root in Australia? Three groups interacted to produce this alliance: the selectors, the squatters, and the shearers. The selectors provided unionists with potential alliance partners. The squatters provided both selectors and unionists with a common enemy. And the shearers provided a bridging agent that was able to act as an alliance broker. Were there groups in the United States that were able to play each of these roles?

Many of the difficulties facing Australian selectors were the same as those confronting homesteaders and other small holders in the United States. Both complained of low prices for their produce, high credit and freight costs, the machinations of merchants and middle men, the sudden and sometimes devastating impact of the weather, and the efforts of speculators and corporations to monopolize the best land.[51] These grievances generated support for some radical reforms, but the typical Australian small holder was no more proletarian in outlook than his American cousin. In neither country were small farmers sympathetic to the unionization of their *own* employees. The *Hummer* complained that "most selectors become very conservative, and hate unions like black snakes."[52] Moreover, in both countries the grievances of small holders varied from region to region. In NSW, for example, farmers in the southern wheatbelt became an important base of support for the Labor party, while dairy farmers along the coast were solidly anti-Labor (Ellem *et al.*, 1988, and Hagan and Turner, 1991, 33–39 and 53–55). In the United States, similar factors produced greater unrest among those growing cash crops, and less among those providing nearby cites with perishable goods (Sanders, 1999, 101–5).[53] Nevertheless, in each country large groups of small farmers were sufficiently aggrieved to consider mobilizing support for a third party, and to this end, they were interested in an alliance with organized labor.

In Australia, squatters provided the labor-populist alliance with a common enemy because they had sharp conflicts of interest with both workers and small holders in an industry that was central to the economy, and because they seemed to symbolize a threat to core egalitarian and democratic values. In the eyes of workers and small-holders, the squatters had four important characteristics. First, they had taken control of vast tracts of the best land (the size and quality of their holdings). Second, they relied on a large workforce of wage-earners to operate pastoral enterprises that were increasingly owned by absentee partnerships and corporations (the corporate nature of their control). Third, they had accumulated economic and political power that enabled them to distort markets and influence parliaments (their monopolistic power). Fourth, and perhaps most important, they had acquired all this through the theft of the public domain, and yet they insisted on nurturing class pretensions (their illegitimacy).

A number of groups in the United States appeared to have similar characteristics. Large landholders and cattle kings provide an obvious analogy. Under the Homestead Act, just as under the Selection Acts in Australia, vast tracts of land that had been intended for homesteaders were rapidly transferred to large land-holders, often by agents posing as settlers.[54] However—both economically and ideologically—the most important common enemies for American labor-populists were the railroad corporations. The railroads were thought to have each of the four characteristics just noted. First, they acquired vast amounts of valuable land. By 1890, over 200 million acres of land had been given to railroad companies: more than four times the amount of land that settlers had "perfected" under the Homestead Act (Shannon, 1936, 638).[55] Second, the railroad companies were corporate enterprises employing large numbers of wage earners. Indeed, they were the prototype for this emerging form of economic organization. Third, the railroads were widely viewed as using monopolistic economic and political power to increase the cost of freight, and corrupt the legislative process. And fourth, the very names that were used to describe railroad owners emphasized their illegitimacy and class pretensions. Just as the Australian pastoralists were widely referred to as the "squattocracy," the men behind the American railroad corporations were widely referred to as "robber barons." Both were labeled this way for the same two reasons. They were seen as thieves ("squatters" or "robbers") who had seized vast tracts of land at the expense of yeoman farmers and the ideal of economic egalitarianism that they represented. And they were seen as having neo-feudal ("aristocratic" or "baronial") pretensions that threatened the political egalitarianism of the New World. They were thus well-placed to play a similar symbolic role.

So, in the United States, there were both potential alliance partners for the unions (to play the role of the selectors) and potential common enemies (to play the role of the squatters). But were there any bridging agents (like the shearers) who could act as alliance brokers? The shearers had three characteristics that helped them play this role. First, they were able to establish and maintain a union organization with a rural base. In part, this was because of the nature of their work. On large properties, shearing sheds brought together one or two hundred shearers and shedhands in a factory-like environment, and the seasonal nature of the work gave them some bargaining leverage, although this should not be overstated (Merritt, 1986, 35–42, 72, and 79). Second, as we have already seen, the ambiguous class location of many shearers made it necessary for their union to take account of the different interests of both small farmers and property-less rural wage-earners. And third, their union provided ideological glue for labor-populism by embracing and promoting a producerist view of class, along with populist policies about monopolies, banks, and land.[56]

Were there any rural-based groups of workers in the United States who could play a similar role?

Hired pastoral and farm laborers were, as we have seen, a large component of the rural population. But it is difficult to identify a group among them who were in a similar position to the Australian shearers. Cowboys seem to invite comparison (Ward, 1958, 10), as do the seasonal groups of workers who harvested wheat and corn. But none managed to organize stable unions in the late nineteenth century (Lopez, 1977, Fahey, 1993). Hauliers and tradesmen based in rural towns did form unions. But they did not have the concentrated numbers needed to provide a rural base for the labor movement. There were, however, two other groups of workers who were sufficiently concentrated to provide such a base.

Miners were frequently located in rural communities. Though most miners were not simultaneously trying to be farmers, some farmers sought to supplement their income by working in the mines during the winter, and some miners did the same in the fields during the summer (Laslett, 1970, 200, and U.S. Industrial Commission, 1901, 407). Many miners also had close personal ties with surrounding farming or pastoral communities, and this made it easier for their union to foster a labor-populist alliance.

Railroad workers were also located in many rural communities, where they too developed close personal and commercial ties. In order to run their steam engines, the companies needed to employ large concentrations of workers in junction towns, rail depots, and roundhouses, which had to be located at periodic intervals along the track.[57] Some railroad workers—especially unskilled construction laborers—were also farmers or farm laborers, although most worked full time for the railroad companies (Stromquist, 1987, 104–15 and 121–22). As Figure 1.3 shows, the men that worked in the roundhouses and railroad workshops, the running crews that were based in them, and the construction and maintenance crews that moved throughout the region, provided a significant base for unionism throughout much of rural America.[58]

Unions of miners and railroad workers were also well-placed to provide the ideological glue for a labor-populist alliance. A producerist notion of class was still strong in both the United Mine Workers and the American Railway Union in the early 1890s (as it had been earlier in the Knights of Labor), and both unions were prepared to embrace a populist program, suitably modified to include specific union demands. Indeed, in the wake of the disastrous industrial defeats of 1894, that is precisely what both unions did. Like the shearers in Australia, each sought to broker a labor-populist alliance, both nationally, and in those states where they were strong. The miners' president, John McBride, brokered such an alliance in Ohio, and the ARU became closely involved in similar efforts in Illinois.

So how distinctive was the role of the shearers' union in Australia? Although no single American union had its particular combination of characteristics, a number of unions were in a position to play a similar bridging role in rural communities. Neither the miners nor the railroad workers had the shearers' large

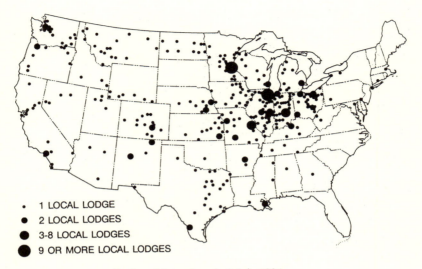

Figure 1.3. American Railway Union Locals, 2 July 1894

Sources: *Railway Times*, 2 July 1894, and Stromquist (1987, 85), *A Generation of Boomers: The Pattern of Railroad Labor Conflict in Nineteenth-Century America.* Copyright 1987 by the Board of Trustees of the University of Illinois. Used with permission of the University of Illinois Press.

small-holder membership, but both could reach deep into rural communities and forge close personal ties between farmers and their members, and both were in a position to help broker a mutually acceptable political program and to provide an organizational base for pursuing it. Had the American Railway Union proved more stable, it would probably have been in the best position to play an analogous role to that of the shearers. Railroad workers stood out because of their widespread presence in concentrated groups throughout rural areas; their mobility, which enabled them to spread ideas and organizations throughout much of the country; the ongoing appeal of producerism and populism among them; and the symbolic importance of their employers to workers and farmers alike.

In some respects, the task of brokering a labor-populist alliance in the United States was easier than it was in Australia. Many farmers were already mobilized and their organizations were actively seeking the support of labor for the People's party. But this also meant that the brokering task of unions in the United States and Australia was somewhat different. Whereas the shearers' union was faced with the task of garnering support from small-holders for a party that was initially established under the auspices of the union movement, their counterparts in the United States faced the task of ensuring that a party, whose principle initial sponsors had been small-holder organizations, could be molded into a vehicle for independent labor politics.[59] In the labor strongholds of the American Northeast and Midwest, this difference was harder to discern. There, farmers were far less organized, and unions had the opportunity to play a similar role to their Australian counterparts by creating labor-led People's party organizations.[60] In 1894, some of the most important proponents of independent labor politics sought to seize the opportunity to do just that.

CONCLUSION

Comparison with Australia leads to different conclusions about the three main economic explanations I have been considering.

Explanations based on the level of prosperity in the United States no longer look very convincing. In the late nineteenth century, the living standards of workers in the United States were indeed higher than in Europe, but the living standards of Australian workers were higher still. Moreover, the standard of living in other countries was not the only, or even the most important, comparative reference point against which Americans judged their economic circumstances. For most workers, internal reference points, like the living standards of wealthier members of their society, the living standards promised by the ideal image of their society, and the domestic living standards that they themselves had previously experienced, were all more important. But, in each of these respects, the cause for discontent in the United States was at least as great, and often greater, than it was in Australia. Since there was sufficient economic discontent to mobilize workers in Australia, it seems unlikely that discontent in the United States was insufficient to allow for a similar development to take place. This is the main negative finding of the chapter. It provides a good illustration of how comparison with Australia can cast doubt on previously well-established or widely accepted explanations.

Explanations based on the weakness of the "new unionism" look more promising. New unions, which were open to unskilled and semi-skilled workers, had both the motivation and the resources to engage in independent labor politics. But these unions organized a far larger proportion of the unionized workforce in Australia than they did in the United States. One of the reasons for this was that top union leaders in Australia were committed to promoting this form of union organization, while their counterparts in the United States tended to resist it. In Australia, the new unions fostered the establishment of a labor party in a number of ways. They pursued policies that strengthened class consciousness. They were at the center of the industrial struggles that cemented union support for the formation of a labor party. And they provided the organizational base to sustain the fledgling party. New unions also tried to foster independent labor politics in the United States, but they had far less influence in the union movement as a whole. Comparison with Australia thus supports the claim that the weakness of the new unionism helps to explain why there is no labor party in the United States. This is the main positive finding of the chapter. Later, I will return to more fully consider the impact of the new unionism, and the causes of its weakness, in the context of a thorough examination of the strike wave of the early 1890s.

Finally, I considered whether it might only have been possible to forge a labor-populist alliance in Australia because of some special class characteristics that were not present in the United States. The demographic and ideological importance of the rural population led proponents of independent labor politics in both countries to seek to establish an alliance between workers and small farmers. In Australia, three groups interacted to foster such an alliance. Selectors provided unionists with potential alliance partners. Squatters provided both with a common enemy. And shearers acted as alliance brokers. But groups that were able to play these roles were also present in the United States. Homesteaders faced many of the same problems as selectors. Large land holders—especially railroad corporations—provided a common enemy. And although there was no one group of workers that had the shearers' particular combination of characteristics, both the miners and the railroad workers were in a position to play a similar bridging role between workers and small farmers. This suggests that a labor-populist alliance was not beyond the reach of American unionists.

CHAPTER 2

Race

RACE HAS BEEN central to many aspects of American social and political development. But what effect did it have on the failure of unions to establish a labor party in the late nineteenth century? Conventional explanations of the effect of race suggest that racial consciousness and racial conflicts reduced the viability of class-based movements in the United States. More particularly, they suggest that the importance attached to racial differences generated divisions between workers that hindered the establishment of a labor party, both directly, by weakening its electoral viability, and indirectly, by making it more difficult to organize the kind of mass, industrywide unions that were most likely to support such a party.

Does comparison with Australia support the conventional explanations? Slavery and its aftermath, and the presence of a significant minority of African-Americans stand out as obvious differences between the United States and Australia. In 1890, close to 12 percent of the population of the United States was African-American, although before the great internal migration that began during the First World War, nine out of ten blacks lived in the South, and the vast majority were tenant farmers or sharecroppers.

But this difference with Australia may be less important than it first appears. For it is not the mere presence of different groups that effects the prospects for working-class solidarity and labor politics. Rather, it is the presence of hostilities towards these groups. Acute, well-entrenched racial hostilities were present in both the United States and Australia, and in both countries they deeply marked the attitude of the labor movement. Indeed, in broad outlines, the racial attitudes of white unionists were remarkably similar. In both cases, blacks were a major target of racial hostility, but in neither case were they the only target. In fact, in both countries, it was a different group—Chinese immigrants—that was the single most important official target of union-led agitation. In addition, in both cases, hostility towards aboriginal inhabitants was pervasive. However, it played a much smaller role in the explicit concerns of unionists, although it must surely have had an important background effect by conditioning settler societies to accept both concepts of racial superiority and the reality of racial violence.[1]

In the next section, I want to take a closer look at the nature and extent of racial hostilities in both countries—looking first at the attitude of unionists towards blacks, and second at their attitude towards the Chinese. Then I will examine the effect of these antipathies, and consider whether or not the Australian case supports the conventional understanding of the impact of race in the United States. Finally, I will consider whether there was a growing tendency to characterize differences between European immigrants in racial terms, and what effect this might have had. I should make it clear, however, that, here, I will only be concerned with the impact of racial hostilities, and not with other types of ethnic conflict. In particular, I will defer discussion of religious conflicts to a later chapter.

THE EXTENT OF RACIAL HOSTILITY

Officially, there has never been any slavery in Australia. But there *was* a group of people whom contemporary whites thought of as occupying an analogous racial and economic position to that of African-Americans. These people, known as "Kanakas," were Melanesians from the South Pacific islands who worked on sugar plantations in Queensland. In legal terms, Kanakas were brought to Australia as indentured laborers on three-year contracts, although some were actually kidnapped (a practice known as "blackbirding"), and many others must have had little understanding of the nature of the contract being proposed to them. By 1891, they formed about 2 percent of the population of Queensland, and in 1901, the importation of Melanesians was banned by the federal Parliament (Hunt, 1978, 82).

The attitude of the Australian labor movement towards the Kanakas was unrelentingly hostile. In some ways, the legal situation of Kanakas was more like that of Chinese contract laborers in America than that of African-Americans. However, contemporary Australian whites saw Kanakas as racially comparable to African-Americans, and as inferior to the Chinese. They also saw them as representing the emergence of a feudal plantation economy in the Australian "Far North," similar to that which had existed in the American "Deep South." The importation of Melanesian laborers into Queensland was a major concern of the labor movement. It was an especially important concern in Queensland itself, but the campaigns that were launched there had the support of unionists and labor-sympathizers throughout Australia.

An article entitled "Australian Slavery" provides a typical account of union attitudes. The article argued that the introduction of black labor was leading both blacks and whites into slavery, and that it would eventually give rise to something like the American Civil War, and the subsequent "race problem," which, it said, "even yet may shatter the great American Republic to its foundations."[2] A front page cartoon in the *Bulletin* made the same point graphically, and linked it to the core union struggle against the employers' demand for "freedom of contract" (see Figure 2.1). The cartoon showed a "degraded" and defeated white worker, chained between a black man and a Chinese man,

Figure 2.1. "Freedom of Contract" — How It Works

Source: Bulletin, 11 April 1891 (State Library of New South Wales)

being lead away by a plantation overseer to a slave-style auction block marked "Free Labour Exchange."

Freedom (like manly independence) was intimately connected to whiteness. Racism and liberalism were typically seen, not as opposed or in tension, but rather, as two sides of the same coin: as mutually dependent and reinforcing. If Australia was to remain a democracy, and avoid sliding into a feudal oligarchy controlled by plantation, pastoral, and shipping interests, it must exclude inferior racial groups whose dependence on their employers would strengthen the political as well as the economic and social power of this would-be oligarchy. This connection between a liberal concern with the conditions for a free society of equals, and a racist concern with the exclusion of certain groups, was a dominant motif of late nineteenth century Australian thought, both within the labor movement and amongst middle-class progressives.

As with the rise of Jim Crow in the United States, these attitudes were also intimately connected to fears about sexuality.[3] A column in the labor press written by "Lucinda Sharpe," ostensibly an American woman in Queensland, gives some feeling for this. "I wouldn't do a black man harm, or a yellow man or a green man for that matter" writes Sharpe, "but I'd rather see a daughter of mine dead in her coffin than kissing one of them on the mouth or nursing a little coffee-coloured brat."[4] The author of the column was actually William Lane, arguably the most influential Australian labor editor and journalist at the time, and a leading proponent of socialism (Wilding, 1980, 50).

Many unionists in the United States also exhibited a deep-seated hostility toward blacks, and a number of unions formally excluded African-Americans from membership, just as some of their Australian counterparts excluded Melanesians.[5] For example, the first annual convention of the American Railway Union rejected the recommendation of its leadership, and decided, by a vote of 112 to 100, to restrict membership to whites. The union congratulated itself on this demonstration of its commitment to democracy.[6] However, as even this episode suggests, there was a certain ambivalence in the attitude of unionists towards blacks in the United States in the early 1890s. This ambivalence was partly a product of the ideological legacy of the Civil War and Reconstruction, which, for a time, went some way towards delegitimizing hostility towards African-Americans. The influence within the labor movement of socialist activists, especially those influenced by Marxism, also had some effect.[7]

AFL policy towards blacks illustrates this ambivalence particularly clearly. Formally, the AFL refused to allow unions that excluded blacks to affiliate with it, and AFL President Samuel Gompers rebuked a number of unions for racial discrimination in the early 1890s.[8] On the ground, however, the AFL soon came to accommodate the heightened racial hostilities emerging in the 1890s. Its attitude toward the machinists' union provides a telling example. In 1890, the AFL refused to admit this union because its constitution explicitly excluded blacks, and an alternative organization open to both blacks and whites was established and given an AFL charter. But in 1895 the machinists were admitted in a compromise that allowed them to continue to exclude blacks in practice, so long as there was no mention of this fact in the constitution.[9] In reality, then, unions were free to decide their own policy towards blacks. In some cases, notably in the industrywide United Mine Workers union (and, for a time, in various unions in New Orleans), black and white workers organized together in the same union. In most cases, however, the segregation of black unionists, or their exclusion from the labor market altogether, became the norm.

So in the early 1890s, deep-seated hostility towards blacks was the norm in both countries. The main difference with Australia was not an absence of hostility towards blacks, but an absence of a sure sense that this hostility was legitimate. Interestingly, this ambivalence about *American* blacks occasionally appeared in Australia as well. At the 1891 Intercolonial Trades and Labor Union Congress, the shearers' leader, W. G. Spence, argued that unions "had to fight the Kanakas, and let the American blacks—many of whom were in unions—so long as they worked for fair wages, have votes." A delegate from Queensland agreed. "By all means, let the American blacks join unions if they are willing and capable," he declared, while in the middle of a diatribe against "Kanakas, Chinese, and Hindoos." Indeed, the 1894 constitution of the shearers' union specifically qualified its exclusion of "alien races" by noting in parenthesis that "This does not apply to Aborigines, Maoris, American Negros, or to the children of mixed marriages born in Australasia." Doubts about the legitimacy of excluding racial groups were strongest in the case of indigenous inhabitants, and the 1891 conference of the shearers' union actually discussed making it easier for aborigines to join the union.[10] However, when it came to the Melanesians (or Kanakas)—the group that white Australians thought of as occupying the position most similar to that of African-Americans in the United States—Australian unions, unlike their American counterparts, had no compunction about establishing a color bar.

However, there was another group about which there was no ambiguity in either country. Whether in Australia or the United States, Chinese immigrants were subject to vitriolic hostility. In both countries, this hostility first came to prominence during the gold rushes of the 1850s, which took place on the west coast of the United States and in southeast Australia. Although there were a large number of Chinese diggers in certain districts, they were never more than a small percentage of either country's population, and once the gold rush ended, that percentage continually declined.[11]

Despite this, from the late 1870s onwards, anti-Chinese agitation came to occupy a central place on the political agenda of both labor movements. This development was given a major boost around the same time by both the California Workingmen's movement, which grew out of a meeting called to support the 1877 railway strike in the United States, and by the popular movement against Chinese immigration, which supported the Australian seamen's strike of 1878. In each case, opposition to competition from Chinese labor merged with general racial objections to the Chinese per se.[12]

In both countries, anti-Chinese agitation quickly became a staple concern of the newly emerging peak councils of the union movement. In Australia, the first Intercolonial Trades Union Congress in 1879 unanimously resolved that the "importation of Chinese is injurious morally, socially, and politically," and demanded "speedy legislation" to exclude them.[13] A similar resolution was passed at each subsequent Congress. Parliamentary committee reports from the various Trades and Labour Councils (TLCs) show that these resolutions were not just rhetorical, and provide an indication of the amount of attention paid to the "Chinese question" throughout Australia.[14] In 1888, at the height of a new wave of agitation, unionists were so exercised by the issue, that delegates invoked the threat of another Boston Tea Party should the British government (which wanted to protect its imperial treaty with China) try to interfere with the right of self-governing colonies in Australia to restrict immigration (ICTUC, 1888, 30).

Likewise, in the United States, the issue was a major concern at the founding convention of the Federation of Organized Trades and Labor Unions (the direct predecessor of the AFL) in 1881. The convention resolved that "the presence of the Chinese, and their competition with free white labor, is one of the greatest evils with which any country can be afflicted," and urged "the absolute necessity" of legislation to prohibit their immigration (FOTLU, 1881, 4 and 20). The resolution passed with only one dissenting voice. It had the full support of Gompers, who introduced an additional resolution the following year to give the Federation's Legislative Committee, which he chaired, a mandate to pursue it (FOTLU, 1882, 17–18 and 19). Gompers was still pursuing the issue during the AFL's 1894 debate. Urging immediate protests against a proposed treaty with China, Gompers wrote that "it is needless here to discuss the impossibility of amalgamation or assimilation of the Chinese in America with our people . . . that immigration of Chinese into this country is undesirable and should be prohibited is . . . self-evident."[15]

In both countries, campaigns to drive out Chinese workers led to the development of "union labels." Because of their ability to help facilitate boycotts, these labels came to be seen, especially by the AFL, as a major tool of organized labor. In the United States, Gompers' anti-Chinese stance had its roots in union campaigns to replace Chinese cigar makers with whites. To assist their campaigns, these unions sought to distinguish cigars produced by their members with a "white label" (Saxton, 1971, 73–75 and 213–18, and Mink, 1986, 79 and 95–96). In Australia, the furniture makers' union was the first to introduce the idea of labeling. It demanded that Chinese-made furniture be specially stamped (Sutcliffe, 1921, 125, and Markus, 1979, 163–68).[16]

In both countries, the consensus about racial hostility towards the Chinese was also reflected in the labor press. In Australia, the degree of hostility varied somewhat from one publication to another in the early 1890s.[17] The *Australian Workman*, the official organ of the NSW TLC, tended to use the most moderate language. It even occasionally—very occasionally—gave space to the defense of genuinely universal brotherhood.[18] The *Hummer* (and later the Sydney *Worker*) printed extraordinary diatribes. In a typical piece that extended the attack on "Asiatics" to outback "Afghan" camel drivers, which the paper viewed as a threat to the carriers' union, it wrote that "like the Chinese and other strong-smelling epidemic diseases, [camels] increase by both breeding and importation . . . and it is about time the Afghan, the Camel, and the Chow were given notice to quit."[19] Most inflammatory of all were the *Boomerang* and the Queensland *Worker*, which were joined in their consistent and obsessive racial vitriol by the highly influential pro-labor *Bulletin*.[20] This same consensus can be found in the labor press in the United States. Racial hostility towards the Chinese was present, not just in the labor papers in California and the West, where it was especially intense, but throughout the United States. It was certainly reflected in the national journal of the AFL, and even the papers of the Socialist Labor party sympathized with it. Indeed, the party's Midwestern papers explicitly hailed the victories of the Australian labor movement over the "evil of Chinese labor."[21]

By the beginning of the 1900s, Gompers could summarize the AFL's position in a pamphlet entitled *Meat vs. Rice: American Manhood vs. Asiatic Coolieism: Which Shall Survive?*, and the Australian Labor party, loudly proclaiming its fear of "racial contamination," had made the maintenance of "White Australia" its first and foremost objective.[22] Gompers had been declaring since the early 1880s that the anti-Chinese campaign was "a question of whether the workingmen of America shall eat rats, rice, or beefsteak."[23] But now the very title of his pamphlet managed to weave together all the fears that helped power the racial antipathy of unionists in both countries. Here were the fears about prosperity ("meat"), freedom ("coolieism"), nationality ("American"), sexuality ("manhood"), and social Darwinism ("which shall survive"), all brought together and merged into the demand for Chinese exclusion.

The Effect in Australia

The Australian case suggests that there may be a problem with the conventional claim that racial hostility hindered the emergence of classwide organization and labor politics in the United States. Though there were some differences in the nature and targets of this hostility, Australian unionists had the same basic racial antipathies as their American counterparts. Yet in Australia, this was quite compatible with the establishment of new industrywide unions and a labor party. But the Australian case also suggests something more. It suggests that the effect of racial hostility may have been the reverse of that which the conventional explanation proposes. Uncomfortable though it is to acknowledge, the Australian case suggests that, rather than hinder the establishment of a labor party, racial hostility can actually serve to foster that development.

In Australia, racial hostility helped to facilitate the establishment of the Labor party both directly and indirectly. Indirectly, it helped to facilitate the formation of the Labor party by helping consolidate some of the earliest and most important examples of the new unionism. In key unions like those of the seamen, the miners, and the shearers, anti-Chinese and anti-black mobilization played an important (though by no means the only) role in consolidating industrywide organization. As we have seen, unlike craft unions, the new unions could not rely on the control of a monopoly of skills in order to exercise power in the labor market. As a result, they were more reliant on mobilizing popular support and political pressure to make industrial gains. Racial hostility helped the new unions do this because it made it easier for them to present their grievances as part of a concern that commanded broad classwide and cross-class support.

In 1878, the recently formed Seamen's Union went on strike against the employment of Chinese labor at below-union rates by the largest shipping company in Australia (Curthoys, 1978, and Markus, 1979, 81–87). Because of the anti-Chinese aspect of the dispute, the seamen rapidly gained support, not only from other unions, but also from large public meetings backed by middle-class politicians, and even eventually from the government. As the union itself noted in a retrospective assessment, it was this broad base of support that enabled it to effectively win the dispute and enjoy a subsequent period of "stability and solidarity" (Ebbels, 1983, 155–56). The Seamen's Union made use of a similar strategy during another major dispute in 1885 (this time linked to the demand for wage rises and a closed shop), and they repeatedly appealed to anti-Chinese sentiments thereafter (Markey, 1988, 288–89, and Markus, 1979, 168–70).

Other unions were quick to learn the same lesson. The establishment and consolidation of the Amalgamated Miners' Union was repeatedly accompanied by appeals to anti-Chinese sentiments (Markus, 1979, 74–78). Likewise, the shearers linked their 1891 campaign for a closed shop to agitation against the employment of Chinese cooks and shedhands (Markus, 1994, 170–76).[24] When the shearers were soundly defeated in the strike that followed, their leader, W. G. Spence, emphasized that the pastoralists had agreed to try to "prevent the employment of Chinese or Kanakas as shearers or shearers' cooks," in order to hold the union together by claiming some kind of victory (Markus, 1979, 174–75).

Writers and journalists aligned with the labor movement were well aware of the effects that racial hostility could have. The labor movement in Queensland was widely viewed as having the strongest commitment to socialism and classwide organization, and William Lane argued explicitly that it was the intensity of feeling about "coloured labour" that had fostered this. "I think that [coloured labour] has made Queensland as progressive as it is," says the socialist didact in his second novel, *The Workingman's Paradise*. "It was a common danger for all the working classes, and from what I hear has given them unity of feeling earlier than has been acquired in the south [of Australia]." (Miller, 1980 [1892], 89). Two months after the Maritime strike, an editorial in the *Bulletin* argued that only an appeal to racial identity could mobilize white workers to limit the ability of capitalists to undermine their interests.[25]

Racial hostility also directly helped consolidate electoral support for the fledgling Labor party. This was particularly clear in Queensland, where the campaign against Melanesian labor helped Labor candidates both solidify classwide support within their core constituency and appeal beyond it to other sections of the community. Some sense of just how important this sometimes was can be gleaned from the reaction to Labor's by-election victory in the sugar-growing district of Bundaberg in 1892. The *Australian Workman* described the win as a "crushing defeat of the slave-trade party . . . by the white labor candidate." According to the paper, "the issue was purely black and white, no other matter being allowed to intrude itself into the contest by the workers party."[26] Likewise in NSW, the campaign against "Afghan" camel drivers helped reinforce cross-class bonds between the shearers' union and the broader community in some large rural towns after the 1891 Shearers' strike (Merritt, 1986, 225). As we have seen, these bonds were crucial to Labor's electoral success in rural areas.

However, it is important not to overstate the significance of racial hostility. Neither the new unions nor the Labor party were established with racial goals as their principle objective. Indeed, in the early 1890s, racial issues were well down on the labor movement's agenda in most parts of Australia, including NSW.[27] In part, this was because the organizational security of the unions became the movement's central concern in the wake of repeated industrial defeats, and in part it was because legislation prohibiting Chinese immigration had already been achieved. Racial issues were not mentioned at all in the draft platform for a labor newspaper that the NSW TLC sent out to its affiliates at the beginning of 1890.[28] Nor were they mentioned in the original platform that the Parliamentary Committee of the TLC proposed for the NSW Labor Electoral Leagues. Before the 1891 elections, a clause demanding the stamping of Chinese-made furniture was added in response to lobbying by the furniture makers' union.[29] But during the campaign itself, labor candidates made little mention of racial issues. For example, a pamphlet issued by the labor candidates in West Sydney did not discuss these issues at all, and focused squarely on the conflict between workers and employers.[30]

However, although the salience of racial issues was relatively low in the early 1890s, the underlying attitude of key labor leaders was not in doubt.

TLC President Brennan—probably the single most important figure within the TLC pushing for the establishment of a labor party—had been a salaried canvasser for the Anti-Chinese League in 1888 (Markus, 1979, 145). TLC Secretary Houghton suggested to the 1891 Intercolonial Trades and Labor Union Congress that "the exclusion of alien races" was one of three core political objectives on which unionists throughout Australia could agree (ICTUC, 1891, 96–97).[31] Moreover, in the population as a whole, anti-Chinese and other forms of racial rhetoric remained popular, and in the late 1890s it returned to prominence and played an important role in consolidating support for the Labor party throughout Australia.

From 1896 onwards, the NSW Labor platform called for the "total exclusion of undesirable alien races," and in 1900 this clause was placed near the top of the Federal party platform.[32] In the first debate on immigration policy in the federal Parliament in 1901, the party's leader made it clear that, while Labor's support for the "White Australia" policy was "tinged with considerations of an industrial nature," the *main* reason for this support was the "possibility and probability of racial contamination" (Ebbels, 1983, 234–35). Racial consciousness had a strong grip on all classes, and there was little difference of opinion about immigration policy among the main parties in the federal Parliament (Markus, 1979, 220–21). By presenting itself as the most fervent advocate of a "White Australia," and by outbidding its opponents in its commitment to racial purity, the Labor party was able to appeal successfully to a broad cross-class electoral coalition and reinforce its credentials as a national rather than a purely class party (Markey, 1978, 76–77, and 1988, 295–96).

So, contrary to the conventional thesis about the United States, racial hostility in Australia fostered the establishment of a labor party, both indirectly, by helping consolidate the new unions, and directly, by helping consolidate the party's electoral support. Labor leaders were able to use racial hostility, and the white racial consciousness it helped generate, to strengthen their industrial and political organizations. White racial consciousness was a kind of identity resource, and labor leaders were able to use this resource both to strengthen the bonds between skilled and unskilled white workers, and to foster a cross-class alliance with sections of the middle class.[33]

The Effect in the United States Compared

Given the presence of a similar degree of racial hostility and white racial consciousness, were there some other characteristics of American society that made the effect of racial hostility different in the United States? The obvious candidate is the larger size of the black population. Racial hostility could only have the effect it had in Australia because the groups that were the targets of racial hostility had a limited capacity to undermine the interests of either the unions or the Labor party. I am tempted to call this capacity their "fight-back capacity," but I want to avoid any suggestion that it had to involve conscious resistance. Of critical importance was whether these groups were large enough to undermine efforts to establish new industrial unions, or to influence electoral outcomes. The presence of large numbers of workers who had been excluded from union membership would pose a threat to union organization simply by providing employers with a pool of labor on which they could draw whenever they felt the need. But the capacity of groups that were the target of racial hostility to resist in this way was not solely determined by numbers. It was also determined by social conventions and legal enactments that limited what jobs they could do and whether or not they could vote.

Did the racial hostility directed against African-Americans and Chinese immigrants in the United States alienate groups of workers who had the capacity to undermine efforts to build new unions or to establish a labor party? The conventional explanation of the effect of racial hostility assumes that they did. At first glance, the aggregate figures for the United States and Australia in Table 2.1 suggest that the far larger proportion of blacks in the United States may indeed have enabled them to have the kind of labor market impact that would have reversed the effect of racial hostility that was observed in Australia.

There can be little doubt this was so in the South. There, where African-Americans constituted 33.8 percent of the population (U.S. Bureau of the Census, 1975, 22), racial hostility undermined the prospects for a labor party both by creating divisions within the working class, which weakened the prospects for a more inclusive new unionism, and by creating divisions between black and white farmers, tenants, and sharecroppers, which weakened labor's potential allies in the populist movement. But the South, with its

TABLE 2.1.
Blacks, Chinese, and New Immigrant Europeans, as a Percentage of the Total Population, 1890 and 1891

	United States				Australia		
	Total U.S.	Pennsylvania	Illinois	California	Total Australia	NSW	Queensland
Blacks	11.93	2.05	1.49	0.94	0.33	0.09	2.39
Chinese	0.17	0.03	0.03	6.01	1.34	1.25	2.18
Slavs	0.82	1.32	1.75	0.39	0.13	0.14	0.13
Italians	0.29	0.46	0.21	1.28	0.12	0.13	0.11
Total Population	100.00	100.00	100.00	100.00	100.00	100.00	100.00

Notes and sources: see appendix

largely agrarian economy, and its small working class, was not the region in which one would have expected to see a labor party emerge in any case.

Of far greater importance were the industrial heartlands of the Northeast and Midwest, where the labor movement was strongest, and the prospects for a labor party were greatest. There, the situation was very different. Blacks were a much smaller proportion of the population in the North. They constituted 1.6 percent of the population in the Northeast, and 1.9 percent in the North Central census regions (U.S. Bureau of the Census, 1975, 22). Indeed, as Table 2.1 shows, in states like Illinois and Pennsylvania, which were the most likely proving grounds for labor party experiments, the combined population of blacks and Chinese immigrants was similar to that in key areas of Australia like NSW. In each case, it was about one to two percent.

In principle, it was possible for blacks to come north and compete with white workers, but in fact blacks were largely excluded from the northern labor market in the late nineteenth century (Cohen, 1991, 78–108, and Fredrickson, 1981, 221). Job competition was severely limited by formal and informal practices that restricted the mobility of black labor. Some of these were imposed in the North, where both employers and unions upheld conventions that sharply circumscribed job opportunities for blacks, and where local ordinances could prohibit blacks from crossing the city limits or remaining in a town after dark (Keiser, 1972, and Lewis, 1987, 84–85). Others resulted from increasing efforts to restrict the movement of black labor within the South.[34] In addition, poverty made the costs of long-distance travel prohibitive for many Southern blacks (Cohen, 1991, xiii, 109–10).

Strike-breaking was the hard cutting edge of the impact that alienated racial groups could have on union effectiveness, and northern employers did sometimes recruit southern blacks (and, more occasionally, Chinese) as strikebreakers. But while the fear of black strike-breaking was frequently invoked by white unionists, its actual extent was quite limited. A recent study counted only 42 instances of strike-breaking by blacks between 1865 and 1894 (Whatley, 1993). One reason why employers did not make more use of blacks as strikebreakers was the availability of white strikebreakers. As in Australia, employers in the United States had no difficulty finding white strikebreakers in any of the major industrial struggles of the early 1890s. Another reason was that they feared that the introduction of black strikebreakers would increase support for the strikers among the white community in general, and make it more difficult for them to gain crucial backing from local and state police and military forces. The experience of employers when they did introduce black strikebreakers showed that these concerns were often well-founded (Lewis, 1987, 82 and 84). In any case, whatever the mix of reasons, the proportion of blacks in the North did not rise significantly during the decade of the 1890s, despite the industrial unrest that marked that period. Indeed, in the Midwest, the proportion of blacks in the population slightly fell.[35]

So, overall, in the 1890s, the labor market clout of the main groups that were the targets of white racial hostility in the United States was similar to that of their counterparts in Australia. In neither case were they large enough to pose a significant threat to the effectiveness of the new unionism.

It is possible, of course, that this general picture did not apply in particular industries that were of crucial importance to the success of the new unionism. To check whether this was so, I want to briefly consider the composition of the workforce in three such industries: rail, coal, and steel. In states like Illinois and Pennsylvania, "colored" workers—almost all of whom were African-American—were typically an even smaller proportion of the workforce in the rail, coal, and steel industries than they were of the total population of the state. In Illinois, 0.7 percent of railroad workers, 2.5 percent of coal miners, and 0.4 percent of steel workers were "colored." In Pennsylvania, the figures were 1.0 percent, 0.7 percent, and 1.3 percent, respectively.[36] While case studies point to occasional examples of larger concentrations of black workers in particular companies, sometimes as a result of earlier strike-breaking incidents, the aggregate quantitative evidence underlines just how marginal the position of African-Americans was in the industrial labor market of the North.[37]

The unions in each of these industries adopted a different approach to black workers. The Amalgamated Association of Iron and Steel Workers rejected attempts to officially exclude blacks, but nevertheless acted to limit the number of blacks in their industry and the kind of jobs that were open to them (Kleinberg, 1989, 18). The American Railway Union—like the older craft-based Railroad Brotherhoods—restricted membership to whites, while the United Mine Workers opened membership to blacks. Both, however, suffered catastrophic industrial defeats in 1894, and there is little evidence to suggest that the ARU found it harder than the Mine Workers to organize and establish itself as a result of this color bar, or that it played a significant role in the union's demise.

So consideration of particular industries does not alter the overall conclusion that, in the industrial North in the early 1890s, neither blacks nor Chinese had sufficient labor market or electoral influence to stop racial hostility from having a similar effect to that which it had in Australia. However, there were a number of factors that may have made this effect less significant than it was in Australia.

First, as we have already seen, labor leaders in the United States were more ambivalent about overtly embracing racial hostility towards blacks. While the AFL was refusing to allow the machinists' union to affiliate until it removed the color bar from its constitution, the Wagga branch of the shearers' union in Australia was fearful that the NSW TLC would refuse to allow it to affiliate, not for having such a clause in its constitution, but rather for not doing enough to uphold it.[38] The ambivalence of American labor leaders was often

little more than rhetorical. But even when it was purely rhetorical, it still limited the ability of these leaders to use the racial identity of white workers to
the same extent as their Australian counterparts.

Second, it may also have been harder to make use of racial hostility towards
blacks to help glue together cross-class support for a union or a labor party. In
Australia, racial rhetoric enabled labor leaders to pose as having broader national concerns, over and above the narrow sectional economic interests of its
class constituency. In the United States, however, racial hostility towards
blacks still suggested slightly dubious national credentials in the North, given
the association of pro-slavery, anti-black sentiments with secession, rebellion,
and war against the Union.[39] These doubts about the national credentials of
racial antipathy were fading fast. Nevertheless, they probably still did something to limit the effectiveness of appeals to racial hostility towards African-
Americans in the early 1890s.

Third, while no ambivalence inhibited the use of anti-Chinese rhetoric by
labor leaders in the United States, the remoteness of the main areas of Chinese immigration from the major industrial centers of the Northeast and Midwest may have limited the effectiveness of such rhetoric. Of course, the extent
of racial hostility towards the Chinese did not necessarily depend on the number of Chinese immigrants who were present in any given area. The enthusiastic participation of workers in anti-Chinese demonstrations in Illinois and
Massachusetts during the anti-Chinese agitations in California, and the AFL's
national campaigns for the restriction of Chinese immigration, provide ample
evidence of that (Parmet, 1981, and Miller, 1969, 176–201). Nevertheless,
the comments of some labor leaders on the west coast suggest that they sometimes felt there was a lack of urgency about anti-Chinese campaigns among
unionists further east.[40]

These factors may have muted the effect of appeals to racial hostility in the
United States, and inhibited the ability of labor leaders to use it to strengthen
their industrial and political organizations. But they were unlikely, overall, to
alter the causal "direction" of that effect. Compared with Australia, the industrial and political advantages of appealing to the racial consciousness of
whites were probably more limited. But given the presence of the same basic
circumstances—a high level of racial hostility among whites, as well as black
and Chinese populations that were too small to threaten the effectiveness of
the new unionism—it seems reasonable to conclude that the conventional
claim that racial hostility hindered the development of the new unionism and
the establishment of a labor party is mistaken—at least in the early 1890s. To
the extent that racial hostility had an effect on these developments in the industrial North of the United States, it could, as in Australia, instead help to
foster them.

In the new century, all this would change. The First World War, reinforced
by subsequent restrictions on European immigration, altered labor market

conditions and encouraged a substantial movement of blacks to the North. Once this occurred, the effects of racial hostility quickly reversed. In the long run, racial hostility undoubtedly helped undermine industrial unions, and racial exclusion would not prove to be a viable strategy for labor leaders seeking to organize them. But in the early 1890s, none of this had happened yet.

EUROPEAN IMMIGRATION

However, before we can reach a final conclusion about the effect of racial hostility in the early 1890s, there is one further argument that must be addressed. According to this argument, racial hostility was able to undermine the prospects for the new unionism and the establishment of a labor party in the United States because it helped define the attitude of many existing unionists towards the so-called "new immigrants" from southern and eastern Europe.[41] Once the racial logic of hostility towards blacks or Chinese immigrants had been widely accepted, these antagonisms were extended by analogy to groups of European immigrants. As a result, Italians, Slavs, and others were increasingly characterized as "continental Chinese."[42] Like the Chinese, they were condemned not only for low-wage "coolie" competition and for supposed "slavish" sycophancy towards employers, but also for being "unassimilable" and somehow morally and physically "degenerate." Characteristics that were originally attributed exclusively to blacks and immigrants from China were transposed to southern and eastern European immigrants.

According to the proponents of this argument, the overall effect of these developments was to weaken an old antagonism between Protestants and Catholics and to strengthen a new antagonism between old and new immigrants (Mink, 1986, 53 and 76–77). Old immigrant Catholics from Ireland and Germany—many of whom were prominent unionists—were now redefined as natives in opposition to new immigrant Catholics and Jews from southern and eastern Europe. This in turn reinforced the solidarity of skilled AFL craft workers, most of whom could trace their origins to northern and western Europe. However, it simultaneously strengthened the cleavage between them and the mostly unorganized, unskilled new immigrant workers from southern and eastern Europe. In short, the emergence of racial nativism strengthened the intra-class divisions between skilled and unskilled workers which were hampering the emergence of a more inclusive unionism. It thereby undermined the prospects for the establishment of a labor party (Mink, 1986, 68, and Saxton, 1990, 313–16).

This is an important argument that raises a number of difficult issues. In retrospect, we can see that the late nineteenth century saw the beginning of a major change in the sources of European immigration to the United States. And it seems likely that, by the early twentieth century, an increasing tendency to characterize differences between European immigrants in racial terms was hindering the emergence of industrial unionism and labor-party politics. But what exactly was the situation in the early 1890s?

At the beginning of the 1890s, immigrants constituted 15 percent of the total population in the United States, and 32 percent of the total population in Australia (U.S. Census Office, 1894b, lxxix, and Vamplew, 1987, 8–9). In both countries, the vast majority of the foreign-born population were immigrants from northern and western Europe. Indeed, as Table 2.2 shows, when these are added to immigrants from other English settler societies (Canada, New Zealand, and either the United States or Australia), most of whom could also trace their origins to northern or western Europe, they constituted about 90 percent of the foreign-born population in both cases. There were, however,

TABLE 2.2.
Birthplaces of Immigrants, as a Percentage of the Foreign-Born Population, 1890 and 1891

	United States			Australia	
	U.S.	Pennsylvania	Illinois	Australia	NSW
North and West Europe	**78.8**	86.7	85.9	**89.3**	87.6
Britain	13.5	23.1	11.3	59.6	59.0
Ireland	20.2	28.8	14.8	22.7	23.2
Germany	30.1	27.3	40.2	4.5	3.0
Scandinavia	10.1	2.8	15.3	1.7	1.5
South and East Europe	**7.8**	11.2	9.0	**1.0**	1.3
Slav	5.5	8.2	8.0	0.4	0.5
Italy	2.0	2.9	1.0	0.4	0.5
English Settler	10.7	1.5	4.7	3.5	4.2
Canada	10.6	1.4	4.7	0.4	0.4
New Zealand	—	—	—	2.4	2.8
Australia/U.S.	0.1	0.1	<0.1	0.8	1.0
North and West Europe and English Settler	**89.5**	88.2	90.6	**92.8**	91.8

Notes and sources: see appendix

some important differences in the composition of these northern and western European immigrants. In the United States, the largest groups of northern and western Europeans came from Britain, Ireland, Germany, and Scandinavia, but in Australia, while there was some immigration from Germany and Scandinavia, the vast majority came from Britain and Ireland.[43] In addition, the proportion of southern and eastern European immigrants was significantly larger in the United States. Moreover, as the 1890s progressed, this proportion continued to increase, with the largest groups coming from Italy, Austria-Hungary, and Russia. By contrast, although there were a small number of Italians and others in Australia in the 1890s, immigration from southern and eastern Europe only became a major factor much later.[44]

Intellectual currents that characterized differences between Europeans in racial terms were becoming influential in both countries. Proponents of Social Darwinism and other "scientific" theories of racial difference posited the idea of a racial hierarchy at the top of which were the so-called Anglo-Saxons and their Nordic and German "cousins." Southern and eastern Europeans were located well down this racial hierarchy, above Africans and Asians, but below the "Teutonic and Celtic stock" of northern and western Europe. Many of these ideas were initially developed by academics and intellectuals in the late nineteenth century. Charles Pearson's role in formulating and popularizing some of these ideas in his book, *National Life and Character*, provides a prime example of the common ideological influences that flowed throughout the English-speaking world. Pearson, a former Oxford don and a liberal Minister for Education in Victoria, both influenced, and was influenced by, intellectuals and politicians in the United States and Britain, as well as Australia. His book, which was published in 1892, made a major impression on figures like Theodore Roosevelt and Henry Adams in the United States, and Prime Minister Gladstone in Britain.[45]

The attitudes of labor leaders and the pro-labor press towards southern and eastern Europeans suggest that these ideas were beginning to have an influence within the Australian labor movement in the early 1890s. But they also suggest that they had not yet been unambiguously embraced. Debates about the immigration of Italians and Russian Jews illustrate the attitudes that were evolving.

The beginnings of a racialized conception can be seen in discussions about the nature of Italian immigration. The Italian Workingmen's Mutual Benefit Society told the NSW TLC that it was concerned that "the Italian name will be brought down to the level of the Chinese" (Markey, 1978, 73), and in the early twentieth century there was indeed a growing tendency for unions to group Italian immigrants with the Chinese and Kanakas (Hunt, 1978, 84 and 94, and Saunders, 1978, 105).[46] But in the early 1890s, this racialized way of thinking about Italians was not yet firmly established. The TLC's ambiguous

attitude is well captured in a convoluted resolution it passed rejecting participation in an International Workingmen's Exhibition in Milan on the grounds
that the Exhibition's sponsor, the Italian government, was "crushing the
labour organizations in Italy and drowning in blood the hopes of the Sicilian
toilers." It resolved "That the Council heartily sympathises with the Sicilian
workers in the heroic struggle for 'Bread and Liberty' wishing them speedy victory and a more humane and democratic government. Furthermore as the
Capitalistic Italian Monarchy tends to drive to America and Australia millions of pauperised discontented men, who if inabilitated to emigrate, would
press the solution of the social question in their own country, [it] calls upon
the Australian workers to agitate to secure some legislation for the restriction
of Italian immigration." In short, the TLC urged Australian workers to assist
the heroic struggle of their Italian counterparts, by agitating for legislation to
prohibit them from immigrating to Australia.[47]

Rumors that Russian Jews who had been driven out of their country by
czarist persecution might be resettled in Australia immediately generated a vi-
cious racialized response from some sections of the labor movement. The *Bulletin* declared that "even the Chinaman . . . is preferable" . . . "If Australia has
to choose between the two Asiatics, the one with the tail is preferable to the
one with the Talmud every time."[48] However, some high-profile labor leaders
rebuked those who peddled these sentiments. Responding to a similar diatribe
in a tailor's letter to the *Australian Workman*, the editor pointed out that Marx
and Lassalle would have been treated similarly by the Russian government,
and J. D. Fitzgerald urged unionists to welcome Jews as fellow workers in the
cause of human emancipation.[49] But these more sympathetic attitudes did not
prevent the TLC from urging the exclusion of Russian Jews. Two years later, it
resolved to "approve of the action of the Government in introducing a Bill to
preclude this class of Immigration."[50]

Understanding the attitudes of Australian labor leaders towards southern
and eastern Europeans is complicated by the fact that these attitudes were
connected not only to racialized stereotypes associated with the anti-Chinese
agitation, but also with a long-standing hostility to immigration per se. The
Australian Intercolonial Trades Union Congress had consistently opposed
"assisted immigration" programs. The principle beneficiaries of these programs, in which Australian governments sought to encourage immigration by
bearing some of the costs, were immigrants from Britain and Ireland. Yet the
opposition of the Intercolonial Congress to assisted immigration was as consistent and longstanding as its opposition to Chinese immigration. Resolutions rejecting both were passed at the very first Intercolonial Congress and
were repeatedly reaffirmed thereafter.[51]

In the early 1890s, this more general opposition manifested itself in anxious
hostility to a proposal by General Booth of the Salvation Army to send poor
British emigrants to start a new life in Australia. Union leaders and the

pro-labor press were adamantly opposed to the proposal. The NSW TLC resolved that it "commends the action of Gen Booth . . . in exposing the sufferings and deplorable conditions of the masses of the people, but deprecates any action which would lead to the deportation of pauper or undesirable classes to the Australian colonies." Labour Councils in other parts of Australia wrote to support this stance and to coordinate their response. A letter from the Melbourne Trades Hall Council linked the immigration of poor Britons to the immigration of the Chinese.[52] And the *Hummer* complained that Londoners were the "dregs" of Europe, and would not provide the right racial material from which to build a great and prosperous Australian nation.[53]

This gives some feeling for the confused currents of ideology that informed the Australian labor movement's attitude towards immigrants in the early 1890s. There was certainly an emerging tendency to racialize the identity of southern and eastern Europeans, and to characterize them as "Continental Chinese." But it was also possible at times for unionists to conceive of a class of immigrants from England who were a kind of "British Chinese." Such a concept made absolutely no sense within the emerging framework of scientific racism. But that is the point. In the early 1890s, this ideological framework was only just emerging. For the moment, the attitudes of labor leaders were left oscillating between the two fixed points of traditional union policy: the general opposition to any immigration that might threaten the labor market conditions of their members, and the racial opposition to immigration by groups like the Chinese.

What were the attitudes towards southern and eastern Europeans that were prevalent in the United States in the early 1890s? And what, more particularly, were the attitudes of labor leaders and the labor press? As in Australia, these questions are difficult to answer. Awareness of the new sources of immigration, and racialized hostility towards it, did not suddenly appear fully formed, rather they developed over time and were in the process of emerging during the 1890s—developing first in some areas of the country and among certain sections of society, before later spreading to others.

Statisticians, as well as some academics and politicians, were certainly aware of the emerging changes in the sources of European immigration at the beginning of the 1890s, although they could not know that this trend would continue, and some thought it would be a passing phenomenon.[54] A handful of academic race theorists and patrician New Englanders were beginning to draw on the racial hierarchy of Anglo-Saxonism and Social Darwinism in order to analyze these changes and offer a rationale for opposing them.[55] But in the early 1890s, many Americans were still unaware of the changing composition of European immigration, and the new arguments of the racial nativists still played only a small role in public debate.[56]

We can trace the broad outlines of the evolution and development of public attitudes in the United States by following the changing assumptions underpinning immigration policy. Responding in part to union pressure, the federal government first excluded Chinese laborers (in 1882), then contract laborers (in 1885), then imposed a literacy test (in 1917), and finally ended up explicitly restricting the immigration of various categories of Europeans (in 1921 and 1924) (Mink, 1986, 108–10, and Tichenor, 2002, 3). It was the shift from the prohibition of contract labor towards the imposition of a literacy test that marked the acceptance of a racialized conception of southern and eastern Europeans. The principle proponent of the literacy test, Senator Henry Cabot Lodge (1891), explicitly justified the measure as a mechanism for excluding southern and eastern Europeans, and explicitly appealed to the new racial arguments to make the case that this was desirable. He argued that these immigrants "are not a good acquisition for us to make, since they appear to have so many items in common with the Chinese." His bill was extensively debated in 1896, passed the Senate by a majority of two, and would have been enacted had it not been vetoed by the President (Tichenor, 2002, 81–83). But after this close call, opponents of immigration restriction fought back, and it would be nearly two decades before a literacy test was, in fact, enacted.

The top leaders of the AFL were certainly aware of the changing composition of European immigration. In June 1894, Gompers told a United States Congressional Committee on Immigration that "now mostly Italians and Slavs were coming instead of desirable immigrants like the Germans and Irish" (Kaufman and Albert, 1989, 513). By then, Gompers was also prone to discussing southern and eastern Europe together with China and treating both as degraded and lacking civilization: a civilization which, he felt, had found its highest expression in England and the United States.[57] Eventually, much like the NSW TLC, he came to argue that the freedom of workers elsewhere was best served by requiring them to "remain within their own countries and help in national struggles" (Gompers, 1925, 157–58).

Elsewhere within the labor movement, awareness of the new immigrants and hostility towards them was variable. It was strongest in the mining and steel industries, especially in Pennsylvania, which had a long history of nativist hostility based on religion. "The situation is alarming" declared the national convention of the United Mine Workers in 1892, referring to the "great multitude" of Italians and Slavs who were coming to work in the coal fields (Laslett, 2000, 136). Likewise, the Pittsburgh-based *National Labor Tribune*, which was the official organ of the Amalgamated Association of Iron and Steel Workers, and had long adopted a strident nativist tone, repeatedly drew attention to the Slav, Italian, Hungarian, Russian, and Polish immigrants who were said to be displacing English, Scottish, Welsh, Irish, German, and American workers.[58]

These unions were undoubtedly hostile to the new immigrants, but the racialization of that hostility was only beginning to emerge. The *National Labor Tribune* criticized Gompers for considering only the "trade" aspect of the immigration question and not paying sufficient attention to its "moral" aspect. But this criticism partly reflected an older hostility towards "undesirable" European immigration in general. The *United Mine Workers' Journal* carefully distinguished between the "character" of different types of Austrians, supporting the immigration of those from Lower and Upper Austria and Bohemia, and calling for the exclusion of Hungarian and Slavonic immigrants. But the journal continued to frame its argument for exclusion in terms of the union movement's longstanding opposition to contract labor.[59] So in areas and industries where awareness of the new immigration was strongest, a tendency to racialize the differences between European immigrants was becoming apparent—although this was still somewhat ambiguous.

Taken as a whole, however, the union movement had not yet embraced racial hostility towards southern and eastern European immigrants in the early 1890s. At its 1894 convention, the AFL reaffirmed its existing policy of opposition to the immigration of contract labor, and then bluntly declared "that further restriction of immigration is unnecessary." It was not until well after the AFL's 1894 debate on the "Political Programme" that the union movement began to debate a change of policy. At the AFL's 1896 convention, a special committee put forward a resolution endorsing Henry Cabot Lodge's literacy test bill. But the resolution provoked strong opposition and the vote was lost. Opponents of the resolution were highly suspicious that the new racial nativism that underpinned the argument for a literacy test was merely a front for the old religious nativism of which many had themselves been victims, and of which there had been a great resurgence in the early 1890s. Their fears were reinforced by the anti-Irish rhetoric that some leading proponents of the literacy test had once embraced, opposition to the bill from German and Catholic organizations, and speeches by Democratic politicians arguing that the "real purpose" of the bill was "hostility to the Catholic Church" (Tichenor, 2002, 82). The resolution itself acknowledged these fears and sought to address them, but the majority of delegates were not persuaded, although in a concession to the leadership, the matter was referred back to the Executive Council for further consideration. Better organized, the leadership returned to the 1897 convention with a resolution that did pass. Only then did the AFL begin its commitment to a racialized logic for the exclusion of southern and eastern Europeans, although the commitment remained controversial for some time. A full-throated racial hostility towards southern and eastern Europeans had to wait for another decade.[60]

So in the early 1890s when the AFL was deciding whether or not to get involved in establishing a labor party, racial hostility towards southern and eastern Europeans was beginning to emerge in the United States, but it had not yet firmly established itself within the labor movement. On the contrary, until the late 1890s, the majority of union leaders were deeply suspicious of further immigration restriction, and the rhetoric of racial nativism that was associated with it. Careful attention to the timing of these developments is necessary in order to assess their impact on the decisions about labor politics that labor leaders made in 1894. This task is especially difficult because change was just around the corner, and, with the benefit of hindsight, it is easy for us to identify the emergence of attitudes that now seem to be the forerunners of subsequent developments. But during the AFL's debate about labor politics in the early 1890s, these developments had not yet taken place.

In any case, there were not enough "new immigrants" in the early 1890s to pose a threat to the organizational success of industrial unions or the electoral success of labor party experiments. There *were* larger concentrations of southern and eastern Europeans in key industrial states, like Illinois and Pennsylvania, than there were in the United States as a whole. But, as Table 2.1 shows, even in these states, Italians and Slavs together were still less than 2 percent of the total population.[61] To place this figure in perspective, note that it is similar to the proportion of African-Americans in these states, and three times less than the proportion of Chinese in California, where hostility, as in Australia, had tended to strengthen labor party experiments. A group of this size had only a limited capacity to influence labor market outcomes and the viability of union organization. These limits on the labor market influence of southern and eastern Europeans were further compounded by their even more limited electoral influence. During the 1890s, very few southern and eastern European immigrants met the requirements of the citizenship and electoral laws that governed the right to vote. Illinois, for example, required five years residency and full citizenship (Jensen, 1971, 188 and 253, Kleppner, 1979, 200, and Nash, 1982, 53).

The size of new immigrant groups also varied from industry to industry. However, although southern and eastern Europeans were sometimes a significant component of the workforce in particular companies and localities, overall they were still only a small proportion of the workforce in major industries. In 1890, Italians, Russians, Hungarians, and Bohemians together comprised 2.8 percent of railroad workers, 2.4 percent of steel workers, and 6.1 percent of coal miners.[62] In short, these workers were not yet a sufficient proportion of the workforce in key industries for their alienation to pose a serious threat to the organizational or electoral success of labor movement initiatives. Coal mining was already a partial exception to this (although, even in Pennsylvania, only about 14 percent of miners were Italians or Slavs, and three quarters were either native-born or from Britain or Ireland).[63] But, in that industry, Slav and Italian miners themselves initiated strike action and rallied to the union in the late 1890s, despite its official hostility to new immigrants (Nash, 1982, 34–40, and Higham, 1955, 72 and 87–88).

Let me briefly summarize the argument of this section. At first glance, the Australian case would seem to offer some support for the thesis that racial hostility towards "new immigrants" from southern and eastern Europe helped undermine the prospects for industrial unionism and labor-party politics.[64]

The late nineteenth century saw the beginning of a racialized hostility towards southern and eastern Europeans in both countries, and these immigrants comprised a significantly larger proportion of the U.S. population than they did that of Australia. But close attention to the timing of these developments suggests it would be a mistake to use this thesis to help explain the decisions of unionists in the early 1890s. There are two main problems with such an explanation. First, racialized hostility towards these groups had not yet firmly established itself within either labor movement in the early 1890s. Indeed, the majority of AFL leaders remained suspicious of the emerging arguments for racial nativism. Second, in the early 1890s, southern and eastern Europeans were still only a small proportion of the American population, even in key states and industries.

All this would soon change. By the beginning of the twentieth century, racialized hostility towards southern and eastern Europeans had become firmly entrenched in the official thinking of the AFL, and these immigrants, most of whom worked in unskilled or semi-skilled occupations, had become a significantly larger proportion of the American population. Together, these developments did indeed reinforce the craft focus of the AFL, and thereby weakened the prospects for industrial unionism and labor party politics. However, in the early 1890s, they had not yet developed sufficiently for hostility towards southern and eastern Europeans to be an important part of the explanation for the AFL's 1894 decision not to establish a labor party.

This does not preclude the possibility that other types of ethnic tensions did have an important effect. In fact, as we will see in Chapter 7, many American union leaders were very worried about such tensions. But it was tensions based on religion rather than race, which were the focus of their concerns. Religious hostilities had the potential to divide workers who hailed from northern and western Europe into large hostile blocks—blocks that were far larger than those formed by hostility directed towards southern and eastern Europeans. While religious hostilities could contribute to hostility towards southern and eastern European immigrants, they also tended to overshadow hostilities that were more specifically directed at this still small group. The most important organization fueling nativist hostilities in the early 1890s was the American Protective Association. But the central focus of its hostility was Catholicism, especially Irish Catholicism, and it seems not even to have been aware that there were growing numbers of southern and eastern European immigrants coming to the United States (Higham, 1992, 86).

CONCLUSION

In this chapter, I have focused on the impact of racial hostilities. I have tried to show that, contrary to conventional wisdom, racial hostility did not play an important role in hindering the establishment of a labor party in the United States. In both the United States and Australia, racial hostility towards blacks and Chinese immigrants was rampant. But the Australian case shows that racial hostility could actually foster the establishment of a labor party, if the targets of that hostility were not sufficiently numerous to disrupt the effectiveness of union organization or electoral mobilization. In the United States, unions in key northern industrial states found themselves in these same basic circumstances. Some other differences, like the greater uncertainty among top AFL leaders about the legitimacy of anti-black attitudes, muted the effect of racial hostility in the United States (relative to its effect in Australia). But these differences were unlikely to reverse the direction of this effect, as the conventional explanation supposes. Racial hostility might also have affected the prospects for labor politics by spilling over into relations between natives and "old immigrants" from northern and western Europe on the one hand, and "new immigrants" from southern and eastern Europe on the other. Racial hostility towards southern and eastern European immigrants was beginning to emerge in both countries, and these immigrants did form a larger group in the United States than they did in Australia. But neither the racialization of hostility towards these immigrants, nor the growth in size of their communities, had developed sufficiently in the early 1890s to affect the decisions about labor politics that were made in that period.

CHAPTER 3

Elections and the Constitution

In this chapter, I want to consider some of the basic institutions around which American politics is organized. A number of writers have suggested that these lie at the heart of any explanation for why there is no labor party in the United States (Oestreicher, 1988, 1286 and 1269, and Steinmo, 1994, 117). Many others argue that political institutions are part of the explanation, even if they are not the most important part. At least four institutional aspects of the American political system are said to have hampered the establishment of a labor party. Some are aspects of the electoral system. Others are aspects of the constitutional division of power. The first concerns the early expansion of manhood suffrage. The second concerns the incentives generated by the electoral system. The third concerns the vertical division of power, or the federal nature of American politics. The fourth concerns the horizontal division of power, and especially the presidential nature of the executive. These institutional features—especially the electoral ones—have been the basis for long-standing and widely canvassed explanations for the absence of a labor party. In this chapter, I will consider the effect of each in turn. Later, I will discuss some other political institutions. In Chapter 4, I will examine the courts, and in Chapter 7, the party system.

Early Suffrage

By the 1890s, universal manhood suffrage for whites had long been a fact of life in the United States. In Europe, by contrast, property qualifications and other class-related measures were still used to deny voting rights to a large proportion of working-class men. This difference is frequently pointed to as the source of one of the main explanations for why the United States failed to produce a viable labor party. According to this explanation, whether or not a state made the class position of workers politically significant had an important effect on whether or not workers chose to organize themselves politically on a class basis. By denying workers the equal political status of full citizenship, European states generated a class-based political grievance around which a labor party could mobilize support. By contrast, because the formation of a large industrial working class in the United States took place after property qualifications had been removed, American labor leaders were unable to mobilize support by appealing to these kinds of grievances.

This line of thought has a long history. Writing in 1907, Lenin attributed the weakness of the socialist movement in the United States to the absence of any "big nationwide democratic tasks facing the proletariat." A similar idea was developed by Perlman (1928). More recent advocates of the importance of the early enfranchisement of the working class include Lipset (1985, 227–29), Bridges (1986, 190–2), Marks (1989, 221–22), and Steinmo (1994, 117–18).[1] However, the comparison with Europe is sometimes overdrawn. In some European countries, property qualifications had been removed by the late nineteenth century, and in some others, the property qualifications that remained had the potential to reinforce divisions between skilled and unskilled workers.[2] In Europe, labor-based parties emerged both where workers were enfranchised early, and where they were enfranchised late. But, whatever the situation in Europe, the importance ascribed to this explanation is not supported by comparison with Australia.

At the beginning of the nineteenth century, almost all American states restricted voting to those who could meet various property qualifications. Change came unevenly since electoral law was solely a matter for the individual states. However, most states abandoned their property qualifications in a wave of democratic reform in the 1820s, '30s, and '40s, though many replaced it with the requirement that voting be restricted to those who paid tax. Although the amount of tax required was usually small, it still served to discourage poor workers from voting and it showed that the principle of universal manhood suffrage had yet to be fully accepted. Typically, however, this tax qualification proved to be a transitional measure, and by the mid-nineteenth century universal manhood suffrage for whites (or something quite close to it) was the norm in the United States.[3]

But by the end of the 1850s, universal manhood suffrage for whites was also the norm in Australia. At the beginning of that decade, the British government had accepted Australian demands for self-government, and legislative and executive powers were transferred from the Imperial Parliament to the parliaments of the separate Australian colonies. As in the United States, electoral laws were different in the various colonies. The constitutions under which self-government was established typically provided for a property qualification, but before the end of the decade, legislation establishing universal manhood suffrage had been adopted in all but two cases.[4] By the 1880s and 1890s, universal manhood suffrage for whites was, as in the United States, a long-standing and widely accepted fact of political life. Indeed, it was an important element of the democratic and egalitarian self-image of both Australians and Americans.

This is not to say that labor leaders and unionists in the 1880s and 1890s were entirely happy with electoral laws in either country. On the contrary, a number of serious shortcomings vexed reformers in both the United States and Australia. Some of these were common to both countries. For example, the unequal size of electoral districts and rural gerrymanders often reduced the value of the votes cast by urban workers; and residence requirements disenfranchised itinerant and mobile workers. These typically required 12 months residence in the United States and six months in Australia.[5] Some shortcomings were specific to Australia. For example, plural voting enabled those with property outside the electorate in which they resided to vote in more than one electorate; and the upper houses of the colonial parliaments (though weaker than their counterparts in the United States) were either appointed or were elected by those meeting a property qualification. Some shortcomings were specific to the United States. For example, poll taxes and other economic restrictions, educational and literacy tests aimed at whites, and complex registration regulations had been introduced in various states; and the absence of official ballot papers and secret voting procedures led labor and populist leaders to demand the introduction of what Americans called the "Australian ballot."[6] In addition, many labor leaders in both countries sought other changes, including the introduction of the referendum and the initiative, and more direct elections. Some also agitated for votes for women.

In Australia, payment of members of parliament was a long-standing demand of many labor leaders. In Victoria, this reform had been introduced in 1870. But in NSW, payment of parliamentarians was only enacted in 1889 (Pernica, 1958, 426), and it is often cited as one of the factors that led union leaders to consider establishing a labor party the following year. Prior to this, members of parliament had to be men of independent means, and unions found that even maintaining one member of parliament was too much of a financial drain (Gollan, 1960, 52, Ebbels, 1983, 213, and Markey, 1988, 174 and 203). However, the payment of members of parliament does not distinguish Australian legislative bodies from their counterparts in the United States, for although the situation differed from state to state, some form of payment was also the norm in the United States in the late nineteenth century (Hayes, 1900a, 72–74, and 1900b, 101–3). So, whatever role the introduction of payments for parliamentarians played in facilitating the establishment of labor parties in Australia, it cannot be a reason for the failure of labor leaders in the United States to pursue a similar course of action.

The continued presence of a property qualification for some Australian upper house elections would seem to be the best grounds on which to build a defense of the conventional early suffrage explanation for developments in the United States. In NSW, however, where the Labor Party first emerged, the upper house was appointed and the party made no mention of the issue in its first election platform. Moreover, in Victoria, where property qualifications were in force, the need to reform the upper house tended to strengthen the predilection of labor leaders to remain within the camp of the established liberal party. Later in the 1890s, the NSW Labor party did address the question of upper house reform, especially after various attempts were made to obstruct legislation backed by labor and liberal politicians. The party called for the direct election of the upper house, or for its replacement by a system of legislative review by referendum.[7] Of course, the United States Senate was also not directly elected at this time.

The NSW Labor party did use electoral reform to mobilize support during its first election campaign in 1891, but its principal demand in this area was the abolition of plural voting. In Sydney and its suburbs, it is possible that as many as 18 percent of those who were entitled to vote were plural voters—that is, they were property owners who could also vote in another electorate. George Grey, a veteran liberal and a former governor of South Australia and Premier of New Zealand, spearheaded a campaign on this issue during a visit to Sydney a couple of months before the election. The NSW Trades and Labour Council (TLC) made a great fuss over the "grand old democrat" and associated itself closely with his campaign. On his arrival, the executive committee was sent to interview Grey in his hotel, and upon his departure the whole council adjourned early and marched to his ship to send him off.[8]

However, similar opportunities were also available to labor leaders in the United States. Contrary to popular belief, the second half of the nineteenth century was marked by "mushrooming upper- and middle-class antagonism to universal suffrage" (Keyssar, 2000, xxii). Not only did some states have ongoing economic restrictions on the suffrage, but others debated proposals to reintroduce such restrictions. These restrictions were debated in the North as well as the South, and while some were principally aimed at the exclusion of racial or immigrant groups, others were aimed more generally at the exclusion of lower-class natives and whites.[9] These debates gave labor leaders the opportunity to not only champion democratic electoral reform but also to act as the defenders of established American political rights. As in Australia, the issues differed from state to state. In New York, for example, an attempt was made to reimpose a property qualification on those citizens who were entitled to elect officials who controlled taxation and expenditure. The measure passed the state legislature in 1877, but failed when it was resubmitted the following year (Beckert, 2001, 18–24). Jurors in New York, however, did have to meet a property qualification. The jurors who convicted the Theiss boycotters, and thus helped launch Henry George's 1886 United Labor party campaign, had to have property worth at least $250. They were all employers (Foner, 1955, 118). Complaints about restrictions like these were often aired in the labor press. A widely circulated speech by Henry Demarest Lloyd (1893, 1) that helped launch the AFL's Political Programme debate at its 1893 convention, began by drawing attention to the latest efforts to restrict the right of workingmen to vote.

The claim that the early introduction of voting rights for workers can explain the absence of a labor party in the United States seems implausible when compared with Australia. Something close to universal manhood suffrage for whites was a well-established feature of both societies in the second half of the nineteenth century. But labor leaders in both societies could still appeal to democratic demands and the defense of classless suffrage rights in order to help mobilize support for independent labor politics. Moreover, even if there had been no such opportunities, the conventional argument would still be misleading because the effect of universal manhood suffrage is more ambiguous than the conventional argument recognizes. Full acceptance of universal manhood suffrage might have left labor leaders without the opportunity to appeal to a democratic cause that many European socialists championed to great effect (Lipset, 1985, 227–29, and Geary, 1981). However, in both the United States and Australia, there were other actions of the state that continued to generate major class-based grievances. A well-entrenched and widely accepted classless system of manhood suffrage offered significant advantages to labor leaders seeking to tackle these grievances. It provided them with regular, fully legitimized opportunities to mobilize workers politically in order to gain some influence, or even control, over the actions of the state. In short, even when universal manhood suffrage removes one opportunity, it provides another.

THE ELECTORAL SYSTEM

There are, however, other arguments about the effects of the American electoral system. These typically focus on two of its features: the first-past-the-post formula for converting votes into seats, and the single-member districts (or constituencies) from which representatives are drawn. This single-member plurality electoral system is then compared with the multiple-member districts and proportional representation of electoral systems that prevail in most of Europe. The basic argument is that, while European electoral systems facilitate the emergence of a multiparty system, the U.S. single-member plurality system reinforces the position of the two main existing parties and makes it extremely difficult for any third party, including a labor party, to gain legislative seats.

Among the proponents of this argument, some—like Lipset (1963, 293–95), Husbands (1976, xxx) and Marks (1989, 217–18)—focus specifically on the effect of the electoral system on labor or socialist parties, while others—such as Schattschneider (1942, 65–84), Mazmanian (1974), and Rosenstone et al. (1984, 16–19 and 48–80)—focus on its effect on third parties in general. In each case, however, the basic argument is the same.

These studies of the United States appeal to a well-known comparative literature that broadly supports the claim that there is a correlation between the electoral system and the number of parties in the legislature.[10] Lijphart (1994, 95–98 and 143), for example, finds that in a plurality system, psychological effects—resulting from the fear that a vote for a third party is a wasted vote—reduce the effective number of parties to three, and mechanical effects—resulting from the formula by which votes are translated into seats—further reduce the effective number of parties to two. These comparative studies also find that the number of seats per district (the "district magnitude") has a significant influence over the effective number of parties in the legislature. The district magnitude creates a threshold—a minimum level of electoral support—that parties must cross in order to gain seats. All single-member districts, irrespective of whether a plurality or a majority formula is used, establish significantly higher thresholds than those established by the multimember districts required for proportional representation. The effective threshold for single-member plurality and majority systems is 35 percent, while the average effective threshold for proportional systems is less than 7 percent (Lijphart, 1994, 50–51).[11]

Does the evidence of these studies allow us to conclude that the electoral system played an important role in hampering the emergence of an American labor party? Comparison with Australia poses an obvious problem. In the second half of the nineteenth century and into the early twentieth century, Australia had a plurality electoral system like that in the United States, and yet, under this system, the unions were able to establish and consolidate a labor party. The same point can be made about other English-speaking countries. Britain, New Zealand, and Canada all had plurality electoral systems, but in all of them, labor parties were established that consolidated themselves either as one of two main parties (as in Britain and New Zealand), or as a permanent third party (as in Canada).

English-speaking countries were not the only places where labor-based parties established and consolidated themselves under high-threshold electoral systems, for proportional representation had not yet been introduced when European social democratic and socialist parties first emerged. In Denmark and Sweden, these parties entered parliament and became an important political force under single-member plurality systems like those in the English-speaking countries. In Germany, Austria, Italy, the Netherlands, and Norway, the same thing happened under single-member majoritarian systems that required two or more ballots with only two candidates in the final round and hence an absolute majority for the winner (Grumm, 1958, 367–73, Rokkan, 1970, 155–58, Carstairs, 1980, 10 and 213). While in France, the socialists consolidated themselves under a similar two-ballot system, but without the requirement for an absolute majority in the final ballot.[12] These two-ballot systems, which grew out of the electoral traditions of the Catholic Church, shared many of the features that make plurality systems inimical to third parties. In particular, they shared the single-member districts that help establish a high threshold for entry into the legislature. Moreover, while they avoided some of the psychological (or "wasted vote") effects of plurality systems, they all (with the exception of France) actually imposed a higher threshold than plurality systems by insisting that a winning candidate gain 50 percent of the vote.

Far from helping to cause the rise of labor-based parties, proportional representation was typically introduced by their opponents as a response to their rise. Proportional representation was introduced in two phases. In a few cases, it was introduced prior to the First World War to ensure minority representation in culturally divided societies like Belgium and Finland. But in the large majority of cases it was introduced after WWI. In this second phase, representation was typically introduced at the behest of established "bourgeois" parties that were attempting to protect their ability to win seats in the face of a rapidly growing labor-based party (Lipset and Rokkan, 1967, 32–33, Boix, 1999).

Similar concerns led the non-Labor parties to introduce the preferential (or alternative vote) system in Australia. This changed the standard plurality system into a majoritarian one and removed much of the psychological fear that a vote for a small party was a wasted vote. Again, far from being a cause of Labor's growth, the introduction of preferential voting was primarily a response to it by opposing parties who were fearful that the divisions between them would deliver government to Labor (Wright, 1980, 53–54). There was a long tradition of property owners seeking to protect their position by urging the introduction of either proportional representation or the limited vote in order to protect "minority interests" (Pernica, 1958, 22–28). Until the rise of the Labor Party, however, these efforts had been in vain. The first successful effort to alter the electoral formula occurred in Queensland in the lead up to the 1893 election. Reacting to the manifest strength of the Labor party in Queensland by-elections, as well as in other parts of Australia, the liberal premier, Samuel Griffith, introduced optional preferential voting.[13] Indeed, so worried was he about Labor's growing strength that he delayed the expected date of the election by two years and, reversing earlier reforms, introduced stricter residential qualifications and halved parliamentary salaries (Murphy, 1975, 138 and 148–50). Elsewhere in Australia, fully preferential systems were introduced for similar reasons in the twentieth century.[14]

There is no doubt that, by imposing a high threshold, single-member plurality (and majority) systems place more obstacles in the way of insurgent parties than proportional systems. But in the late nineteenth and early twentieth centuries, proportional systems were rarely used, not only in the English-speaking world, but also in Europe. Indeed, before 1900 no European country used proportional representation for national elections, and no large European country used it before the end of the First World War (Grumm, 1958, 374, Rokkan, 1970, 157, and Carstairs, 1980, 9).[15] Thus, these obstacles, far from being unique to the United States, were actually the norm. Moreover, as the preceding cases show, whatever effect these obstacles might have had on other parties, labor-based parties repeatedly found that they had the kind of electoral support that enabled them to be surmounted.

The ability of the electoral system to shape the party system is not limitless. In a single-member plurality system, if a party can muster one vote more than

50 percent in a given district, it will certainly win a seat. Usually it requires less. Just how much less depends on the number and strength of its competitors. Where there are closely fought elections between the two major parties (as there were in a number of key industrial regions of the United States in the late 1880s and early 1890s), and where labor draws support from both of the other parties, then a third of the vote will suffice. If additional parties (like the Prohibitionists) are in the race, then even less may be needed. Whatever the threshold though, the single most decisive factor will be the geographical distribution of the party's potential support (Schattschneider, 1942, 70).

A single-member plurality electoral system will not hamper an emerging party if its potential supporters are sufficiently geographically concentrated to cross the threshold in a number of electoral districts. What the emergence of labor-based parties in other countries shows is that the potential support for these parties *was* sufficiently geographically concentrated. It was not only sufficiently concentrated in the most highly industrialized countries (like Britain and Germany), but in a wide range of countries, including many that were far less industrialized, in Europe and beyond. As one of the most industrialized countries in the world in the late nineteenth century, the United States fell in the upper end of this range. If Australia had some electorates with sufficiently large concentrations of workers to support a labor party, then this was certainly also true of the United States. This suggests that it is reasonable to conclude that the electoral system is not an important part of the explanation for why there is no labor party in the United States.

MULTIMEMBER DISTRICTS

However, there is an often overlooked fact that complicates this conclusion. The argument I have been discussing emphasizes the impact of single-member plurality elections, but in the United States, although almost all elections made use of the plurality formula in the late nineteenth century, many were conducted in multimember electoral districts. Indeed, at the beginning of the nineteenth century, multimember districts had been the norm. From 1842 onwards, elections to the federal House of Representatives relied exclusively on single-member districts. But a great many state legislatures continued to make use of multimember districts (or a combination of single-member and multi-member districts), especially for House elections.

In 1870, House representatives elected from multimember districts outnumbered those from single-member districts, and only five states made exclusive use of single-member districts. Moreover, the use of multimember districts was not concentrated in one region of the United States, but was spread throughout the more industrial Northeast and Midwest as well as being used in the South and West. Although there was a slow trend toward single-member districts in the late nineteenth century, multimember districts continued to be widely used, and in 1912 there were still only nine states that made exclusive use of single-member districts. In fact, as late as 1962, just prior to the Supreme Court's reapportionment rulings, 46 percent of house representatives in the states were elected from multimember districts (Klain, 1955, 1113–16, Silva, 1964, 505–6, and Hamilton, 1967, 321 and 331).

The Australian experience suggests that one way in which a labor party might emerge is by first establishing itself in some states, before then spreading to others. Given this, the effect of electoral systems in the states is of considerable importance.

So what is the effect of a multimember plurality electoral system on the prospects for establishing a labor party? As we have seen, the comparative literature on twentieth century elections suggests that the greater the district magnitude, the easier it should be for a new party to establish itself. However, this finding does not apply if comparison is limited to plurality systems. Indeed, when plurality systems alone are considered, increasing the district magnitude might be expected to make it harder for a new party to establish itself. In a three-member plurality system, for example, each voter would have three votes and the three candidates with the largest number of votes would win a seat. If voting is party-based, this is likely to result in a clean sweep for the party supported by the largest number of voters. However, while the winning party might have an overall plurality in this three-member district, it may not have a plurality in each of the three districts into which this district would be split if single-member districts were used. If a losing party in a multimember district would have a plurality in at least one of these hypothetical single-member districts, then the multimember system would deny it a seat that it could have won in a single-member system (Silva, 1964, 312–16, and Lakeman, 1974, 36–40). In the twentieth century, this is precisely what happened to black voters in large American cities with multimember or "at-large" elections (Engstrom and McDonald, 1981).

Would we expect a similar effect to inhibit the formation of a labor party in the late nineteenth century? The Australian case suggests not. Australian legislatures also typically made use of multimember districts. For example, in the 1891 election to the NSW lower house, the Legislative Assembly, there were 36 seats in four-member districts, 30 in three-member districts, 40 in two-member districts, and 35 in single-member districts.[16] This election is especially interesting, not only because it was when the Labor party first established itself, but also because Labor's success was greatest in the largest multimember districts. Labor won four (of the 35) single-member seats with 9.42 percent of the vote, 11 (of the 40) two-member seats with 18.37 percent of the vote, seven (of the 30) three-member seats with 20.53 percent of the vote, and 14 (of the 36) four-member seats with 25.84 percent of the vote (Hughes and Graham, 1968, 428–40).

A closer look at the NSW experience suggests that, as in single-member plurality systems, the prospects for a labor party in a multimember plurality system principally depends on the geographical concentration of its potential supporters. Labor's success in four-member districts is hardly surprising given that many of these districts covered areas of Sydney where large numbers of working-class voters were concentrated. For example, the districts of Balmain and West Sydney, in both of which Labor won all four seats by a substantial margin, were centers of waterfront and craft unionism. Labor won 48.7 percent of the votes cast in Balmain, and 55.8 percent in West Sydney. Similarly, the four-member districts of Newtown and Redfern, where Labor won four of the five seats it contested, were centers of railway unionism. Labor won 27.2 percent and 31.7 percent, respectively, in these districts.[17]

The general point that emerges from the NSW case is that increasing the district magnitude in a plurality electoral system can only have an effect on a party's prospects if it is possible to make the district large enough to swamp the party's potential supporters. Thus, it is not the number of seats per district (or the district magnitude) in itself, but rather the number of voters per district, and the size of a party's support-base within it, that has an effect on the party's prospects.[18] While it was certainly possible to swamp black voters in some citywide elections in the United States, workers in the industrial centers of the Northeast and Midwest could not all be swamped in a similar way. There were simply too many large concentrations of workers.

In principle, the number of voters per district might have been so much greater in the United States that despite its more industrialized economy, it was easier to swamp working class majorities than it was in Australia. But this was not the case. In the 1891 elections in NSW, single-member districts had an average of 2,153 voters, and four-member districts had an average of 10,850 voters, with 8,163 in the smallest district, and 18,704 in the largest (Hughes and Graham, 1968, 429). In the United States, many of the industrialized states of the Northeast and Midwest had electoral districts that fell within a similar range. Massachusetts, for example, had an average of 2,336 voters per district in the mid-1890s (Hayes, 1900a, 66). Illinois, which had unusually large seats, had an average of about 19,000 voters in each district.[19] In short, the presence of multimember electoral districts does not alter the earlier conclusion that the basic problems facing American advocates of a labor party were not connected to the nature of the electoral system.

The Case of Illinois

A final piece of evidence that helps clinch the argument against the importance of the electoral system comes from an intra-U.S. comparison. The focus of this comparison is the state of Illinois. Uniquely among the U.S. states,

Illinois used a semi-proportional multimember system to elect representatives to its lower house (the Legislative Assembly). This so-called "cumulative voting" system was used continuously between 1870 and 1980. The system divided the state into three-member districts and each voter had three votes. As in a plurality election, the voter could give one vote to each of three candidates. But unlike in such a system, the voter could also cumulate his votes by giving one and a half votes to each of two candidates, by giving two votes to one candidate and one to another, or by giving all three votes to a single candidate. Both the intention and the effect of this system were to make it easier for a minority party to win a seat by enabling its supporters to concentrate their votes on one candidate. Under Illinois's cumulative voting system, any party with the support of 25 percent of the voters would be certain to win a seat—and where a third party was competing with two established parties, a smaller percentage would typically suffice. From 1870 until the end of the nineteenth century, third parties were represented in the state legislature in all but two years.[20]

If the plurality electoral system was one of the principle obstacles to the establishment of a labor party in other parts of the United States, then we might expect a labor-based party to have succeeded in establishing a foothold in Illinois.

A serious attempt *was* made to establish a labor-populist party in Illinois in the early 1890s. The high point of this effort was the election of 1894, which took place in circumstances that were similar in many respects to those in NSW in 1891. The Illinois election of 1894 took place in the immediate aftermath of the Pullman strike, just as the NSW election had taken place in the aftermath of the Maritime strike. As in Sydney, workers in Chicago had been at the center of a massive nationwide strike and had firsthand experience of its defeat. In addition, at the time of the election the AFL appeared to be moving to endorse independent labor politics nationally, just as the Intercolonial Trade Union Congress had done in Australia. Yet for those involved in this effort, the 1894 election was a disappointing failure.[21]

Unfortunately, it is not possible to provide data that would enable us to directly compare the class composition of electoral districts in Illinois and NSW.[22] Nevertheless, there is plenty of evidence that these poor electoral results occurred despite the fact that there were more than enough workers to elect representatives in a number of districts. Illinois had a large industrial workforce, both in Chicago—a city that was substantially more industrialized than Sydney—and in other parts of the state where large numbers of rail, coal, and steel workers were concentrated. The problem was not the class geography of the Illinois electoral districts. The problem was that the labor-populists could not muster enough working-class votes.

In Cook County (where the bulk of Chicago's population resided), the potential labor vote was estimated by contemporaries at about 235,000, but only between 34,000 and 40,000 votes were cast for labor-populist candidates (Destler, 1946, 209). According to one estimate, only 13.1 percent of voters in Chicago's lower-class wards, and 14.4 percent of voters in its lower middle-class wards, voted for these candidates.[23] In addition, in the election for the federal House of Representatives, Chicago's second electoral district contained more industrial workers than any other electoral district in the United States. Many of its voters worked in packinghouses, railroads, and factories, and workers in the district had experienced some of the worst confrontations with soldiers and police during the Pullman strike (Tarr, 1971, 38–42). Moreover, according to a police department survey, unemployment in Chicago had been running at 25 percent in the packinghouses, 20 percent in the railroad yards, and 50 percent in the factories (Jensen, 1971, 212). And yet the labor-populist candidate in Chicago's second district won only 18.2 percent of the vote (Allen and Lacey, 1992, 27).

Outside Chicago, rail and coal workers had also suffered severely during the recent strikes. These workers were more likely than others to vote for labor-populist candidates. But even in the towns and counties in which they were concentrated, the populists were unable to prevail. Altogether, populists won 18 percent of the vote in Illinois's coal towns, and their vote in counties like Will, Peoria, and Rock Island, which were both railroad and industrial centers, ranged from about 5 to 7 percent.[24] These results were similar to those in other states with large concentrations of industrial workers. In Pennsylvania, the populists won 14 percent of the vote in bituminous coal towns, and 5 percent of the vote in the state's steel communities. In Ohio, where the president of the United Mine Workers union lead the campaign, the labor-populists still only won 20 percent of the vote in the state's coal towns.[25]

The case of Illinois helps to confirm the argument that factors other than the electoral system were obstructing the emergence of a labor party in the United States. Here was a state in which a unique electoral system significantly lowered the threshold that a new party would have to cross in order to win seats. And yet, despite a serious effort, propitious circumstances, and a large pool of potential labor voters, it still proved impossible to establish such a party.

FEDERALISM

The early development of manhood suffrage and the incentives generated by the electoral system were similar in the United States and Australia, but the constitutional division of power was not. In this section, I want to consider the vertical division of power between the federal and state governments. In the next section, I will examine the horizontal division of power between the legislative and executive arms of government.

Comparison of the vertical division of power is complicated by the fact that the Australian states were preparing to federate in the 1890s. Indeed, the first federal convention met in Sydney a couple of months before the 1891 elections, and the NSW Premier, Henry Parkes, had been busy over the previous two to three years establishing his claim to be the father of federation. But it was not until 1898 that a plan for federation was put to a referendum, and the new federal government was not itself launched until the beginning of 1901. Thus, at the time when the first labor parties were being established, each of the Australian states remained a separate self-governing political unit.

Some writers have suggested that the federal structure of political institutions in the United States played an important role in determining the fate of labor politics (Perlman, 1928, 286, Lowi, 1984, 37–38 and 45–50, Oestreicher, 1988, 1270–2, and Steinmo, 1994, 120–21). These writers argue that, because federalism dispersed authority between so many different political units, it made it nearly impossible to capture sufficient governmental authority to effect fundamental economic or social change. The states had jurisdiction over many of the questions that were of most concern to unions, and so a labor-based party could only achieve decisive, systematic reform if it could gain control over many different governments at once. But this, they argue, would be extremely unlikely.

The problem with this argument does not arise from comparison with Australia. The problem with it is that it addresses the wrong question. The question we are addressing is not "Why have labor parties failed to achieve all their goals?" or "Why have they failed to achieve fundamental social change?" It is not the failure to do these things that distinguishes the labor movement in the United States from its counterparts in Europe, Australia, and elsewhere. Rather, the question we are addressing is "Why has the labor movement failed to establish an electorally viable political party?" and, in particular, "Why has a labor-based party failed to gain a foothold in the political system?" In these respects, federalism helped rather than hindered.

Federalism fostered the establishment of a labor party in a number of ways. First, it lowered the barriers to entry into the political system by increasing the number of points of access for a new labor party. Second, it created political units in locations where such a party might have been able to secure an initial base. This made it possible for a party to first seek to establish itself in those states and regions where the strength of the labor movement was greatest. And third, it enabled the labor movement to engage in strategic experimentation, by offering a wide variety of different opportunities—at federal, state, and local levels—in which to try out different political models. In short, the multiplicity of political units in a federal system may have hindered radical society-wide reforms, but it simultaneously increased the opportunities for those seeking to establish a political foothold.

There is no obvious cross-nation correlation between the presence of federalism and the absence of labor-party politics. Federal systems in countries like Germany, Switzerland, and Canada did not inhibit the establishment of these parties (Lipset and Marks, 2000, 57). Indeed, as the Australian case showed in the early twentieth century, once labor parties had achieved a certain degree of success in a few key states, federalism generated incentives that fostered the spread of labor parties to other states. Once labor parties had established themselves in NSW, Queensland, and South Australia, competition for influence in the federal arena gave them an incentive to strengthen their weak or scarcely existent counterparts in Victoria, Tasmania, and Western Australia (Murphy, 1975, 9, and Loveday et al., 1977, 112–13).

Presidentialism

There are two aspects of the horizontal division of power in the United States that some claim have contributed to the failure to establish a labor party. The first concerns the presidential (or gubernatorial) nature of the executive. The second concerns the powerful role of the courts. In both of these respects, Australia differed from the United States. In each part of Australia, as well as at the federal level, the institutions of government were principally modeled on the Westminster parliamentary system.[26] In this section, I want to consider the effect of presidentialism in the United States. In the next chapter, I will turn to the role of the courts.

Some authors claim that it is not the electoral system alone, but rather its interaction with presidentialism, that helps explain the failure to establish a labor party (Schattschneider, 1942, 83, Lipset, 1963, 294–95, and 1996, 40–41 and 86, and Marks, 1989, 218). They point out that, whatever the effect of the plurality system on legislative elections, it certainly fosters a two-party system in presidential (and gubernatorial) elections. In a parliamentary system, like that in Britain and Australia, a third party might hope to win the balance of power and share control of the executive. But in the United States, only one person can win the presidency (or the governorship of a state), and in order to do so his or her party must be able to attract widespread support across the country (or state). The geographical concentrations of strength that could win a number of legislative seats for a third party would be little help in a presidential election. Worse still, the problems facing a third party would be compounded by a strong psychological effect. Noticing that the two main parties are the only likely winners, third-party supporters are likely to conclude that a vote for their party would be wasted, and may even help to elect the candidate they least prefer.

This line of argument is unobjectionable. But the authors I am discussing go further and argue that the two-party-reinforcing effect of presidential elections "contaminated" the party system that emerged from legislative elections. As a result, they argue, it undermined the ability of third parties to win legislative seats, even where they had geographically concentrated support.

The evidence from comparative studies is limited (Shugart and Carey, 1992, 220 and 227–28, and Lijphart, 1994, 2 and 133–34). But two main arguments have been put forward to defend the claim that presidential elections contaminate the party system that would otherwise emerge from legislative elections. The first concerns the incentives facing party activists. The second concerns the behavior of voters.

The first argument rests on a comparison with parliamentary systems like those in Britain or Australia. In a parliamentary system, a third party can hope to win some control over the executive by gaining the balance of power in the legislature. But, according to this argument, in a presidential system, the only way to exercise some control over the executive is to participate in the election campaign of one of the two main parties. And so activists in the United States had an incentive to channel their activities into one of the two main parties, even when an independent third party was viable in the legislature (Shugart and Carey, 1992, 227).

The general problem with this argument is that it reaches conclusions about the incentives facing party activists in the United States by drawing on a misleading comparison between their situation and that of party activists in parliamentary systems. The question facing activists in the United States was not whether the incentive to establish a labor party was stronger in Britain or Australia, but whether there were sufficient incentives to do so in the United States itself.

While control over the executive was important, it was not the only kind of control that was important, especially prior to the growth of executive power in the twentieth century. Legislative power was also a big prize. Indeed, in many states, the legislature was seen as "the most important and powerful organ of the state government" (Bogart and Mathews, 1920, 288). Given sufficient geographically concentrated support, a labor party (at either a federal or state level) could hope to win the balance of power in Congress, and use it to exercise substantial influence over legislation.[27]

Furthermore, participation in a major party campaign was not the only way to exercise control over the executive. Formally, some legislative bodies had the power to veto executive appointments. Informally, a president or governor needed the support of Congress to pass his own legislative program. A third party holding the balance of power in Congress could use its position to exchange support for a presidential or gubernatorial bill in return for influence over various executive decisions. Activists in such a third party may well have had more influence than activists who chose to work within the president's party. They would certainly have had far more influence than those who chose to work within the party of the losing candidate from the other major party.

In Australia, gaining the balance of power in the Legislative Assembly was the principle initial goal of those who established the NSW Labor party. Their plan was for Labor members of parliament to stay out of government and remain on the cross benches, offering support in return for concessions. One source of inspiration for this strategy came from the success that Parnell's Irish Home Rule party had achieved by following a similar strategy in the British House of Commons. The *Bulletin* urged the Labor party to follow Parnell's tactics, and George Black, who had been an early advocate of the establishment of a labor party (and who was one of the new labor members elected in NSW in 1891), later recalled that the party was "unceasingly exhorted to take pattern from that best known of all third parties—the Home Rule party."[28] But whatever the inspiration, it is clear that both the labor leaders who sought to establish the party following the defeat of the Maritime strike, and those who took part in the initial 1891 election campaign, explicitly advocated the balance of power strategy, and saw its achievement as a viable goal.[29]

In the United States, despite the presidential nature of the executive, many labor leaders favored the same strategy of acquiring a balance of power in the legislature. This was the strategy pursued both by the United Labor parties in 1886, and the labor-populists in 1894. During each of these periods it was seen as a practical goal by supporters of these initiatives as well as by a number of sceptics. It is not hard to see why. For much of the late nineteenth century, the vote for third parties was greater than the lead that the winning party had over its major party competitor, and this was true in the industrial heartlands of the mid-Atlantic and Midwest, as well as in the United States as a whole (Kleppner, 1979, 239).

Parnell's achievements in the House of Commons also inspired labor leaders in the United States. In the wake of the industrial upheaval of 1886, the Washington lobbyist for the Knights of Labor called explicitly for the establishment of "a Parnell party" in the federal congress (Fink, 1983, 27), and in Illinois, the *Chicago Times* agreed with the labor press that the new labor party "may develop sufficient strength to hold the balance of power" in the state legislature (Staley, 1930, 77 and 79). In 1886, the party came close to doing so. If all the labor members of the Illinois House combined with the Democrats, they could just block the Republicans (Staley, 1930, 73–74). In 1890, three populist independents held the balance of power in Illinois. They sought to use their leverage to elect a United States senator, although they proved unable to hold together (Destler, 1946, 167).

In the lead up to the 1894 elections, the possibility of achieving the balance of power in at least some state legislatures was again the focus of much attention. This was the explicit goal of the State Executive Committee of the Illinois People's party, and it was also endorsed by some craft unionists who were otherwise sceptical about independent labor politics (Destler, 1946, 206 and 188). Even some unionists who were close to Gompers, like the leaders of the Coast Seamen's Union, considered pursuit of the balance of power a practical strategy for a labor party, although they rejected the establishment of such a party on other grounds, such as the inability of labor leaders themselves to remain unified.[30]

Union leaders and labor party activists did not see the incentives they faced in the way that proponents of the importance of presidentialism suggest. In both parliamentary Australia and the presidential United States, labor leaders endorsed the idea of achieving a balance of power in the legislature, and saw this as a viable goal for a labor party.

The second argument for contamination concerns the behavior of voters. According to this argument, the parties of the two main candidates for president (or governor) invariably become the main focus for the attention and commitment of voters, and this makes the electability of legislative candidates dependent on the ability to present an electable presidential candidate.

There is no doubt that straight ticket voting poses a problem for third parties, but it is not the interaction between presidentialism and the electoral system that generates this problem. Far from subordinating their legislative to their presidential preferences, voters could just as easily do the opposite. For example, a hypothetical labor party loyalist could be expected to vote for the major party presidential candidate who was most likely to work with, or be susceptible to pressure from, the congressional candidates with whom his or her primary loyalty resided. Moreover, the fact that the election of a major party's presidential candidate is virtually assured may encourage a more uncertain labor party supporter to feel that it is "safe" to cast a vote for the party in congressional elections. In any case, the 1894 elections were mid-term elections. So there was no need for labor or populist supporters to split their ticket and bifurcate their loyalties in order to avoid wasting their vote in elections for the president. Similarly, voters in Illinois could focus on the state legislature that year, without having to decide who should be governor.[31]

During the early years of the twentieth century, a wave of electoral reforms were introduced (including the introduction of primaries), which sometimes made split-ticket voting more difficult, and often had the effect of strengthening the position of the two main parties and weakening the position of third parties. Simply placing candidates before the voters became increasingly difficult as many states introduced complex petitioning rules and other restrictions on third parties' access to the ballot. However, when the AFL was having its 1894 debate, and labor-populists were experimenting with third-party politics in Illinois and elsewhere, these reforms had not yet been introduced (Mazmanian, 1974, 89–101, Rosenstone et al., 1984, 19–25, and Epstein, 1986, 158–74).

The one important reform that did occur prior to these events was the introduction of the "Australian ballot." The first state to introduce the Australian ballot did so in 1888, and by 1893 all 33 non-southern states had followed suit (Wigmore, 1889, Evans, 1917, Fredman, 1968, and Ware, 2000). But the introduction of the Australian ballot made split-ticket voting easier, and proponents of independent labor politics were among the main advocates of these reforms. Prior to its introduction, parties themselves printed lists of their own candidates on distinctively colored strips of paper. Party workers handed these strips to their supporters outside the polling station, and voters registered their choice by (publicly) depositing the strip of their preferred party in a ballot box. Although in principle there were provisions enabling voters to alter some of the names on the party strip, or to arrive with their own independent list, in practice these provisions encouraged straight-ticket voting. After the introduction of the Australian ballot, the opportunity to engage in split-ticket voting, and to do so secretly, was clearly and readily available. States printed a ballot paper listing every candidate for every office, and explaining what a voter must do to register his choices. The voter was handed the ballot by an electoral official, and marked his choice of candidates in a private booth.

This standard interpretation of the effect of the Australian ballot has been challenged by some authors. Reynolds and McCormick (1986) point out that in two states—New York and New Jersey—split-ticket voting initially declined. But this was largely because disgruntled candidates, corrupt local bosses, and spoilers from other parties could no longer disseminate bogus ballots: ballots that looked similar to the regular ones but had one or two names changed. Since these states experienced no major third-party challenge at the time, the removal of this opportunity manifested itself as a decline in split-ticket voting. Argersinger (1980) points out that some parties—usually the Republicans—sought to use government control of official ballot papers in order to outlaw fusion candidates. Laws that prohibited a candidate from being nominated by more than one party could indeed make it harder for a third party to achieve electoral success. But in the early 1890s, these laws had not yet been enacted.[32]

So, at least in the early 1890s, the standard interpretation is right. The introduction of the Australian ballot significantly increased the opportunities for split-ticket voting. This is not to deny that most voters failed to take advantage of this opportunity, and preferred to vote a straight ticket for one of the two main parties. But this behavior can not be attributed to the institutional incentives generated by the interaction of presidentialism and the electoral system. The high incidence of straight-ticket voting is better explained by the intensity of party identification and party loyalty in the late nineteenth century. The decline of party identification in the last third of the twentieth century was accompanied by a large rise in split-ticket voting—by the 1970s, between a quarter and a third of voters split their ticket—in spite of the continuing impact of presidentialism (Stanley and Niemi, 1998, 129). I will return to consider the nature and extent of party loyalty, and its effect on the prospects for the establishment of a labor party, in Chapter 7. Here I want only to note that American presidentialism is quite compatible with widespread split-ticket voting and the election of labor-party representatives to state and federal legislatures.

CONCLUSION

In this chapter, I have considered a number of explanations for why there is no labor party in the United States that appeal to basic institutional characteristics of the American political system. None of these explanations has proved satisfactory, although the reasons for this vary.

Explanations based on the early introduction of voting rights for workers seem implausible in light of comparison with Australia, since something close to universal manhood suffrage for whites was a well-established feature of both societies. In both cases, the retention of some electoral inequalities and class-based restrictions, or the threat to re-impose them, offered labor leaders the opportunity to appeal to democratic demands to help mobilize the political support of workers. These opportunities were not as great as those in European countries where most workers had yet to be granted voting rights. But there were additional opportunities for labor leaders in the United States and Australia that compensated for this, since the suffrage gains that *had* been achieved legitimized efforts to engage in political mobilization, and provided a ready-made electoral arena in which to undertake this task.

The effect of electoral systems on party systems is a favorite and long-established theme of political science. But it would be a mistake to attribute too much significance to this effect in explaining the failure of unions to establish a labor party in the United States. In the late nineteenth century, Australia had a very similar electoral system—with a plurality electoral formula and a mix of single-member and multimember districts—and yet labor parties were quickly able to establish themselves there. Indeed, similar high-threshold plurality or majority electoral systems prevailed throughout Europe at that time. These high thresholds were repeatedly surmounted by labor-based parties because workers were geographically concentrated in particular areas. Since there were also large concentrations of workers in parts of the United States, it is misleading to suggest that it was the electoral system that was blocking the emergence of a labor party. The case of Illinois provides further support for this conclusion. Illinois's unusual semi-proportional cumulative voting system significantly reduced the percentage of votes that a party needed in order to win a seat, and yet proponents of independent labor politics had no more success establishing a party there than elsewhere in the United States.

Unlike the electoral system, the constitutional division of power in the United States differed from that in Australia. While Australia was poised to federate at the end of the nineteenth century, it had not yet done so in the early 1890s. Nevertheless, federalism does not provide a good explanation for the failure to establish a labor party in the United States, for although federalism made it harder to achieve systematic nationwide change, it made it easier for the labor movement to gain a foothold in the party system.

The nature of the executive and its relations with the legislature also differed. While Australia had a parliamentary system, the United States had a presidential one. Elections for president (or governor) did tend to foster a two-party system, but there is no institutional reason to think that this undermined the legislative prospects for a third party with geographically concentrated support. Activists still had an incentive to establish such a party, because the balance of power in the legislature would give them substantial legislative and executive influence. In the late nineteenth century, many labor leaders, in both the United States and Australia, believed that achieving the balance of power was a viable goal. Voters could support the legislative candidates of a third party, without "wasting" their vote in executive elections, by voting a split ticket. Indeed, this had just been made easier by the introduction of the Australian ballot. The fact that most voters did not split their ticket and remained loyal to one of the two main parties requires further examination, but it was not the result of the institutional incentives generated by presidentialism.

So, neither the suffrage or the electoral system, nor the federal or presidential division of power helps explain why there is no labor party in the United States. There is, however, one other feature of the constitutional division of power I have yet to consider. This concerns the role of the judiciary. Arguments focusing on the judiciary have recently received growing attention. And for this reason I will deal with these arguments separately in the next chapter.

CHAPTER 4

The Courts

A NUMBER OF POLITICAL scientists and historians have tried to explain why the American Federation of Labor refused to be involved in any form of party politics by focusing on the special role that courts played in the United States, and on the emergence of systematic judicial hostility towards organized labor. At the core of their explanation is what I will call the "court repression thesis."[1] These authors have made a strong and increasingly influential case. But their case suffers from a number of serious problems. Before turning to these problems, however, I want to first set out the basic argument of the court repression thesis, and then compare the legal basis of repression and the role of the courts in the United States and Australia.

THE COURT REPRESSION THESIS

According to the advocates of the court repression thesis, American unions and their leaders were not initially hostile to political action. On the contrary, prior to the 1890s they had frequently turned to the legislative process in order to advance a wide range of goals (Forbath, 1991, 3 and Hattam, 1993, 8–9). But in the late nineteenth century organized labor was subject to a long wave of intense judicial hostility: a hostility that had become unmistakable by the 1890s, and one which would not be reversed until the 1930s.

The most startling feature of this new judicial hostility was the development of a new doctrine of civil conspiracy and the concomitant deployment of labor injunctions. Labor injunctions enabled the courts to directly suppress strikes by issuing sweeping prohibitions against unionists on pain of imprisonment for contempt of court. In the 1894 Pullman strike, for example, Eugene Debs and the other leaders of the American Railway Union were arrested for breaching a blanket injunction that prohibited them from sending telegrams or communicating in any other way with workers in order to encourage them to strike or aid their efforts to do so (U.S. Strike Commission, 1895, xl, and Lindsey, 1942, 160–63 and 274–75).

There is some dispute about how much of a rupture with past judicial practice this entailed (Archer, 1998, 393). Nevertheless, all agree that with the widespread deployment of labor injunctions, a new wave of judicial hostility broke over the unions in the 1890s. By the beginning of the twentieth century, the use of injunctions had become so widespread that many of the basic forms of collective action—like consumer boycotts—on which even the most conservative unions relied, had been effectively outlawed. Forbath (1991, 61–62 and 193–98), who has gone to a good deal of trouble to build up an overall picture of the use of injunctions, concludes that they were not only issued "in virtually every railroad strike [and] in most strikes in which industrial unionism, 'amalgamation', or 'federation' was at issue," but also "in most major organizing and recognition strikes, boycotts, closed shop or sympathy strikes or anti-union/open-shop lockouts of significant magnitude."

Judicial hostility did not just undermine organized labor's ability to act in industrial disputes. It also undermined the broader social reforms that unions had sought to achieve through the legislative process. Time and again, labor-backed reforms that passed through state legislatures were undermined by the courts. New laws would either be struck down entirely through judicial review, or be interpreted in such a way as to vitiate the legislature's original intention.[2] For example, laws governing working hours had been amongst the most important of the reforms that unions sought. But these laws were repeatedly held to be unconstitutional by state supreme courts unless they were strictly limited to "dependents" like women and children.

To make matters even worse, the courts could also add to their legal arsenal by taking laws that had been passed with labor-backing, and interpreting them in ways that were inimical to the unions (Forbath, 1991, 69–71 and 95–97). The Sherman Antitrust Act, for example, was intended to curb the monopoly power of large corporations, but in 1893 the courts applied it to combinations of workers.[3] Likewise, injunctions were issued against the railroad unions in 1888 on the basis of the Interstate Commerce Act, in spite of the fact that Congress had considered, and specifically rejected, an attempt to apply the act to labor.[4]

According to the court repression thesis, this wave of judicial hostility changed union attitudes towards politics. As the cumulative impact of court interventions made itself felt, union leaders and activists became increasingly skeptical about the effectiveness of political action. The courts, so the thesis goes, effectively placed labor's goals beyond the influence of politics. As a result, when this became clear in the 1890s, many union leaders began to view political action as futile. The only way to achieve anything, it seemed, was to strengthen the economic position of workers in the marketplace by building the strongest possible organizations in order to force concessions directly from employers. This was pure-and-simple unionism. Making a virtue of necessity, the unions embraced it.[5]

Thus, according to the court repression thesis, the rejection of political action by Gompers and his allies at the AFL's 1894 convention was largely a response to the incentives established by the actions of the courts.

It was not merely the fact of judicial hostility that is said to have established these incentives—unions faced some degree of judicial hostility in most countries—rather it was the particular structure of the American state and the role of the courts within it that was important. Whereas in Britain, parliamentary sovereignty ensured that courts would ultimately defer to the will of the legislature, thus giving unions an incentive to seek some control over the legislature, in the United States, the separation of powers, and the importance of judicial review, enabled the courts to obstruct or override the decisions of the legislature.[6] Or that, at least, is what the advocates of the court repression thesis claim.

LABOR LAW AND THE COURTS

Does comparison with Australia help us assess this claim? I want to first compare the legal basis of repression in the two countries, and then turn to some basic differences in the constitutional division of power. In both the United States and Australia, nineteenth-century labor law was rooted in the same English common law traditions. These traditions conceived of individual employment in terms of master and servant relationships, and they conceived of combinations of employees as criminal conspiracies.

In both countries, the common law conception of employment as a master–servant relationship sat uncomfortably with a more egalitarian popular conception of the social status of workers, and with the political pressures arising from manhood suffrage. But, while the use of master and servant law atrophied in the United States in the early nineteenth century, it was reinforced in Australia by the passage of Master and Servant Acts. These statutes allowed magistrates to fine or imprison workers who broke their contract of employment, and they became the predominant means for regulating labor in the first half of the nineteenth century.[7]

Paradoxically, however, the severity of Master and Servant law in Australia was actually testimony to the relatively powerful position workers occupied in the labor market. The shortage of labor and the ease with which workers could find alternative work, lead employer-dominated legislatures to seek to redress this "imbalance" by statute. Whether the Master and Servant Acts succeeded in doing this is a moot point. "Absconding" was by far the most frequent offense committed by workers, but the very frequency of these cases, along with the incessant complaints of employers in local newspapers, suggests that the deterrent effect of the legislation was limited (Quinlan, 1989, 34–36 and 1996, 16–17 and 21–23). In any case, after about 1860 it was usually only rural employers who made use of the Acts, and cases initiated by workers seeking to recover unpaid wages came to dominate proceedings. Between 1845 and 1860, these worker-initiated cases accounted for 29 percent of all cases tried. Between 1881 and 1900, they accounted for 78 percent of such cases (Merritt, 1981, 208–39).

The Australian Master and Servant Acts were not designed to deal with collective action by workers. Nevertheless, clauses against "enticement," which had been originally designed to stop employers poaching workers from each other, could be directed against union organizers who encouraged workers to break their contracts.[8] And strikers themselves could be charged with "desertion" or "disobedience" if they went on strike before the end of their contract (Portus, 1958, 92–93, and Markey, 1988, 123). After 1860, use of the legislation against unions seems to have been limited and relatively ineffective (McQueen, 1987, 89–90). However, its use against unions was (briefly) revived by pastoralists in the shearers' strikes of 1890, 1891, and 1894. Assault, threat, and intimidation were the most common charges brought against unionists in the early 1890s, but significant use was also made of the Master and Servant Acts (Quinlan, 1989, 37–38, and 1996, 25–27, and Hearn and Knowles, 1996, 33 and 45).

For much of the nineteenth century, unions were susceptible to charges of criminal conspiracy in both the United States and Australia. However, while conspiracy laws were rarely used in Australia (Quinlan, 1989, 36–37 and 41), they were a persistent problem for American unionists (Tomlins, 1985, 36–44, and 1993, 101–219, and Hattam, 1993, 30–75). By 1890, a number of state legislatures in both the United States and Australia had passed laws giving unions immunity from prosecution for criminal conspiracy.[9] But in spite of this, conspiracy laws were still invoked, although in quite different ways, during the strike waves that hit both countries in the early 1890s.

In the United States, a decline in prosecutions for criminal conspiracy was accompanied by two other developments that gave new life to court-administered repression of unions: the wholesale recourse to injunctions, and the formulation of a new doctrine of civil conspiracy. Injunctions enabled courts to act preemptively against the unions. At first, they were typically justified on the grounds, either of preventing violations of the Interstate Commerce Act or the Sherman Antitrust Act, or of preventing damages to an employer's "future expectancies." But the latter kind of injunction became the most important, especially after it was endorsed by the Supreme Court following the Pullman strike. In order to place it on a firm legal footing, judges had developed a new doctrine of civil conspiracy. According to this doctrine, future expectancies were a kind of property to which the employer had a right. They were said to be analogous to the "good will" an employer builds up with his or her customers. Just as the employer had future expectations of a continued supply of customers that were a form of property that could be sold when selling the business, so too the employer had future expectations of a continued supply of labor that were also a form of property. Many strikes and boycotts were deemed to be illegal attempts to cause irreparable damage to this property (Commons, 1918, 505–7, Frankfurter and Green, 1930, 5–24, Rayback, 1966, 204–7, and Tomlins, 1985, 46–52).

In Australia, a number of legislatures passed laws that gave unions immunity from prosecution for criminal conspiracy. NSW and Queensland were exceptions, although prosecutions remained most unusual (Portus, 1958, 95–99, Sutcliffe, 1967 [1921], 76–81). However, there were two important strikes in which conspiracy charges were brought against unionists. In the 1891 Queensland Shearers' strike, a number of unionists were charged with conspiracy to intimidate, and in both this strike and the 1892 Broken Hill Miners' strike, unionists were also charged with seditious conspiracy (Svensen, 1989, 156–97, and Markey, 1988, 124–25). The arrests and convictions that resulted certainly had an important impact on these two disputes, but unlike developments in the United States, they did not foreshadow a new ongoing role for conspiracy law in the regulation of industrial relations.

In both countries, conspiracy law was used against unionists in the industrial upheavals of the 1890s. In Australia, however, a system of compulsory arbitration and state-backed union recognition emerged in the wake of these upheavals to provide a new framework for industrial relations, and the use of conspiracy law atrophied (Macintyre and Mitchell, 1989). In the United States, on the other hand, conspiracy doctrines were reformulated and given a new lease of life that placed them at the center of labor law until the 1930s.

So, labor law had common roots in the United States and Australia, although it sometimes developed in different directions. However the most important difference between the two countries arose, not from the development of labor law, but from the basic constitutional division of power between the courts and the other branches of government. In this respect, the role of the courts in late-nineteenth-century Australia was closer to that in Britain than that in the United States. For most purposes, Australian parliaments (and the executives who were responsible to them) dominated the law-making process in the same way as in Britain. Where there was a conflict between the legislature and the courts, it was the legislature that had the final word, and this Westminster-style relationship between parliament and the courts was recognized by both contemporary constitutional authorities and definitive judicial rulings.[10]

However, there were some significant differences between the British parliament and parliaments in Australia. Self-government had been established in Australia by various Acts of the Imperial Parliament in Westminster. These Acts provided what was in effect a written constitution that established certain limits on the sovereignty of each parliament (Castles, 1982, 408–11 and 449–52, and Lumb, 1983, 46 and 100, and 1991, 96–98). In order to police these limits, Australian Supreme Courts claimed the right to exercise a form of judicial review (Lumb, 1991, 8–11 and 14, and Todd, 1894, 302). However, it was a more restricted form than in the United States. In matters of domestic policy, Australian legislatures were usually certain to prevail. As the Privy Council in London had made clear, within its sphere of competence "the

Local Legislature is supreme, and has the same authority as the Imperial Parliament."[11] This was especially true in those areas that dealt with changing economic and social conditions, and it most certainly applied to laws regulating labor and industrial relations (Castles, 1982, 445, 453, and 469–71). Indeed, this was one of the areas in which Australian legislation became particularly distinctive. Thus, in the matters of most importance to unions, the role of the courts was clearly subordinate to that of the legislature. In this respect, Australia was quite unlike the United States.

Union Attitudes towards Politics

The problems with the court repression thesis result, not from comparison with Australia, but rather from its characterization of the American union movement and from the causal mechanism to which it appeals. The thesis offers an explanation for the AFL's attitude to labor politics that is built around three propositions. (1) Unions were initially sympathetic to political action. (2) During the 1890s they were subject to a wave of judicial hostility at the hands of unusually powerful courts. (3) This led them to opt for apolitical pure-and-simple unionism.

In what follows, I want to consider a number of problems with this explanation, but I do not propose to dispute every facet of it. The problem with the court repression thesis does not lie in its account of judicial developments (proposition 2), but rather in its account of union attitudes to politics and of the effect that judicial developments had on them (propositions 1 and 3).[12]

The characterization of the development of union attitudes towards politics offered by the court repression thesis is misleading in a number of respects. To understand why this is so, it is important to recognize that the attitude of the AFL and its leaders was not simply one of being either for or against political action. Rather the attitude of the AFL varied along at least two dimensions.

One dimension concerned the *type of goals* that should be pursued through political action. Most of the goals the AFL discussed clustered into one of two categories. On the one hand were "negative goals," like anti-conspiracy and anti-injunction legislation; on the other, "positive goals," such as the eight-hour day and factory legislation governing working conditions.

A negative goal had two defining features. First, it sought relief from a problem that had emerged because of the actions of the state, and hence it sought to stop the state from using its authority against the interests of labor. Second, it was concerned with the unions' core interest in maintaining their capacities as organizations—in other words, it was not concerned with the substantive ends of unionism (like better working conditions) but rather with the maintenance of the organizational means to achieve such ends.

A positive goal had the opposite two defining features. First, it sought to address a problem that had emerged independently of the actions of the state, and hence it sought to encourage the state to use its authority in the interests of labor. The state was addressed as a potential ally in the solution of a problem rather than as the source of a problem. Second, it was concerned with the substantive ends of the union movement, rather than with the defensive task of maintaining the organizational means.

A second dimension on which the AFL's attitude toward politics varied concerned the *type of political action* that should be undertaken. On the one hand, political action could be limited to pressure group politics. This would principally involve lobbying those in power. Although it would also extend to advising workers to vote for labor's friends and punish its enemies, while carefully keeping the unions themselves out of the electoral arena and refusing to identify the labor movement with any political party. On the other hand, political action could be extended to include union participation in partisan politics. This would involve competing in elections either by backing an established political party or by forming an independent labor party.[13]

Advocates of the court repression thesis tend to elide these distinctions, and it is this that makes their account of union attitudes towards politics misleading. For union attitudes along these two dimensions do not necessarily vary in tandem.

Let me begin by looking in more detail at union attitudes towards the different types of goals. It is true that the AFL did come to reject the use of political action in pursuit of positive goals, and to limit itself to a narrowly defined set of negative goals.[14] Indeed, eventually this rejection became so radical that the AFL actually *opposed* most social legislation, including even legislation to limit working hours.[15] However, this shift in attitude only became clearly apparent in the early years of the twentieth century—somewhat later than the court repression thesis suggests. Arguably, it was not unambiguously entrenched until 1914 when the AFL ruled out the pursuit of a general eight-hour day through legislation (Rogin, 1962, 530–34, and Skocpol, 1992, 210–12). In any case, there was no such shift at the AFL's key 1894 convention. If anything, the opposite took place.

The "Political Programme" proposed a significant expansion of the AFL's commitment to positive political goals. Unsurprisingly, then, it generated vigorous questioning and debate that in some cases lead to the rejection of particular proposals. Advocates of the court repression thesis tend to focus on this questioning as evidence of growing support for a less political strategy, while failing to note the underlying agreement on the need to pursue a wide range—indeed, an unprecedentedly wide range—of positive goals through political action.

The debate on plank 4 of the Political Programme provides one example of this. The plank called for "Sanitary inspection of workshop, mine, and home," and a number of delegates sought to delete reference to the home in order to defend its "sanctity" and "privacy" from government interference. But none of the delegates disputed the proposal that the AFL should seek legislation for the sanitary inspection of the workplace, and ultimately the original plank was passed including its reference to the home.[16]

But perhaps the best example is provided by the celebrated debate on plank 10, which called for "the collective ownership by the people of all means of production and distribution." After hours of debate, the opponents of this plank prevailed and the convention voted to replace it with a plank calling for "the abolition of the monopoly system of land holding." However, note that not only was this itself a positive political demand, but also that, without any opposition, the convention had already passed planks 8 and 9, which called respectively for "municipal ownership of street cars, water works, gas, and electric plants" and "the nationalization of telegraphs, telephones, railroads, and mines" (AFL, 1895a, 25–62). Far from being a retreat from positive political goals, the outcome of the 1894 convention marks the high point of the AFL's commitment to the pursuit of positive goals through political action.

So, with respect to the type of goals, the AFL does shift from a more to a less political attitude by abandoning the pursuit of positive goals and limiting itself to negative ones. But it does this a decade or so later than the court repression thesis suggests. Indeed, just as judicial repression is really beginning to bite in the early 1890s, the AFL makes its broadest-ever commitment to political action in pursuit of positive goals.

Let me turn now to union attitudes towards different types of political action. Along this second dimension, the claim of the court repression thesis that previously political unions moved in the 1890s towards a more apolitical stance is especially misleading. There is no doubt that the question of whether or not to become involved in partisan politics was a central question at the 1894 convention (AFL, 1895a, 4–13 and 62–64). Equally, it is clear that (with some help from rulings by the Chair) the 1894 convention rejected both partisan politics in general, and independent labor politics in particular, and that subsequent conventions continued to reject them thereafter. However, contrary to the court repression thesis, this rejection of any kind of partisan politics was not a new development, rather it was simply the reaffirmation of a long-standing position.

Indeed, it was a position that key leaders of the AFL had adopted before either the AFL or its predecessor, the Federation of Organized Trades and Labor Unions (FOTLU), had been founded. The leaders (like Gompers, Strasser, and McGuire) who played the central role in defeating the call for independent labor politics in 1894 had been wrestling with the question of what role partisan politics should play in the union movement for much of the 1870s. They confronted this question both as socialist activists and as leaders of their own unions.

As socialist activists, they had been schooled in the debates of Marx's International Workingmen's Association. These debates centered on the question of whether a union-based economic strategy or a party-based political strategy should predominate, and many of those who later played a leading role in the AFL became protagonists of the first position. In particular, Samuel Gompers began participating in these debates in 1873 and soon became closely aligned with proponents of the union-based strategy.[17]

The conflicts engendered by these debates spilled over into the unions. Samuel Gompers and Adolf Strasser, for example, sought to put the union-based strategy into practice in the cigar makers' union. In 1877, they warded off an attempt to subordinate the union to the organizational form called for by the protagonists of the party-based strategy. And in 1879, they succeeded in passing a resolution declaring that no union local "shall be permitted to aid, cooperate, or identify itself with any political party whatsoever" (Kaufman, 1986, 71–72 and 139).

Thus, for many of the key union leaders who came together in 1881 to form the FOTLU, opposition to union involvement in partisan politics was already a well-established orthodoxy. It is hardly surprising, therefore, that this orthodoxy was reflected in the stance adopted by the new Federation. At its very first meeting, the newly appointed Legislative Committee, which was established for the purpose of lobbying and was effectively the Federation's executive, unanimously resolved that none of its members "should publicly advocate the claims of any of the parties."[18]

This anti-partisan orthodoxy was reinforced almost immediately by a series of conflicts within the cigar makers' union and between the FOTLU and the Knights of Labor.[19] With one exception, it remained the position of both the FOTLU and the AFL right up to 1893 when the debate over the Political Programme was launched.

The exception occurred in 1886. This was the year when the FOTLU reorganized itself as the AFL, and the founding convention of the AFL (1886, 16) resolved to "urge a most generous support to the independent political movement of the workingmen." Amidst a rash of experiments with independent labor politics in the wake of the "Great Upheaval," even Gompers had suspended his opposition to partisan political action and thrown his support behind the Central Labor Union's campaign to elect Henry George as mayor of New York.[20]

There was, however, a good deal of ambivalence within the AFL about this new stance. The welcoming address to the 1886 convention was a blunt statement in favor of maintaining the traditional opposition to union involvement in partisan politics. The original motion before the convention called for the formation of an independent labor party, but, as we have seen, the resolution that passed limited itself to urging "a most generous support to the independent political movement." It prefaced this with an acknowledgment that: "this subject has, in the past, been a prolific source of dissension and trouble in the ranks of the workingmen" (AFL, 1886, 16, and Kaufman, 1986, 387 and 453–56).

By the following year, the old anti-partisan orthodoxy was already reasserting itself. Gompers disassociated himself from the attempt to establish a United Labor party to capitalize on Henry George's impressive showing in New York, and the AFL reverted to pressure group politics (AFL, 1887, 26 and 29–30, and Kaufman, 1987, 45). Thereafter, the AFL and its leadership made plain their rejection of partisan politics in general, and independent labor politics in particular, year after year.[21]

Thus, the outcome of the AFL's 1894 debate (reconfirmed more emphatically in 1895) was simply the reaffirmation of a long-standing orthodoxy with deep roots in the organization. The decision to reject partisan politics did not mark a new departure. Rather, it marked the rejection of pressure for a new departure, and a cementing in place of the AFL's traditional attitude to types of political action.

The court repression thesis claims that unions shifted from a pro-political to an anti-political attitude in the 1890s. But union attitudes toward politics varied along at least two dimensions, and they did not vary in tandem. What implications does this have for the court repression thesis? With respect to the type of goals, unions did indeed shift from a more to a less political stance as they abandoned the pursuit of most positive goals and limited themselves to negative ones. However, they did this somewhat later than the 1890s, and only after first moving in the opposite direction. With respect to the type of political action, however, unions did not shift from a more to a less political stance. In the 1890s they simply reaffirmed the position to which they had long been committed by continuing to oppose partisan political action and by continuing to favor a more limited pressure group approach. Here, then, there is a serious problem of timing for the court repression thesis. If union opposition to partisan politics was firmly entrenched well before the new wave of court repression became apparent, then there is no longer a *prima facie* case for claiming that it was court repression that caused this opposition.

Of course, this in itself is not sufficient to show that judicial hostility played *no* role in labor's rejection of partisan politics. It could be that the effects of court repression simply reinforced a long-established predilection.

THE EFFECT OF COURT REPRESSION

So what were the effects of court repression? According to the court repression thesis, judicial hostility led unions to reject the option of political action, both because courts had unusually wide-ranging powers that gave them the final say on most of the political issues that were of importance to unions, and because, in exercising these powers, the courts were immune to political influence. These basic constitutional features of the American state established a structure of constraints and opportunities—a "political opportunity structure"—that made it rational for unions to repudiate political action and opt instead for pure-and-simple unionism. Since the courts made the decisions that mattered, and the courts were immune to political influence, it would have been futile and foolish for unions to expend any effort on seeking to exercise political influence. Or so argue the advocates of the court repression thesis.[22]

There are a number of problems with the argument advanced by advocates of the court repression thesis. One problem is that it overstates the constraints and understates the opportunities that confronted the unions. By emphasizing the extent to which courts were immune to the effects of political action, the court repression thesis presents the American state as a political opportunity structure without political opportunities. In fact, the American courts were susceptible to the effects of political action in a number of ways.

First, many judicial decisions rest on statutory interpretation rather than on constitutional interpretation (or judicial review). In these cases, the legislature merely has to clarify its intentions if it wants to overturn the decision of the court. Some of the most important anti-labor decisions that courts made in the late 1880s and early 1890s were of this sort. The authority on which the federal courts relied in order to issue injunctions during the Pullman strike rested largely on their interpretation of the Interstate Commerce Act and the Sherman Antitrust Act. Congress could have overturned these interpretations, but for many years it did not even attempt to do so, and when it did finally address the issue in the Clayton Act of 1914, its intentions were deliberately left ambiguous, enabling the courts to sustain their original interpretation (Fink, 1987, 916, and Ernst, 1995, 165–90). Here then, the root problem for labor was not that the courts were immune to political influence, but rather that labor was unable to exercise sufficient influence over the legislature.

Second, even where judicial decisions do rest on constitutional interpretation, there are various ways in which both the "political" branches of government (that is, the legislature and the executive) and popular opinion can bring pressure to bear on the courts. In principle, these decisions can be overturned by constitutional amendment, or even by altering the size or the jurisdiction of the relevant court. In practice, however, it is the ongoing need of the courts to maintain their legitimacy that is most likely to allow political influences to be brought to bear. These influences can affect not only how a court decides a case, but also whether it will hear the case at all. The courts have to tend their legitimacy with special care because they are almost always dependent on others to implement their decisions. Thus, when issues become sufficiently "emotionally charged," or when they are subject to sustained political counterattack, the courts tend to retreat.[23]

These pressures are likely to be particularly acute during periods of social and political turmoil, or when the courts make controversial decisions on matters that are the subject of partisan conflict (Nagel, 1965). Thus, in the crisis of the 1930s, the effect of overwhelming Congressional support for the Norris-LaGuardia and Wagner Acts, along with Roosevelt's battle with the Supreme Court, showed that political pressure could be made to prevail over even the most recalcitrant court.[24] This legislative and executive pressure was powerfully augmented by the pressure of public opinion. The 1936 election was seen in part as a plebiscite in which people were asked to choose between the New Deal and its political and judicial opponents. The Court responded to Roosevelt's landslide victory by reversing its opposition to state and federal labor laws, as well as to other pieces of New Deal legislation: a process that it began even *before* the president's 1937 court-packing plan had been disclosed (Skowronek, 1993, 314, and Plotke, 1996, 148–49).

To be sure, the 1930s were an unusually tumultuous period, but the 1890s were also such a period. Then, too, the United States simultaneously experienced a deep economic depression, widespread social unrest, and political realignment. The difference in the 1890s was not that constitutional judicial review was immune to political pressure, but rather that the courts were rarely subject to political pressure to act in the interests of labor.[25] During the Pullman strike, for example, the courts were not acting contrary to the wishes of the executive. They were acting in concert with the executive. Indeed, in many respects it was the executive branch that was the initiator. President Cleveland and Attorney General Olney called on the courts to rule as they did, and sent military forces to enforce their rulings.[26] Likewise, there were many cases where it was legislative hostility or legislative passivity that enabled the courts to continue to act unchecked.[27] Even when making rulings based on constitutional interpretation, political pressure could be brought to bear on the courts. In the 1890s, however, it was rarely labor that exerted that pressure.

Third, and perhaps most strikingly, the courts were susceptible to political influence through the selection and replacement of judges. By the late nineteenth century, most state judges were actually elected, and subject to reelection, just like politicians.[28] The election of state judges first became widespread in the 1840s and 1850s.[29] By the 1880s and 1890s, these elections were keenly fought and attracted a particularly high turnout. In fact, however, it was often the party conventions that exercised the real power by choosing which candidates to nominate in the first place. Later, in the early twentieth century, the introduction of direct primaries, nonpartisan ballots, vetting by bar associations and other Progressive reforms weakened the control exercised by parties. Even after these reforms, however, party affiliations remained crucial. Indeed, the vast majority of successful candidates were politicians-turned-judges. Over 70 percent had previously held at least one nonjudicial political office, and most had held two or more such offices.[30]

Moreover, even when judges were not directly elected they were still appointed by politicians and hence susceptible to political pressure. The most important example of this was in the federal courts where the constitution stipulated that judges were to be appointed by the President, but only with the consent of the Senate. Studies of appointments to the federal courts in the late nineteenth century show that partisan considerations were every bit as important as they were in state-based judicial elections. Between 1877 and 1899, 96 percent of all appointees were from the same party as the president who appointed them, and almost 90 percent had been actively involved in politics as presidential electors, delegates to party conventions, or party organizers.[31]

With respect to the selection of judges, many American courts were actually more susceptible to political influence than courts in countries like Britain and Australia.[32] This raises intriguing questions about the attitude of American unions towards political action. Whether through election or appointment, partisan politics played the key role in judicial selection. In these circumstances, electoral mobilization and other forms of partisan political action offered the unions immediate and important advantages.

Overall then, courts were susceptible to political influences in a number of ways. They were susceptible to legislative and executive pressure, to electoral mobilization, and to the demands of partisan politics. None of this is to deny that it could be difficult to influence the courts through political action. The courts were certainly not *as* susceptible to political influences as were legislatures and executives. The point here is simply that meaningful opportunities for unions to influence the courts through political action did exist. American unions did *not* find themselves facing a political opportunity structure without political opportunities.

Of course, the fact that there were opportunities to influence the courts through political action does not in itself mean that unions had an incentive to do so. For whether or not the unions had an incentive to make use of these opportunities also depended on the *importance* that they attached to particular goals, and the *cost* of any alternative strategy for achieving them. Note that two consequences follow from this way of thinking about labor's incentives.

The first concerns the relevance of the main cross-national comparative argument that advocates of the court repression thesis invoke. As we have already seen, this argument revolves around a comparison between political institutions in the United States and Britain.[33] Whereas in Britain, the doctrine of parliamentary sovereignty meant that legislative victories could be used to override the courts, in the United States, the separation of powers and judicial review enabled the courts to override legislative victories.

The comparison with Britain does establish that political action was a cheaper strategy to pursue in Britain than in the United States. But how did this affect the incentives facing American unions? Political action may have been more costly to American unions than it was to their British counterparts, and yet may still have been less costly than any alternative strategy available to them *in the United States*. Presuming that the goals they were pursuing were important enough, they would then still have an incentive to engage in political action. Thus, the question we need to answer is not whether a particular strategy was cheaper in Britain, but whether there was an alternative strategy that was cheaper in the United States.

The second consequence to note is that a union's incentive to engage in political action depends in part on the type of goals it is pursing, and hence that the effects of repression may not be the same for both positive and negative goals. In considering the incentives facing the unions, we should, therefore, consider these two types of goals separately.

In the case of negative goals, unions have a particularly strong incentive to engage in political action, simply because of the nature of these goals. Negative goals are of the utmost importance to unions since they deal with their core organizational interests. If no progress is made towards the achievement of these goals, then the very ability of unions to function is thrown into doubt. At the same time, political action is the only way that unions can hope to achieve negative goals, since it is the state (including the courts) that is the source of the difficulties that these goals seek to overcome. There is no alternative strategy for dealing with state repression, let alone a cheaper one. In short, if unions have negative goals, they have a strong incentive to pursue them, and in order to pursue them they must engage in political action. John McBride, who replaced Gompers as AFL president in 1895, placed recognition of this at the center of his annual report: "As an organization, we may decide to leave politics alone, but unfortunately for the interests of the organization and its members, politics will not let us alone, hence we are compelled not from a sentimental but from a purely business standpoint to consider and act politically . . ." (AFL, 1895, 16). When court repression forces unions to pursue negative goals, it gives them a strong incentive to engage in political action.

Note, however, that while court repression forced all unions to pursue negative goals, it did not affect all unions in quite the same way. In particular, it tended to have a harsher effect on industrial unions than on craft unions (Archer, 1998, 403). While many industrial unionists felt that they had nothing left to lose, craft unionists invariably did still have something to lose. They might have lost their ability to engage in effective industrial action, but they still had the organization itself.[34] I will discuss the differential impact of repression in greater detail in the next chapter. What is important to note here, however, is that court repression still gave these craft unionists an incentive to engage in political action. If attempts to politicize the issue of this repression would have been likely to provoke the courts to make further attacks—attacks that would in turn have lead to the dissolution of the craft unions themselves—then court repression may have given them an incentive to adopt a submissive apolitical posture. This, however, was not the case. The courts repeatedly insisted that they were not opposed to the existence of unions per se (Hovenkamp, 1991, 207, and Ernst, 1995, 165–90), and as we saw earlier, the politicization of an issue was likely to make the courts more cautious rather than more belligerent.

So court repression gave all unionists a strong incentive to engage in political action. Indeed, they had an incentive not just to engage in political action in general but to engage in partisan politics in particular. Each new episode of repression made it ever more apparent that the pressure group politics to which the AFL had long limited itself was failing to provide the unions with sufficient political leverage, and this failure created an incentive to take stronger measures and move towards partisan political action. Occasional changes in union attitudes towards partisan politics bear this out. Each of the periods when the AFL's anti-partisan orthodoxy came under strain followed intense episodes of judicial repression that, accompanied by other forms of state repression, forced negative goals to the fore.

When the whole New York union movement plunged into independent labor politics in the 1886 campaign to elect Henry George as Mayor, they did so in direct response to judicial interventions in the Theiss Music Hall boycott, which threatened the ability of the unions to use one of their key industrial tactics. Gompers's speeches of support were quite explicit about the connection with judicial repression (Kaufman, 1986, 431). Comparable motivations were at work in many of the other cities where unionists engaged in independent labor politics that year (Foner, 1955, 117–19, and Fink, 1983, 25–26 and 30–31).

Similarly, the pressure for a move towards independent labor politics that built up in 1893 and 1894 followed closely in the wake of a series of repressive judicial interventions in major industrial disputes. The strongest advocates of partisan political action in 1894 were those from places like Chicago who had most keenly felt the wave of judicial and military repression during the early 1890s. Citing the urgent need to deal with this repression, they plunged into partisan politics (Perlman, 1923, 139, and Destler, 1946, 165–66).

Moreover, eventually, despite remaining rhetorically wedded to apolitical pure-and-simple unionism, the AFL was itself forced into partisan politics in 1908 following a series of judicial rulings that seemed to outlaw almost any action that a union might take during an industrial dispute. In the 1905 Chicago printers strike, an injunction against the eminently conservative and respectable Typographical Union had prohibited "peaceful picketing, any moral suasion whatsoever" and any "attempt by the printers to induce non-union printers to join the union." Recognizing that its long-standing efforts to convince Congress to pass anti-injunction legislation had come to nought, the AFL leadership responded by drawing up a "Bill of Grievances" and making an unprecedented effort to use labor votes to influence the out-come of the 1906 mid-term Congressional elections.[35] Arguably, this was still just within the boundaries of pressure group politics, but a series of court cases that came to a head in 1908 drew the AFL into political action that was unmistakably partisan.

The most important of these were the Danbury Hatters' case and the Buck's Stove case—both of which had been brought as test cases by militant employ-ers' organizations.[36] In the Danbury Hatters' case, unions found that even the organization of a consumer boycott was outlawed, while in the Buck's Stove case, the AFL's top office-holders, including Gompers himself, were sentenced to jail terms (although the appeals went on for so long that they ultimately avoided jail because the statute of limitations had expired). At the same time, the Supreme Court overturned state legislation outlawing "yellow dog" con-tracts, thereby making it legal for employers to ask workers to sign contracts that stipulated that they would be fired if they joined a union. Gompers and his colleagues responded to these rulings by leading the AFL into a de facto al-liance with the Democratic party. Since the Republican party had effectively controlled Congress and the presidency since 1896, and its attitude to the AFL's demands for legislative relief ranged from indifference to hostility, Gompers sought to take the AFL into the 1908 presidential election on the side of the Democrats.[37] Despite years of rhetoric about the prejudicial effects of partisan political action, the stalwarts of the AFL felt they had little choice.

Thus, there seems to have been a strong incentive to engage, not just in political action, but in partisan political action in response to continuing court repression. Indeed, more than this, there was probably an incentive to move towards independent labor politics. In the late nineteenth century, support for the two main parties was finely balanced both federally and in a number of states. The prospect of holding the balance of power held out the possibility of substantial influence in key areas, and support for union-backed legislation from Republican and Democratic politicians was strongest where there had been a large vote for an independent labor party (Foner, 1955, 145, Friedman, 1991, 8–9, and Montgomery, 1993, 152–53). Arguably then, independent labor politics was the best way to maximize labor's influence. In any case, court re-pression had the opposite effect to that claimed by the court repression thesis. By forcing negative goals to the fore, it gave unions an incentive to engage in partisan political action of one sort or another in order to maximize their polit-ical influence in the hope of protecting the ability of their organizations to engage in industrial action.

In the case of positive goals, the effect of court repression is less clear. At the AFL's 1894 convention, Adolf Strasser, Gompers's mentor from the cigar mak-ers' union, seemed to appeal directly to a version of the court repression thesis in a debate about a plank in the Political Programme that called for a "legal eight-hour workday" (AFL, 1895a, 19–21). Referring to the use of judicial review to overturn previous legislation, Strasser argued that "There is one fact that cannot be overlooked. You cannot pass a general eight hour day without changing the constitution of the United States and the constitution of every State in the Union. . . . I hold we cannot propose to wait with the eight hour movement until we secure it by law. The cigar makers passed a law, without the government. . . . I am opposed to wasting our time declaring for legislation being enacted for a time possibly, after we are dead. I want to see something we can secure while we are alive." Here then, a leading unionist explicitly argues that continual judicial obstruction gives unions an incentive to avoid political action in the case of positive goals and instead seek these goals through direct bargaining with employers: the pure-and-simple approach.[38]

But is this really the effect of court repression? Positive goals certainly did not have the same immediate organizational importance as negative goals. Nor was political action the only way to achieve them. Nevertheless, there are several reasons to doubt that court repression did in fact give unions an incentive to desist from political action in the case of positive goals.

First, Strasser's approach depends exclusively on the organizational strength of the unions and their ability to utilize industrial weapons like the strike and the boycott. This in turn requires judicial tolerance of labor organizations and their industrial strategies. However, judicial tolerance is precisely what was lacking, and as we have seen in discussing negative goals, it is precisely in order to achieve it that political action was most urgently required. Strasser's apolitical strategy presumes the existence of an industrial relations environment that could only be achieved if political action was taken. But in an environment where there is already a strong incentive to undertake political action, the cost of undertaking additional political action in pursuit of positive goals may well be less than would otherwise be the case. The cost of running an election campaign just to win an eight-hour day would be enormous, but if an election campaign had to be run anyway, the cost of including the eight-hour day in the platform would be negligible.

Second, Strasser's approach does not consider the possibility that political action in pursuit of goals like an eight-hour day might have secondary benefits for unions. There might, for example, be an incentive to engage in political action in pursuit of positive goals in order to improve the chances of achieving negative ones. If a political campaign is necessary to deal with court repression anyway, there might well be an incentive to widen the alliance of those opposed to the courts by including middle-class reformers and other proponents of positive social goals, as well as those with an immediate organizational interest in the maintenance of union strength.[39] When judicial obstacles to both positive and negative goals finally did fall in the 1930s, they fell together.[40]

Third, there is conflicting evidence at the state level. Unions at the state level typically faced judicial repression that was at least as bad as, and often worse than, that experienced by unions at a federal level. Yet many state federations of labor continued to engage in political action in support of positive political goals. If judicial repression gave federal unions an incentive to desist from political action in pursuit of positive goals, why did similar or worse repression not give state unions an incentive to similarly desist?[41]

There are thus reasons to doubt whether court repression gave unions an incentive to desist from political action in the case of positive goals. But the case against the court repression thesis does not depend on these doubts.

Advocates of the court repression thesis are particularly fond of citing Strasser's argument against the eight-hour plank as powerful supporting evidence for their thesis.[42] For example, Skocpol (1992, 228–29) moves directly from a discussion of Strasser's intervention to conclude that "interaction with a court-dominated state thus strengthened opponents to labor politics within the U.S. trade union movement." Likewise, Hattam (1992, 163–66) draws on Strasser's argument to conclude that "the option of pursuing workers' interests through a labor party, or its equivalent, was no longer viable in the United States. . . . Short of revolutionary transformation, there was little incentive for workers to mobilize politically, as hard won political victories were continually obstructed by the courts."

In drawing these conclusions, the advocates of the court repression thesis make two mistakes, each of which highlights one of the main problems with the argument about the effects of court repression.[43] First, they mistakenly take Strasser's rhetorical exaggeration about the constitution and the power of the courts literally. But we have seen that the courts were not immune to political pressure and that there were a number of ways to exercise this pressure—all of which were well short of revolutionary transformation. Second, they elide the distinction between positive and negative goals and mistakenly generalize Strasser's argument against political action in pursuit of positive goals to an argument against any political action.[44] But whether or not court repression gave unions an incentive to desist from engaging in political action in pursuit of positive goals, it certainly did give them an incentive to engage in political action in pursuit of negative goals.

Conclusion

The court repression thesis claims that the wave of judicial hostility that struck unions in the 1890s led them to abandon political action, and that this in turn helps explain the AFL's attitude towards labor politics in 1894 and at subsequent conventions. But careful examination of the institutional incentives facing unionists and the record of what they said and did suggests a number of problems with this claim.

Because it elides the distinction between types of political goals and types of political action, the court repression thesis offers a misleading account of the development of union attitudes towards politics. In the wake of renewed court repression, the AFL did eventually restrict the type of political goals it pursued. However, its attitude towards different types of political action did not change at all. The AFL had long been opposed to involvement in partisan politics and in favor of restricting itself to pressure group politics. In the 1890s, it simply reaffirmed that position.

The court repression thesis is right to emphasize the fact that unions were subject to a new wave of judicial repression in the 1890s, but it is wrong about the effects of this repression. According to the court repression thesis, since the courts had the final say on the political decisions that most mattered to unions, and since they were largely immune to external political influence, the unions had an incentive to repudiate political action. In fact, the opposite was the case. Contrary to the court repression thesis, the unions had both opportunities to exercise political influence over the courts and a strong incentive to use them.

The unions had these opportunities because the courts were susceptible to political pressure both directly, through the selection of judges and their need to maintain legitimacy, and indirectly, through legislative and executive pressure. The unions had an incentive to use these opportunities because court repression had forced them to pursue goals that concerned their core organizational interests, and that could only be achieved through political action. Indeed, because of the ongoing failure of pressure group politics, court repression gave the unions an incentive to engage not just in political action in general, but in partisan political action in particular.

CHAPTER 5

Repression

THERE ARE A NUMBER of theories that argue that repression can help explain why no labor party was established in the United States. These theories fall into two groups. In one group are versions of the "soft repression" thesis. In the other are versions of the "hard repression" thesis. These two theses contradict each other in basic respects.

TWO THESES ON REPRESSION

The most venerable of the two is the soft repression thesis. Proponents of this thesis argue that the failure of American unions to establish a labor party resulted in part from the low level of state repression they experienced.[1] According to the soft repression thesis, the greater the level of state repression, the more likely unions are to establish a labor party. Repression gives unions a strong incentive to enter the contest for political power, since, only by doing so, can they protect their core organizational interests from a predatory state. According to the proponents of this thesis, unions in European countries experienced greater repression than their American counterparts, and hence were more likely to establish a labor party. Where repression is severe, unions have no option but to enter the political sphere even if they only aspire to pure-and-simple unionism.[2]

In contrast, proponents of the hard repression thesis argue that the failure of American unions to establish a labor party resulted in part from the high level of repression they experienced.[3] According to this thesis, the greater the level of state repression, the less likely unions are to establish a labor party. Repression undermines efforts to establish a labor party by giving unions an incentive to adopt a strategy of self-restraint in order to avoid antagonizing powerful political elites—elites who might otherwise unleash a repressive backlash that would threaten their core organizational interests. According to the proponents of the hard repression thesis, the unrelenting hostility of the American state ensured that European-style forays into labor politics were a "luxury" that American unions could ill afford. Repression cowed the American unions into adopting apolitical pure-and-simple unionism as a strategy for protecting their organizations.

Note that the soft repression and the hard repression theses differ in two distinct ways. First, they differ about the extent of repression. According to the soft repression thesis, the level of repression in the United States was low, while according to the hard repression thesis it was high. Second, they differ about the effects of repression. According to the soft repression thesis, it helped the formation of a labor party, while according to the hard repression thesis it hindered.

Does comparison of the Untied States with Australia help establish which, if either, of these theses is right? I will start by comparing the extent of repression in the two countries, and then turn to its effects.

THE EXTENT OF REPRESSION

How repressive was the United States when compared with Australia? Although state repression of unions was never absent, it was not a major concern of the emerging union movement in either country prior to the late 1870s. Indeed, far from worrying about repression, one of the main political concerns of the unions in both countries in the 1870s and into the early 1880s was to secure legislation that would enable them to collect outstanding dues and protect their funds from any fraud perpetrated by wayward union officials.[4]

However, in the late 1880s and early 1890s, state repression emerged as a major problem for both union movements. Two kinds of state agency played a critical role: the police and the military (whom I will refer to collectively as the armed forces), and the courts. Since I have examined the role of the courts in the previous chapter, I will focus here on the role of police and military forces, and on the overall impact of state repression. In both the United States and Australia, governments intervened directly in each of the major industrial disputes of the early 1890s by deploying police, or soldiers, or both. In the tables that follow, I have gathered figures that enable us to compare the extent of these interventions in the three most important disputes in each country. These were, in order of importance, the 1890 Maritime strike, the 1891 Queensland Shearers' strike, and the 1892 Broken Hill Miners' strike in Australia; and the 1894 Pullman strike, the 1892 Homestead Steel strike, and the 1892 Coeur d'Alene Miners' strike in the United States.

I want to begin by comparing the Maritime strike and the Pullman strike. These strikes are particularly worthy of attention, not only because they were the largest and most important of the wave of strikes that hit both countries in the early 1890s, but also because each occurred right before the decision was taken about whether or not to establish a labor party.

The Maritime strike started in August 1890 and lasted for two months. It began when the Steamship Owners' Association refused to accept the right of the Marine Officers' Association to affiliate to the Melbourne Trades' Hall Council. This is the issue that gave the strike its name. However, the name is slightly misleading, for this was only one of two issues at the heart of the strike. The other was a dispute between the shearers' union and the pastoralists over the employment of non-union labor. Moreover, the strike rapidly spread to other parts of the economy, as waterside and other transport workers refused to handle non-union wool, and coal miners refused to provide fuel to the shipping companies.[5]

The Pullman strike began in May 1894 when the rolling stock manufacturer, George Pullman, cut the wages of his employees by between a quarter and a third, but refused to lower the above-market rents he forced them to pay to live in the company town he had built outside Chicago. The strike spread nationwide from late June when the American Railway Union (ARU) imposed a boycott on the use of Pullman cars throughout the United States, and continued until it was defeated in early August. It had been preceded by a separate nationwide coal strike involving more than 100,000 miners (Brecher, 1997, 87–95, and Laslett, 1970, 198–203). However, with the exception of a brief and disappointing sympathy strike in Chicago, the Pullman strike did not spread beyond the railroads, and even on the railroads the older craft-based brotherhoods were hostile to the strike.[6]

Contemporaries in both countries saw these strikes as unprecedented, both because of their nationwide scope, and because they seemed to foreshadow classwide war between the forces of organized labor and the equally organized forces of major capitalist employers. The rapid growth and recent industrial success of the new inclusive unions at the center of both disputes—the shearers in Australia and the railway union in the United States—had led employers to establish counter-organizations that coordinated their actions throughout the disputes. In both cases, the unions made it clear they would settle for arbitration. But, seizing the opportunity for a showdown, the organized employers adopted a militant, uncompromising stance.

In both countries, governments intervened directly in the dispute and used their armed forces to help defeat the strike and protect the interests of major capitalists. Table 5.1 sets out the scale and impact of this intervention. Note that in order to give a better sense of how this intervention was actually experienced, the figures in Table 5.1 refer only to the city that was at the center of each strike, and where the outcome of each was decided. The table shows that repression was far greater in the United States than it was in Australia.

Not only were there almost four times as many armed men in Chicago as there were in Sydney, but there were also many more armed men per striker. In addition, the types of armed forces deployed were different. In Chicago, the police were joined by thousands of state and federal soldiers, while in Sydney the military was mobilized but not deployed.[7] In Chicago, two-thirds of the force were trained police and soldiers, while in Sydney the vast majority (almost four-fifths) were temporary recruits.

Moreover, the intensity of repression was not just a function of the number and type of armed forces deployed. It was also a function of what they did

TABLE 5.1.
Police and Military Intervention in Two Critical Strikes

	1890 Maritime Strike in Sydney		1894 Pullman Strike in Chicago	
Population		383,283		1,099,850
Strikers		7,000		18,000
Armed Forces	Police	573	Police	3,500
	Country Police	96	Deputy Sheriffs	250
	Special Constables	3,283	State Troops	4,243
			Federal Troops	1,936
			Federal Dep. Marshals	5,000
	Total	3,952	Total	14,929
Armed Forces Per 100 Strikers		56		83
Union Leaders Arrested		None		All
Workers Arrested		56+		705
Workers Killed		0		13

Notes and sources: see appendix

when they intervened. The last three rows of Table 5.1 provide some indication of the different kinds of intervention that took place. While the Sydney-based Labour Defence Committee was left free to organize the Maritime strike throughout NSW, and later throughout Australia, the leaders of the American Railway Union were all arrested. At the same time, the union's national office in Chicago was ransacked by deputy marshals, all records and correspondence were seized, and communication with members was effectively prohibited (Lindsey, 1942, 278–79, and Foner, 1955, 270). In addition, up to 12 times as many workers were arrested in Chicago as in Sydney, and most striking of all, the 13 deaths and 53 serious injuries inflicted on workers in Chicago simply had no counterpart in Sydney.

Thus, the number and type of armed forces deployed, as well as the kind of interventions they made, all suggest that repression was greater in the Pullman strike than in the Maritime strike. This conclusion does not only apply to the citywide figures presented in Table 5.1. It also holds true if we adopt either a national or a more local perspective.

Nationwide, up to 50,000 workers took part in the Maritime strike throughout southern and eastern Australia.[8] The four colonies most seriously affected by the strike had a total available military force of about 18,000 permanent, partly paid, and volunteer troops (Nicholls, 1988, 148). Of these,

830 troops were called out in two colonies.[9] None of the strike leaders were arrested, and no workers were killed. Coast to coast across the United States, about 150,000 workers took part in the Pullman strike.[10] About 32,000 state troops were called out in 20 of the 27 states affected, and 16,000 federal troops were deployed out of a total available force of 20,000 (Cooper, 1980, 100, Coffman, 1986, 251, and Hacker, 1969, 259). The strike leaders were all arrested and 25 workers were killed (Yellen, 1974, 135, and Foner, 1955, 269).

Comparison of the worst local incidents of repression in each strike is also illuminating. These incidents were given enormous publicity by (typically hostile) newspapers and public authorities, and they could have a critical effect on perceptions of the legitimacy of the strike, and the expected costs of taking part.

The worst incident in the Maritime strike took place on September 19 at Circular Quay in Sydney when the Riot Act was read to a crowd of about 10,000 people. Some in this crowd had been hurling abuse and gravel at an unusual group of strikebreakers who were driving carts piled high with bales of wool to waterfront warehouses. The strikebreakers were prominent pastoralists and businessmen dressed in top hats, morning suits, and white gloves, and there is evidence that their procession was part of an orchestrated attempt to provoke a confrontation in order to put pressure on the government to arrest the Labour Defence Committee and call out the military. Around 300 police and special constables were on the scene, including 36 mounted police who charged and dispersed the crowd. About 15 arrests were made, leading to fines of a pound or two for some, and jail sentences of up to six months for others. No shots were fired, and the foot police did not even draw their batons.[11]

The worst incident in the Pullman strike took place on July 7 at 49th and Loomis Streets in Chicago when a crowd of several thousand confronted a company of state troops in order to stop the removal of a boxcar that had been overturned to obstruct a railway line. Stones were thrown and several shots were fired from the crowd. When the crowd refused to disperse, the troops first charged with fixed bayonets, and were then ordered to shoot at will. Four people were killed and about twenty were seriously wounded. Four soldiers and a lieutenant were also wounded. This was one of a number of confrontations that took place over several days as crowds surged onto railway lines at key points in the city in order to stop the movement of trains. Again, there is evidence that agents of the railroads tried to provoke at least some of this violence. Certainly, the violence helped their cause, as newspapers across the country led with lurid tales of anarchy and revolution.[12]

One other incident is also worth mentioning. Addressing the Victorian Mounted Rifles, who were preparing for possible deployment in the center of Melbourne, Colonel Tom Price told his men that if they were ordered to shoot at "the disturbers of law and order," they should "Fire low and lay them out." This incident is often cited to demonstrate the extent to which the Australian state authorities were prepared to go to repress the strike. But when compared with the American experience, the incident takes on a different significance, because it also helps show that the limits of acceptable repression were different in the two countries. When Price's words became public, there was a huge furor in Melbourne. The Minister of Defence launched an inquiry, a debate was held in parliament, and some 60,000 people attended a public demonstration.[13] Moreover, Price's troops remained in their barracks,[14] and nobody actually was shot. "Fire low and lay them out." This is what Colonel Price said. But in incidents too numerous to name, this is what his American counterparts actually did.[15]

So, whatever the level of analysis—whether nationwide, citywide, or based on the worst local incidents—comparison of the Maritime and Pullman strikes shows that state repression was greater in the United States than it was in Australia. Evidence from the other major strikes of the period reinforces this same basic conclusion. None of these had the national scope of the Maritime and Pullman strikes, but they were all the subject of national attention.

The Queensland Shearers' strike began in January 1891 when the Queensland Pastoral Employers' Association (backed by a national Federal Council) sought to unilaterally impose an agreement that rolled back the terms of employment unions had recently won, and reneged on the promise to establish a closed shop. The strike lasted for over six months. It spread slowly across the vast pastoral districts of Queensland until March, when all shearers and shed hands were called out on strike. Using a mixture of military and judicial measures, the government consciously sought to break the strike. The defense forces had already been deployed alongside police and special constables, and magistrates who were suspected of neutrality were either pressured to conform or transferred (Svensen, 1989, 114 and 145). Most of the strike leaders were arrested for conspiracy, sent before an extraordinarily biased judge, and sentenced to three years imprisonment. Scores of unionists received heavy jail sentences of three months or more for offenses like intimidation, and many others received shorter sentences. In addition, telegrams between union organizations were stopped, and railway workers who expressed sympathy with the shearers were fired (Kenway, 1970, 116).[16]

The Homestead steel strike began at the end of June 1892 and lasted well into November. It was actually a lockout, initiated by Henry Clay Frick, the new manager whom mill-owner Andrew Carnegie had brought in to rid his company of the Amalgamated Association of Iron and Steel Workers. With the exception of some sympathy strikes at a few other mills in the area (Burgoyne, 1979 [1893], 175–77 and 136–37, and Yellen, 1974, 92 and 95), the strike was confined to the mill-town of Homestead, eight miles from Pittsburgh. Frick's attempt to import a private force of 300 Pinkerton agents led to a gun battle with local residents in which at least seven workers died and the Pinkertons were forced to depart. Some days later, the entire Pennsylvania

TABLE 5.2.
Police and Military Intervention in the Queensland Shearers' Strike and the
Homestead Steel Strike

	1891 Queensland Shearers' Strike		1892 Homestead Steel Strike	
Population		45,687		12,000
Strikers		9,000		3,800
Armed Forces	Police	550	Police	13
	Special Constables	1,099	Deputy Sheriffs	30
	Qld Defense Force	1,442	State Troops	8,000
			Pinkertons	300
	Total	3,091	Total	8,343
Armed Forces Per 100 Strikers		34		220
Union Leaders Arrested		Most		All
Workers Arrested		221+		111+
Workers Killed		0		7

Notes and sources: see appendix

National Guard occupied the town. A concerted effort was then made by the company, the state's armed forces, and the courts to arrest all the strike leaders on charges of treason and conspiracy, to indict scores of other unionists, and to drain the union of funds with bail expenses.[17]

Table 5.2 sets out the extent of repression in these two strikes. Although both took place in what was arguably the core industry in each country, it is not my intention to claim that there are especially strong reasons for a *paired* comparison of these strikes. It is still worth noting, however, that the extent of repression was greater in Homestead than in Queensland. The vast areas of Queensland affected by the shearers' strike make comparison difficult, but even if we consider only the towns of Barcaldine and Clermont in which the largest number of police and soldiers were concentrated, it remains clear that the extent of repression was greater in Homestead.[18] The only qualification to this conclusion concerns the number of workers arrested, since it seems that more workers were arrested in Queensland than in Homestead. But doubts about these estimates (set out in the "Notes and Sources"), and the fact that, even using these estimates, the number of arrests *per striker* was still greater in Homestead, militate against giving too much weight to this one qualification.

Comparison of the miners' strikes that took place in Broken Hill and Coeur d'Alene is particularly interesting, because the circumstances surrounding the two strikes were so similar. Silver and lead was discovered in both places in the early 1880s, and the towns that grew up around the mines were extremely isolated and wholly dependent on them. Broken Hill was in the far west of NSW three days by rail from Sydney,[19] and the Coeur d'Alene region was in northern Idaho in a territory that only achieved statehood in 1890. In both cases, unions formed in the late 1880s. The Broken Hill union was a branch of the Amalgamated Miners' Association. The union in Coeur d'Alene was independent but had close ties with the metal-mining unions in neighboring states that would later form the Western Federation of Miners. In both cases, the core union members were longer-term residents with families, occupational health issues were a central concern, and there was widespread local resentment of the big-city absentee shareholders who had bought out the original owner-miners. In both cases, the unions quickly achieved some important victories, which were written into agreements with the mining companies. But international prices for silver and lead fell sharply, and in 1892 the companies opted to unilaterally break the agreements. In response, the unions struck.[20]

The Broken Hill strike lasted from July to November 1892. The Coeur d'Alene strike lasted from April to November of the same year. Table 5.3 sets out the extent of state repression in these two very similar strikes. Again, repression was greater in the United States. The miners in Coeur d'Alene were swamped by state and federal soldiers. There were far more of them, both in absolute numbers, and relative to the number of strikers, than there were in Broken Hill. Moreover, while the armed forces in Coeur d'Alene came overwhelmingly from the military, the NSW government resisted company-pressure

TABLE 5.3.
Police and Military Intervention in Two Silver Mining Strikes

	1892 Broken Hill Miners' Strike		1892 Coeur D'Alene Miners' Strike	
Population		19,789		3,993
Strikers		6,000		800
Armed Forces	Police	285	State Troops	196
		___	Federal Troops	1,300
	Total	285	Total	c.1,500
Armed Forces Per 100 Strikers		5		188
Union Leaders Arrested		All		All
Workers Arrested		26+		600
Workers Killed		0		6

Notes and sources: see appendix

to deploy soldiers in Broken Hill, and instead relied solely on a buildup of police.[21] In both cases, all the strike leaders were arrested and charged with conspiracy. But while union members in Broken Hill were continually harassed and sometimes arrested by a partisan police magistrate, their counterparts in Coeur d'Alene were arrested en masse. With the exception of those who managed to escape across the border to Montana, nearly every union member and every union sympathizer was rounded up and held in a makeshift "bull pen." Martial law was declared and remained in force for four months (Smith, 1961, 80–84, and Rich, 1941, 112), and it was the publicly stated goal of the military to destroy the union and drive its members from the region. Military commanders offered to free imprisoned miners who resigned from the union, and two mines that were continuing to employ unionists were forced to close down and reopen with non-union labor (Cooper, 1980, 166–70, Jensen, 1950, 36, and Smith, 1961, 93). In addition, only in Coeur d'Alene were workers killed. The deaths occurred when shooting broke out between a group of unionists and a group of deputy marshals, strikebreakers and Pinkertons (Smith, 1961, 62–66).

We are now in a position to compare all six strikes. The conclusion that repression was greater in the United States than Australia is not just a function of the way in which these strikes have been paired. A quick look at Tables 5.1, 5.2, and 5.3 shows that each of the American strikes was more heavily repressed than each of the Australian ones. This is true not just for each strike taken as a whole, but also for each of the main indicators of repression considered individually.[22] Whether measured in terms of the number of armed forces per striker, the kind of armed forces deployed, or their impact in terms of arrests and deaths, the extent of repression was greater in the United States than it was in Australia.

This conclusion holds, not only for the biggest and most important disputes, but throughout the late nineteenth century and into the twentieth. Prior to the railroad strike of 1877, the deployment of soldiers in industrial disputes had been quite unusual in the United States. But by the 1890s it had become commonplace. In a number of the most important disputes, federal troops played a critical role, and as the so-called "Indian Wars" wound down, this became their most conspicuous role (Hacker, 1969, 259–61, and Cooper, 1980, 210). However, it was the state militias that were most frequently used to intervene in strikes. Official records report that between 1886 and 1895 state militias were called out on 328 occasions, and that on more than a third of these occasions this was connected to labor disputes. In fact, given the use of euphemistic and ambiguous categories in these records, it seems likely that close to a half of National Guard duty was connected to strikes and strike-breaking (Ganoe, 1924, 501–5, and Hacker, 1969, 259).[23] In contrast, between 1860 and 1900, troops were called out to provide "Military Aid to the Civil Power" in Australia on about 12 occasions (Stanley, 1988, 88, and Gibson, 1994, 12). Six of these involved strikes: three coal mining strikes (in

1879, 1888, and 1890), the Maritime strike (in 1890), and two shearers' strikes (in 1891 and 1894).

Aggregate figures on arrests are not available, but we do know that, in the United States, when armed forces intervened in strikes, workers were frequently killed. The strike wave of the early 1890s was accompanied by a quite extraordinary level of violence. This violence was not limited to the Pullman, Homestead, and Coeur d'Alene strikes. In 1890, private "detectives" killed five people during a strike on the New York Central Railroad. In 1891, the Pennsylvania state militia killed ten fleeing strikers and wounded another 50. In 1892, the militia killed at least one coal miner in Tennessee.[24] In 1894, deputies killed four striking miners in Pennsylvania, and federal troops killed a further two in Illinois (Goldstein, 1978, 15 and 45–51). And the list goes on.[25] Nor did the Pullman strike see an end to the violence. If anything, it became worse. Between 1902 and 1904, a period for which there are unusually detailed and reliable figures, at least 198 people were killed and 1,966 were injured in labor disputes (Taft and Ross, 1969, 380, and Forbath, 1991, 106). By contrast, in all of the strikes that took place during the wave of industrial unrest that gripped Australia from 1890 to 1894, only one worker was killed.[26] And at no time, either before, during, or after this strike wave, did troops open fire on unionists (Gibson, 1994, 12).

According to the soft repression thesis, the extent of repression was less in the United States than it was in Europe. There is evidence that this is simply not true, at least when the United States is compared with western Europe (Mann, 1993, 635, Spiers, 1992, 209–10, and Gibson, 1994, 12, 14, and 18). But whatever the case in Europe, it is the severity of repression in the United States that is most striking when it is compared with Australia. So, with respect to the extent of repression, comparison with Australia supports the hard repression thesis.

Soldiers and Police

Military institutions in both the United States and Australia grew out of the same English citizen-soldier tradition. As a result, in the late nineteenth century, the vast majority of troops in both countries were militiamen not regular soldiers.[27] Police forces in both countries were also strongly influenced by British models. However, there were a number of differences in the kinds of military and police forces that were used, and two of these help explain why repression was greater in the United States. The first concerns the organizational interests of the militia, and, to a lesser extent, the army. The second concerns the use of private police.[28]

Before the civil war, militias in the United States were only occasionally used in industrial disputes, and after the war, many virtually ceased to exist.

They were revived and expanded in the wake of the 1877 railway strike in order to meet the demands of employers. Now known as the National Guard, the primary purpose of this reorganization was to ensure that state governments would have sufficient military strength to quickly suppress industrial unrest.[29] Thus, the interests of militia forces became intimately linked with the interests of major employers. Indeed, many were directly funded and equipped by big industrialists or associations of businessmen. In Illinois, for example, the second regiment was equipped by the manufacturer Cyrus McCormick, and five companies of cavalry were equipped by a "Citizens Association" composed of Chicago businessmen (Reinders, 1977, 95–96). In Idaho, a company was organized and equipped with a donation of $5,000 from the Coeur d'Alene Mine Owners' Association, in the middle of the 1892 miners' strike (Smith, 1961, 92). Vast privately funded armories were also constructed in the middle of major cities, first in New York, and then in Pennsylvania and other states (Fogelson, 1989, 48–62). In addition, many militia units were staffed or lead by businessmen or middle-class professionals, although it is difficult to be sure about the class composition of the militia as a whole (Reinders, 1977, 96–97). In some states, like Pennsylvania, large corporations made a point of ensuring that those who commanded the militia were sympathetic to their interests (Cooper, 1980, 12).

The army also developed close ties to business interests. This is especially clear in Chicago. Following the wave of labor unrest in 1886, the regional commander, General Schofield, arranged for leading industrialists to raise $156,890 to purchase land for a new fort a few miles north of the city so that federal troops could quickly enter Chicago. Among the major donors was George Pullman (Cooper, 1980, 85–6, Coffman, 1986, 252, and Beckner, 1929, 62–63). Schofield, who had overall command of the army from 1886 to 1895, also had a close personal *rapport* with many leading businessmen, and held stock in a number of railroad companies, including, until 1893, the Pullman Palace Car Company. During the Pullman strike, the federal troops in Chicago were under the command of General Miles. When Miles was given overall command of the army in 1896, businessmen raised $50,000 to buy him a suitable house in Washington (Cooper, 1980, 247–49). Given these organizational and personal interests, it is hardly surprising that the army collaborated so closely with the railroad companies during the Pullman strike, at times virtually taking their directions from the employers' strike coordinator (Cooper, 1977, 191–92).

Australian military forces were not built around the same commonality of interests with the business elite. Volunteer militias were first formed in the 1850s in response to Russian and French invasion scares. Like their counterparts in the United States, militias in the Australian colonies were reorganized in the late 1870s and early 1880s. But unlike in the United States, this was motivated not by the demands of business in an era of growing class conflict, but by the complete withdrawal of the British army in 1870, and another Russian invasion scare. The reorganization was part of a longer-term process of reform in which private initiatives and financial support were replaced with direction by regular soldiers from the small permanent forces, government funding, and the partial payment of volunteers. Unpaid, purely volunteer militias did reemerge in 1885. But again, they were motivated by developments overseas. This time the stimulus was provided by imperial enthusiasms following the death of General Gordon in Khartoum, and yet another bout of panic about the Russians. In many other ways, Australian militias were quite similar to those in the United States. Officers were typically from the local elite, although the class composition of the ranks was probably more mixed. But the organizational interests of militia units were not so closely tied to business interests, and their actions against organized labor in the early 1890s were not premeditated and central to their raison d'être, as they were in the United States.[30] While the American militia faced inwards to meet perceived threats from organized labor to the domestic social order, the Australian militia faced outwards to meet perceived threats from foreign invaders.[31]

The second important difference concerns the preparedness of governments to authorize the widespread use of private police forces in the United States. This took a variety of forms. First, employers secured the appointment of deputy sheriffs and deputy marshals whose principal loyalty was to them rather than to the state. During the Pullman strike, for example, 3,600 of the 5,000 deputy federal marshals were selected, armed, paid for, and directed by the railroad companies (U.S. Strike Commission, 1895, xliv, and Lindsey, 1942, 165–69). Second, employers could hire the services of agencies like the Pinkertons that specialized in providing groups of armed men (as well as spies). By the early 1890s, the Pinkertons had 30,000 regulars and reserves at their disposal—a potential force that was larger than that of the federal government's standing army (Burgoyne, 1979 [1893], 42–45, Jensen, 1991, 24–25 and 40–44). Many of its 2,000 regulars were garrisoned in Chicago (Beckner, 1929, 65, and Brecher, 1997, 72). Employers typically sought to have these agents deputized, although after the Homestead strike, some states legislated to restrict the right of local authorities to do so (Beckner, 1929, 63–67). In response, many large corporations simply established their own private armies and arsenals onsite (Goldstein, 1978, 11–12 and 212). Third, certain employers had a special statutory right to establish and control their own private police forces. The Railroad Police and the Coal and Iron Police in Pennsylvania are the best known examples. State legislation gave them the right to act with full public authority, even though they were wholly controlled by individual railroad, coal, and iron companies, and were neither regulated by, nor responsible to, the state (Taft and Ross, 1969, 316–7, and Shalloo, 1933, 28–29, 35–40, and 59–62).

Few of these options were available to Australian employers. The special constables appointed to police industrial disputes were certainly not neutral. During the Maritime strike, for example, the NSW government rejected a union offer to provide special constables and appointed large numbers of managers, company clerks, and public servants instead.[32] There is also evidence of employer involvement in the appointment of special constables. Clerks in some of the companies affected by the Maritime strike were instructed by their employers to volunteer (Svensen, 1995, 127), and during the 1891 Shearers' strike, most of the special constables were pastoralists or their employees, and some were specially recruited by pastoralists and forwarded to the police.[33] However, special constables were not directly controlled by employers, and the extraordinary activities of the Pinkertons, the Railway Police, and the Coal and Iron Police simply had no counterpart in Australia.

These differences in the kinds of armed forces that were deployed against unionists help explain why repression was greater in the United States than Australia. In the United States, both military forces (especially the militia, but also to a lesser extent the army) and the private police had basic organizational interests that made them particularly responsive to the demands of employers. The resurrection of the militia had depended on its promise to meet these demands, and the private police, of course, could only flourish as long as they did the bidding of those who hired them. Whether implicitly or explicitly, these two groups were more beholden to employers than any of the armed forces deployed in Australia.[34] Ultimately, of course, armed forces in the United States were subject to political control. Militias were responsible to elected politicians, and even private police could only operate if permitted by the legislature. Nevertheless, once they were deployed, these forces had a certain degree of discretion. Employers demanded swift and decisive action against organized labor—and this is typically what they got.

THE EFFECT OF REPRESSION IN AUSTRALIA

Let me turn now to the effects of repression. Does increased repression help or hinder the formation of a labor party? The Australian case suggests that it helps. For the most important effect of increased repression in Australia was that it convinced many unionists that they needed to form a party and contest parliamentary elections. In its official post-mortem report on the Maritime strike, the Labour Defence Committee (1890, 17–19) acknowledged that to "steer clear of politics" had been "a golden rule" of the union movement. But it argued that, given the government's role in the strike, it was now imperative to form a party and "secure a substantial representation in Parliament." This, it concluded, was "over and above all others the greatest lesson of the strike."

It was necessary to form an independent party rather than merely to join with the existing opposition, because the opposition was even keener on repression than the government (Gollan, 1960, 134–35). According to the Labour Defence Committee (1890, 17), "it all amounts to this: whilst we have no cause for gratitude to the Government for their attitude during the strike, we have no reason for believing that the Opposition, had they been in office, would have acted more fairly." Indeed, it was liberal politicians, who had traditionally been most sympathetic to the unions, who had called out the police and military against the strikers. The strike showed "unmistakably" that while "both parties are ready to use the working-classes for their own ends; neither is willing for the working classes to use it" (Labour Defence Committee, 1890, 17).

A proposal that the NSW TLC should contest parliamentary elections had been discussed prior to the Maritime strike.[35] The proposal was the initiative of an experienced union organizer, P. J. Brennan. In January 1890, the TLC instructed its parliamentary committee to work on the proposal, and shortly afterwards, it elected Brennan as TLC President. In April, the TLC endorsed the plan to establish a labor party, and sought the approval of its affiliates and some other unions. However, of the 65 unions approached, only 17 replied, and of these, only four supported the plan unequivocally.[36] The TLC had occasionally flirted with the idea of entering the electoral arena in the past, but most unions had long been opposed to involvement in partisan politics.[37]

Throughout August and September the unions were totally preoccupied with the Maritime strike. However, in early October, as it became clear that the strike would be defeated, Brennan's proposal was revived—first in a joint manifesto which he wrote with the shearers' leader W. G. Spence (in their capacity as Chairman and Secretary of the Intercolonial Conference that had been coordinating strike committees throughout Australia and New Zealand), and then in a memo from the NSW Labour Defence Committee to the TLC.[38] In response, the TLC and its parliamentary committee set to work drafting the platform and rules for a new labor party: the Labor Electoral League. TLC Secretary T. J. Houghton, who before the strike had urged a Gompers-style "support your friends and oppose your enemies" approach to elections, now played a key role in the establishment of the new party, arguing that the actions of the government during the strike had "taught us . . . to marshal our forces for the ballot-box" (TLC, 1891, 11, and Nairn, 1989, 33–34 and 45). At three long meetings in March 1891, the TLC gave its final approval to the party's platform and rules. Although a few unions continued with their traditional opposition, most now threw their support behind the TLC's plan and began organizing Labor Electoral Leagues in those constituencies where they had some influence.

The Intercolonial Trades and Labor Union Congress discussed a similar Australia-wide plan in late April 1891,[39] but the delegates could not agree on a common platform and rules. The superficial similarity to the AFL's 1894 debate is misleading. The disagreement in Australia did not stem from Strasser-like opposition to the pursuit of positive political goals. Both Intercolonial Congresses and the parliamentary committees of TLCs had pursued a wide range of positive and negative goals since their inception.[40] Nor did the disagreement stem from Gompers-like opposition to involvement in partisan politics. Intercolonial Congresses had consistently called for the direct representation of labor in parliament.[41] Rather, opposition to the plan came from those colonies that had been at the forefront of establishing their own labor parties and feared that it would disrupt their efforts. Houghton, who lead the opposition, argued that: "it had taken them eight months to formulate their policy in New South Wales, so as to suit it to local requirements. Was it likely they were going to throw this over for a scheme adopted by Congress after one or two days . . . ?" (ICTUC, 1891, 95).[42] Rather than support any particular plan, "a large majority" of delegates resolved (ICTUC, 1891, 98–99) "to urge upon the various labor organizations throughout the colonies the absolute necessity of at once taking steps to secure the direct representation of labor in Parliament."

The unions in each colony were left free to develop their own response to the strikes and repression of the early 1890s. And this is what they did. In Queensland, as in NSW, plans to found a labor party had been drawn up before the Maritime strike. A proposed platform was sent to district councils and their affiliates for approval, but all bar one council opposed it. However, again as in New South Wales, these plans were given a great boost—in this case, a double boost—first by the defeat of the Maritime strike, and then by the still more flagrant bias of the government during the 1891 shearers' strike. In August 1891, shortly after the end of the shearers' strike, a new labor party was formally established. South Australia and Victoria were also involved in the Maritime strike, and in both cases, unions responded to repression and defeat by establishing labor parties. In South Australia, this happened even though repression had been much milder than in the other colonies. In Victoria, however, there was more reticence. As in Britain, some leading unionists already served as liberal members of parliament, and the new labor party effectively remained a wing of the colony's dominant liberal party throughout the 1890s. In Tasmania and Western Australia, union organization was weak, and the strikes and repression of the early 1890s had had little effect. It was a decade or more before labor parties were firmly established in these colonies, under the influence of successful models elsewhere in Australia.[43]

In each colony that experienced it, the repression of the early 1890s gave unions an incentive to abandon pressure group politics and establish independent labor parties. Repression was not the only factor that produced this shift. In the late 1880s, many central union leaders were dissatisfied with the effectiveness of lobbying, and frustrated by the frequent failure of MPs to stand by the pre-election promises that had won them union endorsement.[44] The leaders who were most preoccupied with the need for legislative reform—like those who attended Intercolonial Congresses or served on TLC parliamentary committees—began to advocate the direct representation of labor in parliament. The introduction of payment for MPs made this a realistic aspiration. But it was hampered by the apolitical traditions that permeated many unions. Repression weakened the reticence of these unions, and strengthened the incentive that central union leaders had to launch electoral organizations.

The Effect in the United States Compared

If there was enough repression in Australia to have this effect, why did the even greater level of repression in the United States not have a similar effect? In order for a labor party to have become firmly established in the United States, two conditions would have had to be met. First, a decision would have had to be made to found the party; and second, the party would have had to succeed electorally, and sustain itself organizationally between elections (especially in the wake of setbacks).

These two conditions could, in turn, have been met in two different ways. On the one hand, a party could have been founded and sustained at a national level. On the other hand, a party could have been founded and sustained in one (or more) key states. These states could then have become a model that others emulated, until eventually the party spread nationwide. As we have seen, the Australian experience was closer to this second path, although the decision to establish labor parties *was* given general support at the Intercolonial Congress in 1891.

Table 5.4 sets out the American experience, both nationally and in Illinois. In addition to being at the center of the Pullman strike, Illinois was well placed to be a model state.[45] In the late nineteenth century, most industrial action took place in a handful of states in the Northeast and Midwest. Illinois, New York, and Pennsylvania had by far the largest number of strikes and strikers. Indeed, between 1881 and 1894, over 70 percent of all establishments involved in strikes, and over 80 percent of those involved in lockouts, were in just five states—these same three states, plus Massachusetts and Ohio (Commissioner of Labor, 1896, 17–22 and 1560–63).[46]

Table 5.4.
Conditions for the Establishment of a Labor Party

	Decide to Found a Party	Succeed Electorally and Sustain an Organization
National	No	—
Illinois	Yes	No

Table 5.4 raises two important questions. (1) What was the effect of repression on the AFL's decision not to found a labor party? And (2) What was the effect of repression on the ability of the labor-populist party that *was* founded in Illinois to succeed electorally and sustain itself? In this section, I will focus on the first question, and in the next, on the second.

So what effect did repression have on the AFL's decision in 1894 not to found a labor party? I have already considered the effect of judicial repression in the previous chapter. Consideration of the additional impact of police and military repression, and comparison with Australia, both reinforce the conclusions reached there.

Like judicial repression, police and military repression gave the union movement a strong incentive to engage in partisan political action. It gave unions an incentive to engage in political action because it generated problems that threatened their core organizational interests, and because these problems could only be solved by influencing political decisions. It gave unions an incentive to engage in partisan political action because pressure group politics had proved unable to solve these problems. Indeed, as in Australia, repression gave unions an incentive to engage in independent partisan political action, since, by the end of the Pullman strike, it was clear that both the Republican and the Democratic parties were prepared to deploy police and troops against unionists.[47] In addition, there was already some evidence of the effectiveness of this strategy. In Idaho, the populists who were elected to the State Senate after the 1892 Coeur d'Alene strike used their numbers to effectively disband the state militia by blocking further funding. In Colorado, the labor-backed populist Governor, Davis H. Waite, refused to send the militia to defeat a strike at Cripple Creek in early 1894, and instead used them to force the company to reach a settlement (Foner, 1955, 312, and Reinders, 1977, 99).

However, some unions were more severely affected by police and military repression than others. As with judicial repression, it was typically the "new" inclusive, industrywide unions that suffered the worst. In the early 1890s, this was the case in both the United States and Australia. The American Railway Union and the Australian shearers' unions provide the paradigm cases, although metal and coal miners also suffered severely in both countries, as did maritime workers in Australia. Craft unions, on the other hand, could sometimes avoid the direct effects of repression, by monopolizing the supply of certain skills, and relying on the power this gave them in the labor market. Police and military intervention was frequently connected to the introduction of strikebreakers, and this was less likely to be attempted if those on strike were well-organized skilled workers who were difficult to replace.

The more severely affected a union was by repression, the more enthusiastic it was likely to be about independent political action. As we saw in Chapter 1, inclusive unions, like the American Railway Union (ARU) and the Australian Shearers' Union (ASU), already had some incentive to engage in political action. ARU President Eugene Debs and ASU General Secretary W. G. Spence had expressed interest in independent political action before the Pullman and Maritime strikes, although Spence had moved in this direction more cautiously than Debs (Debs, 1894, 8–10, Salvatore, 1982, 147–48, and Merritt, 1986, 180–81). But the threat that repression posed to their organizations strongly reinforced these developments. In the wake of defeat, both leaders, citing repression, placed independent political action at the center of their concerns.[48] In contrast, those craft unions that were less affected by police and military repression, often—though by no means always—remained skeptical.[49]

These different experiences of repression helped underpin the disagreement between John McBride and Samuel Gompers at the 1894 AFL conference. McBride, who led the miners' union, favored the establishment of an independent labor party, while Gompers, who hailed from the cigar makers' union, was emphatically opposed to it. Within the ranks of the AFL, the miners' union came closest to being a model industrial union, and the cigar makers' came closest to a model craft union. Just prior to the Pullman dispute, the miners' union had been almost destroyed by an eight-week coal strike that involved the widespread deployment of police and troops, and McBride responded by seeking to establish a labor-populist party both nationally and in Ohio (Laslett, 1970, 197–201). The cigar makers did not experience a similar level of repression. Statistics collected by the United States Commissioner of Labor do not record the use of police and troops, but American-wide figures on the success of strikes provide some evidence of the very different experiences of these two unions in the period between the Great Upheaval of 1886 and the AFL's 1894 Conference. In the coal and coke industry (where almost 40 percent of strikes took place in Pennsylvania, and over 70 percent in Pennsylvania, Illinois, and Ohio), strikes succeeded in 17.3 percent of establishments, partially succeeded in 25.1 percent, and failed in 57.6 percent. In the tobacco industry, however, strikes succeeded in 54.2 percent of establishments, partially succeeded in 6.7 percent and failed in 39.1 percent. In its New York stronghold, where the cigar makers' union was based, strikes failed in only 29.5 percent of establishments (Commissioner of Labor, 1896, 1509, 1545, and Edwards, 1981, 101, 105–9, and 115–16). Of course, repression is not the only factor affecting the outcome of strikes, but these figures do give a rudimentary indication of the capacity of unions to stand aloof from politics and still look after themselves.

It is important to emphasize, however, that it was not only the "new" inclusive unions that were subject to severe repression. Craft unions too could suffer. The iron and steel workers' union is a particularly important example. This union was one of the largest, richest, and best organized craft unions in the United States (Burgoyne, 1979, 15, 302, and Yellen, 1974, 72). But the Homestead strike delivered a "knockout blow" to its stronghold around Pittsburgh, from which it never recovered (Holt, 1977, 132, 134, and Ingham, 1991, 136). Although the union did not have the same pre-existing incentives to enter politics as the "new" inclusive unions, repression induced a similar response. At the 1894 AFL conference, Delegate Brentell, of the iron and steel workers, was the only delegate who joined with the Delegate Penna, of the miners, to argue that political action was necessary on pragmatic grounds, simply in order to secure the unions themselves (AFL, 1895a, 42 and 52).[50] Though one was a craft unionist, and the other an industrial unionist, these delegates shared a common experience. Both had recently seen their unions seriously weakened by severe repression.

So, in both the United States and Australia, those unions that were subject to the severest repression, had the strongest interest in effective political action. However, because the severest repression in the United States was far greater than the severest repression in Australia, it also had another effect. In Australia, unions that were subject to the severest repression were *defeated*. In the United States, they were *destroyed*. Judicial repression helped produce this effect. But the far higher level of police and military repression in the United States also strongly reinforced it. It did this in three ways.

First, it vastly increased the *personal costs* of participation. In both countries, the deployment of police and soldiers increased the likely loss of wages and employment by facilitating the introduction of strikebreakers. But these negative selective incentives were vastly increased in the United States by the greater likelihood of arrest, and the fines and jail sentences that followed. And, of course, by the possibility of death. Only one or two strikers had to be killed to make the prospect of union involvement an extremely frightening one. The enormity of the consequences ensured that even a small chance of death was a major disincentive to further involvement. Although there were limits to its financial resources, the union could offset some of these costs by arranging bail and paying fines. But it could not serve a member's jail term, or bring an activist back to life.

While social, psychological, and moral incentives (like friendship, reputation, and duty) may outweigh the usual material disincentives (like lost wages) that inhibit collective action, these may in turn be outweighed by disincentives generated by repression (like arrest and death). A strong collective identity can ensure that the initial response of many union members will not involve calculations of individual utility. Nevertheless, beyond some threshold, very large personal costs will begin to affect the behavior of even the most committed unionists.

Coal miners, however, were regularly prepared to face down police and troops despite these risks. One reason for this may be the already high likelihood of fatalities at work. In the late 1880s and early 1890s, there were about two deaths per thousand miners each year in Illinois (Bogart and Thompson, 1920, 513). In NSW, there were close to twice this number (Gollan, 1963, 96). The risk of simply going to work was actually greater than the risk of confronting the armed forces. Thus, it may have counterbalanced, or at least normalized, the dangers of such a confrontation.[51]

Second, police and military repression in the United States was more likely to directly undermine the *organizational infrastructure* of the union. The arrest of union leaders, especially where this involved central as well as local leaders, the ransacking and closure of offices, the seizure of records, and the disruption or prohibition of direct or indirect communication with members made any sort of coordinated action virtually impossible. These interventions did not all happen in every strike. But all of them happened in the Pullman strike, and none of them in the Maritime strike.

Third, very high levels of repression induced a sense of *hopelessness*. In both countries, strike defeats lead to demoralization.[52] Unions like the ARU were particularly susceptible to the effects of demoralization. For many ARU members, beliefs about the efficacy of the union were not based on stable convictions built up over a period of years, but rather on a sudden surge of optimism following a single recent success—the victory in the Great Northern strike that took place a couple of months before the Pullman strike spread nationwide.[53] Just as one victory had made the union's reputation, one defeat could destroy it. A similar, though less acute, problem afflicted the ASU. Although it was more firmly established than the ARU, members of the union entered the Maritime strike with an inflated sense of its efficacy because of the sudden achievement of a closed shop in the Jondaryn dispute a few months before.[54] But while the demoralization following the Maritime strike was accompanied by preparations for future struggles, and a belief that, if the appropriate lessons were learned, these could be won (Labour Defence Committee, 1890, 7, 17), the demoralization following the Pullman strike turned to despair and induced a feeling of pessimism, impotence, and hopelessness. Even those who were prepared to bear the high personal costs of repression were unlikely to continue their involvement, unless there was some hope that, at least eventually, it would achieve results.[55]

Leadership despair tends to reinforce this sense of hopelessness, since the meaning of a defeat is often influenced by the way in which union leaders interpret it.[56] This effect can be seen in the different responses of Debs and Spence to their respective defeats. While Debs publicly stated that he would "never again have any official connection with a strike," that the Pullman strike had shown that successful industrial action was impossible, and that *only* political action could redeem the situation (Salvatore, 1982, 148 and 169–72), Spence argued that the need for political action was one of *two* lessons of the strike. The other equally important lesson was the need to strengthen the unions themselves by making membership more inclusive and federal organization more effective. These reforms would ensure that "the next strike will have a very different tale to tell . . . Labour will win . . ." (Ebbels, 1983, 152–53).

Further evidence of this difference can be found in the attitudes that leaders of the two unions had towards far-fetched colonization plans. Following both the Pullman strike and the Queensland Shearers' strike, some leaders responded to defeat by abandoning union organization, and instead launching extraordinary plans to establish model socialist colonies. In the United States, this became the major preoccupation of the remaining stalwarts of the ARU (Salvatore, 1982, 162–67). In Australia, although the promoter of the plan, William Lane, had been the main ideologue of Queensland unionism, it remained marginal to the concerns of the shearers' union.[57]

High personal costs, the demolition of organizational infrastructure, and a sense of hopelessness among workers and their leaders all combined to destroy the American Railway Union.[58] The destruction of the ARU gave its leaders an unequivocal interest in effective political action. But it also meant that their voice in the central councils of the union movement was commensurately weaker. Similar Australian unions survived repression, and, consequently, they were able to exert far greater influence.

When the NSW TLC made the decision to establish a labor party in March 1891, the shearers' union represented about 22 percent of all unionists in NSW, and about 34 percent of those affiliated with the TLC. If the ARU had survived and affiliated with the AFL with its 150,000 members intact, it would have represented about 25 percent of all unionists in the United States, and about 35 percent of those affiliated with the AFL, when that body met to decide whether to establish a labor party in December 1894. But, of course, it did not survive. As it was, the three groups of unionists who had suffered the most severe repression prior to December 1894—the railway workers, the iron and steel workers, and the (metal and coal) miners—represented just 6 percent of all unionists and 7 percent of those affiliated with the AFL.[59] Unsurprisingly, they rarely occupied leadership positions in the organization. In contrast, the three groups of unionists that had suffered the worst repression in NSW prior to March 1891—the shearers, the coal miners, and the maritime workers—represented 46 percent of all unionists and 62 percent of those affiliated with the TLC.[60] From 1889 onwards, members of these unions began to regularly occupy leadership positions in the TLC (Wolman, 1924, 32–33, 110–18, and Markey, 1988, 136–46, 152–58, 318–19, 1994, 19–22, 559).

Intra-Australian comparison confirms the importance of the balance of power within central union councils. In Queensland, the influence of the shearers was even greater than in NSW, and the central council of the union movement there was even more enthusiastic about establishing a labor party. In Victoria, on the other hand, the influence of craft unions was much greater, and the shearers' union was weaker than in NSW. There, the Trades Hall Council was less enthusiastic about establishing a party.[61]

Talk of the "balance of power" may be misleading, however. The growing influence of the "new" unions in the late 1880s was certainly crucial in Australia, but support for political action was not just a question of who had the "numbers" at conferences. Rather, it developed through a more subtle process, in which, by interacting with each other, unionists (including skeptics from craft unions who were relatively unaffected by police and military repression) came to identify with broader concerns and a more inclusive range of class interests.[62] This had been going on for some time. We have already noted how delegates to Intercolonial Congresses, and many of those serving on the TLC and its committees, had long acknowledged the importance of independent political action. But the Maritime strike touched a far wider range of unionists and intensified this process through regular day-to-day contact between skilled and unskilled unionists, reinforced by external hostility.[63] Most unionists came to see the conflict as their own.

The leaders of the AFL did not share a similar experience during the Pullman strike. That strike did not become the "property" of the AFL in the way the Maritime strike had become the "property" of the whole Australian union movement. Moreover, the craft identity of the AFL was more deeply entrenched. The organization had been refounded in 1886, not merely to defend the interests of craft unions, but to defend their interests against the efforts of the Knights of Labor to organize both skilled and unskilled workers (Kaufman, 1986, 275–86, and Taft, 1957, 21–42 and 85–94). This left a legacy of instinctive suspicion of noncraft organizations. Some AFL leaders viewed the ARU as "the second edition of the Knights of Labor,"[64] and this, along with the hostility of the craft-based railway brotherhoods, tended to reinforce rather than diminish the importance of sectional differences between craft interests and those of other unionists.

If the ARU had survived, the outcome may have been different. Like the shearers' union, the ARU operated in a key national industry that had the potential numbers, the national spread, and the foothold in both urban and rural society that was needed if the union movement was to successfully underpin a labor-populist party in alliance with small farmers. And like the shearers' union, the ARU also had symbolic advantages, since, for millions of Americans, its industrial opponents epitomized what had gone wrong with their country.[65] Had the railway union survived, Gompers and the AFL would probably have accommodated them pragmatically as they did with the mine workers, and a different attitude toward politics may have emerged from the industrial upheavals of the early 1890s.

But the ARU did not survive. Whereas in Australia, key "new" unions, like the shearers, helped draw the union movement as a whole towards independent party politics, in the United States, their counterparts, like the railway union, were totally destroyed by greater repression, and hence were unable to have a similar effect.

THE EFFECT IN ILLINOIS COMPARED

The case of Illinois provides further support for my argument about the effect of repression on the decision to found a labor party, while raising new questions about its effect on the electoral success and subsequent viability of such a party. In 1894, the Illinois State Federation of Labor decided to run an independent labor-populist ticket under the auspices of the People's party. Unlike the AFL's national decision in December, this decision was taken in July, *before* the railway union had collapsed. Like NSW, Illinois had well-established urban craft unions, and a triumvirate of core industries with interlocking interests, whose workers belonged to unions that had all recently suffered state repression. In NSW, these were shipping, coal, and wool. In Illinois, they were rail, coal, and steel.[66] The decision to build a labor-populist party confirms the importance of both the "crude" point about the "balance of power" within the union movement, and the more "subtle" point about the extent to which major disputes became the "property" of the union movement as a whole.

Police persecution in Chicago and industrial defeats elsewhere had revived interest in independent labor politics in the early 1890s, and in November 1893, the Illinois State Federation of Labor decided to call a conference of all labor and farming organizations in order to launch a labor-populist party. The conference took place in July 1894, just after the defeat of the coal miners, and in the middle of the Pullman strike. Indeed, a sweeping injunction was issued against the ARU, and federal troops were sent to Chicago, just when the conference was meeting. Both the miners and the railway workers played a prominent role in the conference. A subsequent meeting, where representation was based on the membership of each organization, gives some idea of the importance of the ARU. At this meeting, called to organize the labor-populist ticket in Chicago itself, 22 percent of all delegates, and 35 percent of union delegates, were from the ARU (Bogart and Mathews, 1920, 164). In addition, as in Sydney during the Maritime strike, the intense and widespread personal experience of the dispute, and outrage at the one-sided involvement of armed forces and the courts, produced a strong sense of class solidarity between the railway workers and many craft unionists. The fact that the Chicago Trades and Labor Assembly (which was the backbone of the State Federation of Labor) was prepared to call a general strike, shows the extent to which union leaders identified with the dispute and saw it as their own.[67]

Thus, unions in Illinois decided to build a labor-populist party. They committed themselves to independent labor politics, agreed on a platform, nominated candidates, and ran them in alliance with populist farmers—just as their counterparts in NSW had done. But the party did not prosper electorally, and the unions proved unable to sustain its organization. Repression helped produce this outcome as well. It did so in two ways. By delegitimizing the union movement, it undermined the party's immediate electoral prospects. And by weakening the movement's organizational infrastructure, it undermined both the immediate electoral prospects and the subsequent ability to sustain a party organization.

When industrial conflict breaks out, the parties to the dispute simultaneously become involved in a battle of interpretation, the object of which is to define the meaning of the conflict. Governments (as representatives of the "public will" and the "public interest") and police, troops, and courts (as the upholders of "law" and "order") are well placed to arbitrate between the competing interpretations offered by unions and employers. Indeed, when they engage in repression, this is one of the things they inevitably do, for state repression tends to *delegitimize* unions.[68]

For some citizen-onlookers, the very act of using police, troops, and courts against a group will trigger a presumption of illegitimacy. However, to secure the acquiescence of others, the government will have to explain its actions. To do so, it will have to enter explicitly into the battle of interpretation, and offer its own characterization of the conflict and the parties to it. Once it embarks on repression, the government will need to delegitimize union action in order to justify its own action. The stronger the repression, the more it will have to delegitimize union action, since if union action is *not* thought to be illegitimate, then the government itself is open to attack for acting illegitimately. If the government authorizes very severe repression—the kind of repression that might destroy the union—it will need to delegitimize, not only particular union actions, but union organization itself.

Delegitimization of any sort will damage union-sponsored electoral initiatives. Although repression may politicize its targets, and strengthen solidarity within the union movement itself, it will simultaneously isolate unionists from potential middle-class allies. These potential allies, as well as uncommitted workers outside the union movement, will hesitate to vote for a labor party if it is underpinned by organizations they perceive to be at least partly illegitimate. The greater the repression, the greater the delegitimization. And the greater the delegitimization, the smaller the vote from potential allies.

Comparison of the public statements of governments during the Pullman and Maritime strikes suggests that more severe repression was indeed accompanied by the kind of delegitimization that was likely to have this damaging electoral effect. Attorney-General Olney was the key politician masterminding the federal government's involvement in the Pullman strike. On the day federal troops were sent to Chicago, he explained their deployment to reporters (Lindsey, 1942, 245, Ginger, 1949, 137, and Cooper, 1980, 146–7). "We have been brought," he said, "to the ragged edge of anarchy, and it is time to see whether the law is sufficiently strong to prevent this. . . ." In fact, there had as yet been very little disorder.[69] Olney's personal interests had been closely tied to the railroad companies: he had been a railroad lawyer, a railroad director, and a member of the General Managers' Association that was now organizing the employers' side of the strike (Foner, 1955, 266). But his real motivations could not be used to explain the deployment of federal troops. To do that, he had to invent a sufficiently serious threat.

NSW Treasurer McMillan sought to play a similar role. He, too, was close to the employers, as a prominent member and former Chairman of the Chamber of Commerce. While NSW Premier Parkes was recovering from a broken leg, McMillan received a deputation from the Chamber of Commerce immediately after the events at Circular Quay, which were described earlier. Speaking "for the whole Government," he charged that an attempt had been made to set up "a temporary semi-revolutionary Government. . . . This state of affairs cannot remain without absolute anarchy and disorder ensuing." The ground was being prepared for more severe repression.

However, while President Cleveland fully endorsed Olney's approach (Lindsey, 1942, 149), Premier Parkes publicly repudiated McMillan's, and sought his resignation. Although, in the end, McMillan did not resign, and Parkes accepted at one point that "the state of things is little short of a revolution," the Premier's statements made it clear that the government viewed the striking unions as legitimate institutions. Replying to a question in parliament, Parkes said that, "While we will take such measures . . . as will be equal to any emergency, we will not . . . be party to shooting down men or even attempting to shoot them down . . . by far the greater number of real unionists have behaved all through this disturbance with admirable calmness and forbearance . . . [those] representing large owners of property are entitled to all consideration; but in this matter, and from my point of view . . . they are not entitled to more consideration than those persons who own no property." A couple of days later he added that while he had never been a trade unionist, "he would not have considered himself disgraced by being [one]" (Nairn, 1967, 94–96).

These different interpretations were reinforced by the public statements of those who had overall command of the armed forces in Chicago and Sydney. In Chicago, General Miles not only frequently repeated the interpretation of the government, but actually came to believe it. Indeed, this briefly became a problem for the government when, citing the continuing threat from foreign anarchists and foreign revolutionaries, he resisted orders to withdraw troops from Chicago, even though the strike had collapsed (Cooper, 1980, 150–54). Shortly afterwards, he summarized his view of the Pullman strike. It was, he said, "red hot anarchy, insurrectionary, and revolutionary."[70] In Sydney, by contrast, Inspector-General Fosbery (1890) emphasized that "the disorderly element was a very small minority," and that it was not the unions, but elements of the "ill-conducted classes," that were largely responsible for unrest. "In justice to the Unions on strike," he said in his final report, "I must reiterate . . . that a large majority of their number were extremely well behaved and temperate."[71]

The effect of these differences should not be exaggerated. In both countries, unions suffered from what the NSW TLC (1891, 11) described as "the poisoning of the public mind."[72] In Australia, the middle class had recently joined with unionists to donate huge sums to a strike fund for dockers in far off London (Donovan, 1972, 23). But initial sympathy for the unions involved in the Maritime strike quickly dissipated and was replaced by a pro-employer stance as soon as the conflict was redefined in terms of law and order by the intervention of police and troops (Rickard, 1976, 22–4 and 31). In the United States, however, repression generated a more serious problem. Unionists became ensnared in an endless stream of accusations that redefined the meaning of their action in a way that undermined the legitimacy of labor organization itself. The word that summarized this whole effort at redefinition was "anarchy." The word conjured up fears of the most violent and irrational imaginable challenge to the entire established social order. It simultaneously defined a threat to both the democratic and legal institutions of the state (hence the constant charge of "revolution"), and the American cultural identity of the nation (hence the constant talk of "foreigners").[73] Anarchy, said the government, is what the ARU and its leaders threatened.

It was not just during the Pullman strike that unions were redefined in this way. Chicago had been the center of the prototypical anarchist scare in the wake of the Haymarket bomb in 1886. The following year, Democrats and Republicans ran a joint ticket against the union-based United Labor party. They denounced the party as carrying "the virus of anarchism" (Scharnau, 1973, 54) and called on voters to choose between "the red flag and the American flag" (Bogart and Thompson, 1920, 468). Similar efforts were made to redefine unions in most of the major industrial conflicts of the early 1890s. For example, the military general in command of the Pennsylvania National Guard characterized the Homestead strike as a case of "revolution, treason, and anarchy." And the Chief Justice of the Pennsylvania Supreme Court told a Grand Jury that there were a large number of "foreigners" at Homestead who needed to be taught a lesson. "We have reached a point," he concluded, "where there are but two roads left for us to pursue; the one leads to order and good government, the other leads to anarchy" (Foner, 1955, 212 and 215).[74]

Anarchism, anarchism, and more anarchism. Never has such a stable society been so repeatedly warned that it faces complete social collapse. A year after the Pullman strike, a thoughtful lieutenant unintentionally explained why severe military repression was so frequently accompanied by accusations of anarchism and of the total illegitimacy that entailed. There was, he wrote, only one justification for army intervention in relations between capital and labor: the army's "status towards labor depends entirely upon labor's status towards anarchy. The army is opposed to the anarchist; and if labor makes him an ally, not only does the army maintain the imputation of siding with capital, but the laborer must find arranged against him all notion of right, justice, and reason" (Cooper, 1980, 253). So, if the army is to intervene, "anarchy" must be found. And where "anarchy" is found, its "allies" are devoid of all "right, justice, and reason."

The different levels of repression unions suffered left different understandings about their legitimacy in its wake. While the Australian middle class largely saw the "new" unionism as the radical, and increasingly class-conscious, wing of a well-established liberalism, the middle class in the United States tended to see "new" unions like the ARU as harbingers of the most dangerous known threat to the whole established social order.[75] Economic conflicts were redefined as meta-cultural and meta-political ones, and the labor movement was delegitimized to such an extent, that even the quintessentially legitimate act of seeking electoral support, seemed somehow subversive.

Let me turn now to the organizational infrastructure of the union movement. We have already seen how the loss of this infrastructure, brought about by the repression-induced destruction of some of the key "new" inclusive unions, could affect the decision to found a party. But this loss could also affect the prospects of such a party once it *had* been founded. This became clear even before the first elections following the Maritime and Pullman strikes. It was especially clear outside the capital cities, where campaigning depended most heavily on these same key "new" unions: the shearers and the miners in NSW, and the railway workers and the coal miners in Illinois.[76] While the shearers and the mining unions ran strong successful campaigns outside Sydney, the ARU and the coal miners were already collapsing, and were unable to provide a similar level of support outside Chicago (Hagan and Turner, 1991, 42–53, and Destler, 1946, 206–7).

This foreshadowed an even more serious problem after the election, as the wave of popular indignation at state repression began to subside, and the informal networks of activists forged during the campaign began to break up. The extent to which recently founded labor-populist parties depended on the "new" unions for "organizational ballast" then became particularly clear. Independent parties were only sustained where these unions survived with their organizational capacities intact.

The shearers' union had been an important component of the NSW Labor party from the outset. But its proven ability to deliver rural seats, the need for a solution to factional turmoil (especially following the failure of Labor party MPs to vote as a block to bring down the government over its handling of the Broken Hill Miners' strike), and the weakened position of the urban unions as the depression reached its peak in 1893, all made the party increasingly dependent on the shearers' union. In 1895, and for the rest of the decade, the preeminent position of the shearers', now renamed the Australian Workers Union, was implicitly recognized in the new organizational structure adopted by the party (Markey, 1988, 182–89, and Merritt, 1986, 271–76).[77]

The shearers' union was able to play this pre-eminent role, because, in spite of its industrial defeats, it retained sufficient members to maintain a strong bureaucratic infrastructure.[78] The union employed a large full-time professional leadership, paid traveling organizers to tour the country, and published a widely circulated weekly paper, the *Worker*, which became the house journal of the Labor party and its supporters. In addition, it was the single largest source of funding for the party. Given that many party branches scarcely existed once elections were over, this organizational back-up was crucial. Especially in rural areas, the shearers' union virtually *was* the Labor Party. Neither electoral registration nor voting was compulsory until the 1920s (Loveday, 1975, 44, Hagan and Turner, 1991, 43). So a continual effort to keep supporters registered and informed, as well as the election-day effort to bring them out to vote, could make the difference between success and failure at the polls.

Neither the ARU nor the coal miners' union was able to play a similar role in Illinois after the 1894 election was over. The ARU was finished. Its funds were exhausted, its membership dispersed, its offices closed, and its leaders preoccupied with legal proceedings. When he was not in jail or in court, Debs himself toured the country for speakers' fees in order to pay off debts (Ginger, 1949, 172, and Salvatore, 1982, 137–39). The *Railway Times* continued to be published monthly until 1897, but it became little more than a "vehicle for a cult of personality centered on Debs" (Salvatore, 1982, 142). The United Mine Workers' Union was not completely destroyed, but it was in no position to provide organizational resources for a political party. In Illinois, only 500 dues-paying members remained (Phelan, 1994, 20). Nationally, it was so weakened by its defeat in the 1894 strike that it had to suspend publication of its journal, and was unable to pay its affiliation fees to the AFL, or even to cover the cost of its own executive meetings. Indeed, it had to take a $1,000 loan *from* the AFL just to survive (Destler, 1946, 207, Foner, 1955, 245, and Laslett, 1970, 198).

Without the organizational ballast that unions like these could provide, a labor-populist party in Illinois had no hope of surviving setbacks and disappointments in the wake of the 1894 elections. Even if there had been greater initial electoral success, such a party would have been unlikely to sustain itself without this organizational ballast. Despite their initial success in 1886, none of the United Labor parties in Illinois or elsewhere survived the collapse of the Knights of Labor the following year (Montgomery, 1993, 154–55, and Oestreicher, 1986, xviii, 244 and 253).

COMPLEXITIES AND QUALIFICATIONS

The effect of repression on union survival was sometimes mediated by other factors.[79] *Geographical isolation* enabled some unions to survive severe repression. The timing and impact of *depression* could compound the effects of repression. And the *newness* of union organizations could make it easier for repression to destroy them.

In addition, *employer repression* contributed to the difficulties facing unions.[80] Indeed, some writers have suggested that it was employer repression, rather than state repression, that played the more important role in destroying unions in the United States.[81] Employer organization and intransigence certainly had important effects on unions in both the United States and Australia. But it is difficult to attribute the different outcomes following the strike waves of the early 1890s to these factors, since the behavior of employers was itself a function of the political opportunities available to them. Most employers in both countries preferred to be rid of unions, and when opportunities presented themselves, they made use of them. The greater severity, and more systematic use, of military, police, and judicial repression ensured that these opportunities were more readily available in the United States than Australia. As a member of the Sheet Metal Workers' union wrote: "It is the knowledge that they have the militia to fall back upon that induces employers to hold out against just demands" (Reinders, 1977, 99).

Intertemporal comparison of the United States provides striking confirmation of this. When employer repression finally did decline, it was closely related to a decline in state repression. The strike wave that occurred in the early years of the New Deal was accompanied by the full panoply of military and police repression. Some 18,000 strikers were arrested between 1934 and 1936, and between 1933 and 1936, over 100 were killed (Goldstein, 1978, 218). However, 1937 marked a critical turning point. In that year, following the Flint sit-in strike, first General Motors, and then U.S. Steel and Chrysler, suddenly reversed longstanding policies and agreed to recognize unions and concede improved conditions (Rayback, 1966, 351–54, and Goldstein, 1978, 228–31).

What had happened? The resources available to companies and employers' associations had not diminished: the companies involved were among the biggest in the country. And employer hostility towards unionism was as strong as ever: these same companies included some of the most bitter opponents of unionism. What had happened was that the governor of Michigan had refused to send in the National Guard to remove the sit-in strikers at Flint. Of course, this occurred in a larger context, but it was a context defined by political developments. With Roosevelt reelected, the LaFollette Committee exposing private armies, widespread support in Congress for pro-labor legislation, federal and state politicians urging conciliation, and judicial retreat from the government of industrial relations—in this context—large, militant employers moved to recognize the new inclusive CIO unions.

Note, however, that even when employer repression *is* an important independent cause of the defeat and destruction of unions, these unions still have a strong incentive to engage in effective political action. If employers are deeply hostile to unionism, and have the resources to act on their hostility, pure-and-simple unionism will not be a sensible strategy for the union movement. Pure-and-simple unionism can only begin if employers recognize unions and engage in collective bargaining. But this is precisely what capitalist extremists seek to resist. Faced with such intransigence, unions have a strong incentive to supplement their own inadequate organizational strength with political influence in order to force concessions from their mighty corporate adversaries.

CONCLUSION

The soft repression thesis and the hard repression thesis are in conflict about both the extent of repression and its effect on labor politics.

In both the United States and Australia, repression increased in the late nineteenth century. And in each of the major strikes of the early 1890s, governments intervened with armed forces to help defeat unions and protect employers' interests. But the repression of unions was greater in the United States than in Australia. It was greater both in terms of the number and type of soldiers and police deployed, and in terms of what they did once they had been deployed. This is true for each of the major strikes of the early 1890s, and it is true for the late nineteenth and early twentieth century as a whole. In particular, it is true for the critical Maritime and Pullman strikes that occurred immediately before unions in each country decided whether or not to establish a labor party. And it is true whether we focus on the nation as a whole, the cities at the center of these strikes, or the worst local incidents.

Part of the reason for the greater level of repression in the United States lies in the nature of its military and police forces. While troops in Australia faced outwards towards imaginary foreign threats, troops in the United States faced inwards towards imaginary domestic threats. American state militias had been explicitly reorganized for the purpose of dealing with labor unrest, and both state militias and the federal army developed close ties with major employers. Moreover, unlike their Australian counterparts, employers in the United States were permitted to select, arm, and control various kinds of private police forces.

The most important effect of increased repression in Australia was that it convinced most unionists of the need for direct representation in parliament. Proposals to establish a labor party had been discussed before the strike wave of the early 1890s, but many unions had long been hostile to political involvement, and the proposals did not receive much support. However, the role of the government and the widespread experience of solidarity during the Maritime strike changed the attitude of many unionists. With the backing of the 1891 Intercolonial Trades and Labor Union Congress, labor parties were established, first in NSW, and then elsewhere.

Similar initiatives in the United States were undermined by the greater level of repression. This repression helps explain both why the American Federation of Labor decided not to establish a labor party, and why, when the Illinois State Federation of Labor did decide to build a party, it was unable to prosper electorally and sustain itself.

In the United States, repression had a differential effect on both the disposition of unions to act politically, and their organizational capacity to do so. As in Australia, those unions that had been most severely affected by repression were most strongly in favor of independent political action. But unlike in Australia, these unions faced repression of such severity that they were often unable to survive. High personal costs, the collapse of organizational infrastructure, and a sense of hopelessness combined to destroy the "new" inclusive unions that were typically subject to the worst repression. As a result, the influence of these unions in the central councils of the labor movement was weakened, and at the 1894 conference of the AFL, the balance of power between supporters and opponents of independent political action favored the later.

In Illinois, the decision to build a labor-populist party was taken before the collapse of the ARU. There, the effect of repression was felt in a different way. The government, the armed forces, and the courts could only justify very high levels of repression if they could delegitimize the union movement by redefining it as a wholesale threat to the established political and cultural order. This undermined the new party's electoral prospects by isolating the union movement from potential middle-class and working-class allies. In addition, the repression-induced destruction of the organizational infrastructure of the "new" inclusive unions deprived the party of both the resources it needed for an election campaign and the organizational ballast it needed in order to survive thereafter.

The effect that state repression had on the survival of unions was mediated by a number of other factors. In particular, major employers in the United States were unusually hostile to organized labor. But greater employer repression was at least partly a product of the political opportunities that resulted from greater state repression. Moreover, to the extent that employer repression did have an independent effect, it too gave unions an incentive to engage in effective political action.

Neither the soft repression nor the hard repression thesis is satisfactory. Comparison with Australia suggests that while the hard repression thesis is right about the extent of repression in the United States, the soft repression thesis is at least partly right about its effects. But the effects of repression were more complex and ambiguous than the soft repression thesis acknowledges. Repression both helped and hindered the formation of a labor party. It helped by politicizing the unionists who were most severely subject to repression, but it simultaneously hindered by weakening the influence of these unionists through the destruction of their organizational base.

In both the United States and Australia, it was the "new" inclusive unions that typically suffered the most severe repression and became the most politicized in the early 1890s. But whereas in Australia, key new unions like the shearers survived and helped found and sustain an independent labor party, in the United States, their counterparts like the ARU were totally destroyed by the greater level of repression, and hence were unable to exercise a similar influence.

CHAPTER 6

Liberalism

IN THIS CHAPTER, I want to explore the idea that the prevalence of liberal values in American political culture helps explain why there is no labor party in the United States. I will refer to this idea as the "liberalism thesis." As its most influential proponent acknowledges, the liberalism thesis is based on "the storybook truth about American history" (Hartz, 1955, 3), and despite numerous criticisms, it retains a powerful hold on both the popular and the scholarly imagination.

Two interrelated claims provide the starting point for proponents of the liberalism thesis. The first is the claim that feudalism, and the values it left in its wake, had little or no influence in the United States. The second is that liberal values were able to monopolize ideological space. Unlike in Europe, liberal values did not have to compete with the continuing cultural legacy of declining feudalism, and hence they were able to become the ubiquitous and largely unchallenged evaluative criteria for the whole society. According to the proponents of the liberalism thesis, this constrained (or perhaps even precluded) the emergence of a labor party.[1]

The liberalism thesis has been subjected to a number of fundamental criticisms. One of the most important of these rejects the claim that liberalism has been hegemonic, and instead sees it as one among a number of ideological traditions that have constituted American political culture.[2] I am sympathetic to this argument, and will return to it—or at least one aspect of it—in the next chapter. Here, however, I want to set this objection to one side. Whether or not it was hegemonic, liberalism certainly has been an important component of American political culture, and there can be little doubt that in the late nineteenth century, when compared with Europe, the United States was less marked by feudalism and more heavily influenced by liberal values. In this chapter, I want to consider what effect these values had on the American union movement and its decisions.

Comparison with Australia will help facilitate this. Building on the classic work of Tocqueville (1990), all the main proponents of the liberalism thesis take over the New World–Old World comparison that lies at the heart of his work, and place it at the center of their own analysis. But New World Australia shared many core liberal values with the United States, and like the United States, it was less marked by feudalism and more strongly influenced by these values than Old World Europe. Indeed, many contemporary observers and subsequent historians have argued that liberalism was a dominant, even a hegemonic, political ideology in late nineteenth-century Australia. Advocates of the liberalism thesis are fond of quoting H. G. Wells's claim that "all Americans are, from the English point of view, Liberals of one sort or another" (Lipset, 1996, 32). However, numerous commentators have made the very same claim about Australia.[3] Proponents of the liberalism thesis sometimes acknowledge this in passing, and one or two seek to address it at greater length (Hartz, 1964, 4, 9, 11, 40–44, 70–71, 75, and 106–8, and Lipset, 1963, 199–202, and 248–73). But comparison with Australia poses a more fundamental challenge to the liberalism thesis than these authors are prepared to acknowledge.

Simply by establishing the fact that a labor party could be successfully founded in a country with a political culture strongly influenced by liberal values, the Australian case poses problems for the liberalism thesis. But the Australian case does more than that. For it suggests that, to the extent that liberal values were present, they were not a constraint at all, but were instead an opportunity for those seeking to found a labor party.

Systematic comparison of the effect of liberal values must overcome a number of difficulties. The liberal tradition that is said to prevail in the United States is composed of a cluster of different values, and systematic analysis of more than a few of these would quickly become unmanageable. This problem is compounded by the fact that different authors have identified different clusters of values, which, in addition, do not all operate at the same level of abstraction or generality. Even within some of the proposed clusters, some values are more foundational, while others are more derivative.[4]

In order to deal with these problems, I propose to focus on two values that most historians agree were widely held in late nineteenth-century America. These values are social egalitarianism and individual freedom. Here, I will consider each of these values separately.

In each case, I will first consider how labor leaders and opinion-formers responded to the prevalence of the value in question, and whether they treated it as a constraint or an opportunity. The findings I will set out are based on extensive reading of the pro-labor press, the transcripts, minutes, and resolutions of labor meetings, and the speeches and writings of labor leaders in the late 1880s and early to mid-1890s. I have paid particularly close attention to the arguments that were made in the year or so leading up to the decision about whether or not to establish a labor party. In the case of the United States, I will draw on the opinions of a wide range of labor leaders. But I will often focus special attention on the arguments of Samuel Gompers, John McBride and Eugene Debs in order to illustrate this range of opinions in what I hope will be an accessible way. Gompers and McBride were key AFL leaders who respectively opposed and supported independent political action. Debs was the most prominent unionist at the center of the industrial storm that was creating much of the immediate pressure for political action, and he was a clear and articulate spokesperson for the need to undertake such an initiative.

In each case, I will then consider whether the arguments of labor leaders were likely to seem plausible to ordinary workers (and other potential supporters). In order to mobilize potential supporters, all social movement organizations—their leaders, activists, and newspapers—seek to interpret or "frame" contemporary developments in particular ways. These organizations will only be able to succeed in their mobilizing efforts if they can link or "align" their interpretations with those of their potential supporters, and to do this, they must be able to present their goals in a manner that is compatible with the values and beliefs of their target constituency. Viewed in these terms, the liberalism thesis could be translated into the claim that the prevalence of liberal values made this kind of "frame alignment" difficult or impossible.[5] In principle, this raises two questions: (1) whether the interpretation of a given value offered by labor leaders is plausible, and (2) whether the empirical statements that underpin their claim that it is necessary to act in support of this value are plausible.[6] In the absence of direct evidence of the opinion of ordinary workers in the late nineteenth century, I will have to rely on inferences from the evidence that is available in order to answer these questions. I will examine the relative strength of different interpretations of liberal values among influential opinion-formers like middle-class intellectuals and established politicians in order to suggest an answer to the first question. I will examine what we know about the social developments through which contemporaries lived (and about which they were likely to be aware) in order to suggest an answer to the second. Taking these questions as my starting point, I will seek to establish whether there were features of Australian society that made it likely that ordinary workers would find labor leaders more convincing there than they would in the United States.

SOCIAL EGALITARIANISM

Tocqueville (1990, 1:3) begins *Democracy in America* by introducing his major insight. "During my stay in the United States," he writes, "nothing struck me more forcibly than the general equality of condition among the people . . . this equality of condition is the fundamental fact from which all others seem to be derived . . . ." Though some of the proponents of the liberalism thesis feel that Tocqueville is overstating his case, almost all of them agree on the enduring importance of this insight. They agree that, because of the absence of feudal institutions, and relative insignificance of aristocratic influences, American society was in some sense "born equal."

The equality that they have in mind is not an equal distribution of economic resources—though greater equality in that respect was also widely thought to have existed before the Gilded Age. Rather, it is an equality of social status—an equality of standing and manners, and of dignity and respect. Sombart's treatment is representative and has the added advantage of dealing with social mores as they existed not long after the upheaval of the 1890s. Sombart (1976, 105 and 109–10) emphasizes the appearance of workers in the United States, especially their respectable middle-class clothing, their self-assured demeanor, and the confident way they interacted with all strata of society. Unlike in countries with feudal traditions, where "a person only begins to be a person" if he is an aristocrat, an army officer, or a professional, in the United States there was no "bowing and scrapping before the 'upper classes.'" In general, workers treated others, and were treated by them, as social equals.

Of course, this social egalitarianism was open only to men and those who were thought of as white. But the proponents of the liberalism thesis are right to claim that among this group, throughout the nineteenth century, social egalitarianism was far more prevalent in the United States than in Europe, and that, as a result, the "social position" of the typical American wage-worker was better than that of his European counterpart.

Why is this prevalence of social egalitarianism thought to have constrained the establishment of a labor party? The proponents of the liberalism thesis are not always explicit about the causal mechanism that was at work. Nevertheless, their basic argument is clear enough.[7] Two related explanations are put forward. First, it is argued that social egalitarianism mitigated (or even eliminated) the kind of status-based class grievances that might otherwise have given workers a reason to support a labor party. Second, it is argued that, by mitigating these grievances, social egalitarianism weakened class consciousness, and so deprived those seeking to establish a labor party of a ready-made class-based identity around which to mobilize workers.

These are the claims that lie behind Hartz's "no feudalism, no socialism" formula. Stated more formally, his point is that Marx and others were wrong to think that capitalism was a necessary and sufficient condition for the emergence of socialism, since feudalism was also a necessary condition for its emergence. But if, for present purposes, we alter Hartz's formula to "no feudalism, no labor party," then the Australian case provides a clear counter-example.

For social egalitarianism has been repeatedly identified as a key characteristic of Australian society. Throughout the second half of the nineteenth century, it was identified by Australians of all classes, and by travellers from Britain, the United States, and Europe, and it has been identified by historians ever since.[8] All of these observers commented on the absence of deference, the self-confidence, and the "manly independence" of Australian workers.

These characteristics were identified both by those who sympathized with social egalitarianism and by those who bemoaned it. According to R.E.N. Twopeny (1883, 91, 107), a conservative liberal in a Tocquevillean mold, "practically, as well as theoretically, there is no aristocracy in Australia . . . Amongst men, social distinctions are very slight." Twopeny (1883, 56–57) noted that even the daughters of poorer working-class families often rejected domestic service as degrading: "For some inexplicable reason, they turn up their noses at the high wages and comparatively light work offered . . . so great is the love of independence. . . ."[9]

The NSW government itself pointed to similar characteristics—if somewhat apologetically—in an official pamphlet distributed at the Chicago 1893 Columbian World Fair. The pamphlet noted that "non-observance of the restraints on social life" was common to both Australia and America, and concluded that "Australia is America with a chubby face" (Dowling, 1893, 18–19).

The standard comparative authorities of the time also agreed on the significance of social egalitarianism in Australia. "The sentiment of social equality is extremely strong," wrote Bryce (1921, 198) "for there were hardly any distinctions of rank to begin with, and such habits of deference as had belonged to Europe did not attach themselves to those whose only claim was a more rapid rise towards wealth." Dilke (1890, 490) claimed simply that Australia is like Britain "with the upper class left out."

Indeed, according to the 1853 *Emigrant's Guide to Australia*, "the equality system here would stun even a Yankee" (Thompson, 1994, 9). Many nineteenth-century observers, especially those from the United States itself, noticed the common absence of feudal values and institutions, and concluded simply that Australia was "another America" (White, 1981, 47–52, and Bell and Bell, 1993, 17–20 and 28). Commenting on his visit in 1895, Mark Twain (1897, 111) observed that "the Australians did not seem to me to differ noticeably from the Americans, either in dress, carriage, ways, pronunciations, inflections, or general appearances."

Labor Leaders in Australia

What effects did the prevalence of social egalitarianism have on the labor movement in late nineteenth-century Australia? One of the main effects was to establish a widely accepted moral standard against which the legitimacy of social practices could be measured. The social egalitarianism that was prevalent was not just a way of behaving, it was also a value or norm that defined how men *ought* to behave towards one another. When the treatment of workers did not live up to this norm, it provided them with strong prima facie grounds for complaint.

Thus, by clearly establishing the legitimacy of social equality, Australian political culture provided activists and intellectuals associated with the labor movement with a major ideological opportunity. Any sign of an attitude of social superiority was susceptible to stringent attack, and attempts to defend economic privileges and status could easily be interpreted as thinly disguised efforts to establish neo-feudal aristocratic privileges. Both unionists, and radical writers, artists, and poets, used these arguments to great effect. They repeatedly sought to delegitimize opponents of the labor movement by accusing them of having un-Australian pretensions to social superiority. And they linked the economic conflict between workers and employers, and labor's foray into politics, to the need to uphold social egalitarianism and defend it against these pretensions.

These messages were carried to workers in union publications like the *Hummer*, the *Worker*, the *Boomerang*, and the *Australian Workman*. The *Hummer* equated the capitalist and the royalist as the enemy of the worker, and the *Australian Workman* used a report on a trip between "the two democracies of modern times"—Australia and the United States—to highlight the gap between the equality both had supposedly established, and the reality of social class distinctions.[10] However, both within the labor movement and in the wider society, the single most important vehicle for their influence was the Sydney *Bulletin*, which circulated throughout Australia and beyond. Its influence was such that, according to the London *Times*, "it is hard to overestimate the extent to which this journal modifies the opinions (one might almost say the character) of its readers."[11] The full-page cartoons published on the front page of the *Bulletin* provide a good illustration of how social egalitarianism could be used to fix the meaning of some of the key events that gave rise to the labor party.

The cartoon in Figure 6.1 was published in August 1890 at the onset of the Maritime strike. One of the main metaphors of the drawing—the location of the protagonists on a narrow plank over a deep ravine—appeals to an older tradition, which saw cooperation between capital and labor as essential to their mutual well-being, by suggesting that failure to reach a class compromise would be fatal for both.[12] But the central metaphor—the image to which the eye is first and most strongly drawn—is the standoff between the two men. Note the dress of the capitalist with its claim to the superior status of a Victorian "gentleman." Note his haughty demeanor with its demand for deference, and his pointing forefinger expressing his assumption that he should command obedience. And note, too, his stomach and the implication of greed and unnecessary wealth.[13] The worker on the other hand is not impoverished or badly dressed. He has his hands in his pockets, and is making no demands and issuing no instructions to the capitalist. He is merely standing his ground in a don't-mess-with-me sort of way. For the worker, the economic conflict is translated into one about the maintenance of his dignity, his self-respect, and his "manly independence"—in short, his equal social status. All of this he still clearly has. He looks the capitalist square in the eye and stands tall and confident. But if he backs down, this is what he stands to lose.

The implication of this interpretation was that labor's defeat in the Maritime strike had placed the worker's social status in jeopardy. But the same interpretation offered an account of why labor ought to move into politics, for

Figure 6.1. The Labour Crisis
Source: Sydney *Bulletin*, 16 August 1890 (State Library of New South Wales)

shifting the conflict from the industrial to the electoral arena offered the worker an opportunity to redeem the situation. The cartoon in Figure 6.2—the *Bulletin's* comment on the first results of the NSW election of 1891—underlines this message. Not only has success at the polls enabled the worker to regain his dignity and status, but, by winning the balance of power in parliament, he has actually become the master of the situation. Now the leaders of the two main parties, who, for all their differences, had joined to support the employers during the strike, have themselves lost their dignity—their frock coats, bow ties, and pinstriped pants merely underline the child-like nature of the situation in which they find themselves.[14]

Similar cartoons can be found in the labor press. The *Worker*, which became the most important union paper, continued and extended the kind of interpretation offered by the *Bulletin*, in its representation of "Labor in Politics."[15] Here, too, the restoration of the worker's dignity and status is presented as a major purpose, and outcome, of labor's foray into politics, although in this drawing the defense of freedom is also presented as a major concern. Two and a half years after the party's first electoral success, its progress had been marked by difficulties and reversals, but the meaning of labor's political project remained closely connected to the maintenance of social equality.

The Australian case shows how the prevalence of social egalitarianism in a society could provide labor leaders and opinion formers with an ideological opportunity by making any attempt to establish some form of social hierarchy an already indictable offense in the court of public opinion. Of course, in the absence of such an attempt, or any activity that could be plausibly interpreted as such an attempt, social egalitarianism does indeed remove one of the grounds for status-based class grievances. This is the point that the proponents of the liberalism thesis emphasize. But note that the absence of social egalitarianism would also remove the grounds for this kind of grievance. A hierarchical social order does not in itself provide grounds for grievance if that hierarchy is thought to be legitimate.

What is needed then, in order to establish a status-based class grievance, is both the acceptance of social egalitarianism and the appearance of hierarchical behavior. Where the acceptance of social egalitarianism is widespread, even minor instances of hierarchical behavior—behavior that in other countries may appear unimportant or pass unnoticed—can provide grounds for grievance. In such a case, all other things being equal, the more widespread the acceptance of social egalitarianism, the more certain workers will be that they have a legitimate grievance, and the easier it will be for them to find allies elsewhere in the population. What matters, therefore, is not the presence of social egalitarianism per se, but rather the presence of a gap between the promise of this egalitarianism and social relations as they actually exist.

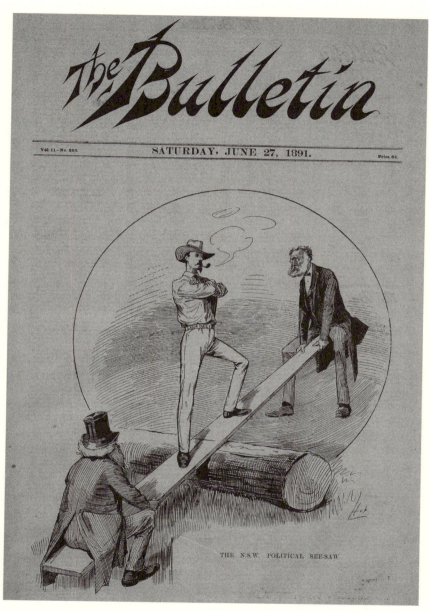

Figure 6.2. The NSW Political See-Saw

Source: Sydney *Bulletin*, 27 June 1891 (State Library of New South Wales)

Labor Leaders in the United States

In the late nineteenth century, American labor leaders argued that such a gap was also emerging in their country. Union leaders and the pro-labor press frequently pointed to the rise of a neo-feudal social order, which they said jeopardized the status of workers as social equals, and threatened them with "degradation." The great industrial upheavals of the early 1890s were often characterized in these terms, and this was especially true during the Pullman strike and its aftermath, when the AFL was in the process of deciding whether to engage in independent labor politics.

This argument was made in a particularly clear and forceful way by Eugene Debs and his colleagues in the American Railway Union. Throughout the Pullman strike, the union's journal, the *Railway Times*, repeatedly emphasized the neo-feudal pretensions of its opponents. George Pullman himself was referred to as "his lordship," "his highness," or "the duke," and the railway corporations and their capitalist allies were described as "plutocrats," "oligarchs," and "aristocrats."[16] In Debs's eyes, the defeat of the Pullman strike freed corporate capitalists to consolidate their drive for a neo-feudal social order and left workers facing humiliation and degradation. "How stands labor itself?" asked Debs in a Labor Day address written from jail, "The answer is humiliating beyond the power of exaggeration" (Debs, 1895a, 5). In its first edition after the union's defeat, the *Railway Times* argued that the strike had commanded such attention because: "It was the first time in the history of our Republic that a president dared to show himself the mere lackey of a rich caste"—a caste that "bade him see to it that the impudent worker was so well humbled that he would cry for mercy." But Debs insisted that all was not lost. For workers could still dispatch these neo-feudal upstarts and regain their dignity and respect by reaching for the power of the ballot. Indeed, he argued that, given their industrial defeat, a move towards independent electoral politics was now essential if traditional American social egalitarianism was to be defended.[17]

In a weekly newspaper column that he wrote from jail, Debs summarized this perspective for the general public. Despite the best efforts of the founding fathers, said Debs, the country had witnessed "the steady increase" of "untitled aristocrats," to such an extent that "a well-founded alarm exists in every section of the land." For, he argued, "the aristocracy of wealth is now as well established in the United States as is the aristocracy of blood in any European country." Like their European counterparts, this American "nobility" sought to "strut and parade before the common people . . . separate and apart from them, above and superior to them, [as if] having a right to direct and control them . . . and 'lord it' over their fellow mortals." To Debs, the outcomes of the Homestead and Pullman disputes were the clearest examples of the growing dominance of this new aristocracy. If the values of the founding fathers were to be defended, it was now an "imperative necessity" for organized labor to make a united stand at the polls.[18]

Debs explicitly noticed that the strength of social egalitarianism made workers more likely to be resentful, and that it was the gap between the prevalence of this value and actual social practices, rather than simply the extent to which social egalitarian values were present, that lead to grievances and class discontent. In another of his weekly columns, he discussed this at length. "In Europe and Asiatic countries, conditions relating to different classes of people excite little concern compared with the United States," wrote Debs. "[There] centuries of despotism have created acquiescence. . . . Here we swept away everything resembling caste. The pomp, and pride, and arrogance of titled nobility and aristocracy we tabooed . . . these lessons have been woven into the fiber of American thought."[19]

Social egalitarian themes were particularly prominent in the ARU, but they were certainly not unique to it. Indeed, they were widely shared by other unions. The Miners' Union had only just experienced a similarly monumental defeat. The union's journal characterized George Pullman as a "hero in all the drawing-rooms of our mushroom aristocracy."[20] And in the wake of the railway workers' defeat, the Miners' President, John McBride, concluded that American laborers had been brought "to the point of serfdom," and that they had to make use of the ballot and mobilize support for a labor populist party in order to retain "respect and independence."[21] Unions who had not recently been involved in massive industrial conflicts, often reached similar conclusions. For example, in a lead article entitled "Against Monarchy," the journal of the Coast Seaman's Union, called on its members to "support the American Railway Union in its fight against commercial kings." The following week it characterized "The Great Issue" at the heart of the strike as the need for "a new declaration of independence . . . independence from the rule of the plutocracy."[22] When the visiting British union leader, John Burns, speaking to a meeting organized by the AFL during its 1894 convention, observed that American capitalists have aristocratic pretensions such that "when they have made their fortune [they] go to England and become the greatest of snobs and toadies," he was greeted by "prolonged cheering" (AFL, 1894, 65).

The fact that the Pullman strike coincided with the annual Fourth of July celebrations served to further highlight the gap between the country's officially professed values and the reality confronting many workers. Appeals to the Declaration of Independence, and especially to its foundational claim that "all men are created equal," were made throughout the year. However, in this context, the labor press was even more than normally disposed to compare "the disgraceful present with the glorious past."[23]

Appeals to social egalitarian themes were not limited to unionists who supported independent labor politics. Similar interpretations were common currency among those who rejected this course of action. In particular, they were explicitly articulated by Samuel Gompers. When Gompers launched issue one of the *American Federationist*, the very first item he included was a poem by a carpenter entitled "Equality," which highlighted America's apparent commitment to social egalitarianism and the grievances that resulted from the failure to live up to its promise. The poem starts with a line from Shakespeare—"The King is but a man as I am." Each stanza then begins with a line like "We are all equal! Can it be true?" or "All men equal! Is it a jest?" In his own writing in the early 1890s, Gompers periodically characterized capitalists as an emerging neo-feudal class. In a paper read before the American Social Science Congress, he argued that "we again face old foes in new uniforms" and compared the capitalist to "his mediaeval prototype, the male baronial lord." These themes can also be found in his leader articles in the *American Federationist* during the coal miners' strike and the Pullman strike, where he referred to the "Striking parallel between the ancient baron on his castled crag and the modern capitalist with his swollen money bag."[24]

Gompers set out his position on these issues particularly clearly in his address to the International Labor Congress at the Chicago World's Fair in 1893. Here he argued that "the separation between the capitalistic class and the laboring mass is not so much a difference of industrial rank as it is a difference of social status. . . . This distinction, scarcely noticeable in the United States before the previous generation, rapidly became more and more marked, increasing day by day, until at length, it has widened into a veritable chasm; economic, social and moral."[25] Gompers must have thought this paper was a good statement of his basic position, for it was one of a handful of papers that the AFL reprinted and circulated widely during 1894.[26]

Gompers did not draw the same conclusions about labor politics as Debs and McBride, but in other respects they shared a similar analysis of the rising neo-feudal threat to social egalitarianism. Indeed, though some gave it more emphasis than others, this analysis was common to most of the schools of reform thought that swirled around the labor movement in the late nineteenth century.[27]

According to the liberalism thesis, the prevalence of social egalitarianism undermined those seeking to mobilize support for class-based political organizations by removing status-differentials that helped underpin class-based grievances and class consciousness in Europe. But leaders and opinion formers in and around the labor movement thought: (1) that recent developments were leading to the emergence of neo-feudal class relationships that threatened social egalitarianism, (2) that these developments were generating class-based grievances and discontent, and (3) that articulating these grievances would help them to mobilize support—both from workers and from potential middle-class sympathizers.[28] In short, in the conditions prevailing in the early 1890s, they saw America's ostensible commitment to social egalitarianism as an opportunity rather than a constraint. Their basic strategy was to identify a subversive neo-feudal threat from capitalist employers, and to position themselves as defenders of the social egalitarian status quo. Labor leaders did not agree on whether the defense of social egalitarianism required the establishment of a labor party. Those like Debs and McBride, whose unions had been thoroughly humiliated in industrial defeats, tended to think it did. Others like Gompers disagreed. But Gompers did not disagree because he felt that the prevalence of social egalitarianism left unions with insufficient class-based grievances on which to draw. How could he when his own union-building project required him to continuously emphasize the importance of these very same grievances?

Were Their Claims Plausible?

We have seen that belief in the value of social egalitarianism was widespread in both Australia and the United States, and that in both countries labor leaders interpreted contemporary developments—especially the strike defeats of the early 1890s—as a threat to this value. But was this interpretation likely to be plausible to ordinary workers and other potential supporters? In particular, were there features of Australian society that made it easier for workers to find this interpretation convincing—easier, that is, than for their counterparts in the United States? Here I want to consider an argument that suggests that there were such features. According to this argument, social relations in Australia may have been far more egalitarian than in Europe, but compared with the United States, they still had some tincture of feudalism. This, according to the argument, was enough to generate the kind of status-based class grievances, and the attendant class consciousness, that could facilitate the political mobilization of the working class.

The most sophisticated treatment of this question has been provided by John Hirst (1988 and 1988a). Hirst argues that many of the leading figures who established self-government in the mid-nineteenth century had an ambivalent or half-hearted attitude towards social egalitarianism.[29] They firmly rejected the idea that position or opportunity should be restricted by privilege or birth, but through their clothing, their forms of address, and in other ways, they were still keen to claim for themselves the superior social status of a Victorian "gentleman."[30] Gentlemen distinguished themselves by wearing top hats, frockcoats, and kid gloves, and they were referred to in correspondence as "John Smith Esq.," not as "Mr John Smith." Hirst claims that these forms of status distinction continued to be practiced into the late nineteenth century, and gave Australian social egalitarianism an uncompleted quality. He suggests that this, in turn, made workers more receptive to the arguments of labor leaders and gave the nascent labor party an important advantage over any American counterpart by enabling it to pose as the only party to be unambiguously committed to full social equality (Hirst, 1988, 70–71).

The *Bulletin* certainly devoted a great deal of space in the late 1880s and early 1890s to satirizing aristocratic and gentlemanly pretensions. It was endlessly pillorying pompous or deferential behavior, especially when it took the form of toadying before royal visitors or vice-regal hosts, and it saw clothing as a key marker of these attitudes. The *Bulletin's* critique of capitalist pretensions during the Maritime strike was thus part of a larger concern with neo-feudal behavior, which was already one of its defining themes. During this period, the journal was consistently hostile to snobbery in general and monarchy in particular, and it adopted a nativist and nationalist tone towards the English. It feared that, if Australia maintained its connection with monarchical Britain, an attempt might be made to saddle it with the "political and social absurdities" of the Old World,[31] and its support for the labor movement was distinctly secondary to its concern with these issues. Indeed, the *Bulletin* insisted that Labor's inaugural electoral success in 1891 should be interpreted as a vote for republicanism.[32] In this, the wish was father to the thought, for the Labor Electoral Leagues had not raised the question, and monarchy was scarcely an issue in the campaign.

However, threats to social egalitarian norms were not just the product of a journalistic imagination, for Australian employers did often behave in ways that must have confirmed workers' fears about their neo-aristocratic pretensions. Indeed, as we have seen in the previous chapter, on at least one occasion during the Maritime strike this was their specific intent. In that episode, leading employers dressed themselves in top hats and tails and rode through the center of the city atop large bails of wool that they moved from the wharves to the wool stores in defiance of the strike. By strike-breaking while flaunting the claim to superior status that was implicit in their dress, they hoped to provoke a level of disorder that would force the government to act more decisively against the unions.

One way to respond to an argument like Hirst's would be to point out that day-to-day experiences in large industrial workplaces, highly conflictual industrial disputes, and high levels of state repression, could have generated class grievances and class consciousness in the United States, even in the absence of any residual culture of status-based class distinctions. However, there is no need to reach for this response. For while there was indeed a strand of ambivalence towards social egalitarianism in Australia, a similar strand of ambivalence was also present in the United States.

The first point to note is that support for class distinctions and a hierarchically based social order had long been an element of American political culture (Ellis, 1993, 95–110). These sympathies, as Hartz (1955, 7–8 and 102–3) himself recognized, were not limited to the plantation societies of the south, but were also found in the Puritan colonies of the north from the outset. In a lay sermon en route to New England, John Winthrop reminded the emigrants that social distinctions were ordained by God, and that in the New World they must be observed even more strictly to decrease the possibility of failure.[33] They were still present at the "second founding" of American society during and after the Revolution. John Adams collaborated closely with Jefferson on the Declaration of Independence, but by the 1780s he had joined Alexander Hamilton and other Federalists in advocating the establishment of aristocratic titles and a hereditary upper house (Greenstone, 1993, 75, 91–93). In a somewhat similar fashion, W. C. Wentworth, who had played a leading role in bringing self-government to New South Wales, sought to establish a hereditary upper house during constitutional debates in the early 1850s. Of course, neither of these proposals met with any success. Wentworth's opponents ridiculed him for attempting to create a "bunyip aristocracy," and the proposal was effectively laughed out of court.[34]

The second point to note is that sympathy for class distinctions and social hierarchy was still present in the late nineteenth century and could be explicitly articulated by influential people. Henry Ward Beecher, who was one of the most influential clergymen of the day, told his congregation that "God has intended the great to be great and the little to be little" (Marty, 1970, 150). A number of other clergymen agreed. For some, inequality was predestined by God. For others, it was "an original, ultimate, unalterable fact" (Marty, 1970, 149–50). In addition, many clergymen endorsed the idea of a "stewardship" of "rank, wealth, learning, or cleverness" (Hopkins, 1940, 90). Elements of these attitudes could also be found among elite reformers (Ellis, 1993, 110–13). More generally, the language of class was regularly used by the wealthy. Alongside the capitalist and working classes, there were "better classes," "respectable classes," "dangerous classes," and "communistic classes" (Beckert, 2001, 2, 217, 232, 237, and 257). Indeed the language of class was ubiquitous. It was used in newspapers, in literature, and in popular culture. And it was used by leading politicians, by legislative inquiries, and by social scientists. According to one social scientist—no friend of the labor movement—"It is commonly asserted that there are in the United States no classes, and any allusion to classes is resented. [But] we constantly read and hear discussions of social topics in which the existence of social classes is assumed as a simple fact" (Sumner, 1883, 13).

Explicit rejection of social egalitarian norms was a minority current in late nineteenth-century America, and labor leaders had little need to worry about whether workers would accept this aspect of their interpretation of egalitarianism. However, in discussing the Australian case, Hirst is less concerned with the explicit rejection of a particular interpretation of social egalitarianism than with the persistence of certain modes of inegalitarian behavior—behavior such as the continued use of frock coats and top hats by the political elite. But these same items of clothing were also prevalent among politicians in the United States. Just as in Australia, the frock coat and top hat were *de rigeur* in the 1850s and 1860s, and remained commonplace for politicians in the 1870s and 1880s, before losing popularity in the 1890s.[35] So, in this respect, too, there is little to distinguish the United States from Australia.

The third and most important point to note is that in the 1880s and 1890s, many of the wealthiest and most prominent merchants, industrialists, and bankers established a distinct class identity and began to consciously emulate an aristocratic life-style. The cultural center of this class was New York, and more and more of its members moved there to hold court, but similar developments could be found in other major cities.[36] They built palatial mansions, attended exclusive social clubs, schools, and universities, developed a taste for hunting and horse racing, and formed societies that attested to their genealogical legitimacy.[37] Many spent their summers in Europe, collected "Old Masters," and, if possible, married their daughters into one of the old noble families of Europe.[38] A *Social Register* was established to identify the members of this class, and each year during "The Season," they held lavish entertainments for each other.[39]

The centerpieces of these entertainments were extravagant balls that provide a striking illustration of the extent of the neo-feudal pretensions of late nineteenth-century American capitalists. A notable example took place in 1883 when one branch of the Vanderbilt family celebrated the completion of their French-style chateau on Fifth Avenue by holding a fancy dress ball to which many of the 750 guests came in the outfits of Renaissance princes and French or English royalty. This new trend-setting home was modeled on the Chateau de Blois, which had been built for a sixteenth-century king of France, and its Louis XV salon was fitted with interiors that had been removed wholesale from a real chateau in France and shipped to New York. But extravagant balls were a regular occurrence. Three times a year, a group of self-appointed "Patriarchs" held a ball that consciously sought to create the kind of exclusive inner circle that, in Europe, was defined by a royal court. Ward McAllister, the man who presided over these arrangements, publicly announced that "Society" was composed of just four hundred individuals. In 1892, he proceeded to name them.[40] The most elaborate ball of the 1890s was organized in 1897 by Mrs. Bradley Martin. For this event, the Waldorf Hotel was decorated to look like Versailles, and the seven hundred or so guests came dressed in court costume from the era of Louis XV. They came as "Kings and Queens, nobles, knights, and courtiers."[41] Bradley Martin came as Louis himself, and his wife sat next to him on a throne, bedecked in the actual jewels of Marie Antoinette. Such was the love of aristocratic symbolism among the super-rich that even at the 1889 Centennial Ball to mark the inauguration of the first President of the United States, many chose to attend in court costumes from the period of Louis XV and XVI.[42]

There can be no doubt that ordinary working people knew about this behavior. Newspapers reported in detail on each of the three annual Patriarchs' Balls, with lists of who attended, what they wore, what they ate, and the floral

Figure 6.3. The Bradley Martin Ball
Source: Harper's Weekly, 20 February 1897 (Princeton University Library)

arrangements and décor of the ballroom. The onset of depression had no effect, and the balls carried on just as before, with each declared to be the most successful and spectacular yet.[43] On the day before the AFL met for its convention in 1894, the *New York Times* announced the opening of that year's social season. "Everything Points to a Season of Quite Unusual Gayety" its headline declared.[44]

Look at the illustration of the Bradley Martin Ball in Figure 6.3, and then recall the claim of Eugene Debs that an "aristocracy of wealth" had emerged that wanted to "strut and parade before the common people . . . separate and apart from them, above and superior to them." Unable to be ennobled in the European fashion, he said, "they take advantage of wealth or position to play the role . . . just the same as if they had been decorated with titles and were under the law permitted to 'lord it' over their fellow mortals."[45] It is not hard to see that many of his readers must have found this claim all too plausible.

One of the reasons why the cartoons in the *Bulletin* and the *Worker* were effective was that, in the 1880s and 1890s, there really were capitalists in Australia strutting around like English "gentry." In the United States at that time, their counterparts began strutting around like aristocrats in absolutist France.

INDIVIDUAL FREEDOM

Why is the prevalence of the idea of individual freedom thought to constrain the emergence of a labor party? Two kinds of mechanisms are suggested by the proponents of the liberalism thesis.

The first sees liberty as an evaluative idea. On this account, the widespread belief in the value of individual freedom served to delegitimize attempts to establish a labor party, because many of the political goals of the labor movement called for greater state intervention in the labor market and in the decisions of economic enterprises. These "positive" goals were not the only political goals of the labor movement. As we saw earlier, some of the unions' most pressing political goals were "negative" ones that sought to stop the state from intervening in the labor market to support employers and to repress unions. Nevertheless, proposals to increase state intervention in the economy were a standard feature of suggested labor party programs.

The second mechanism sees liberty as an affective idea or a source of identity. On this account, the idea of liberty had become intimately connected to the idea of what it meant to be an American: a connection that was articulated in an ideology of "Americanism." Thus, any labor party program that was inimical to freedom was not just illegitimate, but threatened the sense of identity that all Americans shared. This second mechanism plays an important role in Hartz's argument. He repeatedly emphasizes that liberalism is not just a rational moral commitment, but also a nationalist sentiment and an irrational emotion (Hartz, 1955, 6, 29, 30, 205–8, and 231).

However, if it could be shown that labor's political program was compatible with individual freedom, then the constraints posed by either mechanism would prove illusory. Under those circumstances, individual liberty would pose neither an evaluative nor an effective constraint. In the following sections, I will begin by looking at how labor leaders responded to the prevalence of the idea of individual freedom. I will then consider whether ordinary workers and potential middle-class allies were likely to find this response plausible.

Labor Leaders in Australia

How did labor leaders in Australia respond to the fact that the idea of individual freedom commanded widespread support? One of their dominant responses was to see themselves as freedom's defenders. It was a commonplace mantra of union rhetoric that Australia was "the land of the free," and that Australians were a "free people," who could boast that they had turned a "wilderness of political and social slavery" into a "garden of liberty."[46] But the industrial conflicts of the early 1890s suggested to labor leaders that all this was now threatened. In the middle of the Maritime strike, the *Australian Workman*, the official organ of the trade unions of NSW, issued an appeal to "Young Australia" to defend "the liberty which you today enjoy" and "which has had its fullest development in Australia." Drawing on the full force of freedom as an affective as well as a normative idea, it argued that "your heroic ancestors . . . with their great bequest of Liberty . . . also bequeathed to you the sacred responsibility of guarding those liberties." It concluded that "Your country expects this from you; it is included in the patriotic duty which you owe to her."[47]

On this account, the establishment of the labor party was an opportunity to restore liberty to its rightful place. Indeed, according to the *Worker*, the party was literally born of liberty.[48] For the *Australian Workman*, the basic purpose of both the party and the unions was "social equality and freedom for all," and the victory of the party at its first election was seen as vindicating Australia's claim to be a free society.[49]

That this commitment to individual freedom was deeply felt, and not merely opportunistic rhetoric, can be seen from the fact that labor leaders were also prepared to defend it against their own supporters. When speakers like the prominent employer-politician, Bruce Smith, were howled off the platform at election meetings, union leaders and the labor press immediately denounced this as a threat to basic freedoms. Speaking for the Sydney Trades and Labour Council (TLC), its Secretary, T. J. Houghton insisted that "no greater calamity than the stifling of free speech could possibly befall the workers in this or any other land."[50]

Of course, many of labor's opponents also claimed to champion liberty. To deal with these claims, labor leaders regularly deployed a distinction between real freedom and sham freedom, and between real and sham liberals. This distinction was not new in the early 1890s. Unionists and their supporters had been using it for some time to express their enthusiasm for certain established liberal politicians and judges, and their growing disaffection with many others.[51] But in the wake of the great strike defeats of the early 1890s, it gained an added urgency as they sought to respond to employers' attempts to defend a laissez-faire interpretation of liberty that juxtaposed unionism with "freedom of contract," and characterized workers who were not unionized as "free labour."

Unionists and their supporters argued that the supposed freedom offered by "freedom of contract" was a sham because it left most workers with no real choices and simply forced them to accept whatever their employers chose to offer. Labor-supporting publications regularly drove this point home. In a front-page cartoon during the 1891 Queensland Shearers' strike, the *Bulletin* depicted the "free labour" exchange as a slave auction, argued that only with the advent of strong unions had something approaching "freedom of contract" become possible, and presented the pastoralists' efforts to break the shearers' organization as an assault on this partially won freedom.[52] This kind of position developed into a standard argument for state intervention on the grounds that the absence of economic security and the one-sided balance of power between employers and employees were constraints on the individual freedom of most ordinary workers. The state had to intervene to ensure that the weak as well as the strong had meaningful choices in the labor market, and to ensure that all had access to the basic economic resources without which it was impossible to lead an independent life.

These arguments were posed not only in terms of "freedom," but also in terms of "individualism." Many union leaders embraced individualism, and the *Australian Workman* declared itself "individualistic to the backbone."[53] Here, too, a distinction was made between "real" or "true" individualism and the "so-called" individualism defended by labor's opponents.[54] A characteristic example of this type of argument can be found in a letter written by William Morris Hughes in 1891. According to Hughes, the kind of state intervention called for by socialism "will no more superogate the true functions of the individual than any other form of government; on the contrary, it will do much to expand and accentuate the individuality of the members of the community." It will do this by relieving the individual of the constant necessity to think about "how he shall supply himself with the necessaries of life—a process of thought which, so far from being conducive to the retention or development of individuality, tends rather to reduce all men to one pattern."[55] Underlying this defense of "true individualism" is a developmental view of freedom—a view that an individual is only free to the extent that he is able to develop his capacities.[56] On this account, true individualism, like true freedom, requires state intervention to ensure that everyone has access to the economic resources that are a prerequisite for self-development. Those who rejected this kind of state intervention were merely trying to restrict freedom to a privileged few. Labor sought freedom for all.

Australian labor leaders did sometimes worry that freedom or individualism was not wholly compatible with state intervention. William Lane, for example, endorsed the view that state socialism would establish a society in which "individualism finds unlimited scope" (Wilding, 1980, 37). But he also argued that men would be freer under socialism because "nineteen laws out of twenty could then be dropped" (Lane, 1892, 119), and he looked forward to the evolution of socialism into a purely voluntary system of anarchist cooperation. Only anarchism could provide "that free ground whereon true Socialists and true Individualists meet" (Lane, 1892, 113).[57] Overall, however, Australian labor leaders did not accept the anti-statist interpretation of liberty on which the liberalism thesis rests.

But they did worry that their foray into politics might be illegitimate for a different freedom-related reason. Their concern centered on antagonism to the idea of organizing parliamentary parties around the representation of sectional interests, and the pursuit of "class legislation." Parliament, it was said, should rather legislate for the general good by representing the interests of each citizen as an individual. This concern was frequently raised by unionists themselves during the regular debates about the "direct representation of labour in parliament" at the Intercolonial Trades Union Congresses in the second half of the 1880s. According to a delegate to the 1889 Congress, for example, "two wrongs would not make a right. In the past they had had too much class legislation, and now were they to introduce another kind of class legislation."[58] Sometimes—as with this delegate—this allegation was raised in order to uphold the charge. Typically, however, the charge was raised for the purpose of rejecting it. Labor leaders responded to the allegation that the establishment of a labor party would lead to class legislation in one of two ways. These two responses coexisted in the rhetoric of many labor leaders.

One response was to counter-charge that, since every other section had long been pursuing class legislation, they had no choice but to do likewise. "Another great argument against direct representation is that it produces class feeling and class legislation," said a delegate at the 1886 Congress (ICTUC, 1886, 32–33), "We reply that we have it now without it. . . . Land, commerce, and capital are all cared for in our Legislative Assemblies . . . direct representation . . . has been forced upon the working classes from the fact that their interests are studiously ignored. . . . " All this lead him to conclude that "Class questions require class knowledge to state them, and class sympathy to fight for them." A statement that became something of a mantra.[59] Similar arguments were made by many other delegates, and they remained a staple response when a labor party was in fact launched in 1891.[60]

The other response was to deny that labor was a "class party," and to characterize it instead as a "people's party." This response drew on the longstanding liberal juxtaposition of the "people" and the "interests," or the "masses" and the "classes," and it relied on the populist strategy of forging a producers' alliance. Those who saw the labor party in these terms emphasized its similarity with the People's parties emerging in the United States. The shearers' journal, the *Hummer*, was particularly keen on this comparison. The U.S. People's party, it said, "cannot be denounced as a class movement, for behind it stands a labourer, a farmer, an average merchant, and a nationalist . . . the above applies exactly . . . [to] the Labour Party in NSW."[61] But similar comparisons can also be found in other pro-labor papers.[62]

As with social egalitarianism, Australian labor leaders treated the widespread support for individual freedom as an ideological opportunity. They again accused their opponents of failing to honor the shared values of their society, and sought to establish that a gap existed between actual social practices and the social practices that a commitment to individual freedom required. And they confidently portrayed their defense of freedom as the latest episode in the long history of labor's involvement in the patriotic struggle for liberty.

Sometimes, labor leaders used the language of individual freedom to make the case for purely negative goals. These laissez-faire compatible criticisms emphasized the threat to the freedom of individual workers emanating from combinations of employers backed by state repression. At other times, they appealed to individual freedom to support collective bargaining and positive demands for state intervention. In these cases, they faced a more complex task than they had in the case of social egalitarianism, for now they also had to engage in a battle of interpretation over what constituted individualism and freedom with opponents who rejected their claim to champion these values. In this battle, labor leaders emphasized the idea that freedom depended on the availability of meaningful choices, and that individualism depended on the ability to develop one's own capacities. This interpretation allowed them to argue that individual freedom required the kind of state intervention that many unionists demanded.

Although Australian labor leaders did sometimes feel constrained by the liberal political culture of which they were a part, the constraint they felt was not usually the one identified by the liberalism thesis. According to the liberalism thesis, it was not the existence of a labor party per se that was illegitimate, but rather its likely program. The doubts of Australian union leaders tended to run in the opposite direction. They were less concerned that their demands for state intervention may be illiberal, and more concerned that the very existence of a party that pursed class interests may be illiberal. Their response shows that it is not always necessary to set out a philosophically consistent position in order to deal with ideological constraints. Labor leaders overcame their qualms by straddling two different positions: sometimes characterizing their party as a reluctant class party, sometimes as a populist party.

Labor Leaders in the United States

American labor leaders responded to the prevalence of the idea of individual freedom with very similar arguments. Many made a straightforward appeal to the need to defend and restore liberty without reference to the need for collectivism or state intervention. Debs's speech in Chicago on his release from jail in November 1895 is a classic example of this kind of appeal. The speech eulogizes liberty, insists that it is a unique virtue, and emphasizes its special status as a sacred founding principle of American government. Speaking to a vast crowd of over 100,000 people, Debs declared that "the theme to-night is personal liberty; or giving it its full height, depth and breadth, American liberty." But, said Debs, the treatment that he and others received as a result of the Pullman strike showed that this American "birthright . . . has been wrested from the weak by the strong" and "placed in peril." Debs argued that to rescue "American liberties" and to regain their "priceless heritage" workers must reach for the ballot, and they must do this, not just for themselves, but because it is their patriotic duty as Americans.[63]

These sentiments recurred repeatedly in Debs's response to the defeat of the Pullman strike.[64] Indeed, as contemporaries like J. A. Wayland recognized, Debs himself came to symbolize this kind of appeal to the defense of freedom both as a moral value and a source of identity (Salvatore, 1982, 155). Wayland's paper, the *Coming Nation*, ran a special "Liberty" issue to celebrate Debs's release. Under a banner headline declaring that "The Danger to the Liberties of the People from an Organized Plutocracy Cannot be Denied or Disguised," prominent reformers filled the paper with articles that made these kinds of Debsian appeals.[65]

This use of liberty language was certainly not unique to Debs and his confreres. Characteristic AFL unionists—both those who supported independent political action like McBride, and those who opposed it like Gompers—made similar arguments. McBride's call for labor organizations in Ohio to meet to discuss the establishment of a labor-populist alliance, and the resolution he successfully moved at that meeting to establish this alliance, are both framed in terms of the need to restore "that liberty of speech and action for which the founders of the government fought."[66] Likewise, in a Fourth of July editorial published in the midst of the Pullman strike, Gompers identified the struggle of the labor movement with the struggle for liberty, suggested that the values of the Declaration of Independence were in danger of becoming little more than "glittering generalities," and concluded that "the perpetuity of the liberties of our people" depended on "determined action" by the wage workers.[67]

Moreover, an appeal for the defense of liberty is central to the thought of Henry Demarest Lloyd. Lloyd's arguments are especially important because they provided the ideological common ground for the labor-populist party that was established in Chicago in the wake of the Pullman strike. They are set out particularly clearly in a widely circulated speech to the AFL's 1893 convention, and in a major campaign speech in Chicago prior to the 1894 elections.[68] Lloyd argued that a revolution of millionaires and corporate capitalists was already in progress, and that the defense of traditional Jeffersonian liberty was the order of the day. But he also envisaged the political program of the labor movement as a program for the extension of liberty: an extension that was a necessary condition for its defense. Lloyd interpreted the AFL's putative Political Programme as a call for American values to be applied to the government of industry through the establishment of a system of industrial democracy. This, he argued, would add "another great emancipation . . . to the glorious record of liberties achieved by mankind."[69] In this respect, Lloyd's message goes beyond that which Debs was preaching at this time, for Debs's overwhelming concern was with the simple defense of established American values.[70]

Many American unionists also distinguished between "real" or "true" freedom and "supposed" freedom in order to challenge the claims of opponents who deployed the language of individual liberty against them. Those making this distinction typically argued that real freedom requires economic security, and many went on to argue that this in turn would require state intervention in the economy: whether in the form of socialism, or in some more limited form. These arguments appear in a number of contributions to AFL publications.[71] They are also given a prominent place in some socialist papers,[72] where the influence of Laurence Gronlund is often pronounced. Gronlund (1884, 76–77 and 95–97) highlighted the relationship between individual freedom and economic security, and concluded that "State-action and individual Freedom, far from being antagonistic, are really complementary of each other."

Similar arguments were made by appealing to a distinction between "true" and "supposed" individualism. True individualism was said to recognize that some form of state or collective intervention is required in order to remove the need to work long hours just to provide necessities. Only then "would [everyone] be free . . . free to exercise full individualism untrammelled."[73] As in Australia, these arguments are often underwritten by a developmental conception of individual freedom.

However, there were some voices within the union movement that articulated the kind of anti-statist arguments that the liberalism thesis would lead one to expect, and these voices were also present in the AFL's 1894 debate on its Political Programme. In the debate on the plank of the Programme that called for a legal eight-hour day, delegate Weismann suggested that workers would be more independent and self-reliant if they won the eight-hour day without the help of legislation. And in the debate on the plank that called for sanitary inspection, he warned against giving too much power to government (AFL, 1895a, 17 and 25). The delegates, however, voted to endorse both these planks (AFL, 1894, 37).

Anti-statist arguments were also articulated in the debate on plank 10, which called for "the collective ownership by the people of all means of production and distribution." Delegate McCraith, who moved that it be replaced by a plank calling for "the abolition of the monopoly system of land holding," argued that "plank 10 is a menace to liberty fraught with danger" and stated that he was "opposed to any legislation which will tend to increase governmental power." Similar arguments were made by delegates Cohen and Greenhalgh. Delegate Pomeroy went further, claiming that "the cause of our present evils are largely due to the socialistic institutions that already exist," and delegate Sullivan, while seeing some role for state intervention, cited Jefferson's aphorism that "the government which governs the least governs best."[74]

Although plank 10 was defeated, these contributions need to be placed in context. Anti-statist arguments were not the main reason for this defeat. The most important opponents of the plank were Samuel Gompers and his close associates, and they did not deploy these arguments. Indeed, only 5 of the 29 contributors to the debate appealed to anti-statist sentiments, and all of these were either one-time anarchists or single taxers.[75] Moreover, immediately prior to this debate, delegates had voted overwhelmingly for planks that committed the AFL to support an extensive increase in state intervention in the economy in the form of "municipal ownership of street cars, water works, and gas and electric plants for public distribution of light, heat, and power," and "nationalization of telegraphs, telephones, railroads, and mines" (AFL, 1894, 37).

Nevertheless, it is noticeable that Debsian and other liberty-based arguments for state intervention found only a faint echo during this debate. Only delegate Brentell of the steel workers' union made a direct reference to these arguments (AFL, 1895a, 42), although a couple of other delegates, including Penna of the miners' union, drew analogies with the struggle against slavery (AFL, 1895a, 28–29 and 30–31). Why these arguments played such a minimal role, when they were common currency throughout the labor movement, will only become clear in Chapter 8.

The charge of "class legislation" was regularly leveled by labor leaders from all currents of reform thought to draw attention to the extent to which capitalist sectionalist interests had captured control of the legislative process.[76] But fears that the establishment of a labor party might breach the injunction against "class legislation" did not play as large a role in the United States as they did in Australia, although criticisms of this sort did occasionally emerge from within the labor movement. A contributor to the *Official Book* issued for the AFL's 1891 convention rejected calls for labor to enter politics on the grounds that "morally we have no right. . . . Class legislation and administration has no place in a republican form of government." "Are we justified in imitating capital?" he asked. "Since when have two wrongs made one right?"[77] One delegate at the AFL's 1894 convention also briefly alluded to class legislation to reject both Plank 10 and its proposed replacement (AFL, 1895a, 28). However, in the early 1890s, opponents of independent labor politics within the labor movement rarely took up this criticism—and proponents rarely felt the need to address it.

There is plenty of evidence that American labor leaders were committed to the value of individual freedom. But in most cases this did not lead them to conclude that it would be wrong for them or their unions to engage in independent labor politics. Though there were some labor leaders who viewed individual liberty as a constraint. It was far more common for them to see the prevalence of this value as an opportunity that could help legitimize such an initiative. Nor is there much evidence to suggest that labor leaders thought that independent labor politics would compromise their identity as Americans. On the contrary, those for whom freedom was most closely enmeshed with their American identity were often among the strongest supporters of independent labor politics. These leaders often located the labor movement within a narrative that charted the progressive fulfillment of America's promise. Those, like Gompers, who rejected independent labor politics, mostly did so on other grounds. They tended to endorse the claim that liberty was under threat, but rejected the political prescription of their union opponents.

How did the use of liberty language by labor leaders in the United States and Australia compare? There were some differences of emphasis. In the United States, the debate about "Plank 10" socialism played a larger role in the debate about the establishment of a labor party, and so there was somewhat more emphasis on accusations of "statism." In Australia, there was no ready-made populist vehicle through which independent labor politics could be expressed, and so there was somewhat more emphasis on accusations of "class legislation." In addition, rhetoric about real freedom was more often focused on arguments about "freedom of contract" in Australia, because unlike in the United States, the attempt to enforce a closed shop had played an important role in the strike wave there. Overall, however, the use of liberty language by labor leaders and pro-labor papers in the early 1890s is strikingly similar in the two countries.

In both countries, labor leaders saw themselves as defending established freedoms, and the prevalence of the idea of individual liberty was usually viewed as an ideological opportunity. Sometimes their arguments were directed at the negative goal of ending the infringement of these freedoms by employers and governments. At other times they were directed at the positive goal of encouraging certain forms of state intervention. In both countries, labor leaders had to defend themselves against the liberty-based counter-arguments of their opponents. In each case, they sought to do this by deploying a distinction between real and supposed freedom, and they frequently used it to argue that real freedom required state intervention in the economy. In each case, they also made a similar distinction between real and supposed individualism—a distinction that was underwritten by a developmental conception of freedom according to which each person was only free to the extent that they could develop their capacities.

Were Their Claims Plausible?

Were the arguments of labor leaders about individual freedom likely to seem plausible to ordinary workers and other potential supporters? Recall that in principle this raises two questions: one about the plausibility of the interpretation of the value in question, and the other about the plausibility of the empirical assumptions that underpin the claim that the value is threatened.

In the case of social egalitarianism, the plausibility of labor leaders depended principally on the second of these questions. Though there were some who rejected the social egalitarian ideals put forward by labor leaders, this was not because they rejected a particular interpretation of social egalitarianism and sought to defend a different one. Rather it was because they had doubts about social egalitarianism per se.

In the case of individual freedom, however, the plausibility of labor leaders' arguments depended on interpretive as well as empirical questions. "Freedom" could and did have many different meanings in the early 1890s. Some sense of just how many interpretations were current, and how different they could be, can be gleaned from an "extra liberty edition" of the *Coming Nation*, which had asked readers for their definition of liberty. Forty answers were published, ranging from the "full exercise of both mental and physical faculties," and the absence of "man-made laws," to "the right of free access to the bounties of nature," and "the right to do right."[78] In addition, labor leaders had to seek support for their particular interpretations of individual freedom in an environment of charge and counter-charge, amidst a mighty battle of interpretation with their opponents. To the *Chicago Tribune*, for example, it was not the railroad corporations but Debs who was threatening to become a "king" and a "dictator."[79]

So were there features of Australian society that made labor leaders' arguments about individual freedom more plausible? I will begin with the question of interpretive plausibility. Here, three features of Australian society need to be considered.

The first concerns "mateship." In a seminal work, Russell Ward argued that a mixture of frontier conditions, convict origins, and class hostilities in the pastoral industry generated a distinctive "mateship" ethos among the bush workers of the Australian outback—an ethos that eventually spread to the towns and cities, and became the basis for a distinctive national identity.[80] According to Ward (1958, 180, 241–45, and 258), this mateship ethos had a "collectivist, egalitarian bias" that helps explain why the Australian labor movement was stronger and more open to collectivist and socialist ideas than its American counterpart.

At first sight, the statements of new unionists and radical writers seem to support this. For example, in 1893, W. G. Spence urged unionists to practice "mateship in all things" (Ebbels, 1983, 121), and he later recalled that "Unionism came to the Australian bushman as a religion. . . . It had in it that feeling of mateship which he understood already, and which always characterised the action of one 'white man' to another" (Spence, 1909, 78). Likewise, radical authors like Francis Adams and Henry Lawson eulogized the simple moral superiority of bush mateship, and linked this to a positive assessment of the labor movement.

However, there are a number of problems with Ward's argument. First, it is doubtful whether mateship provided the kind of ideological resources that could foster industrial unions and labor party politics. According to Ward (1958, 203), the mateship ethos imposed an obligation on a man to stand by his mates whatever the circumstances. In this, it certainly differed from the stereotypical loner ethos of the American "West." But the literature that portrays these obligations typically highlights interpersonal loyalty between a small group of men—sometimes just two of them—rather than a more expansive class solidarity (Hirst, 1988, 74, and 1988a, 130–31). Second, Ward (1958, 212–17, and 221–28) sees the new unionists and radical writers as nationalizing the mateship ethos by transmitting it from the bush. However, there is a good deal of evidence that—like nationalist intellectuals the world over—they themselves were actually inventing this ethos (Davidson, 1978, 191–209, White, 1981, 85–109, McQueen, 1986, 129–42 and 173–75, and Hirst, 1988, 73). Third, whether invented or not, all agree that it was not until the 1890s that the main effort to nationalize the mateship ethos took place.[81] So it is difficult to see how mateship could help explain the establishment of the labor party at the beginning of the 1890s. Arguably, the nationalization of the mateship ethos was itself a product of some of the same ideological processes that helped give rise to the Labor Party.

In addition, mateship was not just about egalitarian collectivism and solidarity. It also had an intimate relationship with the idea of individual freedom and independence. The bushman, said Ward (1958, 180), "exhibited . . . that 'manly independence' whose obverse side was a levelling, egalitarian collectivism, and whose sum was comprised in the concept of mateship." Mateship was thus a composite concept comprising both independence and collectivism—individual freedom and group solidarity—and it insisted on their mutual dependence.[82]

The mateship ethos that emerged in the 1890s was one aspect of the attempt by unionists and their radical supporters to reformulate the liberal tradition in Australia. "Mateship" was a bridging concept, deployed at the level of popular culture, which sought to combine the widespread commitment to individual freedom with support for some measure of collectivism and solidarity. The success of the efforts to promote this concept provides evidence that it was indeed possible, in a society heavily influenced by liberal values, to interpret individual freedom in ways that were compatible with the requirements of strong unions and labor-party politics. But it does little to explain why similar efforts in the United States did not bear fruit.

The second feature of Australian political culture that warrants attention concerns "colonial socialism." Some have argued that Australians were less resistant to labor's positive demands for state intervention because they were accustomed to colonial governments that had long played an active role in economic and social life.[83]

This argument needs to be treated with caution. For it both overestimates the role of the state in Australia, and underestimates its role in the United States. Australian governments were not significantly involved in the pastoral, agricultural, banking, shipping, retail, mining, or manufacturing industries. But it is true that they were involved in a wide range of economic activities prior to 1890. Most governments did not just run courts, police forces, and schools, but also built and ran water and sewage systems, harbor and river improvements, bridges, administrative buildings, defense works, post offices, telegraph systems, roads, and railways (Butlin, 1959, 35). However, with two notable exceptions— the telegraph and the railroads—these activities were also carried out by governments in the United States. In addition, governments in both Australia and the United States sought to influence the economy through the imposition of tariffs and the sale of land.

In both countries—partly because they were expanding settler societies— there was widespread support for government activities that fostered economic development. In the United States, support for national economic development was a defining policy of the dominant Republican party (Gerring, 1997, 53–66, and 1998, 64–78 and 83–85). In Australia, some forms of government development activity, like infrastructure improvements, were generally accepted. Others, like tariff protection, were a major source of political conflict both within and between states, as they were in America. The single most important difference between the two countries concerned the ownership and control of railways. But Australia's government-run railways were an outgrowth of this common attitude towards economic development. Railroad construction had at first been left to the private sector, but because of a series of ad hoc difficulties and the fact that governments could borrow money more cheaply on the London capital market, government responsibility for constructing and operating railroads became the norm (Butlin, 1959, 39–42).

In both countries, a distinction was drawn in practice between developmental and restrictive government intervention. The former sought to foster the growth of private business activity; the latter sought to regulate it (Butlin, 1959, 35, McCormick, 1981, 21–22, and Gerring, 1998, 74–75). In neither case did support for developmental intervention extend naturally to support for restrictive intervention, and, in particular, it did not extend to support for social and labor legislation. Both countries had extensive public education systems, and beginning in the 1870s, governments in both started to pass Factory Acts on the British model (Nelson, 1995, 136–38, Clark, 1955, 612–13, and Gollan, 1960, 88–92). But beyond that, laissez-faire attitudes towards the regulation of business remained common place.[84]

From the mid-1890s, reforming governments did begin to pass innovative social and labor legislation in Australia (Reeves, 1969 [1902]). But it was only after a new interpretation of liberalism had risen to prominence, and the establishment of the Labor party had altered the incentives facing other politicians, that these changes came about.

The third feature of Australian political culture concerns the influence of the "New Liberalism." Throughout the English-speaking world, laissez-faire interpretations of the liberal commitment to individual freedom were still the received wisdom in the late nineteenth century. But these interpretations were being subjected to an increasingly powerful challenge from middle-class intellectuals who saw themselves as the direct inheritors of the liberal tradition. These "New Liberals" took their inspiration from the work of T. H. Green and his successors.[85] They saw individualism as requiring the fullest development of each individual, and state intervention as necessary to ensure that all were free to undertake this development. Their arguments tended to blur the distinction between liberalism and socialism, and many of them adopted a sympathetic view of the labor movement, and argued that some form of socialism was a precondition for the full realization of liberal principles (Freeden, 1978, 26–72, and 1990, 175–92). The New Liberalism had its greatest impact in the early twentieth century, but from the 1880s onwards its influence began to be increasingly felt. Labor leaders were influenced by New Liberal ideas in both the United States and Australia.

In Australia, these ideas also influenced a significant number of middle-class intellectuals as well as some leading politicians.[86] The politician-intellectual B. R. Wise, who had been a student of T. H. Green at Oxford, and the academic Francis Anderson, whose mentor had been one of Green's inner circle, provided a direct conduit for New Liberal interpretations of freedom. Prominent politicians like Samuel Griffith, Alfred Deakin, and Charles Kingston gave these ideas further exposure.[87] These intellectuals and politicians were "advanced" rather than typical liberals, and they did not always stand by or act on these sentiments.[88] Nonetheless, they helped create an ideological space within an established liberal political culture that made it easier for the interpretations of individual freedom offered by labor leaders to gain acceptance.

Was a similar ideological space available in the United States? Ideas that were influenced by, or analogous to, those of the New Liberalism were promoted by some independent journalists and writers like Henry Demarest Lloyd (Destler, 1963, 12–43, 171–98, and 501). They also gained a degree of support among clergymen influenced by social gospel teachings, settlement movement social workers, and public experts working for the Labor Bureau or the Interstate Commerce Commission, as well as among some academic economists and sociologists (Rodgers, 1998, 52–68, Ross, 1977, 60–61, and Skowronek, 1982, 132–38). But in the late 1880s and early 1890s, "respectable opinion" did not take kindly to the challenge that the New Liberalism posed to laissez-faire interpretations of individual freedom (Ross, 1977, 55).

When a group of up-and-coming academic economists sought to promote the virtues of state intervention, many were subjected to what amounted to academic heresy trials before the wealthy businessmen who dominated the boards of trustees that controlled their universities, and all found it necessary to modify their positions in order to avoid losing their posts (Ross, 1977, 45–52 and 62–63, and Rodgers, 1998, 103–8).[89] Some politicians, like Governor Altgeld of Illinois, were also influenced by New Liberal ideas (Destler, 1963, 197–98), and there was growing attention to railroad regulation and anti-trust issues (Skowronek, 1982, 132–38). However, in the late nineteenth century, it is atypical to find major political figures (like the Australians mentioned above) expressing support for New Liberal ideas.

This was not an inevitable consequence of American political culture. Progressivism (an early twentieth-century relative of the New Liberalism) and New Deal Liberalism (articulated, like the interpretations we are considering here, in the midst of a great depression) succeeded to such an extent that in the United States the very term "liberalism" has now come to mean support for government economic intervention, organized labor, and the welfare state. In addition, labor leaders' interpretations of individual freedom did not all require a justification for state intervention, and for those that did, there were other currents, like Populism, Henry George's Single Tax movement, and Edward Bellamy's Nationalism, which created some ideological space.

Nevertheless, taken as a whole, Australian labor leaders did have some advantages that helped make their interpretations of individual liberty seem more plausible to potential supporters. It is doubtful whether the mateship ethos offered relevant advantages before the labor party was established, and it is also doubtful whether colonial socialism made it easier to win support for state interventionism in the interests of labor. But the stronger presence of New Liberal ideas among middle-class intellectuals and established politicians did provide Australian labor leaders with some advantages that were not shared by their American counterparts.

However, these conclusions about the "interpretive resonance" of labor leaders' arguments have to be balanced against a comparative assessment of their "empirical resonance." In this latter respect, there were three features that, while present in both the United States and Australia, seem to have given a greater advantage to labor leaders in the United States. Each was identified by labor leaders in both countries as one of the main reasons why liberty was threatened. Two have already been discussed.

The first concerns the emergence of neo-feudal behavior among the capitalist elite. This development appeared to threaten not just social egalitarianism, but also individual freedom, by foreshadowing a return to "serfdom" and "slavery." However, as we saw earlier, neo-feudal pretensions had developed much further in the United States than in Australia, and so, all other things being equal, when workers tested the claims of labor leaders against their own experiences and perceptions of social reality, they were likely to be more easily convinced in the United States.

The second feature concerns the emergence of state-backed repression of striking unionists. This development appeared to threaten the freedom of workers to act in defense of their most basic interests and aspirations. Again however, as we have seen, the level of repression was far greater in the United States than in Australia. Moreover, in order to defend state repression, many of labor's opponents tended to set aside questions of liberty, and rested their arguments on their claim to being the party of order. So in this respect, too, the experiences of American workers were likely to make them more easily convinced.

In the view of labor leaders and many other reformers, both of these features were closely connected to a third: the growth of industrial concentration, trusts, and monopolies. Labor leaders in both countries repeatedly invoked these developments as fundamental threats to individual freedom. They were said to turn individual workers and citizens into powerless dependants, and to pose a threat not just to individual freedom in economic relationships, but also to political liberty. In the United States, Lloyd was particularly prominent in drawing attention to these concerns.[90] But they were shared by labor leaders of all persuasions in the early 1890s, including Gompers and the central leaders of the AFL.[91] The same concerns were also repeatedly voiced by Australian labor leaders, and there, too, they were a point of common agreement.[92]

However, industrial concentration had advanced far further in the United States than in Australia. In 1900, there were 443 manufacturing enterprises with over 1,000 employees in the United States. In Australia, there were none.[93] American combinations typically began as cartels formed during the depression of the 1870s to control prices and production. During the 1880s, a number of these cartels reestablished themselves as more tightly organized trusts. The passage of the Sherman Antitrust Act in 1890 spelled the end of this form of combination, but not of combination itself. Indeed, the 1890s saw an unprecedented expansion of company mergers that now took the form of holding companies. This expansion took place in two waves. Its peak occurred during the second wave from 1898 to 1903, but it was already clearly visible during the first wave, which lasted from 1890 until depression struck in 1893 (Thorelli, 1954, 63–96, Chandler, 1977, 315–44, and 1980, 26–28).

Throughout the late 1880s and early 1890s, these developments were the subject of intense public attention and regular stringent attacks (Geisst, 2000, 32, 43, 47, and 52–62, and Thorelli, 1954, 108–63 and 309–68). Content analysis of magazines and journals shows that most middle-class opinion formers were opposed to the emergence of big business at this time (Galambos, 1975, 112–3), and these concerns were further legitimized by prominent politicians (Thorelli, 1954, 159). So, here again, the experience of far greater industrial concentration, reinforced by widespread concern about this development, made it easier for workers in the United States to be convinced of the empirical plausibility of labor leaders' claims that liberty was under threat.

Overall, then, it would be difficult to argue that Australian labor leaders had any decisive ideological advantage over their counterparts in the United States, or that workers were more likely to find the arguments of labor leaders convincing in one country than in the other. True, the greater influence of the New Liberalism gave some interpretations of individual freedom greater "interpretive resonance" in Australia. But the greater display of neo-feudalism, the higher level of state repression, and the far greater development of industrial concentration gave the argument that individual freedom was threatened greater "empirical resonance" in the United States.

Conclusion

Proponents of the liberalism thesis make their case by pointing to a correlation and a causal mechanism. The correlation to which they point is between the prevalence of liberal values and the absence of a labor party. However the United States was not the only country to be heavily marked by liberal values. Liberal values were also prevalent in Australia, and yet there a successful labor party was established. This casts doubt on the correlation. But what about the causal mechanism? The causal mechanism—or rather the mix of mechanisms—on which the liberalism thesis rests suggests that the prevalence of liberal values constrained or even precluded the establishment of a labor party. Perhaps it might be argued that these constraints also applied in Australia, but that unions there managed to establish a labor party in spite of the difficulties they imposed. A closer look at the Australian case suggests that this, too, is mistaken.

In Australia, labor leaders and the pro-labor press treated the prevalence of liberal values as an opportunity rather than as a constraint. They saw themselves as defenders of these values, which, they argued, were being threatened by contemporary social developments. The defeat of the great strikes of the early 1890s highlighted these threats and led opinion-formers in the labor movement to suggest that the only way that unions could defend established liberal values was by forming a party and contesting elections. In the wake of their own strike defeats, many labor leaders in the United States offered very similar arguments. Of course, opponents of independent labor politics did not accept the need to form a party, but in most cases they did not reach this conclusion because they felt constrained by liberal values. Overall, the evidence suggests that in neither country did most labor leaders view the prevalence of liberal values as a constraint.

It is harder to be sure how plausible these arguments seemed to ordinary workers and other potential supporters. Perhaps there were features of Australian society that made it more likely that workers there would find the arguments of labor leaders convincing. A number of possible features have been considered. With respect to arguments about social egalitarianism, the presence of residual support for social hierarchy was found to be present in both societies. Indeed, if there were any advantage, it probably lay with American labor leaders who could point to the striking emergence of neo-aristocratic behavior in the late nineteenth century. With respect to arguments about individual freedom, I have considered the mateship ethos, colonial development policies, and the influence of the New Liberalism, alongside the extent of neo-feudalism, state repression, and industrial concentration. But here, too, there seems no reason to conclude that ordinary workers in Australia were more likely to find the arguments of labor leaders convincing.

So what was the effect of the prevalence of liberal values in these two countries? The short answer is that liberal values tended to help rather than hinder the effort to establish a labor party.

One of the strangest versions of the liberalism thesis is the claim that labor and socialist movements have been weak in the United States because the ideological content of its dominant liberal values was so similar to that of socialism. In effect, according to this argument, "Americanism" became a "substitute socialism" (Lipset, 1996, 87–88, Lipset and Mark, 2000, 25 and 30, and Harrington, 1972, 111). What this fails to see is that, because of the gap between the promise of these values and actual social practices, the prevalence of liberal values gave labor leaders in the United States some important advantages. Unlike their counterparts in countries where feudal values remained influential, they did not have to defend the desirability per se of social equality or freedom for all. Their goals could be presented, not as requiring a revolution or a sharp break with existing values and traditions, but rather as the completion of the American project and the fulfillment of its promise.

CHAPTER 7

Religion

LIBERAL VALUES HAVE had an important impact on American political culture. But the common claim that they were hegemonic is not sustainable, because American political culture was in fact composed of a number of competing influences. One of the most important of these was religion. And central to the American religious tradition has been Puritan Protestantism, which, with its recurring demand for the state to police individual moral choices, has frequently brought it into sharp conflict with liberal values. In this chapter, I want to see whether the religious component of American political culture can help explain why there is no labor party in the United States.

It seems clear that the United States was substantially more religious than Australia. The consensus about the United States is that it has been one of the most religious societies in the "Christian world." Travelers and contemporary observers, as well as historians and sociologists are all in agreement that the United States has long been an unusually religious society by European standards.[1] Indeed, many argue that the United States is "pre-eminently the country of religiosity."[2] The consensus about Australia is that religion has been relatively unimportant. Thus, according to one authority, "Europeans in Australia have not been a religious people" (Jackson, 1988, 1), and with striking frequency, books and articles on Australian religious history begin with similar statements.[3] Many go on to compare this situation with the more vigorous role of religion in the United States. Indeed, some see Australia as the polar opposite of the United States in its attitude to religion: as the "first genuinely post-Christian society."[4] But even among those who are interested in showing that religion has had an important effect in Australia, there is near universal agreement that there was widespread religious indifference (Dilke, 1890, 590, Phillips, 1969, vi, and Hogan, 1987, 286).

The different roles that religion played in the foundation of the two societies and in the national civic cultures that subsequently emerged fit well with this general picture.[5] Religion was central to the mission of those who founded the New England colonies, but it played virtually no role in the decision to found a penal settlement in New South Wales. While the landing of the Pilgrim Fathers at Plymouth was accompanied by much praying and bible reading, there was no religious ceremony to mark the landing of Governor Philip in Botany Bay, but rather a special issue of liquor.[6] In both cases, the colonies began with an established church, but the reasons for this were entirely different. In New England, the puritan desire to build a godly society was the fundamental rationale for the system of theocratic government that was established (Miller, 1956). In New South Wales, state support for the clergy was offered largely in the hope that it might help maintain social order amongst an unruly population.

Observations like these support the general proposition that the United States was more religious than Australia. However, there are many different types of religiosity. In order to understand the impact of religion on the labor movement, we need to look more closely at the religious environment in each country in the late nineteenth century. In what follows, I will begin by comparing the extent of religious involvement, the nature of religious beliefs and practices, the attitudes of the Protestant and Catholic clergy, and the response of labor leaders to these attitudes. Then, I will turn to the political salience of religion in the two societies, paying special attention to its relationship with the party system.

THE EXTENT OF RELIGIOUS INVOLVEMENT

People can involve themselves in religious life to differing degrees. In Australia, at least in NSW, statistics were collected for three kinds of involvement: membership, which required a person to be a communicant or to accept all the obligations and entitlements set down by their church; attendance, which required a person to go to church at least once a week; and affiliation, which required a person to mention the church when asked what their religion was during a census. In the United States, people were never asked their religion during a census, and only statistics for membership are available.

Australians were not irreligious in any absolute sense. In the NSW census of 1891, the overwhelming majority of people (95.9 percent) identified themselves with one Christian denomination or another, and only 1.3 percent specifically claimed to be freethinkers, agnostics, or to have no religion.[7] Had people in the United States been asked, the findings would not have been very different.[8] But these figures provide a poor indication of the extent of religious involvement, for affiliation of this kind could be, and often was, a purely nominal one, quite compatible with an attitude of indifference towards the stated church. A better indicator of the extent of religious commitment is provided by membership figures (Phillips, 1972, 396). As Table 7.1 shows, in the early 1890s, there were more than twice as many church members per head of population in the United States than in Australia.[9] Because membership statistics were collected by churches themselves, and because these churches had widely varying criteria for membership, these figures pose a number of problems. Nevertheless, they do provide a rough guide to the extent of strong religious commitment: one that clearly shows it was far more widespread in the United States than in Australia.

TABLE 7.1.

The Extent of Religious Involvement in Australia (c. 1891) and in the United States (c. 1890)

	Australia		United States				
	NSW	Sydney	Illinois	Chicago	Pennsylvania	Pittsburgh	Total U.S.
Population	1,123,954	383,283	3,826,352	1,099,850	5,258,113	238,617	62,979,766
Affiliation	96.4%	96.4%					
Attendance	26.8%	25.0%					
Membership	13.5%	16.2%	31.4%	35.3%	32.8%	44.3%	32.7%
Churches	1.9	0.9	1.9	0.5	1.8	0.8	2.3

Notes and sources: see appendix

In both the United States and Australia, workers were less likely than members of the middle class to join or attend a church.[10] Systematic comparison is difficult, but the higher overall level of membership, and survey data from the mid-twentieth century (Mol, 1971, 114–15), suggest that American workers were probably less alienated from churches than their counterparts in Australia. However, the level of alienation differed from denomination to denomination, and in both countries, the Catholic church managed to retain a significant working-class following.

THE NATURE OF RELIGIOUS BELIEFS

In broad outline, the nature of religious beliefs and practices around 1890 were similar in both countries. Religious life was dominated by Protestants in both, and in neither was there an established church. South Australia, like Pennsylvania, had been specifically founded without an established church as a "paradise of dissent" (Pike, 1967, Hogan, 1987, 35–44, and Murrin, 1990, 22), but most colonies in both countries had originally had an established church. The Anglican establishment that most of Australia had inherited from Britain was ended in 1836, three years after Massachusetts became the last American state to disestablish its (Congregational) church.[11] Both countries also had strong Catholic minorities. In both cases, the Catholic church was dominated by Irish clergy, and in both cases its minority status lead the church to endorse liberal and pluralist ideas quite different from those it pursued in countries with a clear Catholic majority.

Within this broad outline, however, there were important differences. The most important of these concerns the nature of Protestantism. Table 7.2

compares each denomination's share of total church membership in the two countries. The figures need to be interpreted with caution. The Catholic church, and Protestant churches like the Anglican and Lutheran churches that were aligned with official state churches in Europe, had far less restrictive membership criteria than other Protestant churches. Comparison of the proportion of church members who are Catholics in Table 7.2, with the Australian data in Table 7.3 on the proportion of the total population who are Catholic affiliates, shows how careful we have to be in interpreting this data.[12] Nevertheless, while bearing these qualifications in mind, Table 7.2 does provide an indication of the relative strengths of the different Protestant denominations in the early 1890s.

Three main differences stand out. The first concerns the Anglican church. In Australia, it was by far the largest church, while in the United States it was just one of a number of smaller denominations. The second concerns dissenting or nonconformist churches with roots in Britain, especially the Methodists and the Baptists. These were by far the largest denominations in the United States, while in Australia both were smaller denominations, although the Methodists did have a significant following. The third concerns Protestant churches with roots in continental Europe. Lutheran and Reformed churches were much more significant in the United States than in Australia.

A still more important difference concerns the strength of evangelical-

TABLE 7.2.
Members (or Communicants) of Church Denominations in Australia (1893) and in the United States (1890), as Percentage of the Total Membership of All Churches

	Australia		United States				
	NSW	Sydney	Illinois	Chicago	Pennsylvania	Pittsburgh	Total U.S.
Anglicans	15.4	15.5	1.7	2.3	3.3	3.4	2.6
Catholics	61.4	58.8	39.4	67.6	31.9	53.8	30.2
Presbyterians	6.2	6.6	6.4	3.0	12.5	11.4	6.2
Methodists	7.4	8.1	15.7	4.6	15.1	9.1	22.3
Congregationalists	2.2	4.6	3.0	2.5	0.6	0.5	2.5
Lutherans	0.5	0.1	12.8	11.1	13.7	14.7	7.1
Baptists	1.1	1.8	9.1	3.3	5.0	2.2	18.0
Salvation Army	3.6	3.2	<0.1	<0.1	<0.1	<0.1	<0.1
Disciples	0.5	0.9	5.1	0.3	0.7	0.2	3.1
Reformed	<0.1	<0.1	0.4	0.2	7.2	0.6	1.5
All Churches	100.0	100.0	100.0	100.0	100.0	100.0	100.0

Notes and sources: see appendix

TABLE 7.3.
Affiliates of Church Denominations in Australia (1891), as a Percentage of the
Population

	NSW	Victoria	Queensland	South Australia
Population	1,123,954	1,139,840	393,718	315,533
Anglicans	44.8	35.2	36.2	28.3
Catholics	25.5	21.8	23.6	15.0
Presbyterians	9.7	14.7	11.6	5.8
Methodists	10.0	13.9	7.9	24.3
Congregationalists	2.1	1.9	2.2	3.8
Lutherans	0.7	1.4	5.9	7.4
Baptists	1.2	2.4	2.6	5.6

Notes and sources: see appendix

ism.[13] While evangelical currents influenced Protestants throughout the English-speaking world, they achieved a dominance in the United States that they were never able to achieve in Australia (Rawlyk and Noll, 1993, 18–19). In the United States, the spectacular growth of Methodism and Baptism during the second Great Awakening left evangelical Protestants in a hegemonic position, which enabled them to preside over an "empire of righteousness" for the rest of the nineteenth century.[14] Evangelicals were able to establish this predominance in the United States because of the influence of sect-like religious organization, the strength of Puritan and pietistic traditions, and the success of "revivals." In all these respects, the United States was markedly different from Australia.[15]

The triumph of "unopposed revivalism" (Marsden, 1977, 225) lay at the center of American Protestantism, and provides one of the clearest manifestations of evangelical predominance in the late nineteenth century. Revival meetings, and the evangelists like Dwight L. Moody who starred in them, were emblematic of Protestant activity, and provide a good idea of what was distinctive about it. Evangelicals from different denominations joined together to organize revival meetings, and to promote other causes (like foreign missions and temperance crusades). The interdenominational loyalties that resulted—at times focused on a charismatic leader—often became a more important source of religious commitment than the denominations themselves. As a result, the lines between Protestant denominations became more fluid and people could change with ease from one church to another (Marsden, 1991, 17–22). Revivalism did not take off in Australia. Evangelicals sought to emulate the success of Moody and others, both with imported British and American stars and with local aspirants, and large crowds sometimes turned

up to listen to them. But large crowds also turned up to hear freethought lec-
turers ridicule them, and both sorts of meetings were, in part, a form of enter-
tainment. In general, there were revival meetings, but no revivals. In NSW in
the 1870s and 1880s, church attendance actually declined.[16]

PROTESTANT CLERGY

Throughout the late nineteenth century, most Protestant clergymen and revivalists in the United States were consistently and often vitriolically hostile
to the labor movement. In the 1870s and into the 1880s, they were frequently
hostile to the very existence of unions, and most were also hostile to their
basic bread-and-butter demands for improved wages and an eight-hour workday. By the mid 1880s, many had concluded that unions were not "wholly
evil" (May, 1949, 97), and a few even expressed some sympathy for the labor
movement, but most remained hostile to almost everything that unions did.
The Protestant clergy in Australia also tended to be hostile to the labor movement, but their attitude was less strident. Throughout the 1880s, they recognized that unions had a right to organize, and there was a wider and more
evenly spread range of attitudes—from hostility to sympathy—towards union
demands for social and industrial improvements. However, industrial conflict
was usually deplored.[17]

During each of the critical periods of industrial unrest in the United
States—in 1877, 1886, and again in 1894—the Protestant clergy, and their
main denominational publications, vehemently denounced unions in the
most violent terms. "Bullets and bayonets" and "Gatling guns" were their pre-
scriptions, and "Napoleon" their role model (May, 1949, 92–93, 101). Even
those influenced by the social gospel tended to admonish unions that were involved in industrial action (Hopkins, 1940, 92–96). During the Pullman
strike, prominent Protestant leaders joined a chorus of voices denouncing the
ARU. Some even demanded that "The soldiers must use their guns. They
must shoot to kill" (Lindsey, 1942, 320–21, Lee, 1991, 5–21). During the Maritime strike in Australia, by contrast, most Protestant clergymen adopted a
position of agitated neutrality, and a number of prominent clergymen formed
a Conciliation Committee to help resolve the dispute, although the employers refused to meet with them (Bollen, 1972, 15–23, Phillips, 1981, 162–63,
Hogan, 1987, 135, and Thompson, 1994, 34–36). Beneath this, though, was a
strong undercurrent of hostility, as well as near universal antipathy to the
shearers' demand for a closed shop. The unions were highly critical of the
clergy's role. The Labour Defence Committee (1890, 16) complained bitterly
that, with a few exceptions, "the clergy were afraid to speak out," and that, as
a result, they "took a middle course, and failed to win from the working classes
even the respect accorded to honest opposition." The Pullman strikers could
only wish for such a problem.

During the 1890s, the social gospel led some American clergymen to embrace a form of Christian Socialism, which had its strongest base in the Anglican church (Hopkins, 1940, 150–52 and 173–79). However, these were a tiny minority, and most of the clergy remained deeply hostile to socialism. In Australia, there was also only a small minority of the Protestant clergy who supported socialism, but the range of mainstream clerical opinions was wider. Although some denounced socialism, others sought to show that Christianity was not necessarily incompatible with it.[18] As in the United States, Anglicans—especially high church and broad church Anglicans—provided a conduit for "Christian Socialism," but the effect of this was greater in Australia because of the dominant position of the Anglican Church.[19]

It is tempting to attribute the more hostile attitude of Protestant clerics in the United States to the strength of evangelicalism. Many Protestant clerics certainly drew on the theological resources of the evangelical tradition to support their arguments. Some appealed to a residual Calvinism to suggest that worldly misfortunes were a product of sin.[20] While many others argued that, like other laws governing the material world, the "laws" of political economy were "God's laws," and that it was therefore wrong to interfere with them, especially, it seemed, when they were at work in the labor market.[21] But this same evangelical tradition was equally able to provide resources to support the arguments of the growing social gospel movement, as well as the more radical, egalitarian interpretations proposed by union activists themselves (Hopkins, 1940, and Gutman, 1966). The Christian perfectionism that had driven the evangelical struggle against slavery, and which continued to drive the prohibition movement, could also be turned against the evils of the industrial system (Smith, 1957, 148–62, and Ahlstrom, 1972, 787–9).

An alternative hypothesis might point to the emergence of premillennial ideas within the evangelical tradition. In the early nineteenth century, the United States had been "drunk on the Millennium" (Sandeen, 1970, 42), and the outcome was a consensus among evangelical clergy on the doctrine of postmillennialism. Postmillennialism held that Christ's Second Coming would only occur after the thousand years of bliss that is prophesized in the book of Revelation. It was thus the duty of Christians to pursue moral and social reform in the hope that by doing so they might prepare the way for the millennium to begin. This was the belief that lay behind abolitionism, prohibitionism, and other perfectionist movements. By contrast, premillennialism held that the Second Coming would occur before the millennium. Social reform was thus pointless, since only after Christ's return could any improvements be expected. The urgent task for Christians was to save as many souls as possible before this imminent event. Premillennialism began to gather support in the late nineteenth century. But the vast majority of clergy remained committed to the old consensus, and premillennialism only achieved public prominence in the early twentieth century (Sandeen, 1970, xvi–xviii, Moorhead, 1984, 525, Ahlstrom, 1972, 808–12, and Marsden, 1991, 39–41 and 112–14). In

Australia (as in Britain), a kind of amillennialism was dominant, and neither of these competing doctrines had much influence (Judd and Cable, 1987, 152–53, Piggin, 1996, 76–77, 80, and Bebbington, 1993, 196–97).

Why, then, were the Protestant clergy so hostile towards the labor movement in the United States? No doubt a number of factors were influential. Extra-religious ideological influences like social Darwinism and laissez-faire economic doctrines, the largely middle-class composition of most Protestant congregations, and the middle-class position of the clergy themselves, all played a role. However, each of these factors was also at work in Australia, and yet the hostility there, though present, was not as great as in the United States.

One possible explanation rests on the interaction between the middle-class interests of most Protestant congregations and the institutions through which their churches were governed. In most Protestant churches in the United States, clergymen depended on lay members for their initial appointment, their personal income, support for their projects, and, ultimately, their continued employment. In this they were in a similar position to the dissenting and nonconformist clergy in Australia, but in a very different position to the Anglican clergy. Indeed, these practices of accountability to lay councils had grown out of the Puritan reaction against the hierarchical control exercised by bishops in the Anglican church. Most Protestant clergy had to operate in a competitive labor market in which they had to make, and keep, a reputation among church-goers—a group of people who were simultaneously the consumers of their product, and their employers. Since these consumer-employers were predominantly middle class, and since those who actually served on lay church councils were often prominent local businessmen, it was usually wise to give due weight to the basic economic interests of this group.[22]

This was even truer for revival leaders. Leading revivalists, like the Chicago-based Moody, effectively offered to help protect the interests of wealthy businessmen in return for the financial backing necessary to organize big city crusades. Moody was dependent on wealthy businessmen from the outset (McLoughlin, 1959, 174, 176, 184, 222–30, and 273). Speaking to Christian activists in 1883, he emphasized the importance of converting "the lower classes" before they began to talk of "communism and infidelity." "I say to the rich men of Chicago, their money will not be worth much if communism and infidelity sweep the land." Moody repeated a similar point in a letter soliciting funds from leading businessmen in 1889. "There can," he wrote, "be no better investment for the capitalists of Chicago" (McLoughlin, 1959, 269–70).

CATHOLIC CLERGY

In both the United States and Australia, the Catholic clergy were more sympathetic to the labor movement than their Protestant counterparts. In the early 1890s, the leading prelate in the United States was Cardinal Gibbons of Baltimore. In Australia, it was Cardinal Moran of Sydney. Both were appointed in 1886, and in Rome they were seen as "the two democratic cardinals" (Cahill, 1989, 527). Their attitudes to the labor movement were quite similar, and the hierarchical structure of Catholicism enabled them to exercise a powerful influence on the position of their respective churches. Both were prepared to offer public support to unions, but their support was typically offered in a supercilious and condescending tone and was invariably circumscribed by caveats and conditions. Both upheld the right of workers to organize in order to seek fair wages and working conditions. Both accepted that, in principle, workers had the right to strike, while in practice urging them to shun such action. And both were particularly adamant that socialism was anathema and that private property must be respected. By 1890, these general positions had been widely accepted by Catholic clerics in both countries.[23]

However, during the industrial upheavals of the early 1890s, ambivalence towards the labor movement was greater in the United States than in Australia. The Cardinals' response to the Maritime and Pullman strikes illustrates this. In Australia, Cardinal Moran declared that "the men have right and reason on their side . . . I do not think their demands are unreasonable or excessive" (O'Farrell, 1969b, 154). Following the example of Cardinal Manning during the London Dockers' strike he offered to arbitrate the dispute. In the United States, Cardinal Gibbons endorsed the denunciation of the Pullman strike made by his close colleague and collaborator Archbishop Ireland. Ireland welcomed the deployment of federal troops and spoke forcefully against the strikers for denying the liberties of strikebreakers and threatening the rights of property (Ellis, 1952, 532, Roohan, 1976, 400–1, and Abell, 1960, 86). These were not the only Catholic voices in either country.[24] Nevertheless, in the wake of these strikes, the Catholic church left an overall impression of greater sympathy towards labor in Australia than it did in the United States. During the Maritime strike, cheers went up as workers marched past St Mary's Cathedral in Sydney (Ford, 1966, 74), and afterwards, the Labour Defence Committee (1890, 16) singled out Cardinal Moran as one of a handful of clerics who were worthy of thanks.

There were also significant differences in attitude towards independent labor politics. The church hierarchy in New York set itself against the United Labor party campaign to elect Henry George in 1886, and excommunicated Father McGlynn, a prominent backer of the party (Saposs, 1933, 295, Commons *et al.*, 1918, 2:453, 456, and Roohan, 1976, 334–40). However, Gibbons tried to stop church conservatives from placing George's *Progress and Poverty* on the Index of Prohibited Books (Abell, 1960, 71–72).[25] Intra-church conflicts like these were still unresolved when the AFL was debating its Political Programme in 1894. In late 1892, the excommunication of Father McGlynn was lifted, and the more liberal group around Gibbons seemed to have the upper hand, but by 1895 power was shifting to the conservatives. However, the church's basic attitude to labor politics was not dependent on these shifts. Gibbons and his colleagues gave no indication of sympathizing with labor party experiments. In their eyes, these experiments were dangerous manifestations of the rising threat of socialism. During the 1894 elections, these fears were brought to the fore in Illinois, and Catholics there were warned against supporting the labor-populist ticket (Destler, 1946, 190, 209, Foner, 1955, 324, Jensen, 1971, 218–19, 285, and Schneirov, 1998, 345).

The attitude of Cardinal Moran towards the Australian Labor party was quite different. In 1891, Moran noted the emergence of the party in NSW with approval, while denying any great interest in electoral matters (O'Farrell, 1992, 288). After the election he declared that: "Morally speaking, it is a triumph for Australia that the representatives of the working classes have been elected to Parliament," and that such representation was a "right of the working man" (Hamilton, 1958, 258, and O'Farrell, 1969b, 157). Moran's interest in and support for the Labor party was not consistent in the 1890s, and some other leading clerics—notably in Brisbane—attacked the party vigorously. The Catholic press in Sydney favored the Protectionist party, and shifted from wary support to hostility when Labor decided to enable the Free Trade party to form a government (Hamilton, 1958, 258–62). Nevertheless, support of any sort from the head of the Catholic church in Australia marked a clear difference with the United States, and by the early 1900s, this support had become the norm (Cahill, 1960, 88–101, and O'Farrell, 1969b, 161–64).[26]

It would be difficult to explain why the Catholic clergy in both countries were more sympathetic to the labor movement than the Protestant clergy by appealing to the common theological commitments of late nineteenth-century Catholicism. A more promising explanation is suggested by the similar institutional and economic interests that confronted them in English speaking settler societies. In these countries, the illiberal and anti-democratic tenor of Catholic theological commitments made little sense. In the United States and Australia, the separation of church and state was already entrenched. Moreover, unlike in much of continental Europe, the Catholic church did not stand to lose the privileges that came from close ties to the established order. On the contrary, given its minority status outside the establishment, the church's institutional interests were best served by protecting political liberalism and the space for religious pluralism.[27] In addition, given the disproportionately working-class composition of its adherents, the church could ill afford to completely ignore the demands of the labor movement.

However, ideology and theology may play some role in explaining why leading American Catholics were more hostile to labor party experiments than their Australian counterparts. At first glance, this is far from obvious. Cardinal Moran, ostensibly the more progressive prelate, had in fact been more heavily influenced by ultra-montane attitudes (O'Farrell, 1992, 225–31, Jackson, 1987, 85–91, and Duncan, 1991, 164–67). And key doctrinal statements like the 1891 papal encyclical *Rerum Novarum* could be interpreted as either supporting or opposing a labor party (Inglis, 1963, 314–15, and Abell, 1945, 494). However, the Catholic clergy in both countries did share a common opposition to "socialism," and it could be argued that American hostility to labor-party experiments was greater simply because socialists played a more prominent role in these experiments in the United States. Intra-Australian comparisons provide some support for this claim. Within Australia, the greatest hostility to the establishment of a labor party from the Catholic hierarchy was in Queensland, where the party was seen by contemporaries as being most heavily influenced by socialism. Within NSW, Moran's support for the labor party in 1891 turned first to indifference in 1894, and then to outright hostility in 1897, as the influence of socialists in the party grew (O'Farrell, 1992, 268 and 289). Only after socialist influence had been contained, did Moran return to a supportive stance (Ford, 1966). But care is needed not to overstate this argument. The return to a more sympathetic attitude was also a result— rather than a cause—of the party's success in establishing itself in the 1890s. The party's electoral success among Catholic workers made it increasingly difficult for the hierarchy to oppose it—and the appeal to sectarian themes by Labor's opponents left the church with nowhere else to turn (Hagan and Turner, 1991, 24–26, 40–41, and O'Farrell, 1992, 290).

The Response of Labor Leaders to Clerical Hostility

There is little evidence that differences in clerical hostility influenced the decisions of labor leaders. Late nineteenth-century data on the religious affiliation of union leaders are sparse. In Australia, lay Protestants were probably overrepresented among union leaders, although some of the most senior leaders were Catholics.[28] In the United States, the majority of union leaders were also Protestants, but there is some evidence that Catholics may have been better represented.[29]

In the early 1890s, clerical pronouncements were not a prime concern for labor leaders or the labor press in either country. However, when labor leaders did address themselves to clerical attitudes, their response was remarkably similar. In both the United States and Australia, most labor leaders accepted clerical hostility as virtually inevitable, and their comments varied in tone from weary resignation to sarcasm, cynicism, and amused contempt.[30] In order to explain clerical hostility, they repeatedly pointed to the undue influence that capitalists and the wealthy exercised over churches.[31] Clergymen who were sympathetic to the labor movement were typically viewed as a "noble exception" or a "hopeless minority,"[32] although they were often sought out as speakers at conferences, or for contributions to union journals. Labor leaders were also alert to developments in Catholic social doctrine. But they were suspicious of its real significance, and doubtful that Catholics anymore than Protestants would abandon their alliance with the wealthy.[33]

Although direct discussion of clerical attitudes was a secondary theme, the speeches and writings of labor leaders were suffused with religious language and allusions. The basic stance of most labor leaders in the United States and Australia was that they were *for* "Christianity" but *against* "Churchianity." There were a handful of important exceptions, like Samuel Gompers, who adopted a thorough-going Marxian secularism, but most labor leaders saw Christianity as a mandate for their union organizing activities. Both the railroad workers' leader Debs, and the shearers' leader Spence, explicitly appealed to this kind of argument, and countless labor leaders—both American and Australian, Protestant and Catholic, and conservative and radical—invoked the name of Christ and took up a similar cry. Christ was the "greatest of all social reformers," the "Greatest Agitator," the "ragged socialist of Galilee," or the "first great socialist of the world." "Three cheers for Jesus!" cried J. D. Fitzgerald, a leading NSW delegate at the 1891 Intercolonial Trades and Labor Congress, and a member of the Australian Socialist League.[34]

Overall, then, differences in clerical hostility did not generate substantially different responses in the two countries. And yet religion *did* influence union attitudes towards labor politics. To understand how, it is necessary to examine the relationship between religion and the party system.

RELIGION AND THE PARTY SYSTEM

In the industrializing North of the United States, conflicts between religious subcultures played a central role in electoral competition between the two main parties in the second half of the nineteenth century. The origins of this party system can be traced directly to the strength of evangelical Protestantism in the early nineteenth century. Evangelicals inherited the Puritan commitment to building a Godly society in America. All around them, they saw terrible sins, and, irrespective of their differing sectarian and denominational affiliations, they rallied together to force the government to use its authority to uphold their notion of righteousness, and to enforce what they deemed to be a Godly way of life. Saloons, schools, and the Sabbath were all major concerns, but above all else they sought to end the truly abominable sin of slavery. Evangelical moral crusades soon spilled over into electoral politics, and ultimately, in the 1850s, lead to the establishment of the Republican party, and a realignment of the party system. Evangelical movements were joined in the new Republican party, not only by the remnants of the old Whig party, but also, more importantly, by many activists from the anti-Catholic

Know Nothing movement that had become a powerful political force in the 1840s and '50s. The Know-Nothings grew out of an often-violent sectarian backlash against immigration (especially Irish immigration) following the European famines of the 1840s, and their concerns partly overlapped with those of the evangelical movements.

Those who rejected the call for government intervention to uphold the cultural norms of particular religious or ethnic groups coalesced around the Democratic party. The Democratic party represented itself as the party of "personal liberty." Its core message in the North was that it was not for the government to decide whether drinking alcohol and various other social and religious practices were immoral.[35] Each community should be allowed to follow its own values and its own way of life. Those who responded to this message were typically affiliated with liturgical churches. Liturgical churches rejected the evangelical emphasis on personal conversion experiences and moral activism, and instead placed special emphasis on the practice of formal rituals and the acceptance of traditional authority vested in an organizational hierarchy—practices and beliefs that evangelicals tended to deprecate. Catholics were paradigmatically liturgical, but so too were many Protestants, notably German Lutherans and Anglicans (especially High Church Anglicans). These differences between liturgicals and evangelicals fed into different attitudes towards politics. Liturgical churches believed that it was not for humans to foreshadow the work of God by trying to create a kingdom of righteousness on earth. They were suspicious of evangelical efforts, which they tended to view as fanatical, and they were especially resistant to efforts to draw the state into pietistic moral crusades, since this challenged the paramountcy of the moral authority that they claimed for themselves and sought to impose on their members.

The realignment of the 1850s produced a party system that entrenched the salience of these highly charged ethno-religious conflicts. Each of the two main parties became a kind of "political church," in the sense that they both represented, and helped bind together, two distinct ethno-religious subcultures: an evangelical (or pietistic) one represented by the Republicans, and a liturgical one represented by the Democrats. Each subculture was composed of a complex coalition of different social groups—groups like native Methodists, German Lutherans, or Irish Catholics—each defined in part by national origin and in part by religious affiliation. For most Americans, the act of voting was an expression of their identification with one or another of these ethno-religious groups. Religion was certainly not the only factor underpinning party identification in the industrializing North, but it was undoubtedly a central one.[36]

In Australia, economic conflicts were more important, and religious conflicts were less important, in setting the agenda for electoral politics in the second half of the nineteenth century. Throughout this period, electoral appeals frequently focused on apparently nonideological questions of "good government" and "development," or on meeting the local demands of constituents for roads, bridges, and the like. However, contemporaries also saw politics as a conflict between "parties"—between "liberals" on the one hand, and "constitutionalists" or "conservatives" (as their opponents sought to label them) on the other. The origins of these divisions lay in the formative conflicts that had accompanied the establishment of self-government in the 1850s. These conflicts took place between an alliance of the urban middle and working classes, miners, and smallholders on the one hand, and pastoral and mercantile interests on the other. The most important conflicts concerned democratic reform (to remove property qualifications and other restrictions) and land reform (to improve the position of small farmers or "selectors"). Liberals sought to push these reforms further, while their opponents resisted them. These formative conflicts were soon joined by a third, increasingly important conflict over tariffs. On this issue, however, liberals were divided. While the dominant strand of liberalism in NSW favored free trade, the dominant strand in Victoria favored protection. But all of these conflicts ensured that political divisions would be principally defined in terms of class and other economic interests.[37]

This does not mean that religious conflicts were irrelevant to electoral mobilization in Australia. As in the United States, cleavages between Protestants and Catholics, and between evangelicals and liturgicals (with High Church Anglicans, instead of German Lutherans, as the largest group of liturgical Protestants), both played a role. Conflict over the control and funding of schools was the single most important and enduring factor serving to politicize religious cleavages. But perhaps the clearest example of the electoral use of sectarian tensions occurred after a deranged Irishman attempted to assassinate the Duke of Edinburgh while he was visiting Sydney in 1868. In the hysterical atmosphere that followed, a Protestant Political Association was formed, and with the backing of the Orange Order, it influenced election outcomes in a number of constituencies for the next four years. In this context, Henry Parkes, who was already a leading liberal politician, sought electoral advantage by fanning unfounded fears of a Fenian conspiracy (Loveday and Martin, 1966, 99–100). Private correspondence between Parkes and other politicians reveals that he considered religious affiliation to remain an important motive for electoral behavior well into the 1870s (Martin, 1967 and 1976).[38] Although Parkes publicly denounced sectarianism, Catholics remained disproportionately likely to support his opponents for the rest of his political career.

One factor that restricted the development of ethno-religious electoral blocs was the absence of high levels of residential segregation. Compared with the United States, Catholics were relatively evenly distributed throughout Australia. Although there was some clustering, the 1891 census showed that, with the exception of one small village, there was no district in NSW with a Catholic majority. However, the causal significance of this needs to be treated with care, for less residential segregation could be evidence either that it was harder to make ethno-religious differences politically salient, or that these differences simply were less salient in the first place. The higher level of intermarriage between different ethnic and religious groups in Australia suggests the latter.[39]

There was, therefore, a sectarian strand to Australian politics. But it was a secondary strand. While Parkes was manipulating sectarian animus in NSW in the early 1870s, Victoria was electing a Catholic Premier for the third time.[40] In the United States, Catholics were not even elected as mayors in large cities until the 1880s (Higham, 1992, 60, Kleppner, 1979, 219). Historians who emphasize that sectarianism was important in Australian political development, nevertheless acknowledge that it was much less important than in the United States, and that even the sectarian surge of the late 1860s was relatively mild by American standards (Hogan, 1987, 101, 129–30, and 286). In Australia, it was not the conflicts that accompanied a period of realignment, but rather those that accompanied the establishment of self-government that provided the basis for electoral competition in the second half of the nineteenth century. To the extent that ideologies were important, it was not the strength of evangelical Protestantism, but the strength of liberalism that determined the main lines of political conflict. In contrast with the United States, the outcome was a system in which religious conflicts were less politically salient, and economic conflicts were more so.

This difference in the political salience of religious conflict was reinforced by a second important difference in the age of party organizations and the strength of party identification.

In the United States, the same two parties had dominated electoral competition since the realignment of the 1850s. The longstanding dominance of these parties enabled them to become a focus of loyalty in their own right, and most people came to identify themselves with one party or the other.[41] The pervasiveness and intensity of this party identification was constantly commented upon (and increasingly bemoaned) in the late nineteenth century, and it had a significant independent effect on electoral behavior. Religious affiliations were not the only source of the emotional attachment that underwrote party identification. A second important source was the powerful loyalties forged in the civil war. Well into the late nineteenth century, the Republican party sought to mobilize northern voters by waving the "bloody shirt" and appealing to patriotic sentiments (Kleppner, 1979, 80–89 and 94–96). The American Civil War shared more with the First World War than with previous military conflicts in Europe or the United States. Unlike these earlier conflicts, it involved the military mobilization of an entire society. About 600,000 people were killed throughout the United States (Shefter, 1986, 246–47), and, in the North, 37 percent of men of military age had served in the army by the war's end (Montgomery, 1993, 94). This mass experience of military horror, hatred, solidarity, and conflict had an enduring influence on party identification.

In Australia, party organizations were established later, and so party loyalty had had less time to develop. The situation varied from colony to colony. In

Victoria, a liberal party organization had emerged in the 1860s and 1870s; in Queensland, party organizations dominated politics in the 1880s; and in all colonies, reform leagues were established from time to time that sought to play a proto-party role (Loveday et al., 1977, 23–26, 28–31, and 36). But it was only with the establishment of the Free Trade and Protectionist parties in NSW in the late 1880s that parties became a permanent feature of electoral competition. For most of the period since self-government, politics had been organized around a handful of factional leaders, each of whom had a fluctuating core of supporters in the Legislative Assembly. Although these leaders were associated in the public mind with partisan positions, and newspapers often referred to them as leading "parties," they had no permanent, public organizational presence in the electorate. Agents did operate on their behalf in local constituencies, but they had to do so privately so as not to contravene the ruling idea that members of parliament should be "independent."[42] Not only were the NSW Free Trade and Protectionist parties newer than parties in the United States, but the conflicts that gave rise to them were less emotionally charged. Religious conflict had not played a central role, and the American Civil War was an event that had no parallel in Australia. Consequently, party identification in late nineteenth-century Australia was much less pervasive and intense than it was in the United States.

Because the political salience of religion was greater in the United States than Australia, there was a higher hurdle facing those seeking to promote working-class interests through electoral competition. The party system in the United States did not simply reflect the greater importance of religious cleavages in American society, it also picked out and strengthened the political salience of religious interests and issues, and weakened the salience of class interests and issues of distributive justice. Voters were, of course, concerned about their economic interests, but they were used to the idea that it was ethno-religious interests that were at stake in elections. So, by and large, when they went to the polls, taking their cue from the agenda set by the party system, they voted not for their class, but for their ethno-religious interests. This created a hurdle that Australian unions did not have to jump. Unlike their American counterparts, they did not have to first change the terms of political competition before they could win support. They could simply ask voters to support a radical and more class-specific version of the liberal position that had long helped define the political agenda.

Although the hurdle facing unions in the United States was higher, it was not an insurmountable obstacle. Exogenous shocks could force a shift in the political agenda, and in particular, depression and industrial conflict could greatly increase the salience of class interests. This is what happened in the New Deal realignment of the 1930s, and the enormous economic and industrial turmoil of the early-to-mid 1890s would seem, at first, to promise something similar. In fact, however, just as the effect of this turmoil was about to be felt, the political salience of religion increased still further. The five or six years prior to the AFL's 1894 debate were marked by a proliferation of religious and sectarian conflicts. Moreover, these conflicts emerged with particular intensity in just those states—like Illinois and Pennsylvania—where class conflicts gave independent labor politics its best chance for success. In Australia, by contrast, in the five or six years prior to the decision to establish a labor party, there was an unusually low level of religious and sectarian conflict. Thus, when the opportunity to establish a labor party presented itself in the early 1890s, the political salience of religion posed very different problems in the two countries. While in the United States, a high hurdle had been raised still higher, in Australia, an already low hurdle had actually been lowered.

The Late 1880s and the Early 1890s

How politically salient was religious conflict in each country in the years immediately prior to the decision about whether or not to establish a labor party? The religious issues that became the subject of significant political conflict were the same in both countries. Three sets of issues stand out: temperance and associated "wowser" issues, education, and organized anti-Catholicism.[43] By tracking the waxing and waning importance of these issues, we can track the waxing and waning political salience of religious conflict.

In the United States, conflict over each of these sets of issues followed a similar pattern throughout much of the Northeast and Midwest. In each case, once the lull imposed by the civil war had passed, there was a rising chorus of pietistic demands and political activism. In each case, this reached a crescendo in the years immediately prior to the AFL's 1894 debate. And in each case the surge of political conflict that resulted reinforced the standing ethno-religious image of the two main parties. Here, I will pay particular attention to Illinois and Pennsylvania, but these developments took place in many states.

For evangelicals after the civil war, the "liquor system" replaced slavery as the pre-eminent symbol of the failure to create a godly society. From the late 1870s, campaigning became more intense, urgent, and uncompromising, and by the end of the 1880s a militant, millenarian, prohibitionist stance was the norm. Highly organized activists inside the Republican party forced the issue to the fore, and sought to commit the party to an unequivocal crusade against the demon drink. Their efforts were reinforced by activists in the Prohibition party, who, by taking a small vote away from the Republicans, could make the difference between victory or defeat in the closely fought elections of the period. Democratic party politicians responded by reemphasizing their opposition to sumptuary legislation and their support for "personal liberty," conscious that demographic changes were making this electorally advantageous. Between 1880 and 1890, there were prohibition referenda in 15 of the 30 nonsouthern states, nine of which were held in 1889 and 1890. In addition, many states passed local option legislation that enabled voters in a county or city to decide whether liquor licenses should be granted. The referenda and ongoing licensing campaigns made temperance a matter of permanent mass political concern. In the Pittsburgh area, for example, although a referendum was lost in 1889, Law and Order Leagues "precipitated a kind of guerrilla warfare" by using judicial elections and legal action in one case after another in order to make maximum use of restrictive licensing laws. At the same time, other wowser issues came to the fore. Between 1887 and 1889, there was a federal campaign for a bill against Sabbath desecration, and in 1892 and 1893, a nationwide "pitched battle" took place over whether or not to allow the World's Fair in Chicago to open on Sundays.[44]

The 1870s and 1880s also saw a highly charged debate about education. The conflict was occasioned by the growth of Catholic and Lutheran parochial schools, and by the increasingly assertive demands of the Catholic hierarchy for changes to school-funding, teacher-training, and the curriculum. To evangelical Protestants, this was seen as a threat to the capacity of the public school system to act as an agent of national moral homogenization.[45] The conflict reached its peak in the early 1890s after Republicans sought to strengthen this capacity in a number of states with "Compulsory Education" legislation. In Illinois, for example, such a law was enacted in 1889. This legislation sparked a furious controversy because one of its main effects was to make *English-medium* education compulsory. Since German and other Lutheran schools, as well as many Catholic ones, were often conducted in languages other than English, the controversy strongly reinforced the common interests shared by the liturgical subculture that the Democratic party represented in the North. In the early 1890s, the schools issue dominated elections in a number of states, and the Democratic party used it to rally sufficient votes to edge out the long-dominant Republicans.[46]

Widespread Catholic participation in the civil war had dispelled suspicions of disloyalty and had helped undermine the anti-Catholic organizations of the Know-Nothing era. But the 1870s and 1880s saw a resurgence of political anti-popery, and by the late 1880s, a whole crop of secret anti-Catholic "patriotic" societies had emerged. The most important of these was the American Protective Association (APA). The APA was hostile to immigration, but, above all else, it sought to combat the political influence of Catholics, and especially Irish Catholics. The APA was founded in 1887 and spread steadily throughout the Midwest. In 1891 and 1892, it started to make its influence felt in elections by swinging votes to the Republican party. However, up until 1893 it had no more than 70,000 members. Then, suddenly, in the first half of 1894, it became a nationwide movement. Its own membership grew to about half a million, and the membership of the various patriotic societies that federated under its umbrella grew to about two and half million. The APA blamed the depression on a Catholic conspiracy, circulated bogus encyclicals, and created a flurry of fear by "uncovering" papal plans for a Catholic uprising in the United States that would "exterminate all heretics." In the elections of 1894, the Democratic party, in the middle of a depression over which it had presided, seized on the opportunity to run its own (anti-APA) fear campaign, in an attempt to reignite the loyalties of its traditional supporters.[47]

In Australia, the first surge of sectarian political conflict, in the late 1860s and early 1870s, was associated with education issues. As these conflicts quietened, temperance and Sabbatarian issues found a place on the political agenda. But there was no new surge of religious conflict in the years immediately prior to the 1891 decision to establish a labor party. When a new surge of anti-Catholicism did appear in the first decade of the twentieth century, the labor party was already well established. Here, I will pay particular attention to NSW, but this pattern was broadly similar in most of Australia.

Prior to about 1880, temperance advocates had focused on moral suasion: an approach that commanded the support of Catholic and Protestant clergy alike. The early 1880s saw the formation of groups calling for legal restrictions.[48] However, unlike their counterparts in the United States, who typically pursued prohibition, these groups typically pursued the more moderate demand of local option legislation.[49] They had little success in Victoria. In NSW, where ratepayers had been given the right to veto new liquor licenses in 1882, they made some headway, with a Royal Commission of Inquiry into Intoxicating Drink in 1886, and a campaign for complete local option in 1889 and 1891. But in the late 1880s there was both little opposition to temperance reform and a lot of inertia. Temperance did establish itself as a central Protestant concern in these years, but its political salience as a major source of partisan conflict came later. Sabbath observance was also an issue in the 1880s, although as with temperance, liturgical Protestants were less anxious about this than evangelicals. In NSW, the Lords' Day Observance Society failed to reverse liberalizing legislation that had allowed the Public Library, the Museum, and the Art Gallery to open on Sundays. But their counterparts in Victoria succeeded in warding off similar encroachments. By the beginning of the twentieth century, a visiting American evangelist thought that Sabbath desecration in Sydney was so shocking that it was worse than in Chicago, which, he said, was "the worst city in the world."[50]

Prior to the establishment of the labor party, education was the area in which the political salience of religious conflict was greatest. In the middle of the nineteenth century, there was a dual system of denominational and public (or "national") schools. High Church Anglicans were reluctant to abandon denominational schooling, but eventually, Catholics were left as the only staunch supporters of this system. Legislation to reform education was passed in two waves. The first, in the 1860s, limited the number of denominational schools and subordinated them to common state supervision and regulation.

The second wave, in the 1870s, provided for "free, compulsory, and secular" education, and abolished state aid to the denominational schools. The Victorian Act of 1872 was the earliest and most thoroughly secular, while the NSW Act was passed somewhat belatedly in 1880, and retained a component of "common Christianity" in the curriculum. Afterwards, discussion continued about how to interpret and implement the provisions in this legislation that allowed for religious education, and the Catholic church remained highly critical of public schools and continued to build its own parallel system. But overall, education faded as a political issue in the 1880s.[51]

The educational debates of the 1860s helped create a climate that enabled anti-Catholic organizations like the Protestant Political Association to flourish in the late 1860s and early 1870s. But the temperance and Sabbatarian issues that arose in the 1880s, did not spark renewed anti-Catholic organization in the years before the labor party was established. In 1894, Cardinal Moran himself noted the absence of an Australian version of the APA (O'Farrell, 1969b, 177). A sectarian undercurrent remained, however, and in the early years of the twentieth century there was another outbreak of anti-Catholic organization. The beginnings of this outbreak could be seen in the vociferous Protestant response to Moran's decision to stand for election to the Constitutional Convention in 1897. But the outbreak only reached its peak after the rapid growth of the Australian Protestant Defence Association. The Association was founded in NSW in 1902 by a militant Orangeman amidst the growth of politically assertive temperance agitation. Its aim was to oppose the election of Catholics and their sympathizers, and it played a significant role in mobilizing support for the Free Trade (or Liberal) party in the 1904 NSW elections. More importantly in the long-term, it led many middle-class Catholics to shift their support to the Labor party. These developments help to explain why Labor came to power in its own right in 1910, but they do not help explain why it had already managed to establish itself as a major contender for power. For it was precisely because Labor was now the main established opposition to the increasingly sectarian Free Trade party that middle-class Catholics began to vote for it.[52]

Throughout the second half of the nineteenth century, the political salience of religious conflict was substantially greater in the United States than Australia. By tracking the main issues that fed this conflict, we can see that this difference was further exacerbated in the five or six years immediately prior to the decision about whether or not to establish a labor party. In the United States during these years, the political salience of religion was at a peak. Issue piled upon issue. A great surge of temperance agitation (at the end of the 1880s) was compounded by ethno-religious conflicts over schooling (from 1888 to 1892), and both were in turn compounded by a massive outbreak of organized anti-Catholicism (in 1893 and 1894). In Australia, by contrast, the political salience of religious conflict was in a trough. Temperance and Sabbatarian issues were placed on the political agenda but remained secondary, the earlier political conflicts over education had quietened, and anti-Catholic organization was in abeyance. While American unions confronted the question of whether or not to establish a labor party amidst a great surge of religiously inspired political conflicts, Australian unions confronted this question during a period in which the political salience of religious conflict was even lower than normal.

THE EFFECT IN THE UNITED STATES

How did the greater political salience of religion in the United States affect the decisions of union leaders? The short answer is that it strengthened the fear of many union leaders that, if they adopted any kind of partisan political position, their organizations would be consumed by conflict between workers with opposing party loyalties. The political loyalties of the vast majority of workers, like those of most other citizens, were divided between the Democratic and Republican parties, and union leaders feared that their organizations would be treated as hostile either by members who were Democrats, or by members who were Republicans, or by both.

Repression had given union leaders an incentive to engage in partisan political action. But as we saw earlier, for the majority of union leaders in the AFL, while repression had threatened to disable their organizations, it had not threatened their ongoing existence. These leaders still had something to lose, and they were fearful of losing it.

This was not a new fear. In many unions, it was a long-established orthodoxy backed by constitutional provisions and by-laws that prohibited the union from taking stands on political issues, or endorsing candidates for public office (Shefter, 1986, 242). As the secretary of the bricklayers' union explained in 1872 (Montgomery, 1967, 195): "We have excellent trades' unionists, who are warm Democrats and zealous Republicans . . . and who are ready to point with suspicion to every movement on our part towards the formation of political organizations. . . . The only way we can be successful with our local and national trades unions is by excluding politics from them."

Year after year, Gompers issued similar warnings and urged that, before any involvement in partisan politics could be considered, it was first necessary "to wean our fellow-workers from their affiliation with the dominant political parties" (AFL, 1892, 13, and 1894, 14).[53] A number of his opponents recognized these dangers as well. The leader of the Knights of Labor, Terrence Powderly, consistently sought to ban electoral activity for fear it would exacerbate divisions within the Knights (Fink, 1983, 24 and 26), and John McBride, who defeated Gompers to become AFL President in 1895, seems to have had similar concerns.[54]

The threat that party loyalty posed to union organization was also repeatedly raised by the opponents of independent labor politics in the AFL's 1894 debate.[55] Gompers and his allies did not only fear that party loyalties would cause dissension if the unions entered partisan politics. They feared that this dissension could destroy the unions. They feared this because of the intensity of party loyalties, and the priority that workers gave to them.[56]

Union leaders recognized that the intensity and priority of party loyalty had a variety of sources.

Delegate Pomeroy (AFL, 1895a, 46) highlighted the connection between party loyalty and identities forged during the Civil War: "I want to get a carpenter to join the trades union movement. . . . This carpenter is a Grand Army man, and nearly all carpenters who are old enough are Grand Army men, and he is a Republican. He says, 'I am perfectly willing to join the trades union as such, but I will not join a political party in opposition to my ideas.' He is wrong perhaps; we may all agree that he is wrong, but we want him in the trades union, and you cannot get him in if he has to desert his party and adopt the policy of a new political party . . . advocating against everything for which he fought during the war. The Democrat is the same."

Delegate MacArthur emphasized the connection between party loyalty and national origins. This connection led him to dispute the relevance of the British experience of labor politics (AFL, 1895a, 6). "They are homogeneous and we are heterogeneous," he said, "and it makes all the difference." British unionists "can be got to hold together on political questions. But it is not so in America . . . we have all nationalities in our unions, men who stand together to a unit on wages and conditions . . . but if you mix politics, even a suspicion of them, the spectre of disintegration arises right there and stays there."

However union leaders recognized that the most important connection, and the one that threatened the greatest disruptive effect, was the connection between party loyalty and religious conflict. An editorial in the *Coast Seamen's Journal* summarized the majority position that emerged in the wake of the AFL's 1894 debate. The editor argued that there is an "element of [religious] prejudice which prevents unity of political action among members" and leads to "the most radically opposed views on political affairs." As a result "the trade-union which goes into politics destroys whatever efficiency it may have."[57]

This position recurs repeatedly in the writings, speeches, and resolutions of union leaders and activists. At times, the connection between party loyalty and religious conflict is set out explicitly. Often, however, the connection is implicit, and labor leaders simply reiterate their fear of both party and religious conflict in the same breath.

The AFL regularly highlighted the disruptive effects of religion and party politics. Its 1892 Official Yearbook urged unions "to restrict their efforts solely to industrial ends without doing aught to awaken either political or religious dissensions." This, it pointed out, had been the "traditional policy" of the AFL since its founding (AFL, 1892a). In 1893, the annual convention unanimously passed a resolution deploring "the introduction of any sectarian or captious side issues" and the "religious bigotry" and "rancorous intolerance" that they produced (AFL, 1893, 56). It reaffirmed the "cardinal principle" that neither religion, nor politics, nor various other factors should be allowed to divide the labor movement. The same resolution was passed again in 1894 (AFL, 1894, 25).

Gompers correspondence shows that he was constantly alive to the danger of religious disruption. "It is positively ridiculous and suicidal for us as wage-workers to allow matters of religion to interfere with the progress and success of our movement," he wrote to an AFL organizer in 1893.[58] In his more optimistic Marxian moments, Gompers argued that the salience of religious and political issues was fading as the consciousness of workers evolved in line with their industrial circumstances, and that "year by year the issue is more clearly seen to be purely an economic one" (AFL, 1891b, 69). This helps explain why, in the early 1890s, Gompers did occasionally foresee and endorse the emergence of a political labor movement, although the appropriate time for such a development was always way over the horizon of an ever-receding future.[59] When Gompers's allies returned him to the Presidency in 1895 and entrenched—or re-entrenched—his opposition to the establishment of a labor party as AFL orthodoxy, they continued to emphasize and link the dangers of political and ethno-religious sectarianism.[60]

Many of those who advocated the establishment of a labor party also feared these dangers and the connection between them. Though they did not draw the same conclusions as Gompers, their exhortations to workers to support an independent labor party often showed that they shared similar anxieties. "One thing is certain," wrote a columnist in the *Coming Nation*, "we have our heads stuffed with prejudice and political ignorance." "Rouse yourself," he wrote the next week, "do not be led around by crazy preachers, who are the tools of political schemers. . . . You have a government of your own—run it! Let us get together. Let no religious prejudice stand between us." A contributor to the *Railway Times* urged workers to look beyond traditional loyalties, but noted nevertheless that "the Republican Party has received the support of the Methodist Episcopal Church since 1860." And in a letter to the *American Federationist*, the secretary of the hotel workers union argued that capitalists believed "religious prejudices to be the strongest in the human breast" and aimed to undermine the labor movement by making religion "the great bone of contention." Though he was writing to support independent political action, he seemed far from confident that the capitalists were wrong.[61]

In 1894, both advocates and opponents of labor party politics were particularly fearful of religious conflicts because of the rise of the American Protective Association. The rise of the APA highlighted the connection between party loyalty and religious sectarianism because of the special emphasis it placed on the importance of excluding Catholics from public office. Those who joined swore a solemn oath that ended by repeating an undertaking to "endeavor at all time to place the political positions of this government in the hands of Protestants." Writing prior to the Pullman strike, Debs was deeply concerned about these developments. "Once light the fires of religious fanaticism," he warned, "and nothing short of a miracle can quench them." Even the SLP could agree that there is "nothing fraught with greater danger."[62]

For many leaders of the AFL, these recent developments merely reinforced longstanding anxieties about the disruptive effects of party loyalty. AFL leaders recognized that party loyalty had a variety of sources, but they found its connection with religious conflict especially troubling. August McCraith of the printers union concluded that "the average voter casting his ballot is not a free man, but a one idead, corked up zealot" who is obsessed with "the questions that were fought over in the days of [Queens] Mary and Elizabeth."[63] AFL leaders feared that if they formed a party and entered the electoral arena, they would import this sectarianism into their unions. A labor party would inevitably get drawn into conflicts with the two main existing parties, and because these parties were partly defined by their attitude to religious conflicts, the labor movement would also be seen as taking sides in these conflicts. AFL leaders feared that by forcing their members to choose between loyalty to their unions and partisan loyalties, they would effectively be forcing them to choose between union solidarity and loyalties rooted in conflicting religious commitments. They concluded that, in such a contest, God would prevail and the unions would be destroyed.

The Effect in Australia Compared

Australian union leaders also worried that partisan loyalties would produce dissension and disruption if their unions made a foray into party politics. In NSW, the TLC had been wooed by both the Free Trade and Protectionist parties, and although it had briefly flirted with the Protectionists in 1886, union leaders had come to fear the divisive effects of these preexisting "fiscal" loyalties (Nairn, 1967, 170–73, and 1989, 22 and 24–27).[64]

Indeed, TLC Secretary Houghton believed that this was the main reason why the "great bulk" of affiliates had not looked favorably on the original proposal (made before the Maritime strike) to establish a labor party. "Until the fiscal controversy is definitely resolved one way or the other," he reported, "it is extremely unlikely that the desire of the Council in this forward movement will be ratified" (TLC, 1890, 5). It was not just craft unionists who had these concerns. Even the secretary of the shearers' union, W. G. Spence, was wary of political action because it risked involving his union in conflicts between free traders and protectionists (Merritt, 1986, 180–81). Similar concerns influenced a TLC proposal for the publication of a weekly newspaper. The proposal stated that the paper would maintain "a neutral attitude upon [questions of free trade and protection] that if treated in a party spirit would almost certainly be productive of dissention in the ranks of the workers."[65]

The incentives generated by the defeat of the Maritime strike led most union leaders to look more favorably on the proposal to establish a labor party. But they remained fearful of "fiscal"-based party loyalties and were determined to "sink" all talk of free trade and protection (Nairn, 1989, 52). The TLC Parliamentary Committee responded to a letter "asking which of the rival policies Free Trade or Protection is most in accord with the labor interest" by ruling that the question was "out of order."[66] And P. J. Brennan, the prime mover behind the proposal to establish a labor party in NSW, told the Intercolonial Trades and Labor Union Congress (ICTUC, 1891, 93 and 99) that "if they once raised [the question of protection] at the next elections, the Labor party must fall to the ground."

Like their counterparts in the United States, Australian union leaders feared the disruptive effect of existing partisan loyalties, but the kind of disruption they feared was less threatening. Australian union leaders feared that disruption would doom independent labor politics to failure. But unlike their counterparts in the United States, they did not fear that it would lead to the destruction of union organizations themselves. In this respect, Brennan's comments earlier are typical. It is, he said, "the Labor party"—the party, not the unions—that might "fall to the ground." Thus, after the Maritime strike, union leaders responded to the incentives that repression generated by supporting the initiative to form a labor party. For political representation at least offered some hope that they might be able to contain future repression, and although their efforts might come to nothing if the disruption they feared did indeed break out, unlike their American counterparts, they did not fear that it could make matters worse.

In part, the disruptive potential of partisan loyalties was less threatening in Australia, simply because party identification was newer and less well established than in the United States. However, as we have seen, partisan loyalties were still sufficiently well established for many union leaders to fear their effects. And not without reason. The NSW Labor party went to the polls committed to "Sinking the Fiscal Question." But arguments between free traders and protectionists within the union movement had made it difficult to reach a consensus on a platform for the new Labor party, and some unionists felt that, "despite every effort" to sink it, the fiscal question seemed "only to bob up again corklike."[67] A few months after the election, events seemed to bear this out. Although conflict between free traders and protectionists had not stopped Labor candidates from being elected, it soon lead to splits within the parliamentary party.[68] These splits then made it impossible for Labor parliamentarians to act in a unified way, even when the core interests of the unions were threatened by government repression in the 1892 Broken Hill Miners' strike.

But the main reason for the differences in the kind of disruption that Australian and American union leaders feared were the different conflicts that underpinned partisan loyalties in each case. Australian labor leaders and their supporters were much less likely than their American counterparts to link their concerns about the disruptive effects of party loyalties to fears about religious conflict and sectarianism (and much more likely to link them to fears about tariff conflicts). In a poem, which was first published around 1895 and has been frequently reprinted ever since, Henry Lawson characterized the social egalitarianism of shearers as placing them beyond the reach of sectarian squabbles (Clark, 1955, 797):

> They tramp in mateship side by side –
> The Protestant and Roman –
> They call no biped lord or sir,
> And touch their hat to no man!

Indeed, one of the main historians of the early NSW Labor party goes so far as to claim that "there is no evidence to suggest that religion had played any part in the lively affairs of the Labor party in 1889–1894" (Nairn, 1989, 128). But both the poet and the historian exaggerate the point.

Labor leaders certainly were sensitive to the potential political salience of religious sensibilities. In the 1880s, some had complained that "creed and nationality" and "sectarian tricksters" had weakened unofficial attempts to run labor candidates.[69] In the early 1890s, they continued to be wary of these dangers. One new Labor MP, Arthur Rae of the shearers' union, explained that he "had never, during the late election or since, openly expressed himself on religious subjects . . . He always maintained that religion and politics were safer apart."[70] Another unionist, J. L. Fegan, a teetotaler from the miners union, attributed his failure to be selected as a labor candidate to "resurrectionist" and "beer" votes. Ultimately, however, he was both selected and elected.[71] The *Bulletin* also occasionally drew attention to attempts to rouse sectarian sentiments. Immediately before the 1891 election, it warned workers to beware of both "the Orange Pot and the Roman Kettle" least they be drawn into a "fight for the shadow."[72] Later that year, it denounced the attempt by an afternoon tabloid to link the political conflicts between the Free Trade and Protectionist parties to religious conflicts between Protestants and Catholics.[73]

Nevertheless, overall, labor leaders were relatively unconcerned about religious and sectarian conflict in the early 1890s. One indication of this can be found in the venues they used for both union and labor party meetings. These meetings took place not only in union offices, the Trades' Hall, and the Town Hall, but also in Protestant and Catholic halls, temperance halls, and hotels.[74] In addition, while most union leaders were Protestants, the TLC was represented at the 1891 Intercolonial Trades Union Congress by two Catholics.[75]

On the few occasions when pro-labor papers considered the relative importance of different issues, they tended to agree that religious conflicts played only a secondary role in generating the disruption caused by partisan loyalties. The *Australian Workman* portrayed the 1891 election campaign as a horse race in which "Sectarian Cry fell heavily on receiving a kick from Common Sense and, owing to injuries, had to be shot."[76] The paper agreed that "*if* Prohibition ever became a burning question in this country" it could cause the same kind of trouble as the conflict over tariffs, but it did not seem to think this was currently the case.[77] The *Bulletin* argued explicitly that, when voters went to the polls, religious conflicts over temperance and other wowser issues were subordinated to economic conflicts over class interests and tariff policy. Somewhat more hesitantly, it also argued that, between these two economic conflicts, it was class interests that predominated. Those who placed priority on religious conflicts were "scarcely to be found within the limits of the state." Rather, it was the "great issue between the haves and the have nots; and, again, in a less degree, between the rival fiscal factions" that were determinant. The conflict between Labor and Capitalism was predominant, but were it nonexistent, "the rival fiscal partisans would, swamping all minor issues, divide the country between them."[78]

The economic issues that underpinned conflict between the Free Trade and Protectionist parties in NSW had a very different disruptive potential to the ethno-religious issues that underpinned conflict between the Democratic and Republican parties. Conflicts over tariff questions might stymie cooperation between unions in different industries.[79] But they were unlikely to undermine the cohesiveness of individual unions themselves. Religious conflicts, however, tended to do just that, since most unions needed to maintain solidarity between members with different religious beliefs. Tariff conflicts were also less likely to produce the kind of all-or-nothing moral absolutism that was induced by religious crusades. Where conflicts were rooted in beliefs about God's will, bargaining and compromise often seemed inappropriate. Conflicts over tariffs, however, were more easily susceptible to negotiation. Legislative gains in other areas, like industrial regulation and collective bargaining, might legitimately be traded-off for losses on the question of tariffs. Unlike with the attempt to suppress the conflicts unleashed by neo-Puritan Protestants, the attempt to "sink the fiscal question," did not require a person to compromise their whole moral outlook.

Tariff policy was also an important partisan issue in the United States (Sundquist, 1983, 81, 104, 136, 159, and Brady, 1988, 54–55, 74, and 76–77). Indeed an analysis of electoral pronouncements by the two main parties shows that it was one of the publicly stated issues that most clearly distinguished Democrats from Republicans throughout the 1880s and 1890s (Gerring, 1997, 58, and 1998, 68–9). Although union leaders in the United States were much less likely to link their fears about the disruptive effects of party loyalty to conflicts about tariffs, they did sometimes worry about the disruption that would result if unions were forced to take sides over tariff policy.[80] But like their Australian counterparts, they did not see *this* kind of disruption as leading to

the destruction of union organization itself. It was the intensity of party identification and related religious conflicts that threatened to do that.

Conclusion

Were union leaders right to fear that the Democratic and Republican loyalties
of ordinary workers (and the religious conflicts that played into these loyalties)
had the capacity to unleash dissension that would destroy the unions? Were
their fears well-founded? Nationally, the opposition of Gompers and his allies
meant that the claims underpinning these fears were not really put to the test.
In principle, local and state-based attempts to run labor or labor-populist candidates in Illinois and elsewhere could help answer these questions. In fact,
however, the scarcity of religious data makes this very difficult. Jensen (1971,
85–88) and Kleppner (1979) extrapolate from a unique Iowa census in 1895
that did ask about religious affiliation. But in addition to the obvious difficulty
of relying on data from one Midwestern state in order to reach conclusions
about another, there is the problem of what to do about the 27 percent of respondents who did not give or did not have a denominational affiliation.[81]

There is some evidence that partisan and religious dissension contributed
to the collapse of the labor parties that emerged in 1877 and 1886.[82] In addition, in 1894, although the Illinois labor-populists sought and won support
from both liturgical and pietistic religious communities, they were unable to
completely disentangle themselves from religious conflict. In Chicago, support came disproportionately from Catholics and other liturgicals who were
disgruntled with the Democrats but felt unable to switch directly to the
Republicans (Kleppner, 1970, 216–18, and Tarr, 1971, 40–41). But in major
coal mining areas, Catholics were among the least likely to offer it their
support (Jensen, 1971, 245 and 257–59). In these areas, the People's party
often acquired a pietistic and nativist tone, so that even in mining towns that
had experienced severe industrial conflict and repression, workers remained
politically divided and labor-populists were only just able to win half of the
vote.[83] However it is difficult to determine whether these party experiments
undermined union organization itself. There were undoubtedly some sharp
declines in membership around this time, but the deep economic downturn,
along with industrial defeat and its attendant repression, provide the obvious
primary explanations for this.[84]

There was, however, one kind of political activity that clearly did undermine some union organizations: the sectarian activities of the American Protective Association and similar nativist organizations. At the heart of these
activities was the attempt to exclude Catholics from public office, and conflicts within unions between APA sympathizers and opponents did indeed
lead to the collapse of some local organizations, and seriously weakened a

number of others. Moreover, the APA had the greatest effect in just those unions and in just those states that were most likely to have provided a launching pad for independent labor politics. Centers of strength for the APA could be found among steel workers, coal miners, and railroad workers in Pennsylvania, Illinois, and throughout the Midwest (Kinzer, 1964, 101, 118, 129–31, and 178–79, and Higham, 1992, 57, and 82).[85]

The response to Debs's carefully argued "Americanist" attack on the APA in the *Locomotive Firemen's Magazine* gives some idea of just how prevalent and disruptive sectarian attitudes were within sections of the union movement. The magazine was "deluged with communications," and in reply to this volley of criticism, innuendo, and threat, Debs was forced to adopt a somewhat more defensive tone. While sticking to his basic position, he felt it necessary to state, in a phrase familiar from a later period, that he was not and never had been a Catholic.[86] Debs pointed out that the resurgence of sectarianism was directly undermining unions themselves, and that he personally knew of "scores of lodges, unions and divisions that have perished all but in name."[87] These effects would probably have been felt irrespective of union involvement in independent labor politics, though labor party experiments may have exacerbated them. But they did provide clear evidence of what could happen to unions if the political salience of religious conflict were allowed to infect them.

So there is some evidence—though it is by no means overwhelming—that the strength of party loyalty and its relationship to religious conflict did indeed did pose a danger to unions that entered the electoral arena. But with hindsight we can also see that the AFL's 1894 debate took place during a period when party loyalties were loosening. Though the upsurge in the political salience of religion in the previous five or six years made it hard to see at the time, there were underlying trends that were weakening the foundations on which party loyalty had been built.

Firstly, evangelical Protestantism was facing both an intellectual and a demographic challenge. The intellectual challenge stemmed from the impact of Darwinian theories of evolution, and of new biblical scholarship based on archeological research and "higher criticism." Both were undermining the central evangelical tenant of the inerrancy of the Bible (Marsden, 1991, 3, 16, and 32–39, Ahlstrom, 1972, 764–74, and Handy, 1976, 287–92). The demographic challenge stemmed from the ongoing impact of immigration, which was slowly altering the balance between pietists and liturgicals (Kleppner, 1979, 198–207). These developments were gradually weakening the capacity of evangelical Protestants to set the terms on which electoral competition would take place. Evangelicals succeeded in forcing many states to hold prohibition referenda, but they were rarely able to win them. Outcomes like these, as well as the growth of Democratic party electoral success from 1888 to 1892, made professional Republican politicians increasingly wary of allowing their party to be used as a vehicle for evangelical religious crusades.

Secondly, the lived memory of the Civil War was fading. This was both be-cause the generation that had personally experienced the war was gradually being replaced by a younger generation in the voting population, and because immigration was constantly increasing the proportion of the population that had not experienced the conflict at all—not even vicariously, through the ex-perience of their parents and grandparents. The decade 1885–1895 bore the same relationship to the Civil War that the decade 1965–1975 did to the Sec-ond World War. Both were periods in which generational change weakened the preexisting bases of party identification.

The deep depression and the intense industrial conflict that struck in the early 1890s further weakened traditional party loyalties and provided an oppor-tunity to test whether it might now be possible to pursue an electoral strategy that straddled ethno-religious conflicts and emphasized economic interests in-stead. As the secretary of the steel workers' union noted, "the political parties are losing their grip on labor."[88] However, it was not the AFL but William McKinley and the Republicans who developed such a strategy and put it to the test (Kleppner, 1970, 374, Jensen, 1971, 283–308, and McSeveney, 1972). McKinley's strategy was to emphasize his commitment to the return of prosper-ity and the "full dinner pale."[89] He proposed to achieve this by increasing tariffs (which he said would protect jobs and wages), and by defending "sound money" and rejecting the free coinage of silver (which he said would result in a "53-cent dollar"). The outcome was the realignment of 1894 and 1896, a key aspect of which was a sharp increase in support for the Republicans among urban workers in the industrial regions of the Northeast and Midwest (Sundquist, 1983, 162–65, and Brady, 1988, 65–69). The swing to the Republicans occurred among all ethno-religious groups. Indeed, when the realignment began during the midterm elections of 1894, the biggest swings in the Midwest occurred among Catholics (Jensen, 1971, 229). McKinley's strategy was not class-based. But it did show that the ethno-religious bases of partisan loyalty were not an in-surmountable problem, and that many workers were prepared to think about politics in a new way that gave greater weight to economic interests. McKinley took the risk that the AFL was not prepared to take, and succeeded.

So, perhaps the fears of Gompers and other AFL leaders were misplaced. Some union leaders were certainly aware that voters were increasingly in "a plastic state of mind."[90] However, given the longstanding existence of intense partisan loyalties partly based on ethno-religious conflicts, and the sharp up-surge in the political salience of these conflicts in the years immediately prior to 1894, it is easy to understand why so many of them continued to have these fears. In a sense, this is all that matters. For whether the fears that motivated Gompers and his allies were well-founded is not my principle concern. In order to explain their decision not to establish a labor party, I simply need to establish that these *were* their fears, and that, well-founded or not, they were enough to counterbalance the incentives they had to engage in partisan politics.[91]

CHAPTER 8

Socialism

As we have seen, labor leaders feared the dissension that could result from ethno-religious sectarianism among ordinary workers. But it is impossible not to notice that many also feared another source of dissension: dissension among themselves. Among their fellow activists and leaders they feared, not religious sectarianism, but the secular sectarianism that resulted from factional conflict between left-wing groups. The ideological loyalties of union activists and leaders were divided among various schools of reform thought. There were socialists, anarchists, populists, single-tax followers of Henry George, "nationalist" followers of Edward Bellamy, cooperative colonists, Knights of Labor, and "pure and simple" unionists. Tensions between some of these groups were ever present, and opponents of partisan politics argued that the establishment of a labor party would simply produce a destructive outbreak of faction-fighting, as each struggled to gain control of the party. Indeed, more than this, they feared that this faction fighting would lead to the disruption and dissolution of the unions themselves.

Labor leaders who opposed the establishment of a labor party placed great emphasis on these fears. "Most of us are 'ismites,'" wrote AFL Secretary McCraith in a report to fellow delegates. But, he said, we must not "commit suicide in the attempt" to "get to Heaven." "Experience has demonstrated that in accordance as unionists have gone into politics, they have gone out of labor." A number of union papers made similar arguments. The editors of the *Coast Seamen's Journal* repeatedly warned that if the unions became involved in partisan politics, "the gladiators of the different reform factions" would unleash chaos in the name of a host of "conflicting isms." They reached for one metaphor after another as they tried to capture the extent of their anxiety. Involvement in party politics would be like entering "a hornets' nest." It would draw the unions into "a whirlpool of patented plans." It "would be suicide." The trade union movement was a mighty force, they argued, but it was not strong enough to survive the competing attentions of "fads and faddists" and "irrational enthusiasts with sure-thing reforms." An article in the *American Federationist* by Secretary Foster of the Massachusetts State Federation of Labor warned that the unions would find themselves in a situation like that of the Jews in ancient times. "Whilst the battering rams of the Romans were beating down their walls . . . that great people were engaged in intestine commotions, some advocating the claims of one and some of another to the high priesthood of the nation, and instead of the Romans devouring them, they devoured each other."[1]

A number of students of the American labor movement have suggested that left-wing factionalism helps explain the failure to establish a labor party in the United States.[2] Some have also suggested that, compared with their European counterparts, American labor activists were particularly prone to ideological rigidity and the disruptive factionalism that resulted.[3]

In this chapter, I will first consider whether the left-wing reform ideologies that were present in the United States were different from those in Australia. Then, I will consider how disruptive left-wing factionalism was when labor parties were established. Finally, I will examine, in more detail, the impact of socialist sectarianism, and the specific form that it took.

LEFT-WING REFORM IDEOLOGIES

At first glance, the Australian case seems to support the contention that left-wing factionalism might help explain the failure to establish a labor party in the United States. Drawn by its emerging reputation as a laboratory for social reform, a number of European and American social scientists visited Australasia around the turn of the century and wrote systematic studies based on their findings. These studies typically identified a paradox: that practical social reform was flourishing, even though ideologies of social reform had little influence. The classic statement of this position was set down by Albert Metin, who was commissioned by the Labor Bureau of the French Ministry of Commerce to write a report on his six-month study-tour of Australia and New Zealand in 1899. According to Metin, Australasia "has gone further than any other land whatever along the road of social experiment," and yet "the poverty of theoretical notions is astonishing to anyone accustomed to European polemics."[4] When he republished his report as a book in 1901, Metin gave it a new title that summarized his findings: *Le Socialisme sans Doctrines*, or "Socialism without Doctrine." Americans like Henry Demarest Lloyd and Victor S. Clark reached similar conclusions after their own study-tours. Lloyd (1902, 8, 376) noted that social advance in Australasia "is not the fruit of colonization by religious enthusiasts, or social reformers, or patriots choosing exile," and "one hears little sectarian socialism talked." Clark (1906, 118) observed that "Australian labor leaders know little or nothing of Marxian theories. Few of them know even by title the principle text-books of Continental socialism."

Observations like these suggest that the Australian labor movement was relatively untouched by left-wing reform ideologies. But such a conclusion would be quite misleading. For the Australian labor movement was in fact influenced by a wide range of left-wing reform ideologies in the late 1880s and early 1890s. Evidence for this can be found in: the prominence given to various authors and ideas in the pro-labor press; the reading recommended by unions and their journals; the recollections of labor leaders themselves; and the conclusions of contemporary observers outside the labor movement.

An examination of these sources suggests a striking conclusion. Not only were many left-wing reform ideologies influential, but those with the most powerful influence came from the United States. In particular, the works of three American authors were at the height of their influence in Australia in the years immediately before and after the establishment of the labor party. These authors were Edward Bellamy, Henry George, and Laurence Gronlund. Indeed, "between 1887 and 1894, the works of these three Americans were certainly more widely known and more influential amongst Australian workers than the writings of any English or Continental socialist."[5] Labor papers frequently reprinted their writings and debated their ideas. They also recommended their major works, and distributed cheap copies to union members and other readers. Six of the nine books recommended and sold by the *Hummer* were by Americans, as were three of the four sold by the Queensland *Worker*.[6]

Edward Bellamy's novel *Looking Backward* (first published in 1888) presented a utopian vision of a socialist future. Bellamy (1938, 71) consciously sought to present a version of socialism—which he called nationalism—that was "the legitimate heir to the traditions and spirit of 1776." He saw his socialism as the fulfillment of American morality, and the democratic, egalitarian, and individualist values of American political culture (Bowman, 1958, 116, 153–91). In the United States *Looking Backward* sold 400,000 copies within a decade and spawned a network of reform clubs that began to channel their efforts into the People's party (Bowman, 1958, 115–38).

Of all the American authors, Bellamy's influence on the Australian labor movement was probably the greatest.[7] The *Bulletin* endorsed *Looking Backward* (Gollan, 1962, 126). The shearers' union "repurchased many hundred copies . . . and sent these out amongst the members" (Spence, 1909, 253). The Queensland *Worker* serialized the book in successive issues between March and December 1890. And its influential editor, William Lane, promoted it heavily throughout Australia, and wrote his own fictionalized account of socialism in Australia shortly afterwards (Lane, 1892, and Wilding, 1980, 36–40). Both labor leaders and observers outside the movement, agreed on Bellamy's impact. According to the prominent TLC delegate and Labor MP, J. D. Fitzgerald (1915, 17), "Bellamy's book was a revelation to the working classes . . . and few . . . who claim to be readers at all, have failed to read it." According to the NSW Government Statistician, T. A. Coghlan (1918, 4:1836), "the book had a prodigious circulation throughout Australia . . . wherever a few workers were gathered together, there Bellamy was discussed and approved." He attributed this success to Bellamy's "combination of socialism and individual liberty."[8] Contemporaries testified that tens of thousands, or even hundreds of thousands read the book. Indeed, according to the *Hummer*, "nearly everyone" had read it.[9]

Henry George's *Progress and Poverty* (first published in 1879) offered a searing indictment of contemporary social conditions. George attributed these conditions to the ability of private landowners to continually gain from an "unearned increment" in the value of land. His solution was to force privately held land back into the public domain by replacing all government imposts with a "single tax" on land that was equal to its rental value. In the United States, *Poverty and Progress* was widely read and respected, and it too spawned a network of clubs, and led to George's 1886 mayoral campaign.

George's writings also had a major impact in Australia.[10] His influence began to grow in the second half of the 1880s, building on preexisting support for progressive land taxation and land nationalization leagues. Again, labor leaders like Fitzgerald (1915, 16–17) and observers like Coghlan (1918, 1836 and 1840–41) agreed that George's books achieved a very wide circulation and earned him much influence and respect.[11] This influence reached its peak shortly before the Maritime strike when George himself visited Australia for three months and delivered dozens of lectures. The trip gave rise to a large network of Single Tax Leagues in both urban and rural areas which became closely involved with the establishment of the labor party.

Laurence Gronlund's *Co-operative Commonwealth* (first published in 1884) was, like *Looking Backward*, an attempt to present socialist ideas in a digestible American idiom. Indeed, it explicitly sought to present modern German socialism "in readable English, and applied to American phenomena and American conditions" (Gronlund, 1884, 10). Its reach was never as great as that of Bellamy's novel, but no other analytical work on socialism had as large an audience. For most English-speaking socialist sympathizers in the United States, it provided a basic account of their beliefs: to such an extent that they frequently referred to their goal as the establishment of a "co-operative commonwealth."

The *Co-operative Commonwealth* played a similar role for Australian socialists (Markey, 1988, 243, Churchward, 1952, 258, and O'Farrell, 1958, 157). In the wake of the Maritime strike, one commentator noted that Gronlund "has recently been talking state-co-operation to hard-headed thinkers at a rate that few would imagine. You cannot buy a copy of his book in Melbourne or Sydney today. The book sellers have sold 'clean out.'"[12] When W. G. Higgs, an influential TLC delegate and prominent Sydney socialist, was asked by the NSW Royal Commission on Strikes (1891, 362) to recommend a writer who offers an exposition of socialism, the first book on his list was Gronlund's *Co-operative Commonwealth*.[13] This influence was reflected in the *Australian Workman*, the TLC's official paper, which Higgs edited in the early 1890s.[14]

Other American reform ideologies also had an influence on the Australian labor movement. Populist currents, which focused on banking and plutocratic conspiracies, and the virtues of agrarian smallholding, were influential (Gollan, 1965, 15–21, and Love, 1984, 9–40). One manifestation of this was the popularity of Ignatius Donnelly's *Caesar's Column* (first published in 1890). Donnelly's book was an anti-utopian, not to mention anti-Semitic, novel about the brutalized nightmarish world that would result if current trends were left unchecked. Donnelly was a key figure in the People's party. He was largely responsible for the 1892 preamble to the party's platform, which made a direct appeal for a labor populist alliance (Ridge, 1962, 295–96, and Foner, 1955, 301). The Australian labor press assumed that readers were familiar with *Caesar's Column*, and in 1894 a socialist activist published a short Australian reworking of the novel.[15]

The Knights of Labor were another source of influence. The activities of the Knights were followed with interest in the late 1880s and excerpts from their journals were sometimes reprinted.[16] The Knights sent an organizer to Australia in 1888, and although the branches that were established did not flourish, a parade of prominent labor leaders passed briefly through the organization at the beginning of the 1890s.[17]

Direct personal experience provided a further conduit for American labor reform ideologies. Some, like the prominent socialists S. A. Rosa and W. D. Flynn, had participated in the American labor movement in the 1880s (Burgmann, 1985, 110, Docker, 1982, 82, Bongiorno, 1996, 139, and Scates, 1997, 73). English-born William Lane had spent almost a decade in the United States and had become radicalized there before emigrating to Australia in 1885 (Wilding, 1980, 9–10 and 24–26). By the early 1890s, he was arguably the leading labor ideologue in Australia (Gollan, 1960, 123–24, 173, and 1962, 129 and 133, and Scates, 1997, 179).

Of course American reform ideologies were not the only ones to make an impact in Australia. British, German, and other continental European ideologies also had an influence. And some currents—like the widespread support for cooperative colonies—were the result of a combination of influences (Scates, 1997, 117–35, and Salvatori, 1982, 162–67).

Developments in Britain provided an obvious reference point for the Australian labor movement. The New Liberalism, the new unionism of John Burns and other leaders of the London Dock strike, the Fabians, H. M. Hyndman of the Social Democratic Federation, and William Morris of the Socialist League were all cited as influences by some activists and leaders.[18] But British developments also had a powerful impact on the labor movement in the United States. Indeed leftist writers in both countries were sometimes part of a common transatlantic debate.[19] Many American labor journals followed developments in Britain closely. Some, like the *National Labor Tribune* and the *United Mine Workers' Journal* followed them in minute detail, reporting on the activities of British unions in the steel and coal industries on a district-by-district basis.

Arguments about British developments were central to the AFL's 1894 debate. Leading advocates of independent labor politics, like T. J. Morgan, argued that their strategy embodied the lessons of the "new unionism" that John Burns and his colleagues had pursued on the London docks. Leading opponents, like Gompers and Strasser, argued that it was their strategy of using high fees and benefits to build powerful stable craft unions that embodied the lessons of British experience. Indeed, an extraordinary amount of time was spent arguing about what was actually happening in Britain. The Political Programme explicitly invoked British developments and called on American workers to follow suit, while its opponents accused it of misrepresenting developments in Britain.[20] In Australia, by contrast, arguments for the establishment of a labor party were couched in terms of domestic imperatives.[21] So it would be hard to conclude that British influence was greater in Australia in the early 1890s. If anything—at least in the debate about the establishment of a labor party—it may have been greater in the United States.

Continental European ideologies also had some influence in Australia. Anarchism had a small presence in Sydney and Melbourne. The influence of anarchism had waned in the United States by the early 1890s, but the prominent role that anarchists had earlier played in Chicago, and the ongoing influence within the AFL of union leaders with roots in the anarchist movement, had no parallel in Australia.[22]

A more important source of European influence in Australia was German socialism. Lane's choice of a German character, Geisner, as the "teacher" who educates the protagonists in his novel about socialism, is indicative of these influences (Lane, 1892, 105). Germany was seen as the home of the most advanced socialist thinking, and Bismarck's social policy was thought to foreshadow the potential for state socialism.[23] Some labor candidates even appealed directly to these policies in their electoral propaganda. J. D. Fitzgerald called for an extension of state-provided social insurance with the slogan "What Germans can do, surely Australians can do also!"[24] Socialist electoral success in Germany was also followed with interest (Harris, 1966, 16). Fitzgerald, whom the NSW TLC sent to London during the Maritime strike, also visited Germany and the Netherlands, and initiated an exchange of correspondence between Wilhelm Liebknecht of the German Social Democratic party and the TLC.[25]

Marxist ideas had some influence. Marx himself was typically acknowledged as the leading socialist thinker, and there were brief allusions to him in the labor press.[26] However, prior to the establishment of the labor party, most labor leaders had little or no acquaintance with Marx's writings. A contemporary observer (Pember Reeves, 1902, 68) noted that "here and there might be found some student who knew of Lassalle, or . . . had scrapped acquaintance with Karl Marx." But even well-read leaders like William Lane had probably not read Marx at this time. Indeed, it is not until a year or two later that there is evidence of engagement with Marx's writings. In 1892, the *Australian Workman* recommended a recently published synopsis of *Capital* by Edward Aveling. In 1893, the *Communist Manifesto* was first published in Australia (as an abridged serial) by the Queensland *Worker*. Its editor announced that he had "procured one of the very few copies in Australia." And later that year, the Australian Socialist League arranged the first extensive public exposition of *Capital* in a series of well-attended Sunday lectures by William Holman. However, even among socialist militants, the influence of Marxism remained small. One socialist recalled a discussion with a fellow militant in 1894: "We were discussing *Capital*, not that either of us knew much about the famous work. . . . He had investigated the cover. I had probed further, just turned it over. 'To study Marx,' said he, 'one requires a hard seat, a bare table and a head swathed in wet ice-cold towels.' I agreed with him."[27]

German socialism had a far more significant influence in the United States. Most socialist party members were German-speaking immigrants (Hillquit, 1903, 213–14, Kipnis, 1952, 19, Foner, 1955, 42–44, 46, and Hirsch, 1990, 144–45). Supporters were regularly involved in raising funds for German election campaigns, and socialist papers followed the fortunes of the Social Democratic party in great detail (Hoerder and Keil, 1988, 144–50). An abridged English edition of *Capital* was published in the United States in 1877 (Foner, 1955, 367). And Liebknecht and the Avelings—both Eleanor, who was Marx's daughter, and her husband Edward—went on a speaking tour of the United States in 1886, following an earlier successful tour by two leading German Social Democrats (Hillquit, 1903, 229 and 253).

Both Marx and Lassalle had supporters in the United States, and Marx, in particular, had a profound influence on both socialist party activists, and some important union leaders. In 1872, Marx had moved the headquarters of the International Workingmen's Association—the First International—from London to New York, and the debates that took place under its auspices played a formative role for a small but strategically located group of American labor leaders. A leading member of the International, Ferdinand Laurrell, had personally translated the *Communist Manifesto* for Gompers around 1873 (Kaufman, 1986, 21), and Gompers (1925, 75) then taught himself German so he could study "all the German economic literature that [he] could lay [his] hands on—Marx, Engels, Lassalle, and the others." Gompers (1925, 70) later recalled that his conversations with Laurrell "did more to shape my mind upon the labor movement than any other single influence" and "remained the basis on which my policies and methods were determined in the years to come." But the influence of Marxist ideas on Gompers was not unique. A number of the leaders who were instrumental in establishing the AFL developed their basic ideas about the labor movement as a result of similar influences.[28]

What most struck the European and American social scientists who visited Australia around the turn of the century was the relatively minor influence of

Marxism. Metin, Lloyd, and Clark all placed special emphasis on this observation, and local contemporaries, like Reeves and Coghlan, concurred with them.[29] In this respect, the visitors were undoubtedly correct. But it would be wrong to extrapolate from this to the conclusion that Australia was a land free of left-wing ideology. For in the early 1890s, all the main labor reform ideologies that were present in the United States were also present in Australia. There, too, there were socialists, anarchists, populists, single taxers, Bellamyite "nationalists," cooperative colonists, and Knights of Labor, as well as those who simply advocated trade unionism.[30] What differed was the proportionate influence that each had in the overall mix of reform ideologies in each country, and in some cases, the version that was dominant. British influences weighed heavily in both cases. One might expect British influences to have been more significant in Australia. But in fact, in the early 1890s, they were at least as significant in the United States. The weight of German and other continental European influences, however, was certainly greater in the United States, and this had a paradoxical consequence. American-grown ideological influences were a powerful presence in both countries. But because they faced stronger competition in the United States from European influences, and especially from Marxism, they were actually proportionately less influential there among top labor leaders than they were in Australia. In a sense, then, Australian leftism was more American than American leftism itself.

LABOR PARTIES AND LEFT-WING FACTIONALISM

There was no doubt in either country that single-minded proponents of the various reform ideologies had the potential to generate disruption. Printed under the heading "Cranks and Their Creeds," a letter in the *Australian Workman* characterized the proponents of reform ideologies as having "an incapacity to recognize the virtues of any other emancipatory scheme," and described the dangers of being drawn into the "vortices of enthusiasm" that they created. An editorial, "On Reformers," in an American union journal offered a similar, if more vivid, characterization. One minute, it said, the reformer is expounding on a future state of "angelic bliss," the next minute he "waxes wrath, throws his arms heavenward, rumples his hair, and denounces such and such another reformer in the language of the slums." Both journals simultaneously recognized the virtues of reformers and enthusiasts, but they feared their intolerance, and their inability to work together.[31]

However, the argument made by Gompers and his colleagues, was not merely that sectarian attitudes existed, but rather that the establishment of a labor party would lead to a great upsurge in factionalism that would destroy the unions themselves. So, how disruptive was left-wing factionalism when labor parties were established?

Figure 8.1. Let Them Fight It Out—The Labor Convention in Syracuse
Source: New York Daily Graphic, 17 August 1887 (Samuel Gompers Papers)

The campaign to elect Henry George as mayor of New York was the most prominent of all the United Labor party campaigns in 1886. Initially, factional squabbles were kept to a minimum. But when an effort was made to establish a more permanent party organization in order to build on George's strong showing, a bitter struggle over the platform immediately broke out between single taxers and socialists. Contemporaries portrayed them as fighting each other like Kilkenny cats (see Figure 8.1). George moved to turn the party into a one-issue single-tax organization, and the socialists, who had been instrumental in establishing it, were expelled. In response, they set up a second "Progressive" labor party. Neither party flourished at the polls, and within a year both had collapsed.[32]

Similar problems broke out in many other cities and states. The establishment of a United Labor party was typically accompanied by intense factional struggles between proponents of different labor reform ideologies: struggles that then contributed to the party's failure and collapse.[33] In Chicago, a promising beginning was soon overwhelmed by these conflicts. There, conflicts involving single taxers were less important than the repudiation of the party by Terrence Powderly, the national leader of the Knights of Labor. Attempts by Democrats to use the party for their own ends also contributed to its collapse. In the end, no less than three separate labor parties were formed to compete for the support of Chicago's workers.[34]

The same pattern seemed to be repeating itself in 1894. Severe factional conflict accompanied the effort to build a labor-populist party in Illinois. Attempts to apportion delegates, to settle on a platform, and to nominate candidates, all repeatedly degenerated into "extreme bitterness" (Destler, 1946, 172) and an "indescribable state of turmoil" (Staley, 1930, 117). A last-minute intervention by Henry Demarest Lloyd produced a compromise on the platform that kept the socialists onboard. But the compromise passed by the narrowest of margins—51 votes to 50—and it did not really settle the matter. Encouraged by Henry George, single taxers repudiated the effort to build a party. In addition, Chicago Democrats who felt threatened by independent labor politics sought to capture the nascent organization for themselves. With the help of William Pomeroy and his "labor skates," they sought to take it over by storming the hall where a nominating convention was taking place, and when this failed, they tried to establish a separate party. At the Illinois State Federation of Labor convention, the single taxers joined with Pomeroy's faction to vote down the socialist "plank 10" of the AFL's proposed Political Programme, and replace it with a commitment to the single tax. Pomeroy's delegates then paraded around chanting (Staley, 1930, 124):

> We are the people—we are the men,
> We are the people who killed plank 10.
> They were easy—just like wax;
> We knocked them out with the Single Tax.

Constant inner-party turmoil contributed to poorer than expected electoral results and helped lead to the rapid disintegration of the labor-populist alliance.[35]

The establishment of the labor party in NSW was also accompanied by disruptive factionalism between socialists, single taxers, and others. The TLC had tended to be wary of these groups. Even at the height of the enthusiasm for Henry George, during his visit to Australia, it decided to keep its distance, and resolved to take no official part in the welcome planned for George, nor to attend a banquet in his honor.[36] However, the need to settle on a platform for the new party brought conflict between different reform ideologies to the fore. The focal point for this conflict was plank 13 of the proposed platform. This plank reflected the influence on the drafting committee of Frank Cotton, a representative of the shearers' union and a leading single taxer. Debate over the plank was heated, and a special extra meeting had to be called to resolve the issue. Eventually, with different delegates interpreting the meaning of the plank in different ways, it was incorporated into the platform by a vote of 29 to 18.[37] Labor leaders were certainly aware that ructions between single taxers and others had led to the collapse of the ULP experiments in the United States. Indeed, a number of them drew attention to it explicitly, and some cautioned their colleagues about Henry George's ambiguous attitude to trade unionism.[38] Nevertheless, in the wake of the party's success in the 1891 election, factional conflict became more acute, both inside and outside the parliamentary party.

Unable to win the new party as a whole to their side, first the Protectionists and then the Free Traders sought to split it. In this, they were successful. The number of Labor MPs who stood by the majority decision of their parliamentary caucus fell rapidly from 35 in July 1891, to 27 in September, and then to just 17 in December (Loveday, 1975, 27–29). But these splits were not only the result of residual free trade and protectionist sympathies. They were also the product of a struggle between single taxers and socialists within the party.[39] Henry George's free trade commitments made the single taxers natural allies of the Free Trade party, while the socialists tended to align themselves with the Protectionists.[40] The overlapping influence of these commitments is apparent in some of the anguished parliamentary speeches that Labor MPs made, one by one, as they tried to explain and justify their decisive split in December 1891 (Picard, 1953, 56–60).

Extra-parliamentary efforts to address these splits, and to impose tighter discipline on Labor MPs, imported a series of conflicts into both the unions and the Labor Electoral Leagues (LELs). Tension within the unions was reflected in the labor press. When the *Hummer*, which was generally sympathetic to the single-tax movement, printed correspondence between its editor (the Wagga shearers' leader, W. W. Head) and Henry George, it sparked months of debate.[41] The greatest factional struggles, however, took place in the LELs. Though only a handful of single taxers and socialists became MPs in 1891 (Loveday, 1975, 25, and Markey, 1988, 242 and 299), their numbers in the extra-parliamentary party were much larger. The single taxers reached the peak of their influence at the first annual conference in January 1892.[42] But in the ongoing struggle to impose discipline on current and potential future MPs in 1893 and 1894, they lost their influence to an alliance of socialists and trade unionists. Socialist influence reached a peak in 1896 and 1897. But thereafter, those who wanted to commit the party to a more explicitly socialist objective, were marginalized by an alliance of unions—notably the shearers' union—and moderate socialists.

So labor party experiments did generate left-wing factionalism, but the principle disruption this caused was to the parties themselves. Before an election, the problems were similar in each case: notably the need to agree on a platform and choose candidates. But the level of factional conflict was greater in the United States. In NSW in 1891, arguments over the platform led to an extra evening of debate. In Illinois in 1894, these arguments led to threatened walkouts, attempts to storm the hall, and the establishment of a rival party list. After the elections, the U.S. and Australian parties faced somewhat different problems. In the United States, in the wake of electoral failure, left-wing factionalism contributed to the collapse of the newly formed party organizations. In Australia, in the wake of electoral success, it contributed to limited effectiveness and parliamentary splits. In both countries, however, left-wing factionalism became more acute. In each case, the single taxers and the socialists were major contributors to this factionalism. But it was also exacerbated by the efforts of established politicians to manipulate the new parties for their own purposes.

The impact of this factionalism on union organizations is less easy to establish. As we have already noted, declining union membership in the mid 1890s was primarily a product of recession and repression. Nevertheless, left-wing factionalism did cause some additional disruption in unions and union federations. In 1895, a number of unions left the Chicago Trades and Labor Assembly and formed the Chicago Trades and Labor Congress (Bogart and Thompson, 1920, 165–67, and Destler, 1946, 235). However the causes of this split were complex. The new Congress involved many conservative union leaders who were primarily concerned with taking a stand against the corrupt leadership of William Pomeroy. Moreover, for the socialists involved, it was not the establishment of a labor-populist party in Illinois that motivated them to split from the older Assembly, but rather the AFL's rejection of this course of action at the 1894 convention, and Pomeroy's role in making this decision. In Australia, fear of growing factionalism led some union leaders to argue in early 1892 that the TLC should sever its ties with the party it founded. The TLC vice-president, J. C. Watson, who later became the first Labor Prime Minister of Australia, argued that this was necessary in order to avoid infecting the TLC itself with these factional disputes. But the council eventually decided to remain on the party's central executive committee and try to reunify it (Loveday, 1975, 30–31, and Scates, 1997, 92–93).

So the left-wing factionalism generated by labor-party experiments certainly helped undermine attempts to establish these parties in the United States. It also spilled over into the unions, and may sometimes have weakened them or led to the establishment of rival federations. But the level of disruption that this caused within the unions is not sufficient to explain the fears of destruction—of consequences "too portentous for contemplation" (AFL, 1894, 14)—that were repeatedly voiced by Gompers and his allies. To explain this, we need to take a closer look at the relationship between these union leaders and one particular faction: the socialists.

SOCIALISTS AND UNIONISTS IN THE UNITED STATES

In order to understand why Gompers and his allies feared that left-wing factionalism threatened to destroy the unions, we need to understand the "either-or" mentality that informed the 1894 debate. According to this mentality, union-based and party-based strategies were mutually exclusive, although protagonists did not always pose their positions in quite such stark terms. Gompers, for example, still spoke in the late 1880s and early 1890s as though a union-based strategy might lay the ground for the eventual pursuit of independent labor politics (Kaufman, 1987, 161). He was also prepared to acknowledge that in Britain an independent political movement of workers might be compatible with the maintenance of strong trade unions.[43] However, underlying his position was a deep-seated assumption that, for the foreseeable future in the United States, labor could have a union-based strategy or a party-based strategy, but not both. In the minds of leaders like Gompers, this assumption was of such longstanding and had been reinforced by so much personal experience that by 1894 it had become unchallengeable.[44]

The either-or mentality had its roots in ideological conflicts within the American section of Marx's International Workingmen's Association (IWA), and in an American version of the debate between Marx and Lassalle over the relative importance of economic and political organization. These conflicts came to a head in the early 1870s (Gitelman, 1965, 71–77, Dick, 1972, 9–26, and Kaufman, 1973, 3–55). Those who emphasized the importance of trade union organization claimed to be following the lead of Marx, and argued that enthusiasts for political organization were being led astray by Lassalle.[45] However, though some advocates of political organization were indeed followers of Lassalle, many claimed that it was really *they* who were following Marx. As a result, by the early 1870s, the debate between these groups increasingly came to revolve around competing interpretations of Marx's writings (Kaufman, 1973, 43–48 and 131–35). For example, the rules Marx had drafted for the IWA stated "that the economical emancipation of the working classes is therefore the great end to which every political movement ought to be subordinated as a means." One group interpreted this to mean that the establishment of economic organizations of workers ought to be the focus of activity, and that political action would have to wait until a sufficient level of class organization and class consciousness had been achieved. The other group interpreted it to mean that the establishment of a working-class political party was the essential prerequisite for economic emancipation, and that party organization should thus be the focus of activity.

This ideological conflict took on an organizational form. The protagonists of a union-based strategy formed the nucleus of what eventually became the AFL, and the protagonists of a party-based strategy formed the nucleus of what eventually became the Socialist Labor party (SLP). The conflict was reinforced by increasingly bitter factional struggles within the cigar makers' union in the early 1880s, between the unions and the Knights of Labor in the mid-1880s, and between the leaders of AFL and the SLP in the late 1880s and early 1890s.[46] Of special significance was the AFL's lengthy debate in 1890 about whether it should uphold Gompers' decision to refuse to issue a charter to the New York Central Labor Federation because the SLP was one of its affiliates. The debate focused on the appropriate relationship between unions and parties, and it foreshadowed many of the arguments that were later deployed in 1894. Gompers saw the issue as one of high principle, and employed a stenographer to record the entire debate. His decision to refuse the charter was upheld by a majority of more than 3 to 1 (AFL, 1891a, 40). It was Socialist party factionalism above all else that worried Gompers and his allies. For these leaders, the socialist-backed Political Programme and its proposal to establish an independent labor party was just the latest attempt to subordinate the unions to a party—and this, they were sure, would destroy them.

Despite their claim to be "pure and simple unionists," the hostility of Gompers and his allies towards the SLP was in fact fueled by a history of ideological and organizational ties with the very people they were opposing. Indeed, many of the key union leaders who opposed the socialists repeatedly sought to affirm their own ongoing commitment to socialism. Speaking during the AFL's 1890 debate, Gompers declared that "the man who would accuse me or charge me with being an anti-socialist, simply . . . does not know Sam Gompers . . . there is not a noble hope that a Socialist may have that I do not hold as my ideal" (AFL, 1891a, 22).[47] A similar, if less emphatic, position was adopted by the convention as a whole (AFL, 1891a, 7 and 39–40). Gompers continued to affirm the value of socialism in the early 1890s.[48] But alongside their affirmation of socialism, "pure and simple unionists" sought to draw a sharp distinction between themselves and supporters of the SLP. Though their goals might be similar, their methods, they insisted, were "inherently" different: economic organization on the one hand, party organization on the other. (AFL, 1891a, 22). "Please remember the contrast I make between socialism and the Socialistic Labor Party," appealed Gompers (AFL, 1891a, 35). "I want to accentuate that with all the force and whatever little ability there may be within me."

Thus, to a significant extent, the 1894 debate on the Political Programme was driven by more than two decades of intra-socialist sectarianism. Adolph

Strasser acknowledged this explicitly. He insisted that there was "a vast difference between socialism and socialists," and attacked the Political Programme
as the work of men "who have been fighting the trades union movement in
the United States for over 20 years" (AFL, 1895a, 36). Strasser was arguably
one of the two key protagonists in the 1894 debate. He was important not just
because of the prominent role he took in opposing the program, but also because he had played a leading role in originally formulating the idea of "pure
and simple unionism," and because Gompers had risen to leadership as his
protégé (Gitelman, 1965, 71–72 and 80–83). The other key protagonist was
Thomas J. Morgan. Morgan had taken the lead in proposing, promoting
and defending the Political Programme, and he felt a proprietary relationship
to it. Yet these key protagonists had once been members of the same Social
Democratic Workingmen's party (Kaufman and Albert, 1989, 711 and 721).
The relationship between activists that had once shared such bonds, and the
hostilities that resulted from breaking them, could sometimes be intensely
personal and emotional. "I was a convert, a student of this man here," said
Morgan, pointing to another opponent, the carpenters' leader P. J. McGuire,
who had founded the Social Democratic Workingmen's party with Strasser in
the 1870s (AFL, 1895a, 45, and Gitelman, 1965, 74–75).

The result was a conflict that had all the intensity of sibling rivalry. Gompers, Strasser, and others were at pains to appeal to the authority of the
common ideological parents that they shared with the socialists. They believed that a correct reading of Marx's writings led to the "pure and simple
unionism" position they espoused (Gitelman, 1965, 73–79 and 82). Gompers
thought that Marx (along with the eight hours advocate, Ira Steward) was the
greatest economic and social thinker of the age (Kaufman, 1987, 426). Indeed, after the 1890 conflict over a charter for the New York Central Labor
Federation, Gompers wrote directly to Engels, setting out his case and appealing for support.[49] In the last issue of the *American Federationist* before the
AFL's 1894 debate, Gompers printed an article from Karl Kautsky on the ongoing importance of trade unions, implicitly appealing to Kautsky's authority
as the keeper of the flame of orthodox German Marxism.[50] And during the
debate itself, Strasser appealed directly to the authority of Marx, and challenged his socialist opponents to show how their conclusions could arise from
his writings: "I shall take their own books and beat them" (AFL, 1895a, 36).

The slightly exasperated and bemused comments of Delegate McBryde, the
secretary-treasurer of the miners' union, give some sense of the "insider" status
of much of this factional conflict.[51] McBryde had come to the convention
mandated to support the Political Programme, but he was neither an "SLP-so-
cialist" like Morgan, nor an "anti-socialist socialist" like Strasser. Referring to
the intense factional "feeling" on display at the AFL's 1894 debate, he said: "I
came to this convention without any feeling in the matter. I have no feeling
in reference to Brother Strasser or Brother Morgan or anybody else." As a

labor leader unaligned with either faction, McBryde's comments are particularly revealing. "I notice," he went on, that "the very delegates that assailed socialism and claim to being pure and simple trades unionists, every one are confessed socialists. I am a trades unionist that never was anything else, and know nothing about the socialistic party or anything in connection with the disputes" (AFL, 1895a, 40).

The contributions of Gompers and his allies were characterized by a number of features that bring out the quality of entrenched factionalism that marked the AFL's debates in the early 1890s. First, there was a tendency towards *personal recriminations*. In part, this took the form of ad hominem attacks, and a tendency to be less concerned with what was being proposed than with who was proposing it. In part, it took the form of a tendency to become absorbed in reacting to real or perceived slights that might impugn one's personal honor or integrity (AFL, 1895a, 4–5, 9–10, and 35).[52] Delegate Penna of the miners' union protested that some delegates seemed to be seized by a desire to take their opponent "by the throat . . . and choke the life out of him" (AFL, 1895a, 11).

Second there was deep *distrust of opponents* and a presumption that many were acting in bad faith. Gompers often warned fellow unionists that the socialists were enemies disguised as friends. He used the first editorials in the *American Federationist* to argue that the purpose of the journal was to defend workers alike against the attacks of "avowed enemies" and those acting "under the guise of friendship." In the convention debate itself, this theme recurred repeatedly. Gompers and his allies accused the socialists of engaging in "subterfuge," of using socialism "merely as a cloak," of being "secret foes," and of keeping their real beliefs "hidden." Those who supported the establishment of an independent labor party found that their commitment to unionism itself was constantly called into question, and implicitly or explicitly, the socialists were accused of effectively siding with the capitalist class.[53]

Third, the *certainty* with which key protagonists held their opinions made them prone to dogmatism and intolerance. These qualities must have been particularly noticeable in Strasser. In a testimonial marking Strasser's retirement from the presidency of the cigar makers' union, even Gompers felt it necessary to observe that "he makes few friends, and in consequence of his aggressiveness for the ideas he believes right, has made strong enemies" (AFL, 1891b, 49–51). But Gompers himself had some of these characteristics. In 1890, he told the AFL that "there is not one word in my whole life that I have uttered in connection with the labor movement, or one act that I have done or one step that I have taken, that I would take back" (AFL, 1891a, 35–6). "When I know that I am right," he said, "there is no one . . . who could swerve me one jot."[54] By the end of 1894, Gompers's position on trade unionism had become a demand for "absolute faith," and his opponents had become "men who worship other Gods."[55]

Finally, there was a tendency for protagonists to become *obsessed* with factional conflicts. Occasionally, Gompers seemed to recognize this danger himself. In a private letter replying to a union leader who was visiting the Trades Union Congress in London on behalf of the AFL in 1894, he apologized for inappropriately spending so much space harping on about SLP factionalism. He had to be careful, he said, to resist the temptation "to open the floodgates of my tongue" (Kaufman and Albert, 1989, 516).

I have focused on the presence of these characteristics in the contributions of Gompers and his allies, since it is their decision to block the establishment of a labor party that I need to explain. But the contributions of their socialist opponents were at least as marked by the same characteristics. Indeed, especially following De Leon's rise within the SLP, it must have been hard for Gompers and his allies not to take umbrage at the abuse and vitriol frequently directed at them. According to the SLP's English-language paper, the *People*, labor leaders who were committed to pure and simple unionism were "half sea-horse and half dog-face fakirs, traders, and quacks." They were "ignorant," "corrupt," "perverse," "weaklings," "agents of the capitalists," and "traitors." The SLP, the paper declared, "must march over the bodies of each and every one of them." The AFL, it argued, "has no reason for being . . . it is deader than dead." To drive the point home, the paper published a cartoon showing Gompers and the bakers' leader Weismann on a hand-powered railroad trolley being plowed down by a locomotive marked SLP. The caption suggested that if they did not get out of the way, they would be "crushed or killed." The promised destruction was not merely rhetorical and metaphorical. In December 1895, as if to prove Gompers' point, the SLP sought to break up the AFL by forming a short-lived rival trade union center.[56]

The point here is not to apportion blame to the leaders of the AFL and SLP. Rather, it is to identify the deep-seated mutually reinforcing culture of factional conflict that both shared. This culture of factionalism was rooted in over two decades of ideological and organizational conflicts: conflicts that stemmed from a shared concern with German socialist debates, and especially with Marxism. Unlike religious sectarianism, which tended to decline towards the top of the union movement, this secular sectarianism increased the closer one got to the top.

Why left-wing factionalism took such an acute form in the United States is open to debate. After all, the influence of Marxism elsewhere was not inevitably associated with debilitating sectarianism. One possible explanation concerns the influence of German-speaking political exiles, who, like many exiles, tended to adopt an uncompromising stance. However this effect was waning in the early 1890s, following the repeal of the anti-socialist laws in Germany, and local efforts to "Americanize" the Socialist Labor party.[57] Another possible explanation concerns the diffuse influence on American reform thought of evangelical perfectionist extremism. However, evangelical language was far more common among non-Marxist radicals like Bellamy, George, Lloyd, and Debs, who, with the possible exception of George, were less sectarian, and often sought to bridge the differences between different reform ideologies.[58]

Whatever the explanation, by 1894 the either-or mentality had become a kind of common sense for many AFL delegates. Trying to "mix trades unionism in politics" was like trying to "mix oil and water" (AFL, 1895a, 55).[59] The consequence was that many delegates opposed the Political Programme on the grounds that it would enable socialist factionalism to overtly or covertly undermine the unions. In a typical contribution, Delegate Weismann (AFL,1895a, 38) predicted that: "If we are unsuccessful to rescue [the AFL] out of the hands of these men who come here under disguise to cut the life out of the trades unions, if we let it be surrendered into their hands, disintegration will follow."[60] In response, the proponents of the Political Programme were forced to spend much of their time defending their bona fides as unionists.

The either-or mentality also helps explain why more prominence was not given to the argument that involvement in partisan politics was necessary to control the use of repression. On one side of the debate, the socialists focused on the need to seek legislative power in order to socialize the means of production. On the other side, their opponents focused on the need to maintain strong union organizations by pursuing the immediate needs of workers. The either-or mentality predisposed both to see these as the only alternatives. Thomas Morgan, the socialist who was the leading proponent of independent labor politics, saw the need for a partisan political strategy, but did not even include anti-injunction relief in his proposed political program. Adolph Strasser, his leading opponent, saw the need for anti-injunction legislation and moved an amendment to include it in the program, but he did not see the need for a partisan political strategy to pursue it (AFL, 1895a, 15 and 62). A tantalizing opportunity to find common ground was missed. Only two delegates made any attempt to occupy this ground. Delegate Brentell of the iron and steel workers' union contrasted the claim that partisan politics will disrupt unions with the observation that unions are already being broken up by political repression against which organization alone is powerless (AFL, 1895a, 42). Delegate Penna (AFL, 1895a, 52) of the miners' union argued that "we are trade unionists first, last and all the time, but . . . There is one class of privations we can remove by trades unionism. There is another class that can only be removed by political action, and we cannot remove anything by politics without going into politics."[61] Brentell and Penna represented unions in industries where the destructive effect of repression had been felt to the full, and fear that partisan politics could generate further disruption made little sense. But their voices were drowned by the dominant either-or mentality that informed so much of the debate.

Finally, the either-or mentality helps explain why little attempt was made to articulate a "New Liberal" argument for the establishment of a labor party. Morgan recognized the force of New Liberal arguments in his private correspondence with Henry Demarest Lloyd, and he occasionally appealed to them in Illinois.[62] But in the debate within the AFL, he was too locked into the prevailing either-or mentality, and the common heritage of sectarian conflict he shared with his opponents, to pursue them.

On the contrary, he explicitly counterposed collectivism and individualism (AFL, 1895a, 34). It was almost as if he thought that the use of New Liberal language would leave him open to accusations of lacking integrity. Morgan noted that some would be shocked that an unambiguous socialist commitment lay at the heart of his program, but, he wrote, "instead of concealing the fact, we would have your whole attention and thoughts directed to it."[63] Morgan and his socialist allies were not as vitriolic about the AFL leadership as De Leon and his followers. They had broken with the national SLP leadership in New York in 1893, both because they thought that socialists should continue to work within the AFL, and because they favored a labor-populists alliance (Foner, 1955, 287 and 316–17). However, they continued to be influenced by the either-or mentality and its associated sectarianism. Morgan and his allies argued that union organization and industrial action were either already outmoded or were becoming so, and instead emphasized the importance of legislation (AFL, 1895a, 33–34). Morgan was fixated on Plank 10 of the platform, declaring in the *American Federationist* that "this alone will be the vital test" and casting aspersions on the ability and integrity of those who opposed him.[64]

Between them, the anti-socialist socialists and the SLP socialists framed the terms of the AFL's debate around the either-or mentality they shared. These terms were rooted in leftist ideological disputes that owed more to Marxism than to liberalism. They were forged in a debate that was originally more concerned with the desirability of allegedly incompatible strategies for achieving labor's goals than with the desirability of those goals themselves. As we saw when discussing the liberalism thesis, some delegates did make the kind of criticisms of the Political Programme to which a New Liberal response may have been effective, but the attention of Morgan and the socialists was not focused on these criticisms. Instead, it was focused on what they saw as the main debate—the debate they had long been having with their erstwhile socialist brothers.

Socialists and Unionists in Australia Compared

In Australia, relations between central union leaders and socialists were less fraught during the period in which decisions about the establishment of a labor party were being taken. Members of the Australian Socialist League

(ASL) had been energetic and reliable supporters of the TLC during the Maritime strike. In its wake, although the TLC remained somewhat wary, relations between the two organizations were friendly and becoming friendlier (O'Farrell, 1958, 161–62, and Markey, 1988, 240–42). In 1891, for example, they hosted a joint reception to welcome home J. D. Fitzgerald, who had gone to Britain to rouse support during the strike.[65] Nevertheless, some tensions between union leaders and socialists did exist. The *Australian Workman* noted that in late 1890 and early 1891 "there was much complaint among some of the unions of the socialistic tone of the paper, and the *Workman* was officially asked to give a little less Socialism and a little more Trades Unionism."[66] However, taken as a whole, the paper was a symbol of the relatively friendly relations between unionists and socialists. After all, although the *Australian Workman* was the official organ of the TLC, the editorship of the paper was entrusted to a series of leading ASL members. It is impossible to imagine Gompers handing the editorship of the *American Federationist* to a member of the SLP.[67]

Elsewhere in Australia, relations between union leaders and socialists varied. In Victoria, tensions were somewhat greater. In 1891, the Melbourne Trades Hall Council insisted they were too busy—even for ten minutes—to hear from a socialist delegation, although leading socialists were soon absorbed into the new Labor party. In Queensland and South Australia there were less tensions than in NSW. In Queensland, the more overtly socialist stance of the labor movement left socialists feeling little need for a separate organization, while in South Australia, unionists, socialists, single taxers, and others cooperated amicably within the so-called "Forward Movement."[68]

Overall, socialist sectarianism was not a major preoccupation of Australian union leaders in the early 1890s. Indeed, when the decision to establish a labor party was being debated in the second half of 1890 and the first half of 1891, there was little or no mention of left-wing factionalism in the reports of union leaders and the minutes of their meetings. It was not mentioned at all in the debate on labor's political program at the 1891 Intercolonial Trades and Labor Union Congress,[69] even though this Congress confronted an issue that was quite similar to that which had roiled the AFL's 1890 convention. As in the United States, it had to decide whether or not to accept the credentials of a delegate seeking to represent a socialist organization.[70] However, while in the United States, the decision to reject the credentials of an SLP delegate dominated much of the convention, and was still generating vituperative exchanges years later, in Australia, the issue was quickly and amicably resolved to the unanimous satisfaction of the Congress. A similar conclusion was reached, but without the rancor and set piece confrontation that dominated the AFL convention.[71]

The either-or mentality was largely absent in Australia. Occasionally, the kind of sentiments that would have had Gompers up in arms *were* expressed.

Here and there, a socialist would argue that "unionism . . . has positively *out-lived its usefulness*" and that workers should turn instead "to the proper source of relief—*the state*."[72] But sentiments like these, and the reaction against them, were atypical, and they neither fed into a preexisting either-or mentality, nor gave rise to one. On the contrary, following the Maritime strike, labor leaders typically called simultaneously for measures to reform and strengthen the unions themselves, and for measures to form a party and enter parliament. There was scarcely any dispute about the idea that union organization itself remained vitally important. The underlying assumption of most labor leaders was that the reinforcement of union organization and the establishment of a party were *both* essential, and that they would be mutually supporting.[73]

In order to explain the absence of an either-or mentality, and the less fraught relations between unionists and socialists that resulted, we need to examine the ideological commitments of both prominent union leaders and prominent socialist organizations, and compare them with those of their counterparts in the United States.

Let me begin with the socialists. The most prominent socialist organization—and the one that set the tone for relations with the union movement in NSW—was the Australian Socialist League. Founded in 1887, the ASL was a newer and smaller organization than the SLP in the United States, and unlike its American cousin, it did not contest elections. Its sudden burst of activity during the Maritime strike attracted a wave of new activists, including some who were destined to play a central role in the labor movement. By 1893, it had about 15 urban and rural branches in NSW, and around 2,000 members.[74]

In the early 1890s, the ideological commitments of the ASL were less dogmatic and more fluid than those of the SLP in the United States. Its most important public activity was its regular program of Sunday lectures and debates. These covered a wide and sometimes eclectic range of subjects, and according to those who participated, they were "packed to the doors with men and women of all shades of advanced opinion." New members sometimes occupied uncertain ideological positions. William Morris Hughes, who joined the ASL in 1892, and soon became a frequent lecturer, had equivocated about the relative merits of socialism and the single tax. Another frequent lecturer, the journalist and labor MP, George Black, found something good to say about most of the radical ideologies and movements he reviewed. The undisciplined behavior of ASL members of parliament, some of whom refused to bring down the Protectionist Dibbs government over its actions in the Broken Hill Miners' strike, also suggests loose ideological ties. But, perhaps most importantly, ASL members were enthusiastic supporters of both the unions and the new Labor party, despite the lack of a commitment to a specifically socialist objective on the part of either.[75]

I do not want to exaggerate this point. The relatively tolerant attitude towards the programmatic pragmatism of the Labor party and its union backers did not last, and in the mid-1890s, a push to commit the party to a clear socialist objective led to major factional conflicts. These culminated in 1898 when the ASL left the Labor party to reestablish itself as an explicitly socialist competitor. Sharp conflicts also took place earlier: first in 1889 and again in 1891–92. However these conflicts were not construed as a struggle between union leaders and socialists. Rather, they were either internal ideological conflicts between proponents of state socialism and proponents of more cooperative or libertarian forms of socialism, or they were conflicts with single taxers. While socialists often seemed fractious and dogmatic to contemporary Australians, the fact remains that during the period in which the labor party was being established, their principle organization was less recalcitrant and more fluid in its ideological commitments than its counterpart in the United States.[76]

What were the ideological commitments of key union leaders at the beginning of the 1890s? Here I will try to bring out some important differences with the United States by focusing on three influential leaders: P. J. Brennan, T. J. Houghton, and W. G. Spence. Each was in a major position of leadership during the period when the TLC was deciding whether to establish a political party. Brennan was President and Houghton was Secretary of the TLC, while Spence was the leader of its largest affiliate. All three were centrally involved in coordinating the Maritime strike and in formulating the union movement's new attitude towards politics in the wake of its defeat.[77]

As we saw in chapter 5, Brennan had favored the establishment of a labor party before the strike, and he used his position as TLC President to push the issue to the fore in its aftermath. If anyone can claim to be a founding father of the Labor party, it is him. Brennan had been drawn into the union movement through his work as a ship's steward. His experience of the appalling conditions in the shipping industry lead him to organize the Stewards' and Cooks' Union in 1884, and since then he had been continuously active in the TLC, and had helped form a number of other unions. By 1890 he had become one of the TLC's most experienced organizers. Brennan was not a proponent of any of the left-wing reform ideologies. "Trade unionism, rather than single taxism or socialism, was his working creed" (Nairn, 1989, 39). His ideological commitments stemmed from his belief in class cooperation, protectionism, and Catholicism. Brennan saw capital and labor as having mutual interests that could, and should, enable reasonable men on both sides to conciliate their differences. He saw unions as character-building organizations of respectable working men, and always maintained that employers had nothing to fear from organized labor.[78] In 1892, he accepted appointment as labor's representative on a new voluntary Arbitration Council. As a TLC leader, Brennan sought to keep his protectionist leanings out of official union business, although his loyalty to the Catholic Church was occasionally apparent.[79]

Like Brennan, the basic ideological commitments of Houghton and Spence were not rooted in left-wing reform ideologies. Houghton's background was that of a typical craft unionist. He had been a printer all his life, and throughout the 1880s he was an active member of the Typographical Association. Like Brennan, he tended to look hopefully towards a "conciliatory spirit" to solve conflicts between workers and their employers (TLC, 1891, 8). He was also a protectionist, and, at least nominally, an Anglican. Prior to the Maritime strike, he had opposed the establishment of a labor party and had advocated a Gompers-style policy of endorsing labor-friendly candidates (Nairn, 1989, 45). Spence had mostly worked as a miner before becoming a union organizer, and he, too, was less than enthusiastic about the establishment of a labor party prior to the Maritime strike (Merritt, 1986, 180–81). His case is a little more complex, however, since the self-conscious "new unionism" he fostered among miners and shearers did provide a conduit for a number of contemporary reform ideologies, and from late 1892 he sometimes claimed to be a socialist. But for Spence, socialism was more a frame of mind—"more of a spirit and a temper than a system"—and at the core of his ideological commitment was a belief in a Christian moral obligation to serve others.[80] A deeply religious man, Spence was active in the Presbyterian Church, and was also a temperance advocate and a lay preacher. Like Brennan and Houghton, he hoped for cooperation and mutual respect between employers and workers. Asked by the NSW Royal Commission on Strikes (1891, 45) about the objectives of the "new" unions he had helped establish, Spence replied that "they have set before them no definite aim, except the general one of improving the conditions of the masses."[81]

Spence's comments to the Royal Commission sound remarkably like Strasser's comments to a similar inquiry before the United States Senate. Asked about his union's ultimate ends, Strasser replied that "We have no ultimate ends. We are going on from day to day. . . . we want to dress better and to live better, and become better off and better citizens generally." But this superficial similarity masks an important underlying difference. For as we have seen, Strasser's stance was in fact a product of his earlier socialist commitments and a profound engagement with Marxian ideological controversies. Strasser's insistent disavowal of "theories" and "theorists" led the inquiry Chairman to comment that "I see that you are a little sensitive lest it should be thought that you are a mere theorizer." Strasser was "sensitive" because his protestations were disingenuous. His rejection of theories and theorists was itself a theoretical conclusion. Gompers was somewhat more forthcoming. He told the same inquiry that many of the best unionists "subordinate their theories or convictions" to work in the interests of the union movement as a whole. They have "socialistic convictions," he said, but these "remain in the background."[82] Gompers and Strasser claimed to be "pure and simple unionists." But they were only pure and simple unionists in the sense that they were committed to a theory of "pure and simple unionism"—a theory that began as a version of Marxian socialism.

However, in an important sense, their Australian counterparts really were pure and simple unionists. They were pure and simple unionists in the sense that their beliefs about the union movement, and how it should proceed, were not based on left-wing reform ideologies. In particular, they were not based on commitments that had emerged from conflicts over the appropriate interpretation of Marxian socialism. There had been ideological ruptures in the Australian Socialist League. But neither Brennan and his colleagues nor the organizational origins of the TLC were connected to these ruptures, and neither were connected to conflicts about the relative importance of trade union and party political forms of organization. This does not mean that Brennan and his colleagues were wholly uninfluenced by left-wing reform ideologies. Like other unionists in Australia, they were aware of the various left-wing reform currents we examined earlier, and some were influenced by them more than others.[83] But their attitude towards these debates did not provide the bedrock on which they built their understanding of what unions were for, how they should organize, and what they should or should not attempt to do. Rather, their understanding of these questions was principally a result of their experience within the union movement itself, augmented by the impact of widely held liberal, religious, and "fiscal" beliefs.

Some, like Brennan, had seen the potential for a labor party before the Maritime strike, but most, like Houghton and Spence, only became proponents afterwards. Uninhibited by the either-or mentality of their counterparts in the United States, Australian union leaders were free to respond to the incentives that government repression had generated. Leaders who had previously been skeptical about the establishment of a labor party moved to back such an initiative, largely because this now seemed to be necessary simply in order to defend the basic organizational interests of unionists. In the United States, socialists proposed the establishment of a labor party, and AFL leaders claiming to be "pure and simple unionists" resisted them. But in Australia, precisely because they really were pure and simple unionists, TLC leaders themselves took the initiative to establish a party, and socialists played only a secondary supporting role.

Conclusion

Were Gompers and his allies right to place such great emphasis on the dangers of left-wing factionalism and socialist sectarianism? If they had taken the lead in establishing a party themselves, how great would the disruption of union organization have been then? There is no doubt that in the 1890s the Socialist Labor party could be a particularly destructive sectarian force. But many of its members were uneasy about its growing hostility towards established unions. Many other proponents of independent labor politics were in no way associated with the SLP. And there was no reason to assume that a labor party backed by the union movement as a whole would be controlled by such a small sectarian organization.

The Australian experience is suggestive in this respect. The conflicts involving unionists and socialists that did eventually erupt in NSW were not about the value of union organization, but about the program of the Labor party; and the damage these conflicts inflicted was not on the unions, but on the Australian Socialist League. When the Labor party retreated from adopting more explicitly socialist objectives, following an electoral reverse in 1897, a long-simmering conflict broke out between the moderate and radical wings of the League. The moderates were intimately involved in the leadership of the party and had close ties to key unions. Some were members of parliament. They argued successfully that the Labor party must not get too far ahead of public opinion in order to remain electorally viable, and eventually they left the League. Those remaining in the ASL withdrew from the Labor party and amalgamated with a left-wing splinter group to form a small explicitly socialist party in order to contest elections separately. They received negligible support. Their new organization was modeled on, of all things, Daniel De Leon's Socialist Labor party.[84]

The Australian experience suggests that the establishment of a labor party may have had the opposite effect to that which Gompers and his allies feared. The incentives generated by participation in elections would probably have moderated the stance of some socialists, and may well have marginalized many of the rest. Instead of weakening the unions, the establishment of a labor party may have weakened some of Gompers' bitterest opponents. Indeed, the Australian experience suggests that the fear of factionalism and socialist sectarianism in the United States was partly a self-fulfilling prophecy. Gompers and his allies were blinded to the range of options available by the either-or mentality that framed their understanding of the labor movement and its activists. It was as if they were wearing lenses that polarized the world of the labor movement into party-supporting and union-supporting activists. But because they really did look at the world this way, they really did fear that union organizations might be destroyed if a labor party were established—and so they used their influence to resist this development.

The either-or mentality that generated this effect had been produced by over 20 years of sectarian conflict between different branches of the socialist movement—conflict that had roots in an ongoing ideological dispute over the correct interpretation of Marxism. In Australia, by contrast, the influence of Marxism was negligible in the early 1890s, and the American conflict between SLP socialists and anti-socialist socialists had no parallel. However, most of the other left-wing reform ideologies that influenced American union leaders *did* have some influence among their Australian counterparts, and this was especially true of those ideological currents that had emerged from within the United States itself. In Australia, these American schools of thought helped make the ideological climate within the labor movement more conducive to the idea of establishing a labor party. Though they certainly could not have generated this outcome on their own, the overall impact of these left-wing reform ideologies helped rather than hindered the establishment of a labor party. In the United States, sectarianism fostered by intense conflicts over Marxism outweighed this effect.

It is commonplace to suggest that the weakness of socialist thought in general, and Marxism in particular, is part of the explanation for why there is no labor party in the United States. But the Australian case suggests that it was the strength of Marxism among a strategically located group of leaders—or, rather, the strength of a mentality founded on particular interpretations of it—that had the more important effect.

Conclusion

So why is there no labor party in the United States? Conventional explanations, based on comparison with Europe, have highlighted a number of potential explanatory factors. In this book, I have tried to reassess these, and develop a new more satisfactory explanation, by undertaking a systematic most-similar comparison of the United States and Australia. Australia is a good candidate for a most-similar comparison because it shared many underlying characteristics with the United States. It is an especially good candidate because Australian unions decided to establish a labor party just when their American counterparts came closest to doing something similar, and because in each case they took these decisions against a similar backdrop of events.

The main potential explanatory factors I have considered are listed (in Table 0.1) in the Introduction. In order to assess their explanatory significance, I have first examined the extent to which they were present in the two countries, and have then examined their effects. I have examined the extent to which they were present in order to determine whether they differentiate the United States from Australia, and I have examined their effects by considering whether there is a plausible causal mechanism that links them to the failure to establish a labor party.

Here, I want to draw together my findings. First, I will summarize the negative findings. These are negative in the sense that they concern potential explanatory factors that can be eliminated. Second, I will summarize the positive findings. In this section, I will pay special attention to the interaction that took place between those factors that *are* a part of the explanation for why there is no labor party. And third, I will consider the implications of these findings for the wider debate about the character of American politics and society.

NEGATIVE FINDINGS

Comparison of the extent to which the main potential explanatory factors were present in the United States and Australia casts doubt on many of them by demonstrating that they were common to both countries. An examination of the effects of these common factors confirms that each of them should indeed be ruled out. There is, of course, a sense in which no factor can be definitively eliminated or placed beyond further debate, given that my approach, like that of all comparative studies, involves unavoidable trade-offs and compromises. Nevertheless, I have tried to show that there are good reasons for ruling these factors out.

The level of prosperity in late nineteenth-century Australia was even higher than it was in the United States. So arguments that there were insufficient economic grievances to support a labor party seem implausible. However economic discontent was not simply a product of the level of prosperity. Rather, it was a product of the gap between actual and expected living standards. Expectations about living standards were generated by a number of different comparative reference points. For most workers, it was not comparison with Europe but internal reference points that were the most important source of their expectations. These included the living standards of wealthier people in the country where they lived, the living standards promised by the ideal image of that country, and the living standards which they themselves had previously experienced there. But for each of these reference points, the gap between actual and expected living standards, and the discontent it generated, was likely to be at least as great in the United States as Australia.

The ability to forge a labor-populist alliance between workers and small farmers was important to the prospects for labor-party politics in both countries. A labor party based on such an alliance was the kind of labor party that was most likely to emerge in the United States, and it was the kind of labor party that actually did emerge in Australia. But the class characteristics that could facilitate a labor-populist alliance were present in both countries. Both had a large class of discontented small farmers. Both had a common enemy against which workers and small farmers could unite. And both had unions that could act as bridging agents to facilitate this alliance.

There was intense racial hostility towards black and Chinese people in both countries in the late nineteenth century. However the Australian case shows that this could actually foster the establishment of a labor party. Labor leaders were able to use racial hostility, and the white racial consciousness that it helped generate, to strengthen their industrial and political organizations. The circumstances that made this possible were also present in the northern industrial areas of the United States. In these areas, as in Australia, the targets of racial hostility were not sufficiently numerous to disrupt the effectiveness of union organization or electoral mobilization. This began to change during the First World War. But in the late nineteenth century, these changes had not yet taken place.

The racialization of hostility towards immigrants from southern and eastern Europe was also beginning to emerge in both countries at the end of the nineteenth century. These immigrants formed a larger group in the United States than they did in Australia, and in the early twentieth century, hostility towards them did come to affect the prospects for labor party politics. Here again, though, close attention to the timing of developments is important. For in the early 1890s, neither the racialization of hostility towards southern and eastern European immigrants, nor the growth in size of their communities, had developed sufficiently to have this effect.

Manhood suffrage for whites was an entrenched and long-established feature of both the United States and Australia in the early 1890s. But early manhood suffrage did not hinder the establishment of a labor party. For in both countries, it provided labor leaders with important opportunities, by legitimizing efforts to engage in political mobilization, and providing a ready-made electoral arena in which to do this. In addition, the retention of some electoral inequalities and class-based restrictions, or the threat to reimpose them, enabled labor leaders in both countries to appeal to democratic demands to help mobilize the political support of workers.

The electoral system in both countries was based on a first-past-the-post formula, and a mixture of single-member and multimember districts. This created a high electoral threshold for most third parties. But in Australia, as indeed in most of Europe, labor-based parties were established despite the presence of majority or plurality electoral systems. This was possible because workers were geographically concentrated in particular areas. However this was also true of the United States. Had the electoral system been a significant factor hindering the emergence of a labor party, the outcome should have been different in Illinois, where an unusual semi-proportional system significantly lowered the electoral threshold. But there, too, labor party experiments were unsuccessful.

Egalitarian ideas about social status were much stronger in both the United States and Australia than they were in Europe. However, far from being a constraint, these values provided important opportunities for those seeking to establish a labor party. Labor leaders in both countries argued that social egalitarianism was being subverted by the emergence of neo-feudal class relations. Attempts to establish and maintain class distinctions were present in both countries. But the aristocratic pretensions of prominent merchants, industrialists, and bankers in late nineteenth-century America made it especially likely that the arguments of labor leaders would seem plausible to ordinary workers and other potential supporters.

Ideas about the importance of individual freedom were also prevalent in both societies. Again, however, these values provided those seeking to establish a labor party with opportunities rather than constraints. Labor leaders in both countries argued that individual freedom was under threat. Some pointed to infringements resulting from collusion and repression by governments and employers. Others stressed that true freedom required the establishment of conditions that would enable all individuals to develop their capacities to the full. Either way, they saw themselves as patriotic defenders of established values. There were some features of Australian society that made these arguments more convincing, and some features of American society that did so. But overall, it seems that American workers were at least as likely to find them plausible as their Australian counterparts.

So, each of the factors that are common to the United States and Australia, and the explanations that are built around them, can be ruled out. This leaves us with a number of factors that do distinguish the United States from Australia. But an examination of the effects of these remaining factors suggests that some of them can also be excluded. Those concerning the constitutional division of power fall into this category.

The United States had a presidential system of government. Australia had a parliamentary one. Elections for president or governor did tend to foster a two-party system. But this did not generate institutional incentives that undermined the strategy favored by the proponents of labor-party politics: the strategy of winning the balance of power in the legislature. Activists had an incentive to pursue this strategy because the balance of power would give them substantial legislative and executive influence. And voters could support labor candidates, without "wasting" their vote in executive elections, by voting a split ticket. Indeed, this had just been made easier in the United States by the introduction of the "Australian ballot."

The United States had a federal system. Australia was poised to establish a similar system, but had not yet done so. However, while federalism made it harder to achieve fundamental nationwide change, it made it easier for the labor movement to gain a foothold in the party system. A federal system increased the number of points of access for a new labor party, created political units in industrial areas where such a party could more easily secure an initial base, and made it possible for the labor movement to experiment with different models of political mobilization.

The United States had a system of judicial review that made the courts unusually powerful. Australia had a system of parliamentary sovereignty in which the courts could be overruled by legislation. In the 1890s, American unions experienced a wave of intense judicial hostility. This has led some to argue that union leaders concluded that, since judicial review gave the courts the final say on the decisions that mattered most to the unions, and since the courts were largely immune to electoral influence, it was either futile or foolish to engage in electoral politics. In fact, however, the courts were susceptible to electoral pressure, both directly through the selection of judges and their need to maintain legitimacy, and indirectly through legislative and executive pressure. Moreover, hostile rulings gave unions an incentive to engage in electoral politics in order to exercise this pressure, since this was the only way they could protect their core organizational interests from judicial threats.

So, in addition to all the factors that are common to the United States and Australia, some of the factors that are distinctive characteristics of the United States can also be excluded. Taken together, this rules out most of the main conventional explanations. Explanations based on the level of prosperity, the prospects for a labor-populist alliance, the intense racial hostility towards black and Chinese people, the emergence of similar attitudes towards new European immigrants, the early introduction of manhood suffrage for whites, the electoral system, the strength of social egalitarianism, and the prevalence of ideas about individual freedom can all be ruled out, not simply because they are built around factors that were also present in Australia, but because of what, in addition, we have discovered about their effects. To these can be added explanations based on presidentialism, federalism, and the judicial system, which can be ruled out because of their effects alone.

These negative findings are important in their own right. Two points are especially worth underlining. The first is that they suggest that many of the best known and most widely accepted conventional explanations are not sustainable. Some of these explanations—like those based on prosperity, early manhood suffrage, the electoral system, and the values of social egalitarianism and individual freedom—have been widely accepted for the better part of a century or more. Others—like those based on racial hostility—have only become widely accepted more recently. The second point is that, rather than hampering the establishment of a labor party, many of the excluded factors actually fostered this outcome. Factors like early manhood suffrage, social egalitarianism, the value of individual freedom, federalism, the judicial system, and possibly also racial hostility, each had effects that were—to a greater or lesser extent—the opposite of those that are usually ascribed to them.

POSITIVE FINDINGS

We are left, then, with just a handful of factors: the weakness of the new unionism, the level of repression, the political salience of religion, and socialist sectarianism. These are the only factors that were both distinctive characteristics of the United States and were linked to the failure to establish a labor party by a plausible causal mechanism. They interacted with each other in important ways to produce different outcomes in the United States and Australia. Comparison with Australia highlights two proximate causes of the outcome in the United States: causes which, in turn, were in large part the result of other more deeply entrenched features of American politics and society.

The first proximate cause was the weakness of the "new unionism." In both the United States and Australia, the labor movement was originally dominated by craft unions. However, in the late nineteenth century, efforts were made in both countries to organize new unions that were open to unskilled and semi-skilled workers. But, in the United States, these new unions found it difficult to survive, and by the early 1890s they organized a far smaller proportion of the unionized workforce than they did in Australia. The new unions had both the motivation and the resources to help establish a labor party. In Australia, they fostered the establishment of a labor party in a number of ways. They pursued policies that strengthened the classwide identity of workers. They were at the center of the industrial struggles that cemented union support for the formation of a party. And they provided an organizational base to sustain the party and to enable it to survive some early setbacks. In the United States, new unions also tended to favor the establishment of a labor party, but because they found it difficult to survive, they had far less influence in the union movement as a whole.

Repression was one of the main reasons for the weakness of the new unionism in the United States. It was not just judicial repression that effected unionists. During the strike wave of the early 1890s, governments in both the United States and Australia intervened with soldiers and police to help defeat the unions and protect the interests of employers. But the repression of unions was greater in the United States, and its effects were more complex than is often recognized. In Australia, repression convinced most unionists of the need to establish a labor party. In the United States, the greater level of repression undermined similar initiatives. This greater level of repression both helped and hindered the formation of a labor party. It helped by giving those unionists who had been subject to the most severe repression a strong incentive to engage in independent political action. But it simultaneously hindered by destroying the organizational base of these unionists and weakening their influence within the union movement as a whole.

In both the United States and Australia, it was the new unions that were typically (though not exclusively) subject to the most severe repression. This further strengthened the incentive that they already had to help establish a labor party. But whereas, in Australia, key new unions survived and helped found and sustain such a party, their counterparts in the United States were either seriously damaged or destroyed by the greater level of repression, and were hence unable to exercise a similar influence.

Repression was not the only reason for the weakness of the new unionism in the United States. The ambivalence of Gompers and some other top leaders of the AFL also contributed. Gompers was not opposed to the organization of unskilled workers in principle, but he was opposed to adopting the kind of organizational strategies that might have helped bring this about. Repression also had other independent effects on the prospects for the establishment of a labor party. It could affect the legitimacy of the labor movement, and isolate unionists from potential allies, as governments sought to justify their use of armed force. In addition, repression could seriously affect craft unionists. As a result, these unionists also had some incentive to enter the electoral arena.

The second proximate cause for the failure of unions to establish a labor party in the United States was the fear of dissension that gripped many labor leaders. If repression gave even craft unionists an incentive to engage in partisan politics, why did so many union leaders resist it? The short answer is that these leaders feared that, bad as things were, they could get even worse.

Dissension, disruption, dissolution, and destruction. Over and over again these were the fears voiced by Gompers and his allies. They were voiced in public and in private.[1] And they were voiced before, during, and after the

AFL's great debate in 1894.[2] Gompers himself set the tone for this debate in his presidential report, where he placed these fears at the center of his argument against partisan politics, urging the convention "to steer our ship of labor safe from that channel whose waters are strewn with shattered hopes and unions destroyed."[3]

But it was not just Gompers who voiced these fears. Delegate after delegate raised similar concerns as the debate unfolded. Delegate Macarthur feared the "spectre of disintegration." Delegate Weismann feared "tremendous disruption." Delegate Lennon feared "the disruption of organization." Delegate McGuire thought that forming a party was "suicidal." Delegate Strasser feared it would "split up the labor movement." Delegate Hysell feared the loss of "a large proportion of the membership." Delegate Pomeroy foresaw "dissension" and "disruption." Delegate Daley foresaw unions that had "gone to pieces." Delegate Mahon feared that partisan politics would "destroy this great machine." Delegate Croke feared the introduction of a "disease" that would "kill the association." Delegate Hart feared that the unions would be "torn asunder." And delegate O'Sullivan felt simply that he had to "defend trades unionism."[4]

These fears made no sense to those unionists whose organizations had already been destroyed, or almost destroyed, in the wake of repression. These unionists had an unequivocal interest in political action. Since effective political action was a prerequisite for their organizational existence, nothing could counterbalance the incentive to engage in partisan politics that repression had given them. But for the majority of unionists in the AFL, while repression had threatened to disable their organizations, it had not threatened their ongoing existence. These unionists still had something to lose, and they were fearful of losing it. In particular, they were fearful that the establishment of a labor party, and involvement in partisan politics, would produce the kind of dissension that would lead to the destruction of their unions. These fears had two sources. One was the intense Democratic and Republican loyalties of ordinary workers—loyalties that were in turn fueled by religious identities and conflicts. The other was socialist sectarianism among labor leaders and activists.

Compared with Australia, the United States was both more religious and more heavily influenced by evangelicalism and revivalism. There were also differences in the hostility of the Protestant and Catholic clergy towards the labor movement. On their own, however, these differences do little to explain why there is no labor party in the United States. To understand the impact of religion, we need to examine its relationship to the party system.

The political salience of religion was much greater in the United States than Australia, and this difference was particularly great in the late nineteenth century. Labor leaders in both countries feared that partisan loyalties would produce dissension if unions entered the electoral arena. But whereas party loyalties in the United States were underpinned by religious conflicts, as well as identities forged in the Civil War, in Australia they were underpinned by economic conflicts (like those between free traders and protectionists), and the parties themselves were less well established. Economic conflicts over tariffs could stymie cooperation between unions and threaten the effectiveness of a labor-party experiment, but they were unlikely to threaten the existence of the unions themselves. By contrast, religious conflicts threatened to do just that. Many AFL leaders feared that if they formed a party and contested elections, they would be seen as taking sides in the religious conflicts that helped define the electoral arena. In effect, they would be importing potentially lethal conflicts into their unions. Unions needed to maintain the support of workers who were Republicans and Democrats, Protestants and Catholics, Evangelicals and Liturgicals. Labor leaders feared that if workers were forced to choose between union solidarity and their partisan and religious loyalties, they would choose the latter, and the unions themselves would be destroyed.

Socialist sectarianism was the other reason for the fear of dissension. The loyalties of American union leaders were divided between numerous left-wing factions and reform ideologies. Conflict between the proponents of these ideologies led many to fear that the establishment of a labor party would lead to a destructive outbreak of factional conflicts between activists. American reform ideologies were also influential in Australia, and factional conflicts between socialists, single taxers, and others were present in both countries. But European socialism, and the ideas of Marx and Lassalle in particular, had little influence in Australia, and it was the proponents of these currents that engaged in the most rancorous and destructive conflict in the United States. Both the main advocates and the main opponents of independent labor politics could be found amongst their number. After over two decades of conflict, their positions had hardened into a dogmatic "either-or" mentality that had acquired the status of common sense. According to this mentality, the labor movement could pursue either a union-based strategy or a party-based strategy, but it could not pursue both. Because of this, a number of top leaders viewed the proposal to establish a labor party as an overt or covert attempt to undermine the unions. These leaders claimed to be "pure and simple unionists," but their position was in fact based on a particular interpretation of Marxian socialism. In Australia, their counterparts, who in a sense really were pure and simple unionists, set about establishing a labor party.

So there were two main proximate causes for the failure of American unions to establish a labor party, each of which was, to a significant extent, the result of other more deeply entrenched features of American politics and society. One was the weakness of the new inclusive unions. This resulted, at least in part, from repression. The other was the fear of disruption that gripped many unionists. This resulted from intense party loyalties among ordinary workers—loyalties that were in turn fueled by religious conflicts—and from a particular form of socialist sectarianism among activists. Paradoxically then, in a land that often defines itself as democratic, secular, and liberal, it is the importance of repression, religion, and socialism that helps explain the failure to establish a labor party.

AMERICAN POLITICS AND SOCIETY

Like the conclusions of all social and historical studies, each of these answers raises a new set of questions—questions that can themselves only be answered by looking deeper into the roots of American politics and society. The high level of repression, the political salience of religion, and the strength of a particular form of socialist sectarianism help explain why there is no labor party in the United States. But why was there such a high level of repression? Why was religion so politically salient? And why were socialists so sectarian? To do them justice, each of these questions would require a study of its own. However, I have tried to indicate the beginning of some possible answers. I have examined the evolution of police and military institutions, and the unusually close ties with business interests that developed in the United States. I have considered the role of religious conflicts in establishing the party system that emerged from the realignment of the 1850s, and the sources of the heightened salience of these conflicts in the late 1880s and early 1890s. And I have examined the ideological and organizational conflicts that helped generate the particular type of socialist sectarianism that afflicted the American labor movement.

In the course of exploring why there is no labor party in the United States, I have had to consider each of the main characteristics that have been highlighted by the wider debate about American exceptionalism. The contributors to this wider debate have sought to identify what, if anything, is distinctive about American politics and society. The best known contributors have identified characteristics—like prosperity, democracy, and liberalism—that have often been associated with a celebratory attitude towards the United States and its achievements (even when that was not their original intention). Positions like these have long been influential in both American scholarship and in American public life, and they have undoubtedly had a major influence on the perceptions of outsiders. They have become, in a sense, the textbook wisdom about the United States. Of course, there is no reason why distinctive characteristics must be admirable ones. In recent years, accounts of American political development that focus on the pervasive influence of racial hostility have become increasingly important. These accounts usually avoid exceptionalist claims, although they sometimes come close to treating the extent and influence of racial hostility as a peculiarly American fatal flaw.

A systematic most-similar comparison suggests that none of these characteristics actually are distinctive. Certainly none of them are exceptional. The characteristics that differentiate one country from another can, of course, change over time. But in the late nineteenth century, neither prosperity, nor democracy, nor liberalism differentiated the United States from Australia. Nor did racial hostility. Each of these *were* important characteristics of the United States, and each had important social and political effects, although these effects were not always the same as those that are typically ascribed to them. But my findings suggest that conventional accounts of American politics and society have overemphasized the importance of these characteristics, and underemphasized the importance of others. From the vantage point of comparison with Australia, a number of observations stand out.

The American economy appears distinctive, not because of the prosperity it generated, but, rather, because of the weakness of union organizations in certain areas of the labor market. Despite the fact that the United States had one of the most industrialized economies in the world, new inclusive unions of unskilled and semi-skilled workers found it difficult to survive.

American political institutions appear distinctive, not because of the precocious commitment to democracy that they embodied, but, rather, because of the extensive use of state repression. Representative institutions and the early expansion of manhood suffrage did give ordinary people real opportunities to exercise control over the actions of governments. But judicial rulings, and police and military repression made it difficult or impossible for some groups to maintain organizations that could pursue their interests.

American political culture appears distinctive, not because of the prevalence of liberal values, or the pervasive influence of racial hostility, but, rather, because of the strength and sway of religion. American political culture was not monochromatic. Rather, it was composed of multiple competing traditions. Liberal values competed, not only with racial identities and racial consciousness, but also with powerful religious identities and commitments. Of course religion does play a role in the textbook account of the United States. But that account sees American political culture as a haven for religious minorities, rather than as a cauldron of religious conflicts.

Liberal values also marked the political culture of American social reformers and activists, but in comparison with Australia, it is the influence of socialist thought, and especially Marxism, that was distinctive. American reformers are often portrayed as if they were inoculated against the influence of socialism by the prevalence of liberal values. But far from inhibiting demands for intervention in the economy, liberal values provided social reformers and left-wing activists with powerful ideological resources. Strange though it may seem, it was the strength of European socialist influences—or, rather, of particular interpretations of them—and not their weakness, that did more to obstruct the effective pursuit of these demands.

In this book, I have been primarily concerned to explain why there is no labor party in the United States. But answering this question has led to some striking broader conclusions. These conclusions turn much of the conventional wisdom about American exceptionalism on its head. They also suggest that the most important underlying characteristics that have shaped the United States are not always those that are most commonly emphasized. High levels of prosperity, a precocious democracy, the prevalence of liberalism, and the pervasive influence of racial hostility all had important effects, although they sometimes promoted the very changes they are said to have retarded. But comparison with Australia makes it clear that these were not exceptional characteristics of the United States. Instead, it draws attention to the importance of state repression, the political salience of religion, and even to particular strands of socialism. Of course, we can not, on this basis, go on to conclude that it was really these characteristics that were exceptional. But we can conclude that they helped make the United States exceptional in at least one respect. For they helped leave it without a labor party.

Appendix: Notes and Sources for the Tables

TABLE 1.1 GDP PER CAPITA

Maddison (1991), *Dynamic Forces in Capitalist Development*, Tables A.2, A.6, and B.2.

TABLE 1.2 CONSUMPTION OF FOODS

NSW (Australia): For 1891, see Coghlan (1893a, 837 and 841). For 1901, see Coghlan (1902, 765 and 768).

United States: For 1889 and 1899, see Montgomery and Kardell (1930). For slightly different figures for some items in 1899, see U.S. Bureau of the Census (1975, 330–31).

Meat: The figures for meat include those for beef. The U.S. data for meat and beef are for 1900. There does not appear to be U.S. data for the period around 1890.

Flour: Figures from the United States are for wheat flour. NSW figures seem to be for wheat flour as well, although this is not stated explicitly.

Potatoes: Coghlan (1893a, 841, and 1902, 768–69) suggests that these Australian estimates are too high since part of the potato crop used to calculate these figures was not used for human consumption.

TABLE 1.3 URBAN AND RURAL POPULATION

The figures refer to the percentage of the total population living in towns or cities with a population size greater than that specified. Rural refers to those living either on farms or in towns of 1,000 or less. The U.S. data are for 1890. The Australian data are for 1891.

United States: U.S. Bureau of the Census (1975, 12).

Illinois: U.S. Census Office (1894b, lxx). Illinois figures for these categories of town size are not readily available. 38.8 percent of the population lived in towns with more than 8,000 people, and 44.9 percent in towns of more than 2,500.

Australia: Coghlan (1898b, 61), and Vamplew (1987, 41).

NSW: Coghlan (1894a, 126–7).

TABLE 1.4 GEOGRAPHICAL DISTRIBUTION OF LABOR PARTY SEATS IN NSW

Markey (1988, 189). The 1895 and 1898 totals include seats won in later by-elections.

TABLE 2.1 BLACKS, CHINESE, AND NEW IMMIGRANT EUROPEANS

All Data: All figures are derived from the 1890 census in the United States, and the 1891 census in Australia.

Blacks: All U.S. figures refer to African-Americans. See "all persons of negro decent" in U.S. Census Office (1894b), *Report on the Population of the United States at the Eleventh Census: 1890. Part I,* xcv and 397. All Australian figures refer to South Pacific Islanders. For Australia as a whole, see "Total Pacific" in Vamplew, ed. (1987), *Australians: Historical Statistics,* 8–9. For NSW, see "Polynesia," "British Polynesia" (including Fiji), and "French Polynesia" (including New Caledonia) in Coghlan (1894a), *General Report on the Eleventh Census of New South Wales,* 187. For Queensland, see Coghlan (1898b), *A Statistical Account of the Seven Colonies of Australasia, 1897–8,* 59.

Chinese: All figures refer to the total Chinese population (most of whom, though not all, are immigrants). For the U.S., see U.S. Census Office (1894b), *Report on Population, Part I,* 397. For Australia, see Coghlan (1898b), *Statistical Account,* 58.

Slavs and Italians: These figures are for the foreign-born. For the United States, see U.S. Census Office (1894b), *Report on Population: Part I,* cxlii, cxxxviii–cxxxix, 606–9. For Australia as a whole, see Vamplew, ed. (1987), *Historical Statistics,* 8–9. For NSW, see Coghlan (1894b), *Results of a Census of New South Wales . . . 1891,* 439–40. For Queensland, see Coghlan (1898b), *Statistical Account,* 62. Slavs in the U.S. include those born in Russia, Poland, Hungary, and Bohemia. Slavs in Australia include the figures for those born in Russia (which include those from Poland), and for three-quarters of those born in Austria-Hungary (which is an estimate for those born in Hungary and other non-German-speaking parts, including Bohemia). Australian census takers did not distinguish between those born in different parts of Austria-Hungary until 1921. In addition, prior to this, many German-speaking Austrians were probably counted as Germans. Given this, and given the figures for Austria-Hungary and its component parts in 1901, 1911, and 1921, I have made a rough estimate that about one quarter of those counted as Austro-Hungarians in the 1891 census were German-speaking Austrians, and that the rest were Hungarians, Bohemians, and others. See Jupp (2001, 178) and Norst and McBride (1988, 12 and 201).

TABLE 2.2 BIRTHPLACES OF IMMIGRANTS

U.S., Pennsylvania and Illinois: See U.S. Census Office (1894b), *Report on the Population of the United States at the Eleventh Census: 1890. Part I,* cxxxviii–cxxxix, 606–609.

Australia: See 1891 census data in Vamplew, ed. (1987), *Australians: Historical Statistics,* 8–9.

NSW: See Coghlan (1894b), *Results of a Census of New South Wales . . . 1891,* 439–40.

North and West Europe: This refers to Britain (England, Scotland, and Wales), Ireland, Germany, and Scandinavia (Sweden, Norway, and Denmark), as well as Austria, Holland, Belgium, Luxembourg, Switzerland, and France.

South and East Europe: This refers to Slavic countries as defined by the U.S. census (Russia, Hungary, Bohemia, and Poland), and Italy, as well as Spain, Portugal, Greece and a number of Balkan and Mediterranean countries defined by Vamplew (1987, 8–9) as southern and eastern European and from which only small numbers of immigrants arrived. For the division of Australian figures for Austria-Hungary, see the note to Table 2.1 on "Slavs and Italians."

English Settler Societies: This refers to all of Canada and New Zealand, as well as Australia for the United States, or the United States for Australia. The U.S. census has no data for immigrants from New Zealand.

TABLE 5.1 TWO CRITICAL STRIKES

The Maritime Strike

Population: This figure is from the 1891 Census (Coghlan, 1894a, 127). The same census found that 425,720 people lived in "Sydney and environs" (Coghlan, 1894a, 108).

Strikers: This estimate is based on the membership of those unions in Sydney that depended on strike allowances paid by the Labour Defence Committee

(1890, 39). These unions were the Marine Officers, Vanmen, Sydney Wharf Labourers, Sydney Coal Lumpers, Stewards and Cooks, Seaman, and Trolly and Draymen. According to figures in the *Australian Star* on October 6, 1890, these unions had a combined membership of 6,870. According to figures in the Literary Appendix to the NSW Royal Commission on Strikes (1891), they had a membership of 7,667. These unions represented only about a half of the 14,000 unionists who were dependent on the Labour Defence Committee (1890, 20). Most of the other half worked on coalfields within a hundred-mile radius of Sydney. There were also other strikers (like the shearers) who did not receive financial support from the Defence Committee. Support was only available when a union's own resources had been exhausted, and those engaged in wildcat sympathy strikes were told to return to work (Labour Defence Committee, 1890, 10 and 20). For some evidence that favors a lower estimate of about 6,000 strikers in Sydney, see Spence (1909, 120) who suggests that there were 4,748 on strike in Sydney on September 12. They were joined by some 1,221 trolly and draymen three days later (NSW Royal Commission on Strikes, 1891, 138, and Walker, 1986, 63). See also Coghlan (1918, 1595) and Gibson (1994, 119), who estimate that 4,500–5,000 waterside workers and seamen stopped work at the beginning of the strike, which then grew as more joined.

Armed Forces: See Fosbery (1890, 630) and Gibson (1994, 117–39). Of the Special Constables, 162 were country troops called to Sydney.

Union Leaders Arrested: None of the 27 members of the Labour Defence Committee who ran the strike were arrested.

Workers Arrested: In Sydney, 56 people were sentenced for offenses arising out of the strike (Walker, 1986, 63). Presumably, there were other arrests that did not lead to sentences, although I have been unable to establish this. However, given that the Inspector-General of Police emphasized that the strike was largely orderly, there may not have been many other arrests (Fosbery, 1890, 628).

The Pullman Strike

Population: This figure is from the 1890 census (Bogue, 1985, 120). By 1900, the population of Chicago was 1,698,575.

Strikers: For this estimate, see Lindsey (1942, 134). Later in the strike, the railway workers were briefly joined by other unionists when the Chicago Trades and Labor Council called a sympathy strike. However, with the railway workers near defeat, the response was disappointing and not more than 25,000 took part (Lindsey, 1942, 225).

Armed Forces: See Lindsey (1942, 165, 173–74, 182–83, 196, 199, and 234). Lindsey's figures are similar to those of the United States Strike Commission

(1895, xix). The Strike Commission, however, seems to have mistakenly rounded down the number of state troops to 4,000 and to have left out 500 police reserves who were involved in the strike. For Lindsey's evidence on the involvement of police reserves, see the *Report of General Superintendent of Police . . . of Chicago*, 1894, pages 18 and 22. On the law in Illinois governing the appointment of deputy sheriffs, see Beckner (1929, 65–66). On the composition of the force of Federal Deputy Marshals, see the United States Strike Commission (1895, xliv), Lindsey (1942, 165–69) and Cooper (1980, 145). 3,600 of them were selected, armed, paid for, and directed by the railroad companies.

Union Leaders Arrested: All nine members of the American Railway Union's board of directors were arrested for conspiracy and President Eugene Debs and the union's other top three officials were arrested and jailed for contempt (Lindsey, 1942, 278–82).

Workers Arrested: See United States Strike Commission (1895, xviii). Of those arrested for strike-related offenses in the vicinity of Chicago, 190 were arrested under federal statutes (although only 71 of them were actually indicted), and 515 were arrested by the police. These figures include arrested union leaders.

Workers Killed: According to the United States Strike Commission (1895, xviii), 12 workers were shot and fatally wounded. The figure of 13 comes from the *Report of the General Superintendent of Police . . . of Chicago*, 1894, pages 26–7. In addition, 53 workers were seriously wounded (Lindsey, 1942, 214).

TABLE 5.2 THE QUEENSLAND SHEARERS' STRIKE AND THE HOMESTEAD STEEL STRIKE

Queensland Shearers

Population: This is an attempt to estimate the population in the pastoral districts affected by the strike. It represents the population in the nine census districts in which more than 300 people were employed as pastoral workers in 1891 as defined in class V, order XXI, sub-order 2, item 3 (Queensland Registrar-General, 1892, 12 and 218–19). It can only be considered a very rough estimate because not all pastoral workers were shearers, the borders of census districts did not always coincide with pastoral districts, and the strike itself affected data collection during the 1891 census, especially in the western districts (Camm and Sumner, 1982, 54, and Queensland Registrar-General, 1892, xlv–xlvii).

Strikers: This estimate draws on Kenway (1970), Merritt (1986), and Svensen (1989). At the end of 1890, the two unions that went on strike—the Queensland Shearers Union (QSU) and the Queensland Labourers Union (QLU)—had 3,721 and 7,635 members, respectively (Merritt, 1986, 172, and Svensen,

1989, 49). The strikers were camped at around 50 sites. Svensen, who has gone to a good deal of effort to build up estimates of the population of each camp, concludes that between 9,000 and 10,000 workers were on strike (Svensen, 1989, 131, 253, and 297–300). In April, 8,507 unionists voted in a plebiscite about whether to continue the strike, but it seems likely that there were also a number of unionists who did not vote because they were traveling between strike camps at the time (Kenway, 1970, 117 and 125, and Merritt, 1986, 175).

Armed Forces: For these estimates, see Svensen (1989, 4 and 296). The Queensland Defence Force was predominantly a militia of unpaid, part-time soldiers alongside a small permanent force. See Drury (1891). The largest numbers of police and soldiers were concentrated around the towns of Barcaldine (where there were about 1,650 strikers in four camps) and Cleremont (where there were about 1,300 strikers in three camps). For example, up to 1,000 police and soldiers were sent to the area around Barcaldine. On Barcaldine, see Svensen (1989, 18 and 297–300), Kenway (1970, 116), Hearn and Knowles (1996, 50), and Coulthard-Clark (1981, 73). On Cleremont, see Svensen (1989, 297–300) and Kenway (1970, 114).

Union Leaders Arrested: Ten members of the Barcaldine-based Strike Committee, as well as the Secretary of the QLU and a number of other local leaders, were arrested, charged with conspiracy, and sentenced to three years in jail. The Secretary of the QSU was also arrested but later released. See Spence (1961 [1911], 42–43 and 53), Kenway (1970, 117–18), Merritt (1986, 174) and Svensen (1989, 50, 302).

Workers Arrested: This figure is based on a list of union prisoners compiled by Svensen (1989, 197 and 302–4). Svensen's figures show that 93 were arrested but not convicted, and 128 were sentenced to jail terms of one month or more. He suggests that dozens more were sentenced to shorter terms or fined. Compare this with the smaller estimates of Kenway (1970, 118), who suggests that at least 161 unionists were arrested, and Merritt (1986, 175), who suggests that about 80 unionists were sentenced to jail terms.

Workers Killed: There was, however, one murder carried out by an insane man (Svensen, 1989, 4).

The Homestead Strike

Population: For this estimate of the population of Homestead in 1892, see Burgoyne (1979 [1893], 3 and 303) and Yellen (1974, 73). According to the 1890 census, the population of Allegheny County as a whole was 551,959 (Forstall, 1996, 136).

Strikers: All 3,800 workers at the Homestead works went on strike even though only the 800 skilled craft workers were members of the union: the Amalgamated Association of Iron and Steel Workers. See Krause (1992, 308 and 332), Burgoyne (1979 [1893], 5), Yellen (1974, 73 and 81, and Goldstein (1978, 45–46).

Armed Forces: On the county police, including the sheriff, see Burgoyne (1979 [1893], 48–49) and Yellen (1974, 83). On the Deputy Sheriffs, see Burgoyne (1979 [1893], 211). On State Troops, see Burgoyne (1979 [1893], 111), Yellen (1974, 90), and Krause (1992, 334). Note that the entire National Guard was mobilized and sent to Homestead. On the Pinkerton agents, see Burgoyne (1979 [1893], 46–47). The company claimed that the sheriff had agreed to deputize this private armed force, though the sheriff later disputed this.

Union Leaders Arrested: Warrants were issued for the arrest of all 33 members of the Advisory Committee that was running the strike in Homestead, charging them with treason and conspiracy. However, a few of these local leaders avoided arrest by going into hiding. In addition, the three main local leaders were charged with murder and aggravated riot. The central leaders of the steel workers union were not arrested. After three failed attempts to gain a conviction for murder, all the cases were dropped. See Burgoyne (1979 [1893], 38, 197, and 241–95), Yellen (1974, 94–7), and Foner (1955, 213–15).

Workers Arrested: This figure, which includes the arrested union leaders, is based on a list of those facing grand jury indictments compiled by Burgoyne (1979 [1893], 194–97). Ultimately, none were convicted. The figure must significantly underestimate the number of workers arrested, since none of those arrested for lesser offenses are included.

Workers Killed: This figure is based on the county coroner's report cited in Burgoyne (1979 [1893], 92), Yellen (1974, 86), and Krause (1992, 409, n2). It may be an underestimate. According to a Senate report, at least nine workers were killed (Foner, 1955, 210). In addition, three Pinkerton agents were killed. All these deaths took place during a battle between strikers and Pinkertons. It is difficult to establish how many workers were seriously wounded.

TABLE 5.3 TWO SILVER MINING STRIKES

Broken Hill

Population: This figure is from the 1891 Census (Solomon, 1988, 126–27).

Strikers: For this estimate, see (Solomon, 1988, 244, and NSW Legislative Assembly, 1892–93, 284). There were 5,806 employees of the mines in 1890, and compulsory unionism had been conceded in the 1889 strike (Solomon, 1988, 136 and 238). The largest company alone employed 3,202 workers immediately before the 1892 strike, and it is estimated that over 5,000—and perhaps over 7,000—men and women attended the mass meeting that voted to call the strike (Dale, 1918, 25, and Kennedy, 1978, 67 and 71).

Armed Forces: See NSW Legislative Assembly (1892–3, 309). For other references to police numbers, see Walker (1986, 58), Kennedy (1978, 66 and 68), and Dale (1918, 33 and 49). The government resisted employer demands that it call out the military (Dickey, 1966, 43–44).

Union Leaders Arrested: All seven local leaders who formed the Defence Committee that ran the strike were arrested and charged with seditious conspiracy, though they were immediately replaced by other unionists. One of them was acquitted and the other six were sentenced: two to two years, two to eighteen months, one to nine months, and one (who turned out to be an informer) to three months, although none served more than nine months before being released. See Solomon (1988, 241–2), Dale (1918, 47–49, 55, and 65), and NSW Legislative Assembly (1892–93, 305–6).

Workers Arrested: Correspondence which police, prosecutors, and magistrates sent to the government from the beginning of the strike until October 5, 1892 was tabled in parliament. According to this correspondence (NSW Legislative Assembly, 1892–3), there were 18 workers arrested (including union leaders) during this period. Two strikebreakers wielding revolvers were also arrested. The strike, however, continued until November 6. Dale (1918, 52–60) refers to another eight arrests during this last month, and there were probably a few others. Accounts of the strike give the general impression that strikers and pickets were increasingly subject to petty legal harassment by the Police Magistrate and his men (Dale, 1918, 57, and Dickey, 1966, 48–50). For example, the Police Magistrate responded to queries about one case by explaining to the Under-Secretary for Justice that: "Boohooing and groaning and coughing at persons in public appeared to me to be not only riotous behaviour but indecent behaviour under the 'Towns Police Act' and I inflicted a small fine to show that such behaviour could not be tolerated . . . (Dickey, 1966, 49).

Coeur d'Alene

Population: This is the 1890 census figure for the precincts of Shoshone County around the South Fork of the Coeur d'Alene river where the silver and lead mines were located. In 1890, the largest town in this area was Wallace with a population of 913 (Smith, 1961, 6).

Strikers: This is an estimate of the number of union members left in April 1892 when they were officially locked out. The mines had already been closed since January because of a dispute between the mine owners and the railroad companies over freight rates. Prior to this there may have been up to 2,000 union members in the Coeur area (Smith, 1961, 38, and Jensen, 1950, 28–32).

Armed Forces: See Smith (1961, 59, 74–79, 82, and 90). For more on these troops, see Cooper (1980, 167–69) and Rich (1941, 110–12). There were also perhaps 50 deputy constables and an unknown number of deputy marshals in the area. These are not shown in the table because of uncertainty about the number and the status of these men. In particular, it is not clear what the deputy constables did, or how long they were deployed. Both the sheriff and the justice who appointed the deputy constables were sympathetic to the miners, and were removed from office and arrested by the incoming troops. The deputy marshals on the other hand were probably mostly strikebreakers (Smith, 1961, 55, 100, and 103, Foner, 1955, 238, and Jensen, 1950, 36). In addition, the mining companies employed at least 54 private armed guards and a number of Pinkerton agents who made no claim to be agents of the state and have not been included here (Smith, 1961, 45, and Foner, 1955, 231–33).

Union Leaders Arrested: All the unions leaders and prominent supporters were charged with criminal conspiracy (Smith, 1961, 99–100).

Workers Arrested: This figure includes the arrested union leaders. With the exception of those who fled across the border to Montana, practically every unionist as well as many union sympathizers were taken prisoner. Most of these prisoners were held in a "bull pen," and the largest number held at any one time was about 350 (Smith, 1961, 86, and Cooper, 1980, 168). In federal cases (Smith, 1961, 97–101), 25 were charged with contempt of court, of whom 13 were sentenced to between four and eight months, and two groups—one listing 84 defendants and another listing 116—were indicted for criminal conspiracy, of whom 14 stood trial and four were sentenced to between 15 and 24 months (until the convictions were overturned on technical grounds by the Supreme Court). In state cases (Smith, 1961, 102–5), 42 were charged with murder and destruction of property. However, only one case was heard, and when that defendant was found not guilty, the other cases were dropped.

Workers Killed: See Rich (1941, 110) and Smith (1961, 66, 102 and 118). Three of these workers were unionists, and three were strikebreakers. All were killed before the arrival of troops when shooting broke out between unionists and a group of deputy marshals, strikebreakers, and Pinkertons. In addition, about 25 workers were seriously injured (Foner, 1955, 231–32, and Schwantes, 1996, 157).

TABLE 7.1 THE EXTENT OF RELIGIOUS INVOLVEMENT

Population: For NSW and Sydney, see Coghlan (1894a, 214 and 127). For Illinois, Pennsylvania, and the U.S., see U.S. Bureau of the Census (1975, 27 and 33). For Chicago and Pittsburgh, see Carroll (1894, 91).

Affiliation: Figures refer to the percentage of the population who mentioned a church or denomination when asked their religion during the 1891 census. Like the membership figures collected in the U.S., the Australian figures here include Jews but do not include Buddhists, Confucians, and Muslims. For NSW, see Phillips (1969, 439) and *General Report on the Eleventh Census of NSW* (Coghlan, 1894a, 213–19). For Sydney, see Coghlan (1894b), *Results of a Census of NSW . . . 1891*, pages 370–77. For other Australian colonies, see Vamplew (1987, 420–25). There are no U.S. figures for affiliation, but these numbers were probably similar to those in Australia. For some estimates, see Carroll (1893, xiii and xxxiv–xxxvi), and Finke and Starke (1992, 8).

Attendance: Figures refer to the percentage of the population "generally attending" a church service each week. For NSW, see Phillips (1969, 446). For Sydney, see Phillips (1972, 389). Note that both these figures are for 1890. For some of the difficulties with attendance figures, see Phillips (1972, 385–94). See also Coghlan (1891b, 581–84, and 1893a, 545–48). For Victoria, see Phillips (1982, 30–31 and 36). Attendance figures are not available for the United States.

Membership: Figures refer to the percentage of the population who are communicants of a church or who accept all the obligations and entitlements of a church. For Australia, see NSW Statistician, *Statistical Register* for 1893, 641–51. For the United States, see U.S. Census Office, *Report on Statistics of Churches at the Eleventh Census: 1890* (Carroll, 1894, 44 and 91). Note that the NSW figure is a high estimate. For figures that produce estimates of 13.5 percent and 12.7 percent, see respectively Vamplew (1987, 428–29) and Phillips (1969, 446, and 1972, 395). On the definition of communicants and the problems of generating comparable data, see Phillips (1969, 54, and 1972, 394–96), Vamplew (1987, 428–29 and 464–65), Carroll (1983, xl–xli and lxii, and 1894, xii and 233), and U.S. Bureau of the Census (1975, 389–90).

Churches: Figures refer to the number of church buildings per thousand head of population. For Australia, see Phillips (1969, 449). For the United States, see Carroll (1894, 44 and 91).

TABLE 7.2 MEMBERS OF CHURCH DENOMINATIONS

Australia: All figures are from *The NSW Statistical Register for 1893*, (Coghlan, 1894c, 641–53). This was the first time that figures for members and communicants were compiled on a statewide and citywide basis. Australia-wide figures are not available because of major gaps for some denominations (Vamplew, 1987, 428–29).

United States: All figures are from U.S. Census Office, *Report on Statistics of Churches . . . at the Eleventh Census: 1890* (Carroll, 1894, 38–42 and 94–99).

Columns: These do not add up to 100 percent because minor churches are not included. Churches with less than 0.1 percent of the total membership of all churches are shown as <0.1.

Anglicans: This refers to the Church of England in Australia and the Episcopal Church in the United States.

Lutherans: This refers to both Lutheran and German Evangelical Churches in both countries.

Disciples: This refers to the Church of Christ in Australia and the Disciples of Christ in the United States.

Rows: Other denominational names refer to all churches within that family of churches for which data are available. For details regarding membership data, see Coghlan (1894c, 641–53) and Phillips (1972, 394–96) on Australia, and Carroll (1894, 38–42 and 94–99) on the United States.

TABLE 7.3 AFFILIATES OF CHURCH DENOMINATIONS IN AUSTRALIA

NSW: Figures based on 1891 Census (Coghlan, 1894a, 218) as amended by Phillips (1969, 439).

Other states: Figures based on Vamplew (1987, 422–24).

Columns: These do not add up to 100 percent because minor churches and the unaffiliated are not included.

Rows: For the meaning of denominational categories, see the notes and sources to Table 7.2. For details regarding affiliation data, see Coghlan (1894a, 213–19) and Vamplew (1987, 420).

Notes

INTRODUCTION

1. AFL (1895, 100).

2. See, among others, Stephens (1979), Korpi (1983), Esping-Andersen (1990), Baldwin (1990), Garrett (1998), and Goodin (1999).

3. Other parties might have a trade union wing, like many Christian Democratic parties, or the Liberal party in late nineteenth-century Britain, without giving priority to this relationship.

4. Among many others, see Sundquist (1983), Davis (1986), Lichtenstein (1989), and Brinkley (1998).

5. Skocpol (1979) and Skocpol and Somers (1980).

6. Verba (1967), Lijphart (1971), Sartori (1970 and 1994), Collier (1991), and Evans (1995).

7. See Ragin (1987, 48) on the problem of illusory commonality.

8. On causal mechanisms, see Elster (1989, 3–10), Stinchcombe (1991), Little (1991), Hedstrom and Swedberg (1998), and King *et al.* (1994, 85–87 and 224–228). On the related concept of "process tracing," see Mahoney and Rueschemeyer (2003) and George and Bennett (2005).

9. On the limits to Australian authority over foreign affairs, and the partial limits to authority over the armed forces, see Castles (1982, 401 and 413).

10. In Australia, the Labor party was formed in 1891. In Britain, the Independent Labour party was not formed until 1893, and the union-based Labour Representation Committee (the forerunner of the Labour party) was not formed until 1900.

11. In 1932, unions joined with farmers' organizations to form the Cooperative Commonwealth Federation (which later became the New Democratic party). This party had been preceded by a short-lived labor party established in 1917, as well as by experiments with farmer parties (which had some labor participation) in a number of western provinces.

12. Lipset (1950, 1990, and 1996, 88–109).

13. Foner (1984, 73–74), Somers (1989, 325), Halpern and Morris (1997, 7), Katznelson (1997, 37), Katznelson and Zolberg (1986, 24), and Wilentz (1984, 2).

14. Fredrickson (1997, 49), Wilentz (1984, 1), and Breuilly (1990, 6).

15. This would remain true even if some labor-based parties were to subsequently change their character (Lipset and Marks (2000, 273–294). However, developments in newly industrializing countries could raise some interesting questions. If some of these countries also fail to establish labor-based parties, the American experience may need to be reexamined afresh. But the question of why, alone among the first wave of advanced capitalist countries, the United States did not establish a labor-based party in the late nineteenth and early twentieth centuries would remain.

16. See the speech that chairman Ferguson of the strikers' Defence Committee gave in Broken Hill on September 6, 1892 (NSW Legislative Assembly, 1892–93, 300).

The Broken Hill strike began on July 3, 1892. The speaker was almost certainly referring to the Homestead strike (which began three days later) or the Coeur d'Alene miners' strike (which began on July 11).

17. Especially those associated with the shearers' union and its journals. See also Markey (1988, xi) and Nairn (1989, xiii). In this book, the proper names of parties and other organisations have been retained, and in all quotations the original spelling is unaltered. In other respects, however, American spelling conventions have been adopted.

18. Kaufman (1986, 318–320), AFL (1892, 16), and AF, July 1894, 104.

19. For the NSW pamphlet, see O'Sullivan (1892). For the World's Labor Congress and Lloyd, see Destler (1963, 242, 258–259, 265, 275, and 400). For Lloyd's speeches, see Lloyd (1893) and Destler (1946, 197 and 213–21).

20. For occasional articles, see Goodrich (1928) and Churchward (1952 and 1953). For American exceptionalism, see Hartz (1964) and Lipset (1963). For brief mentions in comparative treatments, see Foner (1984) and Davis (1986).

CHAPTER 1

WORKERS

1. For the origins of the idea of a workingman's paradise, see Kingston (1988, 277).

2. See Snooks (1995), Thomas (1995), Jackson and Thomas (1995), McLean (1999), and Haig (1989).

3. For some problems with Williamson's series, see Pope and Withers (1994, 245–6). For additional comparative data on wages, see Fischer (1988) on seamen, and Dowling (1893, 96) on coal miners.

4. Kelly ended "I am going back to Australia next March." See the *Bulletin*, November 7, 1891.

5. Additional sources of data are provided by the surveys conducted in the United States in 1901 (U.S. Commissioner of Labor, 1904, 648), in Germany in 1907–1908 (Trivett, 1914, 960), and in Australia in 1910–1911 (Knibbs, 1912, 1177–79).

6. I have included potatoes in Table 1.2 because Sombart seems to have a bit of a "thing" about them. At one point, he suggests that German workers may be being "merely obstinate in sticking to a diet consisting exclusively or predominantly of potatoes" (Sombart, 1976, 87). And at another point he even seems to suggest that American workers may be inured to socialism because they are "not acquainted with the discomforts that must necessarily result in the long run from the mixing of potatoes and alcohol" (Sombart, 1976, 105). Since the consumption of alcohol in Australia was somewhat less than in the United States (Coghlan, 1893a, 848 and 1902, 774 and Trivett, 1913, 977), the Australian case provides no support for this alternative "potato and alcohol" hypothesis.

7. For example, the *NLT* and *UMWJ* in the United States took a particularly close interest in developments in the British steel and coal industries.

8. These comparisons sometimes drew on the very same sources. For example, in the United States, the *NLT*, August 29, 1891, 1, reported that "Australasia . . . leads the way and surpasses the rest of civilized nations in industrial remuneration." Two months

later in Australia, the *Hummer*, October 31, 1891, 3, reprinted a piece from the Knights of Labor Journal that reported that "the highest average wages are paid in the Australian colonies." Both items were based on U.S. consular reports. For other comparisons, see the *Bulletin*, July 18, 1891, 6, and the *UMWJ*, May 28, 1891, 2.

9. See the speech of W.G. Spence in the *Hummer*, May 28, 1892, 2. See also the *Bulletin*, January 31, 1891, 5. Interestingly, Australian labor papers also took umbrage at those who suggested that American workers were quite satisfied with their conditions. When a member of parliament sparked a debate on this, they went to great lengths to disprove his assertions. See *AW*, February 20, 1892, 1 and 4, and *Hummer*, December 5, 1891, 3.

10. *AF*, February 1896, 223, and *AW*, January 17, 1891, 1.

11. Sombart is far from alone in this. In Australia, just as a new wave of unionization was about to begin, and a few years before the establishment of the Labor party, Twopeny (1883, 110) made a similar assumption about workers there.

12. See "Ethics of Trade Unions" in *AF*, January 1896, 198–9.

13. See, for example, the report on William Holman's lecture in *AW*, November 26, 1892, 1.

14. See, for example, Sombart (1976, 115–119) who rests heavily on the argument of Turner (1920, 259, 275 and 321) about the availability of cheap land on America's expanding western frontier. Against this, see Shannon (1966, 356–9), and Hofstadter and Lipset (1968).

15. On urban social mobility, see Thernstrom (1964 and 1974), and Laslett and Lipset (1984) for the U.S., and Markey (1988, 20 and 46), Fitzgerald (1987, 103–37), and Davison (1979b) for Australia.

16. *AW*, January 24, 1891, 1, and Commons (1918, vol 1, 510 n19). See also *Hummer*, March 12, 1892, 3.

17. These large firms employed 38 percent of the city's workforce (Schneirov, 1998, 344). In late 1893 and early 1894, unemployment in Chicago as a whole may have been between 40 and 60 percent (Kleppner, 1970, 215). For industry by industry details, see *Chicago Daily News Almanac 1894*, 360–74. See also Jensen (1971, 211–12). A police department survey in late September 1893 reported that 25 percent of those in meatpacking, 20 percent of those who worked in railroad freight yards, and 50 percent of Chicago's factory workers had been laid off. On wage cuts, see Destler (1946, 177–9). Coal miners' earnings fell even further. In 1894, coal miners were earning 77 percent of what they had earned in 1890. In 1897, they were earning 69 percent of what they had earned in 1890 (Nash, 1982, 163). For unemployment in Sydney, see Markey (1988, 39–41).

18. For a clear formulation of this position, see Marks (1989, 45–8, 204–10).

19. For an influential version of this standard account, see Gollan (1960, 99–109).

20. For details of the organizational base of the new unions: on the Maritime industry, see Markey (1988, 89–99); on mining, see Markey (1988, 67–82) and Gollan (1963); on the railroads, see Markey (1988, 99–104) and Docherty (1973); on the pastoral industry see Markey (1988, 57–67) and Merritt (1986); and on the building industry, see Sheldon (1989). For details of fees and benefits, see NSW Royal Commission on Strikes (1891), Literary Appendix, 132–57. See also Markey (1985, 21–22, and 1988, 147–9).

21. Lightfoot and Sutcliffe (1915, 55, 64), Turner (1965, 250), and Peetz (1998, 25, 203). An ambitious project undertaken by Michael Quinlan and his colleagues aims to

create a database of every instance of workers' collective action in nineteenth-century Australia. The database is still incomplete for some states, and it includes participants in informal events as well as the members of formal organizations. But it certainly supports the claim that union membership grew rapidly in the 1880s, peaked in a sudden surge in 1890–91, and then fell back sharply to retain perhaps a third of its peak in the mid-1890s. I am grateful to Michael Quinlan for showing me some of his unpublished data. For other preliminary findings, see Quinlan *et al.* (2003).

22. According to the AFL, the number of affiliated unionists did not change greatly between the end of 1894 and 1897. My estimates here assume that the same was true also for the total number of unionists. See Wolman (1924, 32–33, 118). For labor force data, see *U.S. Historical Statistics*, Table D 11–25. I have assumed that about 65 percent of the labor force were wage earners. For this estimate, see the 1900 data in Table D 182–232. Note that my estimates in this and the next paragraph refer to the period after the collapse of the American Railway Union.

23. See data in Schneirov (1998, 254, 299, 306–7, and 344) and the Illinois Bureau of Labor Statistics (1904, 314).

24. There are three main sources for union membership figures in NSW at this time. The first is a list published in the *Australian Star* on October 6, 1890. The second is the data from June 1891 published in the Literary Appendix to NSW Royal Commission on Strikes (1891). And the third is the sustenation fund reports of the TLC, which record dues paid to it by its affiliates. For these, see the TLC's Half-Yearly Reports for 1890, and its Account Books and Sustenation Fund for 1891 to 1894, both held at the Mitchell Library in Sydney. See also Markey (1988, 318–9). The figures in this paragraph are drawn from the first source. The second source produces higher percentages. I have included the members of the Newcastle, Illawara, and Western District coal miners, the Hunter colliery surfacemen, the shearers, the Sydney and Newcastle wharf laborers, and the trolley and draymen, as well as the unaffiliated Broken Hill metal miners, the all-grades rail union, the coal lumpers, and the seamen.

25. These figures are rough estimates only. They draw on three sources for membership figures. The first is the "Register of the National Trade Unions of the United States" in AFL (1892a). The second is the 1897 membership data in Wolman (1924, 110–119). And the third is the list of the number of votes to which each representative to the AFL's 1894 Convention was entitled in AFL (1894, 7–8). Each union was entitled to one vote for every 100 members. See also Marks (1989, 206–7). There were only two significant industrial unions in the AFL in 1894: the mine workers and the brewers. For the preceding estimates I have added the seamen, the longshoremen, and the (unaffiliated) trainmen. Each of these shared some of the characteristics of the Australian new unions, even though some, like the seamen, insisted they were craft-based organizations. The vote to which the new unions were entitled in 1894 was larger than their membership because, the votes of the miners union had not yet been adjusted to take account of the collapse in its membership following the coal strike earlier that year. Thus, the miners commanded 15 percent of the AFL's vote at the end of 1894, but by then they may have only had as little as 4 percent of its affiliated membership.

26. The resolution was passed unanimously. However, the draft federation plan that was brought back to the 1889 congress was shelved until 1891, for fear of its effect on union autonomy (ICTUC, 1889, 38–49, and Gollan, 1960, 104, 106–7)

27. The critical role of this contribution was widely noticed, and, especially in the English-speaking world, led to discussion of the possibility of pursuing a new policy of international working class solidarity that was sometimes referred to as "Hands Across the Sea." See, for example, *UMWJ*, July 16, 1891, 2.

28. Though a plan to do this was passed by the ICTUC (1891), it was only ever fully implemented in Queensland (Sutcliffe, 1921, 113–23 and 241–47).

29. See the "Report of the General Secretary" in Ebbels (1983, 152). For similar comments by Spence, see his 1892 lecture on the *Ethics of the New Unionism*, and his address on "The New Unionism" in Bourke reported in the *Hummer*, May 28, 1892. See also the conclusion of the Brisbane *Worker*, November 1, 1890: "Unorganised labour broke the strike, and not only unorganised labour but unskilled labour . . . high entrance fees . . . [and] the flimsy partitions which now separate the various occupations should go" (Ebbels, 1983, 149–50).

30. See NSW TLC (1891, 11), ICTUC (1891, 15 and passim), William Lane, writing under the name Miller, in *Hummer*, January 16, 1892, 1, and George Black, who was by then also a labor member of parliament, in *AW*, December 31, 1892, 1.

31. On the Wharf Labourers, see Markey (1988, 148); on the Trolley and Draymen, see NSW Royal Commission on Strikes (1891, 138); and on the Shearers, see Merritt (1986, 142, 178).

32. See "Cheap John Unions" I and II in the *AF*, February 1896, 223 and 226, and March 1896, 14–15.

33. *UMWJ*, July 19, 1894, 4.

34. See the masthead of each edition of the *CSJ* in the early 1890s. This is all the more interesting because the Coast Seamen's Union had watched the Maritime strike in Australia particularly closely, and was well aware of its lessons. Indeed, it endorsed them. See *CSJ*, December 3, 1890, December 10, 1890 and January 14, 1891.

35. This was especially true of those in and around the shearers' union. For other examples, see Markey (1985, 17–18) and the NSW Royal Commission on Strikes (1891).

36. For the emergence of this use of the term, and the response of Gompers and his allies to it, see AFL (1891a) and the articles, letters, and speeches in Kaufman and Albert (1989, 77–8, 113–14, 181, 403, 503). See also Foner (1955, 280–81), and *AF*, August 1894, 191–3.

37. Gollan (1960, 129, 139–40), Rickard (1976, 43–4, 51, 119) and Tanner (1982, 48–51). The Victorian unions behaved more like the British than the American unions. As in Britain, they did not eschew party politics *per se*. On the contrary, they had a long-standing alliance with the liberal party. But they were cautious about independent political activity. For Victoria, the main source of data on membership is the record of subventions paid to the Trades Hall Council (Macarthy, 1967 and 1970). See also Docherty (1973).

38. This was typical of both advocates and opponents of the new unionism in the United States, although Gompers at first resisted this characterization. See the note before last. For Australian examples, see Labour Defence Committee (1890, 18), Black in *AW*, December 31, 1892, 1, and Spence (1892, 3–5, 8–10), as well as his comments in *Hummer*, May 28, 1892, 2 and NSW Royal Commission on Strikes (1891, 45).

39. ICTUC (1884, 129–30, 1886, 29–42, 1888, 64–8, and 1889, 34–6).

40. *Trades and Labour Advocate*, December 21, 1889, 6. See the report of the meeting of the Sydney Wharf Labourers' Union.

41. For the NSW case, see Hagan and Turner (1991, 41–53) and Markey (1988, 182, 185). For more on this and the previous paragraph, see Chapter 5.

42. On the iron and steel workers, see Secretary Kilgallan's report, *AF*, July 1894, 105. On the carpenters, see Galenson (1983, 70), but note that while the union's convention voted to endorse the "Political Programme," its delegates to the AFL convention did not all vote this way. On the boot and shoe makers, see Laslett (1970, 56–9).

43. For the mine workers before the strike, see letters and articles in *UMWJ*, December 15, 1892, December 22, 1892, January 26, 1893, June 1, 1893, August 24, 1893, December 28, 1893, and for official decisions of the union see Laslett (1970, 199–201) and *UMWJ*, April 12, 1894, 1–2, and April 19, 1894, 2. For the railroad workers before the strike, see the convention minutes in *RT*, July 2, 1894, 3. After the strike, see *UMWJ*, July 19, 1894, 4, and August 23, 1894, 4, and *RT*, August 15, 1894, 2, September 15, 1894, 2, and March 1, 1895.

44. See Table 1.3. For Australian data, see Coghlan (1898b, 61), Vamplew (1987, 40–41) and Coghlan (1894a, 126–7). For U.S. data, see U.S. Bureau of the Census (1975, 12) and U.S. Census Office (1894b, lxv).

45. See "Manifesto to the Electors of the Murrumbidgee" in the Supplement to the *Hummer*, June 18, 1892. Rae was also one of the two founders of the *Hummer*, the original paper of the shearers' union, and through it his ideas reached a wide audience. The analogy between the NSW Labor party and the People's party in the United States appeared in the very first issue of the paper. See *Hummer*, October 19, 1891, 3. On the "treaty of the tillers and the toilers" between the Farmers' Alliance and the Knights in the U.S., see Sanders (1999, 53–4, 122–3).

46. For estimates of the proportion of shearer-selectors, see Merritt (1973, 595 and 1986, 44 and 48), who is the leading authority on the shearers' union. See also Markey (1988, 57–67 and 141–4).

47. In 1891, there were over 100 million sheep in Australia. About 60 percent of these were in NSW, and about 20 percent in Queensland. See Coghlan (1898b, 307) and Merritt (1986, 5). In 1894, there were about 45 million sheep in the United States. Illinois had around 1 million of these, and no state had more than 4 million. See *Chicago Daily News Almanac, 1896*, 56.

48. These Acts remained at the center of political debate until the 1880s. For the Acts, see Clark (1955, 116–26). For the debate, see Gollan (1960, 33–49).

49. For NSW, see Coghlan (1894a, 293, 299, and 1893a, 253). For the U.S., see Shannon (1966, 361), Adams (1997, 556), and Holmes and Lord (1896, 42). For Illinois, see Engerman and Goldin (1994, 102), and Bogart and Mathews (1920, 63). Note that wage-earners were only a slightly smaller percentage, about 42 percent, in Victoria than in NSW (Merritt, 1986, 46). But compare this with Fahey (1993, 96), whose data for Victoria gives a figure for males of 24 percent.

50. On Australia, see Merritt (1986, 44, 46–7). On the U.S., see Engerman and Goldin (1994, 104).

51. For summaries of these grievances in the U.S., see McMath (1993) and Sanders (1999, 101–33). For how shearers' unionists percieved these problems, see "Selectors and Laborers" and "The Farmer as a Laborer" in the *Hummer*, January 30, 1892, 1, and February 6, 1892, 1.

52. On Australia, see Merritt (1986, 89–91) and compare with Ward (1958, 238–45). For the *Hummer*, see January 30, 1892, 1. For hostility towards farm laborers' unions in

the U.S., see Foner (1955, 305–8). AFL President Samuel Gompers (1892, 93) rejected a labor-populist alliance as "unnatural" on the grounds that the People's party was concerned with the interest of "*employing* farmers" rather than "*employed* farmers." Emphasis in original.

53. In Illinois, for example, the wheatbelt provided the People's party with a rural base, even though elsewhere in the state farmers offered very little support (Destler, 1946, 167, 208, and Nelson, 1995, 22). In more than half of the 15 years up to 1894, the Illinois state board of agriculture reported that Illinois farmers had lost money on the production of wheat (Bogart and Thompson, 1920, 237).

54. Between 1882 and 1890, in the United States, one third of all final entries were commuted—that is, sold on after a short period (Shannon, 1936, 647). During the same period in NSW, about half of selections were transferred (Coghlan, 1893a, 250).

55. In California, the Southern Pacific owned 11 percent of the entire state (Gates, 1975).

56. For a clear example of this producerism, see *Hummer*, January 30, 1892, 1: "We want the genuine toilers, the wealth-producers (whether working 'hands' or small employers), to see that their interests are really identical. It is monopoly and class rule which robs both." See also "The Farmer as a Laborer," *Hummer*, February 6, 1892, 1, which consciously seeks to "inculcate" a similar message. On the importance of the Labor party's land policy in rural areas, see Hagan and Turner (1991, 36–9).

57. Roundhouses had to be located every 140 miles or so to clean and refuel engines (Ellem *et al.* 1988, 29), and division towns had to be located every 200 to 300 miles (Stromquist, 1987, 144)

58. For discussion of the factors effecting solidarity between railroad workers in rural towns and the surrounding community, see Stromquist (1987, 145–7, 174–86).

59. At the Congress of Industrial Organizations in St. Louis that launched the People's party in February 1892, 29 percent of the delegates represented labor organizations and about two-thirds represented farmers (Foner, 1955, 301, and Sanders, 1999, 129–30).

60. The Farmers Alliance was strong in the south, west, and part of the Midwest. In the Midwest, it was strong in the west north central states, but weak in the east north central states like Illinois and Ohio. See Sanders (1999, 121–2) for membership figures.

CHAPTER 2

RACE

1. The comment of the NSW Government statistician (Coghlan, 1894a, 196) that "the aboriginal race is fast disappearing before the march of settlement," conveys the general attitude of whites in both societies in the late nineteenth century.

2. *Hummer*, April 2, 1892, 1.

3. See Williamson (1986) and Gilmore (1996).

4. *Hummer*, April 9, 1892, 3.

5. On Australia, see Hunt (1978, 80).

6. See the convention minutes in the *RT*, July 2, 1894, 1 and Stromquist (1987, 81). Foner (1955, 255) gives the vote as 113 to 102. The ARU convention decided instead

to establish an auxiliary union for "colored" workers. See *RT*, July 15, 1894, 1. These decisions were immediately noticed by black unionists. See the letter by R.L. Davis, the black mine workers' leader, in *UMWJ*, July 19, 1894, 8.

7. The influence of Marxism alone was no guarantee of immunity to racist influences, as the anti-Chinese attitudes of some of these same socialist activists showed all too clearly. See also the debates within the Socialist Party in the early twentieth century (Miller, 1984, and Leinenweber, 1984).

8. See, for example, Gompers' letters in Kaufman and Albert (1989, xix–xx, 166–68), and Mandel (1955).

9. When the newly admitted union refused to allow the nonracial alternative union that the AFL had established to amalgamate with it, Gompers simply revoked the alternative union's charter. Note that the Secretary of the alternative union was T.J. Morgan, the principal architect of the AFL's putative "Political Programme," and a leading opponent of Gompers (Mandel, 1955, 37).

10. For the 1891 Congress, see ICTUC (1891, 97). For the shearers' constitution, see Markus (1978, 140–41). On ambivalence towards aboriginals, see Curthoys and Markus (1978, xvi), and Markus (1979, 138–41).

11. Markus (1979) provides a good comparative account of the development of anti-Chinese campaigns in both countries, which pays close attention to the role of the labor movement. See also Markus (1994, 59–72).

12. On California, see Saxton (1971, 113–56) and Mink (1986, 81–88). On the seamen's strike, see Curthoys (1978, 48–65).

13. See ICTUC (1879, 36–40). The debate referred repeatedly, and in some detail, to developments in California and especially San Francisco.

14. For Congress discussions, see ICTUC (1879, 29–46, 1884, 45–50, 1885, 70–74, 1886, 53–62, 1888, 26–35, 1889, 62, 1891, xvi, 92 and 97) and Sutcliffe (1921, 124). Though the "Restriction of Asiatic Immigration" appeared on the agenda in 1891, this item seems to have been swamped by the debate on a political platform. See also Markus (1979, 177) for a quantitative analysis of the frequency with which issues about non-Europeans were discussed in various TLCs.

15. *AF*, May 1894, 50–51. See also his President's report (AFL, 1894, 12).

16. See also the more general discussion about establishing a trade union mark in ICTUC (1891, 30–2, 60–1, 82–3, and 110).

17. For similar conclusions, see Markus (1979, 204).

18. For example, a Victorian correspondent argued that "no worker, whatever his nationality or colour, should be refused our fellowship" (*AW*, May 23, 1891, 4), and a poem called for international solidarity and argued that differences between races are "mere surface shadow" (*AW*, January 9, 1892, 4).

19. "The Camels are Coming," *Hummer*, December 5, 1891, 1–2. See the similar reference in Markey (1978, 73): "the camels must go; the chows must also leave; and Indian hawkers must hawk their wares in some other country. This country was built expressly for Australians, and Australians are going to run the show." Presumably, many of the camel drivers were not Afghan at all since the 1891 census counted only 20 Afghans in the whole of NSW (Coghlan, 1894a, 184). For other examples, see *Hummer*, April 2, 1892, and June 18, 1892, and the paper's platform, published on February 6 and subsequently, which places "black and yellow labour" as the first item on the list of things it opposes.

20. William Lane, the editor of the *Boomerang*, serialized his first novel in it between February and May 1888. The novel, in which an alliance of the white upper class and Asian capitalists is defeated by armed white trade unionists, was called *White or Yellow: A Story of the Race War of 1908* (Wilding, 1980, 32–33).

21. *St Louis Labor*, August 11, 1894, 5, and September 29, 1894, 5.

22. See Gompers and Guttstadt (1902) and Ebbels (1983, 222 and 234–36).

23. See Gompers' 1883 comments to the U.S. Senate Committee on Education and Labor (1885, 1: 282). For similar comments on May 1, 1890, see Kaufman (1987, 312).

24. The Amalgamated Shearers' Union abandoned an earlier policy of recruiting Chinese workers in 1888. A few of the unions' Victorian leaders objected to the change (Markus, 1978, 139, and 1979, 172).

25. The *Bulletin*, January 17, 1891, 4.

26. *AW*, June 18, 1892, 2. The headline in the Queensland *Worker* was "Bundaberg Goes White." See McQueen (1986, 38) and Markus (1979, 207–22).

27. Markus (1979, 176–9) provides quantitative evidence for the decreasing frequency of TLC discussions about racial issues in the early 1890s in various parts of Australia. See also Markus (1994, 176–222).

28. See TLC General Council Minutes, June 27, 1890, and the appended flyer.

29. See TLC, General Meeting Minutes, March 31, 1891, and the report in the *SMH*, April 1, 1891, 8. For the full platform, see Ebbels (1983, 211–2). For earlier lobbying of the TLC by the furniture makers' union, see TLC Parliamentary Committee Minutes, May 4, 1889, and TLC General Meeting Minutes, February 6, 1890, and February 20, 1890. When the platform was revised again in 1892, a clause calling for the "Prohibition . . . of the use of camels" was also added (Ebbels, 1983, 215–7).

30. Ebbels (1983, 213). See also Markus (1979, 205–7).

31. However, as a Member of Parliament in 1891, Houghton urged that votes should be given to naturalized Chinese immigrants—a stance for which he was roundly lampooned by the *Bulletin* (August 22, 1891, 7).

32. See Ebbels (1983, 118) and Markus (1979, 219). In 1905, it was placed at the top (Ebbels, 1983, 222).

33. The ability of Australian labor leaders to link the cause of labor with white racial consciousness in such a way that they could simultaneously reinforce working class identity and appeal beyond it may have helped them avoid what Przeworski and Sprague (1986) call "the dilemma of electoral socialism" when, in the late 1890s and early 1900s, their aspirations began to shift, from achieving a balance of power, to winning a parliamentary majority.

34. On the effectiveness of Southern labor control laws, see Wiener (1979), Woodman (1979), and Cohen (1991).

35. In the Northeast, the proportion of blacks in the population rose from 1.55 percent to 1.83 percent between 1890 and 1900. In the north central census district, the proportion fell from 1.92 percent to 1.88 percent (U.S. Bureau of the Census, 1975, 22).

36. U.S. Census Office (1897, 552–3 and 602–3). By comparison, 7.8 percent of all miners in NSW were Chinese (though these were largely alluvial gold and tin miners), as were 5.1 percent of station laborers in the pastoral industry (Coghlan, 1894b, 717–9 and 696–8).

37. For examples of larger concentrations of black workers in the Pennsylvania steel industry, see Kleinberg (1989, 18) and Couvares (1984, 89).

38. See the NSW TLC Executive Committee Minutes, March 4, 1890. The Wagga shearers sent a letter to the TLC "asking if any objection will be raised to affiliation to the Council in view of the fact that the union included several Chinese among their members." In a "long explanation of the matter," which the TLC decided to accept, the branch explained that the Chinese members had been recruited before the constitutional ban had been introduced.

39. It may also have made them appear to be taking sides in partisan conflicts between Republicans and Democrats—something many union leaders wanted to avoid.

40. See, for example, the letter in *CSJ*, November 22, 1893, 5, from a regional organizer urging all Pacific Coast Labor Councils to send delegates to the forthcoming AFL annual convention to ensure sufficient attention and support for their campaign to amend the Geary law.

41. For this argument, see especially Mink (1986), as well as Saxton (1971, 273–8, and 1990, 293–319) and Jacobson (1998, 42, 76–7).

42. Lane (1987, 69, 85). In the discussion that follows, I will use the term "Slavs" as it was used in late nineteenth-century America. The U.S. Census Office saw immigrants from Russia, Poland, Bohemia, and Hungary as the principal groups of Slavs.

43. The largest concentrations of Germans were in South Australia and Queensland where they constituted 9.3 percent and 7.9 percent, respectively, of the foreign-born population.

44. First in the 1920s, when the United States began to restrict European immigration, and then, on a much larger scale, after the second world war (Price, 1963, 9–11, and Jupp, 1991, 69–81).

45. On racial ideas in Australia, see White (1981, 66–72). For Pearson's book and the reaction to it in the United States, Britain, and Australia, as well as Roosevelt's correspondence with Pearson, see Pearson (1892) and Tregenza (1968, 226–235).

46. See also the *Bulletin*, December 12, 1891, and comments in the *AW* on the role of an Italian socialist in the Circular Quay riot during the Maritime strike (Svensen, 1995, 196–7).

47. See the TLC Parliamentary Committee Minute Book, February 12, 1894, and the TLC General Meetings Minutes, March 29, 1894, where the Committee's recommendations were received and adopted. See also the minutes for December 11, 1893 and January 8, 1894. The resolution was suggested by Secretary Sceusa of the Italian Workingmen's Mutual Benefit Society, who was a radical member of the Australian Socialist League.

48. The *Bulletin*, May 9, 1891, 7. See also the anti-Semitic cartoon on page 13 of this issue.

49. See *AW*, May 9 and May 16, 1891. Like the *Bulletin*, the tailor thought that the Russian Jews "are more to be frightened of than Chinamen." In a subsequent reply, he adopted a slightly less strident tone, and sought to place more emphasis on labor conditions and economic interests. See *AW*, June 6, 1891.

50. See the resolution of delegate Kelly "that this Council views with alarm the proposal to Colonize the Islands of the Pacific with exiled Russian Jews" in TLC General Meetings Minutes, April 30, 1891, and the report on correspondence with the NSW government about this in the General Meetings Minutes of May 14, 1891. For the resolutions two years later, see TLC Parliamentary Committee Minute Book, February 20, 1893, and TLC General Meetings Minutes, March 2, 1893.

51. For resolutions on assisted immigration see ICTUC (1879, 29–35, 1884, 108–16, 1885, 63–9, 1886, 98–100, and 1888, 49–52). In 1889, the Congress did not pass a resolution on the topic, and in 1891 it was included in the debate on Political Reform (ICTUC, 1891, 92). The original resolution in 1879 "that this Congress most emphatically condemns the principle of appropriating any portion of the public moneys for the purpose of immigration" was passed with only two dissentients. This condemnation extended to American as well as British immigrants. During the debate, particular mention was made of the NSW government's practice of paying its immigration agent in the United States five shillings per head for every immigrant from America.

52. See TLC General Meetings Minutes, November 28, 1890, December 11, 1890, and January 22, 1891.

53. *Hummer*, November 7, 1891, 4. See also the *Hummer*, October 31, 1891, and the *Bulletin*, January 17, 1891 and February 7, 1891.

54. U.S. Census Office (1894b, lxxxi and cxli), and the *Nation*, LII, 1891, 108 cited in Higham (1992, 65). Census findings also took some time to disseminate. For example, the 1890 Census Report, which noted these changes, was only published at the end of 1894.

55. On the intellectual progenitors of this approach in the United States, see Higham (1992, 139–44), Mink (1986, 124–7), and Tichenor (2002, 77–80). Higham (1992, 95 and passim) shows that a form of Anglo-Saxonism was present earlier, but argues that it was only during the 1890s that it was crafted into a tool for differentiating between European immigrants and justifying the exclusion of southern and eastern Europeans.

56. On awareness, see Higham (1992, 64–5, 67, 86–7, and 168). On the emergence of racialized hostility, see Higham (1992, 87–96, 138–9, 159, and 165–75). Opponents of immigration typically remained more broadly opposed to immigration. See, for example, Atchinson (1894, 52–5, 102, and 109–10), who complained not just about southern and eastern European immigration, but also about Irish, German, and even British immigration. The book argued that the United States was in danger of becoming "the Botany Bay of Europe" (Atchinson, 1894, 2 and 19).

57. See his 1890 May Day speech on the demand for an eight-hour workday (Kaufman, 1987, 310–12).

58. See, for example, the report of testimony by Terrance Powderly of the Knights of Labor before a Congressional Committee in *NLT*, April 19, 1890, 2, or the editorial on "Wholesale Immigration" in *NLT*, September 21, 1891, 2. The paper followed legislative debate on immigration in detail.

59. See *NLT*, April 26, 1890, 1, and *UMWJ*, September 24, 1891, 3. See also *NLT*, November 12, 1892, 3, "A Change in the Character of Immigration," which explicitly characterized the differences between the old and new immigrants as racial.

60. For these debates, see AFL (1894, 47, 1896, 24, 49, 81–2, and 1897, 88–91). See also *AF*, February 1897, 257, as well as Higham (1992, 72), Mink (1986, 123), and Tichenor (2002, 70, 82–3, 85, and 118–9).

61. Most Italians and Slavs had only arrived in the previous decade, and few had been present long enough to add U.S.-born members to the adult population (U.S. Census Office, 1894b, lxxxi). So these figures are a reasonable indication of the size of these communities. Indeed, in one respect, they may overstate the size of the new immigrant population. The U.S. Census includes Bohemians as Slavs. But native-born and old immigrant communities did not usually *perceive* them in the same way as Hungarians,

Russians, and Poles. A number of them were German-speakers, and they were rarely mentioned in unionists' complaints about Slavic immigration. In Illinois, Bohemians were about 40 percent of the Slav population.

62. U.S. Census Office (1897, 304–5, 354–9, and 484–9). On specific companies and localities, see U.S. Industrial Commission (1901, 392), Jensen (1971, 253), Kleinberg (1989, 12–7 and 43–6), Couvares (1984, 88–92), and Schneider (1975, 268–9).

63. Parentage data from 1900 suggests that, perhaps 12–14 percent of Pennsylvania coal miners were Italians or Slavs in 1890 (U.S. Census Office, 1897, 602–3, and 1904, 262–5 and 370–5).

64. In earlier work, I myself argued that this was so (Archer, 1997).

Chapter 3

Elections and the Constitution

1. In their most recent work, Lipset and Marks (2000, 44 and 58–63) have moved away from this position.

2. For details, see Flora (1983, 89–151), Rokkan (1970), Rose (1974), Carstairs (1980), and Mackie and Rose (1991).

3. Porter (1918, 110–111) and Keyssar (2000, 51). In a few states, a tax qualification remained in force until into the twentieth century.

4. Clark (1955, 345–353 and 376) and Gollan (1960, 1–32).

5. This bald statement understates the difficulties in the United States. The triple restriction imposed in Illinois was typical. To qualify to vote, one had to have resided in the state for one year, in the county for 90 days, and in the electoral district for 30 days. By contrast, in NSW—and subsequently in other colonies—a single residential restriction was reduced first to three months in 1893 and then to one month in 1895, under strong pressure from the new Labor party. On the U.S., see Argersiner (1989, 67–70) and Keyssar (2000, Table A.14). On Illinois, see Bogart and Mathews (1920, 350) and Keyssar (2000, 153–5). On Australia, see Gollan (1960, 177), Crowley (1974, 149–150), and Markey (1988, 176).

6. On plural voting, see Clark (1955, 377–384) and Gollan (1960, 83 and 176–7). On the upper houses, see Gollan (1960, 52, 67, and 180) and Markey (1988, 203–4). On U.S. restrictions, see Keyssar (2000, 117–36, 141–6, and 151–9). On demands for the "Australian ballot," see Fredman (1967, 210–1 and 218–9), and AFL (1889, 19).

7. See Gollan (1960, 52, 67, and 180) and Markey (1988, 203–4). On the abolition of the upper house, see "The Lion in the Path" in the *Hummer*, "Supplement" June 18, 1892, and the 1892 platform in Ebbels (1983, 218).

8. For details of the plural voting provision, see the Electoral Act of 1880, 44 Victoriae, No. 13, in the Thursday, July 15, 1880 Supplement to the *NSW Government Gazette*, 3595–6. For the estimate of plural votes in Sydney, see Nairn (1989, 274–5, n17). On Grey, see Nairn (1989, 55 and 61). For the reaction of the TLC, see *AW*, April 11, 1891 and June 6, 1891.

9. Keyssar (2000, 117–62). Restrictions aimed at lower-class voters variously took the form of property or tax requirements, education or literacy tests, residency restrictions, or special registration requirements.

10. Duverger (1954), Rae (1971), and Lijphart (1994).

11. For definitions of the "effective number of parties" and the "effective threshold," see Lijphart (1994, 11–12, 25–28, and 67–72).

12. Single-member districts were the norm, but in some elections, multimember districts were used. For the details of France's constantly changing electoral laws in the late nineteenth and early twentieth century, see Carstairs (1980, 175–8) and Campbell (1958, 69–90). In Belgium, Switzerland, and Luxembourg two-ballot majoritarian systems with multimember districts were the norm (Carstairs, 1980, 213).

13. Although this had very little effect on electoral outcomes (Hughes and Graham, 1968, 503–15).

14. In addition, proportional representation was also introduced in Tasmania in 1907, and for elections to the Federal Senate in 1949.

15. Belgium was the first to use a proportional system, in the general election of 1900 (Rose, 1974, 53–4). This point is worth emphasizing because there is a persistent tendency for American authors to assume (falsely) that proportional representation prevailed in Europe during America's late nineteenth-century "Gilded Age." See, for example, Argersinger (1989, 62).

16. For other legislatures in the early 1890s, see Hughes and Graham (1968).

17. Hughes and Graham (1975, 1–15). Labor's larger share of the vote in four-member constituencies was partly a function of the fact that it stood more candidates in these seats. But that in turn was partly a function of the fact that Labor organizers thought that these were the seats in which they had the best chance of winning. On the class geography of Labor seats, see Nairn (1989, 65–6), Hagan and Turner (1991, 15–16), and Fitzgerald (1987, 13–49).

18. Hamilton (1967, 324–8) provides additional support for this conclusion in his study of multimember districts in mid-twentieth-century America.

19. This estimate is based on the number of votes cast in 1894 and the turnout figures (for Cook County) reported in *Chicago Daily News Almanac for 1895*, (1895, 255, 356, and 426). The number of voters in a district ranged from 11,000 to 25,000.

20. Moore (1909, 20–1). See also Thorpe (1909, 1017–8), Blair (1960), and Hamilton (1967, 336–9).

21. For state house and senate results, and for statewide offices by counties and towns, and, in Chicago, by wards and precincts, see Chicago Daily News Company (1895, 253–7, 272–85, and 350–61). For a breakdown of house and senate results by county, see Illinois Secretary of State (1894). For federal election results, see Allen and Lacey (1992, 27–8 and 230–2).

22. For problems with the data and some proxy measures, see Fitzgerald (1987, 42–3) on Sydney, and Kleppner (1970, 381–4) and Tarr (1971, 317–8) on Chicago.

23. See Kleppner (1970, 216–7). In the city as a whole, the labor-populists won 12 percent. In 1886, the United Labor party had won 27.5 percent of the vote in Cook County, and had elected seven state congressmen (Allen and Lacey, 1992, 212).

24. On coal towns, see Nash (1982, 54–5), Destler (1946, 208), and Jensen (1971, 245 and 257), whose estimate of 17 percent is made on a slightly different basis. On railroad centers, see Destler (1946, 208), and on "markedly industrial counties," see Bogart and Thompson (1920, 400). Only citizens could vote in Illinois, but Nash (1982, 53) estimates that less than 10 percent of coal miners in Illinois were not citizens. For the number of miners by county, see Illinois Bureau of Labor Statistics (1894).

25. For Pennsylvania, see Nash (1982, 20–21, 54, 171, and 174), and for Ohio, see Kleppner (1970, 237 and 248) and Nash (1982, 54 and 172).

26. Although the upper house of the federal parliament was modeled on the U.S. Senate.

27. Indeed, a small cohesive party could have been influential even without the balance of power, given the fractious nature and weak internal discipline of the two main parties.

28. See the *Bulletin*, June 20, 1891, 8, and Black's undated pamphlet *Labor in Politics*, 22 and n27 [in ML at Q329.31/P]. But see also Black (1926, 25), in which he notes that "Perhaps I overestimate the influence which the Irish plan of campaign in the House of Commons had on Australian opinion, but I am confident the Parnell's tactics inspired me with ideas as to the possibility of a third party."

29. See Labour Defence Committee (1890, 19), and the flyer of the West Sydney Labor Electoral League in folio 2 of "Political Labor League of NSW. Handbills, press cuttings, platforms, etc" [in ML at Q329.31/P].

30. See CSJ, November 2, 1892, 4, December 28, 1892, 8, and January 10, 1894, 8.

31. The most significant election for a statewide office that year was for Treasurer.

32. The exception was South Dakota, which introduced the first anti-fusion law in 1893. For Illinois, where the Australian ballot was introduced in 1891, and anti-fusion laws in 1897, see Bogart and Mathews (1920, 307, 355–6 and 371–2).

CHAPTER 4

COURTS

1. Versions of this thesis appear in Fink (1987), Forbath (1991 and 1991a), Hattam (1992 and 1993), and Skocpol (1992).

2. Forbath (1991, 37–58 and 177–87) and Hattam (1993, 152–3) provide lists that show that the courts undermined far more labor-backed legislation than they upheld.

3. Hovenkamp (1991, 229) argues that Congress may have intended the Act to apply to labor as well. However, according to Perlman (1923, 154), few thought it did at the time.

4. Gompers himself made this point to the U.S. Strike Commission (1895, 188–205). See also Kaufman and Albert (1989, 576). These developments were also raised by a couple of delegates during the AFL's 1894 debate on the Political Programme (AFL, 1895a, 30–1).

5. Similar conclusions are drawn by Shefter (1986) and Voss (1993), although Shefter focuses on a broader range of instruments of state repression, and Voss focuses on state acquiescence in the face of employer repression.

6. This comparison with Britain is developed at length in Hattam (1992, 166–71, and 1993, 180–203). See also Forbath (1991a) and Archer (1998, 415, n12).

7. On the United States, see Orren (1987 and 1991), Tomlins (1993), and Montgomery (1993, 25–51). Note, however, that Tomlins and Orren argue that some of the concepts that underpinned master and servant law reappeared in a different guise in later American judicial decisions. On Australia, see Clark (1955, 678–682), Portus (1958, 90–94), Merritt (1981), McQueen (1987), and Quinlan (1989 and 1996). Merritt's study

of all the surviving bench books in NSW provides the most thorough overview we are likely to get of the application of Master and Servant Acts.

8. Orren (1991, 123, 124, 129, and 138) discusses a number of attempts to use enticement doctrines against unionists in late nineteenth-century America.

9. Although in both countries prosecutions focusing on "intimidation" continued (Hattam, 1992, 159–162, and Markey, 1988, 124–5).

10. Todd (1894, 301) and Lucy (1990, 90). For an overview, see Castles (1982, 445, 449, 450, and 452).

11. Cited in Lucy (1990, 90).

12. I should also make clear that I will focus on only one aspect of the argument that advocates of the court repression thesis have developed. Advocates like Forbath and Hattam have offered a rich and nuanced interpretation of the role of the judiciary in the shaping of the American labor movement, and there are many aspects of their argument on which I will not touch.

13. Gompers himself often made this distinction. See Kaufman and Albert (1989, 143) and AFL (1896, 20–21).

14. The AFL's persistent efforts to achieve immigration restrictions are one major exception to this.

15. Skocpol (1992, 206–17). The AFL was only prepared to accept social legislation for "dependent" workers like women, children, and government employees.

16. AFL (1895a, 21–5). This relatively short but intense debate is worth further attention in its own right. It reveals much about various delegates' attitudes towards family life and the relationship between individuals and the state. It also reveals a widespread sense of superiority towards less respectable unskilled and insecure workers and their families.

17. Kaufman (1986, 22, 28, and 83–4) and Gompers (1925, 75). For more on these debates, see Chapter 8.

18. Kaufman (1986, 235). The resolution went on to say "that this shall not preclude the advocacy to office of a man who is pledged purely and directly to labor measures." So, here, from the outset was the pressure group conception of politics—opposition to any involvement in partisan politics alongside legislative lobbying and a limited electoral strategy of supporting labor's friends and punishing its enemies—the same conception which Gompers defends in his 1894 Presidential Report (AFL, 1894, 14).

19. For the cigar makers, see Kaufman (1986, 247–74). For the conflict with the Knights, see Kaufman (1986, 275–86).

20. Speaking to a mass meeting of tobacco workers, he made it clear that while he had always opposed independent political action by unions in the past, he now thought that the time had come for workers to select candidates, as well as to vote for them (Kaufman, 1986, 433–4).

21. See the annual proceedings of the AFL (1888, 13, 1889, 23, 1890, 12–21, 1891, 40, and 1892, 12–3 and 29). The AFL's rejection of partisan politics was strongly reinforced by a debate in 1889 and 1890 about the affiliation of the New York Central Labor Federation. On one level, the debate was about whether the Socialist Labor party, as a party, should be allowed to affiliate to a union organization. But this question drew the delegates into explicit discussion of the relevance of independent labor politics (AFL, 1891a).

22. This argument is set out particularly clearly by Hattam (1992, 166, and 1993, 74–75). Similar arguments can be found in Forbath (1991, xi and 97) and Skocpol

(1992, 226–9). Note that the argument does not discriminate between different types of political action. If it is right, then neither pressure group politics nor partisan politics would be worth pursuing since the courts are said to be immune to political influences whatever their source.

23. McCloskey (1960, 111 and 151–5). For similar observations, see Bickel (1962), Choper (1980), and Murphy (1962). For a contrary view, see Lasser (1988).

24. On the Norris-LaGuardia Act, which put an end to the widespread use of labor injunctions, see Forbath (1991, 163). On the Wagner Act, which established the right of unions to organize and to bargain collectively, see Leuchtenburg (1963, 150–2) and Finegold and Skocpol (1984, 180).

25. On the influence of business interests on late nineteenth-century courts, see Burch (1981, 103–10).

26. Lindsay (1942, 147–75) and Foner (1955, 266–67). Lindsay concludes that "Between the Department of Justice and the federal judiciary there seemed to be a sympathetic understanding, and almost every move initiated by the former received the hearty support of the latter."

27. In one extraordinary case in 1902, the Colorado legislature refused to pass an eight-hour law even after the state's constitution had been amended to ensure that such a law would be constitutional (Perlman, 1923, 214, and Forbath, 1991, 47). For other examples, see Dubofsky (1994, 13), Montgomery (1993, 153), and Forbath (1991, 49 and 148–50).

28. There was, however, a strong presumption in favor of reelecting sitting judges. See Hurst (1950, 130) and Hall (1984, 362–5).

29. For the history of judicial selection, see Haynes (1944), Hurst (1950), Niles (1966), and Friedman (1973).

30. On turnout, see Hall (1984, 356–9 and 361); on nominations, see Hurst (1950, 129–34) and Hall (1984, 354 and 365); and on politicians-turned-judges, see Friedman (1984, 65) and Tarr and Porter (1988, 55).

31. Hall (1980, 448, 456, and 464) and Friedman (1973, 328, and 1984, 65).

32. Indeed, Australian union leaders hoped to move closer to the American system. In its first platform in 1890, and again in 1892, the NSW Labor party called for the direct election of magistrates (Ebbels, 1983, 212 and 216).

33. All the advocates of the court repression thesis appeal to this comparison. See Fink (1987), Forbath (1991 and 1991a), Hattam (1992 and 1993), and Skocpol (1992).

34. Gompers emphasized this in his 1892 presidential report (AFL, 1892, 12).

35. Marks (1989, 71–2), Forbath (1991, 110), and Ernst (1995, 131). Since 1894, the AFL had lobbied every session of Congress about anti-injunction legislation (Marks, 1989, 71, and Karson, 1958, 29–30).

36. For a detailed analysis of the legal and political effects of these cases, see Chapters 6, 7, 8, and 9 of Ernst (1995). See also Mink (1986, 185–6 and 212), Marks (1989, 71–3 and 202–3), and Forbath (1991, 92–4).

37. Perlman (1923, 198–207), Karson (1958), Scheinberg (1963), and Ernst (1995, 111, 135–7, and 146).

38. In his autobiography, Gompers (1925) himself makes a similar point in an oft-quoted passage from a chapter entitled "Learning Something of Legislation." Commenting on attempts by the Cigar Makers' Union in the early 1880s to secure legislation outlawing sweatshop production in tenements, Gompers writes: "Securing the enactment of a law does not mean the solution of the problem . . . The power of the courts to pass on

the constitutionality of a law so complicates reform by legislation as to seriously restrict the effectiveness of that method." Having twice had legislation overturned by the courts, the union decided to adopt a new strategy and place pressure on the employers directly through industrial action. In this way, he claims, "we accomplished through economic power what we had failed to achieve through legislation." These comments by Gompers and Strasser are repeatedly cited by advocates of the court repression thesis. See Forbath (1991, 40–2, 54, and 1991a, 17–8), Hattam (1992, 163–6, and 1993, 157–60), and Skocpol (1992, 227–9).

39. Skocpol (1992, 206–7, 229–31, and 242) shows how an incentive like this helped draw state federations of labor into support for a number of broad positive social reforms. AFL wariness of middle-class proponents of positive social reforms in the Progressive era weakened not just the social reformers but also the AFL's own ability to gain the legal immunities it desperately sought.

40. Minimum wage regulations, the Wagner Act, and the Social Security Act were all upheld one after the other in 1937 (McCloskey, 1960, 175–6).

41. Skocpol (1992, 233–9 and 258). Having argued in favor of the court repression thesis to explain federal union policy, Skocpol (1992, 317–33 and 239–45) points to the different internal institutional structures of state and federal union organizations and the different interests that result in order to explain their different attitudes to positive political goals. But this is to shift from an explanation based on judicial repression and the political opportunity structure to one based on the different kinds of working class interests that the state and federal labor organizations represented.

42. For references, see n38 above.

43. In addition, they fail to note that Strasser had long opposed political action for reasons that had nothing to do with court repression. Originally a pro-political "Lassallean," he began to oppose political action around 1876 (Kaufman, 1973, 65). The fact that Strasser was now appealing to something like the court repression thesis does not necessarily imply that this was in fact the main reason why he opposed the Political Programme. They also overemphasize this one piece of evidence and fail to give sufficient attention to the fact that the majority of delegates rejected Strasser's argument and voted for the eight-hour plank.

44. Arguably, Forbath is less inclined to do this. In a footnote to an article, he seeks to distinguish his position from Hattam's (Forbath, 1991a, 20–1). But see also Hattam (1993, 164–5), where she also seems to be aware of the problem.

CHAPTER 5

REPRESSION

1. Proponents of the soft repression thesis include Lipset (1985, 220–1 and 230–246), Marks (1989, 12–5, 52–5 and 68–76), Geary (1981, 54–65), and (in a more ambivalent way) Mink (1986, 35–6). Geary does not discuss the United States and only applies the thesis to European countries. See also Perlman (1923), Hartz (1955), and Grob (1961), who emphasize the low level of repression.

2. Germany, under the anti-socialist laws of 1878–1890, is often viewed as the paradigm counterpoint to the United States in discussions of the soft repression thesis.

However, the anti-socialist laws were primarily directed at the social democratic party rather than the unions themselves.

3. Those who argue that workers' organizations in the United States were subject to relatively high levels of repression include Jacobi (1991, 292–5) Shefter (1986, 232–66), Montgomery (1993), Voss (1993), Sexton (1991), and Mann (1993, 628–91).

4. For details and references to primary sources, see Archer (2001, 190–1).

5. See NSW Royal Commission on Strikes (1891) for contemporary evidence, and Svensen (1995) for a booklength treatment. For shorter accounts, see Gollan (1960, 129–35), and Hagan and Wells (1992).

6. See the United States Strike Commision (1895) and Carwardine (1894) for contemporary evidence, and Lindsey (1942) for an authoritative booklength treatment. For shorter accounts, see Foner (1955, 261–78) and Ginger (1949, 87–183, and 1958, 143–167).

7. Although 162 of the special constables were troops based in the bush who had volunteered to come to Sydney, and some troops were deployed elsewhere in Australia (Fosbery, 1890, 630–31, and Gibson, 1994, 106–189).

8. For this estimate, see Philipp (1967, 144) and Scates (1992, 37). Buckley and Wheelwright (1988, 183) estimate that, excluding the shearers, 25,000 to 30,000 workers were involved. Freudenberg (1990, 34) estimates that 30,000 were involved simultaneously at the peak of the strike.

9. Seven hundred of these were called out in Victoria over a period of nine weeks, and 130 in South Australia for a day (Coulthard-Clark, 1981, 72–3, Calder, 1985, 61, and Gibson, 1994, 177–8). In addition, about 50 permanent artillerymen in Sydney, and about 200 permanent artillerymen in Melbourne were held "in readiness" (Gibson, 1994, 124 and 143).

10. For this estimate, which is based on the number of ARU members, see U.S. Strike Commission (1895, xxiii).

11. For full accounts of this incident, see Svensen (1995, 176–181) and Gibson (1994, 127–132 and 136–7). See also Fosbery (1890, 629–30), Spence (1909, 137–40), Clark (1955, 776–8), and Walker (1986, 63).

12. For a full account, see Lindsey (1942, 205–209 and 215–19). See also Wish (1939, 306–8), Ginger (1949, 141–3), Foner (1955, 269), Yellen (1974, 117), and Cooper (1980, 146–52).

13. A huge number in a city with an 1891 population of 474,440.

14. They were also assigned to guard public buildings (Gibson, 1994, 149).

15. See Svensen (1995, 128–36 and 191–92), Gibson (1994, 152–55), Spence (1909, 140–41), and Calder (1985, 59–66).

16. For the fullest treatment of the strike, see Svensen (1989). See also Kenway (1970, 111–20), Merritt (1986, 169–75), and Spence (1909 and 1961 [1911], 45–62). For background on the shearing industry, see Merritt (1986, 3–91).

17. For the fullest treatment, see Krause (1992) and, for a contemporary account, Burgoyne (1979 [1893]). See also Yellen (1974), Foner (1955, 206–18), and Ingham (1993). For background on the union and the industry, see Ingham (1978 and 1991).

18. For example, in Barcaldine, where the strike committee and the Pastoral Employers' Association had their headquarters, there were about 60 armed forces per 100 strikers. In Homestead, there were nearly four times that number. See "Notes and Sources" for Table 5.2.

19. There was no direct line and travel was via Melbourne and Adelaide.

20. On Broken Hill, see Kennedy (1978, 21–72) as well as Solomon (1988, 235–45) and Dale (1918, 21–72). On Couer d'Alene, see the authoritative account by Smith (1961), as well as Jensen (1950, 25–37) and Foner (1955, 230–34).

21. This was in part because the newly formed Labor party now held the balance of power in the Legislative Assembly.

22. With the one exception noted earlier.

23. There are no precise figures on the number of times state militias were called out. Reinders (1977, 98) estimates that between 1877 and 1903 they were called out to deal with civil disturbances on over 700 occasions. Cooper (1980, 13) suggests that, on a conservative estimate, the militia were called out to deal with industrial disputes on at least 150 occasions between 1870 and 1900.

24. See Montgomery (1993, 102) and Foner (1955, 228).

25. According to one estimate, 92 people died in strikes from 1890 to 1897 (Green, 1980, 10).

26. During the 1894 shearers' strike (Merritt, 1986, 243, 401, and Spence, 1961 [1911], 72–3).

27. In the mid-1890s, there were over 100,000 militia (plus 9,000 officers) and 25,000 regular soldiers (plus some 2,000 officers) in the United States (Fogelson, 1989, 41). In Australia, there were a total of 18,925 militia and volunteers and 1,280 permanent soldiers and staff in 1891–92 (Nicholls, 1988, 148).

28. For a fuller discussion of these and other differences, see Archer (2001, 200–3).

29. See Skowronek (1982, 85–107), Reinders (1977, 81–101), Montgomery (1993, 89–104) and Cooper (1980, 83–93). The repression of labor unrest continued to be a central function of the militia until state police were established to take over this role in the early twentieth century (Smith, 1969 [1925], 28–42 and 54–65).

30. The possibility that military aid to the civil power might at times be needed was considered by those charged with reorganizing the militia, but it was not a central concern. See, for example, Sir William Jervois' 1877 report to the Victorian government, which, while hinting at this need, does not even mention it directly (Gibson, 1994, 5).

31. For an overview of Australia developments, see Stanley (1988), Nicholls (1988), Grey (1990, 43–47), Gibson (1994, 4–12), Dennis et al. (1995, 159–65), and Wilcox (1998).

32. Fosbery (1890, 635–6) and Svensen (1995, 146). For the similar situation in Victoria, see Gibson (1994, 151) and Svensen (1995, 127). In South Australia, however, 40 of the 200 special constables appointed were unionists (Svensen, 1995, 142).

33. Kenway (1970, 114), Spence (1909, 148–150), and Svensen (1989, 92, 114–5 and 146–7).

34. These same two groups were probably responsible for all of the deaths in Tables 5.1, 5.2, and 5.3. In the Pullman strike, five workers were killed by the militia, and eight by deputy marshals or unknown persons. At Homestead, all seven were killed by Pinkertons. And at Coeur d'Alene, all six were killed in a conflict with deputy marshals and strikebreakers.

35. For this and the following paragraph, see NSW TLC General Meeting Minutes and Parliamentary Committee Minutes for 1889–1891. These are held in the Mitchell Library, Sydney at A3829–A3831 and at A3823 and A2761, respectively. See also Nairn (1989, 22–56), Markey (1988, 171–6, and 1994, 36–48), Rickard (1976,

26–52), and Gollan (1960, 80–98 and 128–36). For early historical accounts written by participants, see Roydhouse and Taperell (1892), Spence (1909), Fitzgerald (1915), and Black (1926–29).

36. The four unions were the Typographers, the Smelters, the Miners, and a branch of the Shearers. Two more unions (the Balmain Labourers and the Furniture Trades) supported the plan but were unable to provide the necessary funds, and another (the Boot union) would only support the plan if a protectionist platform were adopted. Ten unions rejected the plan: the United Labourers, Stonemasons, Quarrymen, Tinsmiths and Sheet Iron workers, Sydney Wharf Labourers, Cooks and Stewards, Printers, Newcastle Wharf Labourers, Trolley and Draymen, and Railway and Tramway workers. See the TLC's General Meetings Minutes for April 24 to June 5, 1890. See also TLC (1890, 5), and Nairn (1989, 40), who cites slightly different figures.

37. In 1874, 1880, and 1885. For opposition, see "Trades-unionism and Politics," *TLA*, December 21, 1889, 4.

38. Spence (1909, 126–32) and TLC General Meetings Minutes, October 9, 1890.

39. The Congress met while the Queensland Shearers' strike was in full swing, a month after the arrest of the Barcaldine strike committee. The preamble to the plan explained that it was motivated by a sense of "political insecurity" that had been awakened by "recent events" (ICTUC, 1891, 90).

40. See the minutes of each ICTUC (1879, 1884, 1885, 1886, 1888, and 1889), including reports of the various parliamentary committees from 1885 onwards.

41. The issue was not mentioned at the first congress in 1879, but from 1884 onwards resolutions calling for the direct representation of labor were passed at every congress, ususally unanimously (ICTUC, 1884, 129–30, 1886, 29–42, 1888, 64–8, and 1889, 34–6). In 1885, there was no resolution on direct representation, but it was called for in the President's report and support for direct representation underpinned much of the debate on a resolution calling for the payment of MPs (ICTUC, 1885, 17 and 50–60).

42. For further comments by Houghton, and similar remarks by Brennan, as well as by the leading Queensland delegate, William Lane, and the President of the United TLC in Adelaide, S.H. Buttery, see ICTUC (1891, 93, 95–9, 102 and 104). These delegates represented the three colonies—NSW, Queensland, and South Australia—in which efforts to establish a labor party were furthest advanced.

43. For all states, see Murphy (1975), Gollan (1960, 109 and 128–50), and Sutcliffe (1967 [1921], 126–40). On Queensland, see also Harris (1966). On South Australia, see Walker (1968) and Moss (1992). And on Victoria, see Bongiorno (1996), Rickard (1976), and Tanner (1982). Note also that, in NSW, the 1892 Broken Hill miners' strike reinforced the lessons of the Maritime strike. The failure of recently elected Labor MPs to unite to bring down the government over its handling of the strike led to the introduction of rules to ensure that these MPs would vote as a unified independent party in the future (Nairn, 1989, 94–7, and Markey, 1988, 181–2). On the political impact of the strike in Broken Hill itself, see Kennedy (1978, 75–84).

44. For an early example, see ICTUC (1884, 129–30).

45. Union activists themselves explicitly acknowledged this (Destler, 1946, 177).

46. In 1890, over half of all manufacturing establishments, and a third of the entire United States population, were in these five states (Commissioner of Labor, 1896, 21, and Bogue, 1985, 72–3).

47. In the lead up to the 1892 presidential elections, with the Homestead dispute just over, Henry Clay Frick wrote to Andrew Carnegie that "I cannot see that our interests are going to be affected one way or the other by the change in administration" (Kehl, 1981, 175–6).

48. See Debs's (1895, 9–11) speech in Chicago on his release from jail. "What is to be done," asked Debs, in the face of "Russian injunctions . . . a deputy marshal's clubs . . . the government's machine guns and . . . judicial traps." The answer was to reach for the redeeming power of the ballot: "There is nothing in our government it can not remove or amend. It can make and unmake Presidents and Congresses and Courts . . . To the unified hosts of American workingmen fate has committed the charge of rescuing American liberties . . . by seizing the ballot and wielding it . . ." On the "redeeming power" of the ballot, see the Labor Day message which Debs (1948, 6) wrote in jail a couple of months earlier. For Spence, see his reports to the 1891 and 1893 Conferences of the ASU (Ebbels, 1983, 120–1 and 152–3), and his later account in Spence (1909, 220–1): "The industrial war which saw the Government siding with the capitalists . . . had at last brought home to the worker the fact that he had a weapon in his grasp stronger than Governments or capitalists. The idea of self-government came to him in a new light, and he saw that he must not only vote, but must make the platform, and select his own political war-cry. Labor set about becoming a new force and a new party in political life."

49. Marks (1989, 204–7), Rickard (1976, 51), and Markey (1988, 181).

50. The steel workers and the miners both sent delegates to the 1894 AFL Conference mandated to vote for the political program in full, although some of them failed to do so (Commons et al., 1918, 511–2).

51. For the risk of death while working on the railroads, see Commissioner of Labor (1890, 41), Bogart and Thompson (1920, 326), and Markey (1988, 99, 102–3).

52. The arrest of leaders, in particular, could have a demoralizing effect, in addition to its disorganizing effect. In Australia, this was noticeable in both the Queensland Shearers' and Broken Hill strikes. See SMH, March 27, 1891, and NSW Legislative Assembly (1892–3, 305–6).

53. Foner (1955, 257–9 and 261–3). The railway workers 1885 victory over Jay Gould had similar effects on the Knights of Labor (Voss, 1993, 75).

54. Gollan (1960, 108–9). Indeed, the rapid growth of the "new" unionism in the late 1880s had produced a mood of "confidence bordering on euphoria" and the whole union movement entered the Maritime strike on a "wave of emotional optimism" (Rickard, 1976, 26 and 31).

55. Part of the power of Marxism as a mobilizing ideology was that it offered workers precisely this promise of future success, even in in the face of terrible defeat. But Marxism had little influence amongst ordinary workers in either country. For its influence amongst union leaders, see Chapter 8.

56. McAdam et al. (1996, 6), and Tarrow (1994, 118–34). For an innovative application of the concepts of "cognitive liberation" (McAdam, 1982) and "cognitive encumbrance" in order to explain the collapse of the Knights of Labor, see Voss (1993, 75–9 and 225–8).

57. The "Equality" colony was eventually established in Washington state (Fogarty, 1990, 135–9 and 160–6, and LeWarne, 1968, 137–48), and the "New Australia" colony in Paraguay (Souter, 1981). Both soon collapsed. See also the efforts of the Australian

Shearers' Union and its successor to gain legislative backing for efforts to establish agricultural cooperatives in Australia (Walker, 1970).

58. For a similar assessment, see Lindsey (1942, 338).

59. Only the coal miners and iron and steel workers were affiliated to the AFL, and the coal miners—the only major industrial union that was affiliated to the AFL—was close to collapse following their own defeat early in 1894. Note, however, that these two unions had 18.8 percent of the votes at the AFL's 1894 convention. The iron and steel workers had 3.5 percent of the votes, and the miners had 15.3 percent (AFL, 1894, 7–8). The miners' share of the votes had yet to be adjusted for their recent loss of membership.

60. The Australian figures in this paragraph are based on the membership data published in the *Australian Star* on October 6, 1890. For even higher estimates based on the data published by the NSW Royal Commission on Strikes in June 1891, see Archer (2001, 210). On union membership sources, see Chapter 1, note 24. "Maritime workers" here include the various "new" unions in the Maritime Labour Council.

61. For details, see Archer (2001, 210, n124).

62. For a good example from the printers union, see Hagan (1966, 77–9) and Archer (2001, 210, n125).

63. Rickard (1976, 31–4) describes a process that could be characterized as the emergence of a kind of negative class consciousness in which unionists "of the better class" found themselves repudiated by the respectable society of which they had always felt themselves a part.

64. This was Strasser's phrase in a private letter to Gompers (Foner, 1955, 274).

65. See Chapter 1 on the similar symbolic role of "robber barons" and the "squatocracy."

66. Pittsburgh and Chicago were the two main steel-making districts in the United States. Although the iron and steel workers union had lost control of the Pittsburgh mills following the Homestead strike, it retained its lodges in Chicago (Holt, 1977, 130–2).

67. For this paragraph, see Destler (1946, 165, 171, 179–80, and 183–6, and 1963, 243–4 and 269–70), Staley (1930, 112–25), Bogart and Mathews (1920, 160–65), and Goodwyn (1976, 411–21).

68. On "frame battles" and their effects on "bystander publics," see McAdam *et al.* (1996, 338 and 343). Della Porta (1996, 64 and 85) focuses explicitly on the effects of police repression.

69. That came later, after the deployment of troops (Lindsey, 1942, 205).

70. See Miles (1894, 186–7) and Wooster (1993, 198–201). Miles continued: "Men must take sides either for anarchy, secret conclaves, unwritten law, mob violence, and universal chaos under the red or white flag of socialism on the one hand; or on the side of established government, the supremacy of law the maintenance of good order, universal peace, absolute security of life and property, the rights of personal liberty, all under the shadow and folds of 'Old Glory' on the other." For similar, if sometimes less strident, views from other officers, see Cooper (1980, 250–7). Miles later became Chief Guardian of the Guardians of Liberty: a secret anti-Catholic, anti-immigrant society (Lipset and Raab, 1971, 102).

71. The Superintendent of Police in Chicago actually made a similar point, but his voice was drowned out by contrary claims (Lindsey, 1942, 219).

72. The press and the pulpit also contributed to this. The *SMH* was quite capable of comparing the Maritime strike with the "horror" and "frenzy" of the Paris Commune (Gollan, 1960, 134). For the consistently wild and lurid headlines in most Chicago newspapers during the Pullman strike, see Lindsey (1942, 308–19), Ginger (1949, 141–2), and Foner (1955, 269). For the more sympathetic role of the *Chicago Times*, see Destler (1946, 190–3). For the pulpit, see Chapter 7.

73. Note how economic conflicts were translated into political and cultural conflicts, and meta-conflicts at that. Charges that unions were seeking to overthrow the economic order were less prominent. This was not accidental. In that sphere, as Henry Demarest Lloyd pointed out during the Chicago election campaign of 1894, a revolution really *had* come, and the established economic order was already being overthrown. However, it was not the unions but the large capitalist corporations who were the revolutionaries (Destler, 1946, 212–21).

74. On the great upsurge of law-and-order rhetoric during the election campaigns of the mid-1890s, see Gerring (1997, 80).

75. The Australian interpretation was reinforced during the Maritime strike by a handful of established liberals, like Chief Justice Higginbothan of Victoria, who publicly sent ten pounds a week to the Melbourne strike fund, and Attorney-General Kingston of South Australia, who acted in court on behalf of arrested unionists. When Governor Altgeld of Illinois had the temerity merely to question the deployment of federal troops, he too was branded an anarchist and subjected to the most extraordinary attacks. According to the *Chicago Tribune*, for example (Lindsey, 1942, 192): "This lying, hypocritical, demagogical, sniveling Governor of Illinois does not want the law enforced. He is a sympathizer with riot, with violence, with anarchy." The successful redefinition of the ARU as a harbinger of alien anarchism is all the more striking because Debs in fact preached a very American message rooted in Jeffersonian republicanism (Salvatore, 1982, Debs, 1895).

76. Rural campaigning was heavily dependent on unions in Illinois because of the weakness of the Farmers' Alliance in that state (Goodwyn, 1976, 415 and 582–7).

77. The Queensland Labor party became even more reliant on the shearers' union (Murphy, 1975, 149, 150, 152, and 154–5), while in Victoria, where the shearers' union was much weaker and the miners' union was dissaffected, it proved difficult to sustain an independent party (Rickard, 1976, 51, 119).

78. Loveday (1975, 45–55), Merrit (1986, 264–71), and Markey (1988, 182, 185, and 189).

79. For a fuller discussion, see Archer (2001, 215–8).

80. Following the Pullman strike, suspected unionists were summarily dismissed, and active members were given an apparently normal reference with a secret watermark showing a crane with its head cut off (Wish, 1939, 311, Lindsey, 1942, 338–9, Ginger, 1949, 178–80, and Salvatore, 1982, 138).

81. See Commons *et al.* (1918, 495–6), Holt (1977, 141–4 and 146), Jacobi (1991), Mann (1993, 634, 640, and 647–8) and Voss (1993, 12, 202–5, 223–6, 232, and 237–8, and 1996, 241–3). In particular, Voss, like me, sees the repression of "new" inclusive unions as central to any explanation of the exceptional nature of labor politics in the United States. But her focus is on the role of employer repression against the Knights of Labor in and around 1886.

CHAPTER 6

LIBERALISM

1. Among the most important proponents of this thesis have been Sombart (1976), Hartz (1955 and 1964), Lipset (1963, 1977, and 1996), and Greenstone (1986 and 1993).

2. For example, see Smith (1993), though note that he still accepts that liberal values were unusually potent and had a constraining effect on labor politics (Smith, 1999, 20).

3. According to Wedderburn in 1876, "most of the objects for which Liberals in England have hitherto struggled . . . are . . . so much a matter of course . . . that they are hardly regarded as questions of controversy" (Ebbles, 1983, 44), and according to Macintyre (1991, 12–3), "deprived of its natural enemy," liberalism spread "like the rabbit . . . run wild because of the absence of ecological checks." For similar comments, see Dilke (1890, 490), Adams (1893, 48–9), Reeves (1969 [1902], 1:60), Serle (1971, 22–4), Loveday et al. (1977, 12, 477–81), Loveday and Martin (1966, 56–7), Philipp (1967, 131). Some also suggest that liberalism generated an ideologically based identity: a kind of "Australianism" (White, 1981, 52 and 81). According to the Bulletin, July 2, 1887, "all men who leave the tyrant-ridden lands of Europe for the freedom of speech and the right of personal liberty are Australians before they set foot on the ship that brings them hither."

4. Sombart (1976, 20, 39–40, 55–58, and 109–110) identifies egalitarianism, democratic radicalism, and a capitalist spirit as important, though he does not refer to a liberal tradition, but rather to an over-arching "American" or "Anglo-Saxon" spirit. Lipset (1996, 19 and 31) identifies liberty, egalitarianism, individualism, populism, and laissez-faire. Lipset and Marks (2000, 30) substitute anti-statism for liberty. Greenstone (1993, 35, 36, and 48) identifies individual freedom, private property, and government by popular consent. But these categories also vary: sometimes it is individual freedom, sometimes individual rights, sometimes it is private property, sometimes private enterprise, and so on. Smith (1993, 563) identifies limited government, individual rights, and a market economy, and treats democracy as part of a separate republican tradition. Katznelson (1997, 43) identifies equal respect, individualism, rights, consent, toleration, the distinction between public and private, democracy, and markets. Gerstle (1994, 1046) identifies emancipation, rationality and progress. And Hartz (1955), in the single most influential statement of the liberalism thesis, does not clearly specify the nature of liberal values at all, relying instead on suggestive associations and allegorical categories like Lockeanism and Algerism. In his later work, he identifies egalitarianism, individualism, democracy, and capitalism (Hartz, 1964, 71, 102, and 109). Similar problems attend discussions of a "republican" (or a "labor republican") tradition.

5. On frame alignment, see Snow et al. (1986), Snow and Benford (1988), and Morris and Mueller (1992).

6. Compare this second point with the idea of "phenomenological constraints" in Snow and Benford (1988, 207–11), and of "reality-testing" in Klandermans (1988, 175).

7. See Sombart (1976, 109–10), Hartz (1955, 6, 9, 205–6, 219, 234, 246–7, and 254), Lipset (1977, 35–8 and 50–4, and 1996, 36, 79, and 84), Lipset and Marks (2000, 25–7), and Greenstone (1993, 37–8 and 40).

8. For summaries, see White (1981, 47–52, 62, 76–7, and 83), Kingston, (1988, 277–82), and Thompson (1994, 5–9).

9. Twopeny later founded and edited the *Pastoralist Review* at the behest of employers in the pastoral industry who were seeking to establish an organ to promote their interests during the 1891 Shearers' strike (Ward, 1973, 7).

10. See *Hummer*, January 2, 1892 and elsewhere, and *AW*, May 9 and 16, 1891.

11. *Times*, August 31, 1903. See also Clark (1955, 806) and Lawson (1987, ix, 103, 122–3, and 212–3).

12. This ideal of class cooperation can frequently be found in union resolutions and addresses.

13. The *Bulletin* first used a similar figure to portray the capitalist during the 1888 coal miners' strike (Hirst, 1988, 72).

14. The Free Trade leader Parkes is on the ground, while the Protectionist leader Dibbs is in the air. The cartoonist who produced the illustrations in both Figures 6.1 and 6.2, Livingston Hopkins, was born in Ohio and had originally practiced his craft for various magazines in New York before moving to Sydney as a staff artist for the *Bulletin* (Lawson, 1987, 102–3).

15. *Worker*, December 23, 1893.

16. *RT*, June 15, July 2, and August 15, 1894. Pullman actually had been granted a noble title by the King of Italy (Lindsey, 1942, 31), and sometimes the paper suggested that their opponents literally wanted to reestablish an aristoratic order. "They want a king," ran one headline (*RT*, April 15, 1895), "The Plutocrats are tired of the Sovereignty of the People: And Demand a Royal Family and a Titled Nobility with Aristocratic Trimmings."

17. *RT*, August 15, 1894, 1, and *Evening Press and Chicago Mail*, November 4, 1895 in Debs Papers, reel 14.

18. *Evening Press*, November 4, 1895.

19. *Evening Press*, October 14, 1895.

20. *UMWJ*, July 19, 1894, 4.

21. *UMWJ*, August 23, 1894, 4. This is how McBride closed his speech to the conference of labor organizations in Ohio that he had convened for the purpose of undertaking independent political action in the state.

22. *CSJ*, July 4, 1894, 6, and July 11, 1894, 6.

23. *RT*, July 2, 1894, 2. See also the *Chicago Times* cartoon on July 4, 1894 with George Pullman and George III (Schneirov, 1998, 99). For some other July 4 commentaries, see *CSJ*, July 4 and 11, 1894, and *AF*, July 1894, 98. For other appeals to the Declaration of Independence, see the Steelworkers' resolution in AFL (1893, 72), or the appeal to Jefferson and Lincoln in Swinton (1894, 405–6).

24. AFL (1891b, 73), *AF*, June 1894, 72, and July 1894, 98.

25. "What Does Labor Want?" in Kaufman and Albert (1989, 388–9). Gompers made similar comments to a Senate inquiry ten years earlier (Kaufman, 1986, 348–9).

26. *AF*, April 1894, backcover.

27. Bowman (1958, 166, 173, 177, and 183–5), "Plutocracy or Nationalism: Which?" in Bellamy (1937), Aaron (1951, 74), Destler (1963, 232–3), and Swinton (1892). See also the SLP article on "Snob-dom" and the cartoon of "King Capital" in *People*, December 3, 1893. I do not want to deny that Gompers and his AFL allies placed less emphasis on "labor republican" themes than the Knights of Labor and others had in the past (Hattam, 1993, 112–37). I simply want to point out that social egalitarian themes

did regularly arise during the period leading up to the AFL's 1894 debate, and draw attention to the effect that they had when they did.

28. Note that Gompers and Debs appealed to social egalitarian themes both when addressing unionists, and when crafting their message for a broader audience. See the preceding references.

29. See also Thompson (1994, 14–22).

30. On this status and its "democratisation" in Australia, see Hirst (1988, 61–4, and 1988a, 106–13).

31. The *Bulletin*, June 27, 1891, 6. For similar sentiments, see *Hummer*, February 13, 1892.

32. The *Bulletin*, June 27, 1891, 6 and 13.

33. "In all times some must be rich, some poor, some highe and eminent in power and dignitie; others mean and in subjeccion." (Miller, 1956, 4–5.)

34. Clark (1955, 334–342). A "bunyip" is something like a yeti: an imaginary creature of aboriginal legend that was subject to occasional "sightings," but whose existence could never be reliably confirmed.

35. This reflected the common influence of men's fashions in London. For the development of men's dress in the United States, see Shaw (1982, 5–13 and 53–7), Schlesinger (1947, 37–8) and Godkin (1895, 217). For illustrations of the clothing worn by politicians, see Dole (1989), Byrd (1988), Josephy (1975), and the front of the official *Congressional Directory*.

36. For New York, see Hammack (1987, 60–79), Beckert (2001, 237–72 and esp. 255–65), and Burrows and Wallace (1999, 1071–88). For other cities, see Balzell (1958) and Jaher (1982).

37. The Sons of the American Revolution was founded in 1889 and the Daughters of the American Revolution in 1890. In the 1870s, Tiffanys established a heraldry department to design coats of arms (Beckert, 2001, 258 and 270).

38. This practice began in the 1870s. By 1915, there were 42 American princesses, 17 duchesses, 19 vice-countesses, 33 marchionesses, 46 ladies, wives of knights, or baronets, 64 baronesses, and 136 countesses (Brandon, 1980, 1). For more, see Montgomery (1989) and MacColl and Wallace (1989). See also the list of "Titled American Women" with their husband's title and the amount of money each had brought to the marriage in *Chicago Daily News Almanac for 1896*, 239–40.

39. The *Social Register* first appeared in New York in 1888, then in Boston and Philadelphia in 1890, Baltimore in 1892, Chicago in 1893, and then in various other cities (Balzell, 1958, 19).

40. *NYT*, February 15, 1892, 5.

41. *NYT*, February 11, 1897.

42. For the Bradley Martin Ball, see Muccigrosso (1994) and Beckert (2001, 1–2, 258, and 334). For illustrations, see these and Churchill (1970, 190–1). For the Vanderbilt ball, see Burrows and Wallace (1999, 1071–2). For illustrations of the Vanderbilt mansion and others that emulated it, see MacColl (1989, 55) and Churchill (1979, 139 and 172). For the Centennial ball, see Burrows and Wallace (1999, 1085).

43. See *NYT* on January 14, February 16, and December 13, 1892, on January 10, February 14, and December 14, 1893, and on January 9, February 6, and December 11, 1894. See also the New York *Daily Tribune* on the same days. The expansion of "society pages" in the 1890s led to saturation coverage of some events (Muccigrosso, 1994,

305). Newspapers in cities hundreds of miles from New York regularly assumed that their readers were familiar with details of various neo-aristocratic episodes. See, for example, "Mrs Vanderbilt and the Duke" and "Plebian still on the Continent" in *Evening Press and Chicago Mail*, October 21 and November 4, 1895.

44. *NYT*, December 9, 1894, 19.

45. *Evening Press and Chicago Mail*, November 4, 1895.

46. *AW*, June 20, 1891, 2, ICTUC (1891, 90), ICTUC (1885, 15).

47. *AW*, September 7, 1890, 6. In a similar fashion, the President of the Intercolonial Trade Union Congress (ICTUC, 1891, 15) declared in his inaugural address at its first meeting following the Maritime strike that "we look to our young men to defend our liberty."

48. See the cartoon in the *Worker*, December 23, 1893, which shows a young (sans coulotte) woman, "Liberty," handing the new born baby of "Politics" to a man representing Labor.

49. "Why You Should Join a Union" and "The Labour Victory," *AW*, June 20, 91.

50. *SMH*, March 5, 1891 and Nairn (1989, 56). For similar responses, see *AW*, March 7, 1891, and the *Bulletin*, May 23 and May 30, 1891.

51. ICTUC (1884, 130). See also Joyce (1978, 172), and the *Bulletin*, April 28, May 9, and July 11, 1891 on sham liberals. For enthusiasm, see reports on George Grey in *AW*, April 11 and June 6, 1891, and *Bulletin*, February 28, 1891.

52. *Bulletin*, April 11, 1891, 1 and 7. (See cartoon in Chapter 2.) See also Ebbels (1983, 137), *AW*, January 24, 1891, and *Bulletin*, September 19, 1891.

53. *AW*, December 24, 1892, 4.

54. *AW*, January 3, 1891, and *Worker*, March 31, 1892.

55. Fitzhardinge (1964, 32). Hughes, who later became Prime Minister, was then just beginning his involvement in labor politics. For his mature articulation of this point, see Hughes (1910, 59–65), but cf Hughes (1910, 140–44). Socialists often argued that they were the only true individualists (Burgmann, 1985, 60). For similar arguments, see "Socialism," *AW* January 23, 1892, and Spence's undated election pamphlet "Private Enterprise: Is It Possible under Present Conditions" held in ML at 335.0901 I.

56. For other examples, see Labour Defence Committee (1890, 19) and the *Bulletin*, March 21 and September 19, 1891.

57. See also "Mates," *Hummer*, January 16, 1892. Lane wrote both this article and the novel from which the preceding quotes are taken under the pseudonym John Miller.

58. ICTUC (1889, 34). See also Delegate Elmslie (ICTUC, 1889, 36).

59. ICTUC (1885, 11, 1886, 33, and 1891, 90).

60. See delegates Kirkpatrick, Barrett, Trenwith, Spur, and Gibson (ICTUC, 1886, 29–42), though note that Gibson also hopes that labor MPs "will only legislate for the general good, independent of class interests." For 1891, see the party's election flyer in Ebbels (1983, 213), *Bulletin*, July 11, 1891, 6, and September 19, 1891, 7, and ICTUC (1891, 90).

61. *Hummer*, October 19, 1891, 3. See also *Hummer*, November 7, 1891, 2 and the election manifesto supplement on June 18, 1892.

62. *AW*, August 8, 1891, 4, and *Bulletin*, July 11, 1891, 7, and July 18, 1891, 7. When the United Labour party was founded in Victoria, many wanted to call it the People's party (Love, 1984, 10).

63. Debs (1895, 3, 6–7, and 10–11). For the atmosphere at this meeting, see Salvatore (1982, 153–55).

64. *RT*, March 1, 1895, *Evening Press and Chicago Mail*, October 14, 1895, and *CN*, November 23, 1895.

65. See *CN*, November 23 and 30, 1895. The *Coming Nation* was the forerunner of the *Appeal to Reason* which became the most widely circulated left-wing paper ever in the United States.

66. *UMWJ*, August 23, 1894. See also "Declaration, Notice, and Invitation," *UMWJ*, August 9, 1894, and *UMWJ*, June 1, 1893.

67. *AF*, July 1894, 98. See also *AFL* (1896, 11–12), and his angry letter to one of the judges who issued the injunction against the ARU (Kaufman and Albert, 1989, 560).

68. "The Safety of the Future Lies in Organized Labor" (Lloyd, 1893), and "The Revolution is Here" (Destler, 1946, 212–221).

69. (Destler, 1946, 221). See also Lloyd (1893, 8).

70. In his Chicago speech, Debs (1895, 11) only once briefly mentions the possibility that the ballot may lead to something more: the cooperative commonwealth.

71. See Boyle in *AF*, December 1894, 215, who combines them with a Debsian invocation to "rebuild the temple of liberty." See also Weissman in *AFL* (1891b, 29–37), Gross in *AF*, October 1894, 166–7, and "What Is Liberty?" in *UMWJ*, December 21, 1893.

72. St. Louis *Labor*, October 7, 1893, *Labor News*, March 10, 1894, and *Labor News*, March 24, 1894.

73. "Mr Populism" in *RT*, February 1, 1895. See also "Individuality" in *Labor News*, March 24, 1894; Debs, "Individualism vs. Socialism" in *CN*, January 23, 1897; Lloyd, "Why the Workmen Should Organize" in *AFL* (1891b, 19); Foster in *AFL* (1891b, 21–5); Flynn in *AF*, July 1894, 103; and Myer in *AF*, December 1894, 126–7.

74. *AFL* (1895a, 27–8, 29, 29–30, 30–31, and 46–48).

75. Cohen was a "philosophical anarchist," and it seems likely McCraith and Greenhalgh were, too. Their position was elaborated in a series of three articles in *AF*, August, 1895, 103, and September, 1895, 116–8 and 120–1. Sullivan was a single taxer (Kaufman and Albert, 1989, 721), and Pomeroy had opportunistically aligned himself with the single taxers earlier in the year (Staley, 1930, 123–5, and Destler, 1946, 201). Weismann had also been an anarchist (Kaufman and Albert, 1989, 726). His arguments are echoed in an AFL-circulated pamphlet by another former anarchist (Lum, 1892).

76. See Gros in *AF*, December 1894 and August 1895; Miller in *AF*, August 1895; Lloyd in Destler (1963, 232–3); and Louise in *RT*, February 1, 1895.

77. *AFL* (1891b, 8).

78. *CN*, November 30, 1895, 2–3.

79. *Chicago Sunday Tribune*, July 1, 1894, 1 and passim. However, as we saw earlier, the strongest and most vociferous criticism of unions during the strikes of the early 1890s was not that they were a threat to liberty, but rather that they threatened to introduce "anarchy." In a sense, it was not a fear of the loss of liberty so much as a fear of the undue love of liberty. Order, not freedom, and civilization, not individualism, were the values to which labor's opponents gave the highest priority. At times it seems as if their response was rooted in a fear of "Americanism."

80. Hartz (1964, 11) sought to incorporate elements of this argument. He also emphasized the influence of Chartist radicals transported to Australia. But in fact, only a tiny percentage of convicts were in any sense political prisoners (McQueen, 1986, 129).

81. Ward (1958, 209, and 1978) himself has reiterated this in response to criticism.

82. In the early 1890s, the most elaborate effort to deploy the concept of mateship within the labor movement was made by William Lane. Lane saw mateship as a way of making socialism compatible, not just with individual freedom, but with an anti-statist interpretation of that idea. Addressing himself to "men who want to do what is right [but] object to socialism because they think it will tend to turn the state into a tyranny," he argued that "Socialism is being *mates*; and you can't be made mates by legislation." For Lane, mateship played the role of a Rousseauian civil religion: the same role that Bellamy ascribed to his "religion of solidarity." See "Mates," *Hummer*, January 16, 1892. Similar arguments appear in Lane (1892, 112–9). See also *Worker*, March 31, 1894.

83. O'Sullivan (1892, iii), Reeves (1969 [1902], 1:63), and Gollan (1960, 86).

84. See NSW Premier Parkes' rejection of unemployment relief, workplace regulation, coal regulation, and an eight-hour law (Parkes, 1892, 310–7, Nairn, 1989, 41–2, and Bollen, 1972, 39), as well as the full-scale defense of laissez-faire by employer-affiliated politicians and journals (Loveday *et al.*, 1977, 177 and 478, Nairn, 1989, 296, and Sawer, 2000, 83).

85. See Green (1881), Ritchie (1891), Hobhouse (1893 and 1911), and Hobson (1909).

86. Campbell (1976, 27–30), Docker (1982, 60–4 and 79–81), Evatt (1918, 49–77), Melleuish (1995, 19 and 26–49), Rowse (1978, 6–11 and 37–41), and Wise (1892). For a good overview, see Sawer (2000).

87. Joyce (1978, 172), Rickard (1976, 66), Sawer (2000, 74), and La Nauze (1965, 106–7).

88. Both Deakin and Griffith mobilized government forces against the unions in the early 1890s.

89. Union leaders were well aware of these developments (AFL, 1895a, 59, and Debs, 1895, 17).

90. Lloyd (1910), Destler (1946, 215, and 1963, 290–314), and *AF*, March 1894, 4.

91. Gompers in AFL (1891b, 73), Kaufman and Albert (1989, 389), and *AF*, March 1894, 5.

92. Labour Defence Committee (1890), Ebbels (1983, 205 and 213), *AW*, June 20, 1891, 2, *Bulletin*, September 19, 1891, 7, the "Monopoly" cartoon in *Worker*, July 14, 1894, Murphy (1975, 35, 129), and Evatt (1942, 185–6).

93. U.S. Census Office (1902, lxxiii and 582–3), and Coghlan (1902b, 660 and 664).

CHAPTER 7

RELIGION

1. Lipset (1963, 141–50, and 1996, 19, 60–7, and 79–80) and Tiryakian (1993) cite multiple sources including Marx, Weber, and Bryce. See also Tocqueville (1990, 1: 308).

2. Marx in Lipset (1996, 80).

3. "In Australia . . . what is most significant historically about religion is its weakness" (O'Farrell, 1976, 67). "In Australia religion has been of moderate importance" (Bollen, 1972, 1). It was "a country not so Christian" (Gilbert, 1988). "In a sense European Australia . . . has always been a secular society" (Hogan, 1987, 287 and 293).

4. O'Farrell (1976, 70). For later qualifications, see O'Farrell (1988).

5. On how religion and nationality became more closely entwined in the U.S. than Australia, see O'Farrell (1988, 8), Ely (1981, 558–9), and Inglis (1967, 35).

6. Mol (1971, 1). The first religious service was held eight days later.

7. Of the rest, 0.5 percent were Jewish, 1.0 percent were Buddhists, Confucians, and Muslims, and another 1.0 percent objected to stating their religion: an option that was available on request (Coghlan, 1894a, 213–9, Phillips, 1969, 439, and 1972, 384).

8. Carroll (1893, xxxiv–xxxvi) suggests, as a *very* rough estimate, that Christians were about 90.5 percent of the U.S. population in 1890.

9. This was not simply a function of the higher proportion of rural residents in the United States. Contrary to widespread belief, in both countries, there were more church members in urban areas than in rural ones. See Table 7.1, Carroll (1894, xxvi–xxvii and 91–99) and Finke and Stark (1992, 203–7).

10. See Phillips (1985), Thompson (1994, 25–8), Gladden (1886, 146–79), Perry (1898), Abbott (1903, 1–50), AF, December 1894, 210–11, and the exchanges between Gompers and Stauffer, and Gompers and Perry, in AF, June 1894, 80–81, and AF, August 1896, 119–20.

11. I will use "Anglican" to refer to both the Episcopal church in the United States and the Church of England in Australia.

12. Especially about claims that there were Catholic majorities in large American cities (Christiano, 1987, 176–9).

13. For definitions, see Bebbington (1989, 1–19, and 1993, 185), Rawlyk and Noll (1993, 17–18), Noll *et al.* (1994, 6) and Marsden (1991, 4–5).

14. Handy (1976, 274–281 and 1991), Marty (1970), and Marsden (1991, 9–17).

15. On sect-like organization and Puritian traditions, see Finke and Stark (1992), Miller (1956), Bebbington (1989, 34–47), Murrin (1990) and Hatch (1990) for the U.S. For Australia, see Bollen (1972, 9), Judd and Cable (1987, 111–158), Piggin (1994, 291), Dickey (1993), Hilliard (1988, 15–18), Phillips (1969, 6, 1972, 383, and 1981, 15) and O'Farrell (1976, 66).

16. From 34.6 percent in 1870 to 29.7 percent in 1880 and 26.8 percent in 1890 (Phillips, 1969, 446–7, and 1981, 84). For revivalism in the U.S., see McLoughlin (1978) and Marsden (1991, 9–24). For Australia, see Phillips (1972, 383, and 1981, 59–86), Piggin (1994, 289, and 1996, 57–64), and Jackson (1988, 3, and 1988, 48–76).

17. On the United States, for Protestant clerical attitudes, see May (1949, 91–111). For revivalists, see McLoughlin (1959, 267–71, 274). For the Social Gospel, see Hopkins (1940, 67–78 and 171–83). For Protestant hostility in Chicago, see Pierce (1957, 437–40). On Australia, see Phillips (1981, 148–55 and 159–60).

18. See the lecture on "true socialism" by the Anglican bishop of Sydney in the late 1880s (Phillips, 1981, 155).

19. On the U.S., see Hopkins (1940, 67–78, 150–52, and 171–83) and Schlesinger (1932, 540–1). On Australia, see Phillips (1981, 155–60 and 166–68) and Thompson (1994, 41). On England, see Inglis (1963, 251–52 and 271–87).

20. May (1949, 53, 67, and 69). Presbyterians with a strict Calvinist attitude were among the most hostile to the labor movement in both the United States and Australia (Bollen, 1972, 18–19 and 39–42).

21. On "clerical laissez-faire," see May (1949, 6–16 and 44–45).

22. Inglis (1963, 299–304). Usually, but not always. In isolated, overwhelmingly working-class communities, the same mechanism encouraged local clergymen to support unions, as happened at Homestead, in the Pullman township, and in some mining villages. Likewise, clergymen without a slave-holding constituency had been more likely to support abolition, and many denominations had split along this line of economic interest.

23. On union organization, see Abell (1945, 473–4, and 1960, 54–60), Roohan (1976, 328–31 and 398), Ellis (1952, 528–9, and 1962, 440–53), Phillips (1981, 164–6), O'Farrell (1969b, 153–8, and 1992, 286) and Hogan (1987, 138–45). On strikes, see Roohan (1976, 399–400), Will (1922, 1: 344), O'Farrell (1969b, 154 and 158, and 1992, 285) and Hamilton (1958, 257). On socialism, see Abell (1945, 481–2, 494), Will (1922, 1, 217–9, 300–1), Karson (1984, 83–7), O'Farrell (1969b, 177), Ford (1966, 81), and Thompson (1994, 49–50).

24. In Sydney, the Catholic *Freeman's Journal* withdrew support as the strike progressed (Hamilton, 1958, 257). In Chicago, the *New World*, which had recently been founded by the city's Archbishop, defended Debs throughout, though it also supported the intervention of federal troops (Lee, 1991, 10–11, 17, 18, and 20, and Schneirov, 1998, 318–9).

25. Ultimately, the authorities in Rome settled on a compromise: they decided that *Progress and Poverty* was worthy of condemnation, but ordered that their finding should not be publicized (Roohan, 1976, 363).

26. The differences between Gibbons and Moran grew wider over time. See their correspondence in 1910 about Labor's plan to nationalize monopolies. Gibbons wrote, alarmed at the "alliance of [the] Roman Catholics of Australia with the party of the Socialists" (Cahill, 1989, 528). Moran replied that the leaders of the Labor party held views he considered to be "quite orthodox" (Ellis, 1952, 1, 536).

27. Despite their common theological commitments, Catholics have tended to support right-wing or authoritarian parties in countries like France, Italy, and Austria, where Catholicism is dominant, but left-leaning parties in countries like United States, Britain, and Australia, where it is not.

28. Spence was a Presbyterian elder, although Anglican and Methodist affiliations were more common (Rickard, 1976, 29, O'Farrell, 1962, 141, 142, Bollen, 1972, 72–75, Hogan, 1987, 137–8, and Thompson, 1994, 37–39, 50). TLC President Brennan was a Catholic. Of the Labor members elected to the NSW Parliament in 1891, 41 percent were Anglican, 21 percent Methodist, 15 percent Presbyterian, and only 15 percent were Catholic (Nairn, 1989, 38–9, 69).

29. Van Tine (1973, 10) and Fink (1984, 23).

30. For the U.S., see *AF*, April 1894, 28–34; *AF*, June 1894, 80–81; *AF*, December 1894, 210–11; *LFM*, November 1893, 904–05; *Evening Press*, November 18, 1895; and *CSJ*, September 16, 1891, 1. For Australia, see *AW*, January 24, 1891; *AW*, August 22, 1891; *AW*, September 26, 1891; *Bulletin*, March 14, 1891; *Bulletin*, March 21, 1891; *Bulletin*, September 26, 1891; *Hummer*, January 16, 1892; and *Hummer*, April 9, 1892.

31. *AF*, August 1896, 119–20; *Evening Press*, September 30, 1895; *AW*, November 29, 1890; and *Hummer*, February 6, 1892.

32. *AF*, June 1894, 80 and *RT*, March 1, 1894, 1.

33. See Debs's response to Gibbons's address on Christ and labor in *LFM*, November 1893, 904–05, and the NSW TLC's vote against a resolution thanking Moran for an address on *Rerum Novarum* in *AW*, August 22, 1891, 3, and Ford (1966, 103). See also *NLT*, August 2, 1890, 2 on Cardinal Manning; AFL (1895, 25) on a speech invoking Gibbons and Manning that was "frequently interrupted by outbursts of applause"; and *AW*, April 8, 1891, and *Bulletin*, May 16, 1891, both on *Rerum Novarum*.

34. On "Churchianity," see Perry (1898, 622), Abell (1962, 64), and *AW*, January 24, 1891, 1. On Gompers, who was born into a Jewish family, see Gutman (1966, 87). On Debs and Spence, see *LFM*, November 1893, 905, and *Hummer*, May 28, 1892, 2. For invocations of Christ, see *Hummer*, May 28, 1892, 2; *UMWJ*, November 10, 1892, 8; *Bulletin*, June 13, 1891, 7; *RT*, March 1, 1894, 1. On Fitzgerald, who was also a Catholic, see *AW*, May 16, 1891, 1.

35. The core Democratic message in the South was often framed in similar terms. It was not, they said, for the government to decide whether slavery (or, later, segregation) was immoral.

36. For influential treatments, see Kleppner (1970 and 1979), Jensen (1971), and Mc-Seveney (1972). For shorter versions, see Kleppner (1978 and 1981) and Jensen (1970). For a wider summary, see Oestreicher (1988) and Swierenga (1990). On the political effects of evangelical and liturgical beliefs, see especially Kleppner (1979, 180–97) and Jensen (1971, 63–8). For other factors, see Gerring (1998) and Bensel (2000).

37. For standard treatments, see Gollan (1960, 1–68) and Loveday *et al.* (1977, 5–43).

38. The upsurge in sectarian politics was also fueled by papal denunciation of liberal politics in the 1864 Syllabus of Errors, and by the 1871 declaration of papal infallibility. In addition, it was fueled locally by bitter Catholic hostility towards Parkes's 1866 Public Schools Bill, and a Catholic ban on mixed marriages in 1869 (Thompson, 1994, 19–20, and Hogan, 1987, 117).

39. For residential segregation, see Hirsch (1990, 36, 98–103, and 125–26) on Chicago, Laslett (2000, 136) on Illinois coal miners, and Kleinberg (1989, 43–44) on Pittsburgh, as well as Davis (1986, 43–44) and Lieberson (1963). On Australia, see Hogan (1987, 124–27), O'Farrell (1993, 116), and Akenson (1988, 66). For intermarriage, see Kleinberg (1989, 204–05) and Kleppner (1979, 368) on the U.S., and McConville (1985, 6), Jackson (1987, 82–102), and O'Farrell (1992, 204) on Australia.

40. Gavin Duffy was elected in 1871. Another Irish Catholic, John O'Shanassy, had already served two terms in 1857–59 and 1861–63 (Thompson, 1994, 19).

41. Indeed, widespread party identification had already emerged in the 1830s and 1840s (Silbey, 1991, 125–30, 139, and 218–21).

42. Loveday and Martin (1966, 91–105 and 121–148). There was some similarity between this idea of "independence" and the "anti-party" ideology of many Republican activists in the United States (Kleppner, 1979, 70, 80–2, 252–7, and 331–3).

43. In Australia, advocates of state action on "puritan" issues like temperance, sabbath observance, gambling, and sexual purity (which was pursued through the regulation or prohibition of dance halls, mixed bathing, and contraceptive devices), were often described as "wowsers" (Dunstan, 1968, 1–6). Wowsers were typically portrayed as black-frocked kill-joy preachers and busybodies. The very fact that a term like this gained popular currency is suggestive about the role of religion.

44. On temperance, see Kleppner (1979, 66–67, 129, 131–42, 211–17, 239–57, and 335–4), Jensen (1971, 186, 191–4, 197–8, and 201–2), Colvin (1926), Fanshawe (1893), and Kerr (1985, 35–65). On sabbatarianism, see Schlesinger (1932, 533–6), Kleppner (1979, 210–1), and Handy (1991, 71–4). For Pittsburgh, see Courvares (1984, 51–5 and 75–9). The Law and Order Leagues also engaged in repeated litigation to enforce Sabbath observance. For Chicago, see Schlesinger (1932, 535).

45. The common school movement, which had established the public school system in the antebellum period, was, like the temperance and abolitionist movements, closely connected to the Second Great Awakening (Jorgenson, 1987, 20).

46. On education, see Jensen (1971, 122–50), Kleppner (1979, 221–31 and 349–55), Jorgenson (1987), Handy (1991, 51–3), Kinzer (1964, 101), Couvares (1984, 71–2), and Krause (1992, 215–7). In Pennsylvania, there was a different controversy over whether nuns wearing their habits should be allowed to teach in public school.

47. This campaign was particularly vociferous in Chicago, where it was specifically aimed at stopping defections to the labor-populists. On anti-Catholic organization, see Higham (1992, 28–30, 61–3, and 77–87), Kinzer (1964), Jensen (1971, 222–7 and 232–7), Kleppner (1979, 68–70, 214–21, and 231–8), and Bennett (1988, 169–79 and 441).

48. The Local Option League was founded in NSW in 1882, and the Women's Christian Temperance Union, modeled directly on its U.S. sister organization, was established in 1882 in NSW and in 1885 in Victoria.

49. Where local option elections were held in the United States, they were usually attempts by professional politicians to avoid activist demands for prohibition legislation (Colvin, 1926).

50. Phillips (1981, 192). On temperance, see Phillips (1981, 144–48 and 167–68), Hogan (1987, 145–54), Thompson (1994, 17), and Bollen (1972, 70–71). The growing interest in temperance in the early 1890s is also reflected in the attention labor journals paid to it. On sabbath observance, see Phillips (1981, 175–93), Hogan (1987, 97), and Thompson (1994, 12–13, 16–18, 22, 26, and 32–33). See also *Bulletin*, January 31, 1891, 4–5 on Parkes's move to forbid the Australian Socialist League to hire a theater for its Sunday lectures.

51. On education, see Austin (1961, 107–210), Phillips (1981, 207–40), Hogan (1987, 83–95), and Thompson (1994, 18–21).

52. On anti-Catholic organizations, see Bollen (1972, 145–51), Hogan (1987, 144, 150, and 165–66), and Thompson (1994, 44–48). On the Catholic shift to Labor, see also Hamilton (1958, 262–67), and Hagan and Turner (1991, 24–26).

53. In January 1887, just weeks after Henry George's strong showing in New York, Gompers was already doubting whether the workers who voted for George had really "sever[ed] their connection with the two dominant parties" (Kaufman, 1987, 9). Every year thereafter he can be found warning against the dangers posed by divergent party loyalties. See Kaufman (1987, 121, 364, and 391), AFL (1892, 9 and 13, 1893, 12, 1894, 14, and 1896, 22), and AF, August 1896, 118–19 and 129–30.

54. However, whereas Gompers (AFL, 1894, 14, and Kaufman and Albert, 1989, 203) thought that "it is ridiculous to imagine that the wage-workers can be slaves in employment and yet achieve control at the polls," McBride (AFL, 1895, 15) thought that it was a "self-evident truth . . . that wage workers cannot hope to be free in the

shops, mines, and factories while trudging in party slavery to the polls." See also *UMWJ*, August 19, 1894.

55. See the remarks by delegates Macarthur, McGuire, Lennon, and Pomeroy (AFL, 1895a, 6, 12, 43, 45, and 46). See also McGuire on the disruptive effects of "sectarian side issues" and "the deviltry of party politics" (Finn, 1973, 254). On his changing attitude to politics, see Galenson (1983, 67–73).

56. Gompers noted that "our fellow-workers have to too large an extent been partisans first and wage-workers after" (AFL, 1893, 12). He made a similar point the previous year (AFL, 1892, 9).

57. *CSJ*, October 30, 1895. Subsequent editorials suggest that the editor has racial as well as religious prejudice in mind. See *CSJ*, March 4, 1896 where he argues that politics "exists almost solely by virtue of the contention between races and religions."

58. Kaufman and Albert (1989, 408). For other correspondence, see Kaufman and Albert (1989, 154, 354, 378, and 476).

59. See Kaufman (1973, 172–3 and 211–2). For McGuire's similar position, see Galenson (1983, 72).

60. See Treasurer Lennon (AFL, 1895, 66), Delegate O'Sullivan (AFL, 1895, 79), and First Vice-President McGuire in Galenson (1983, 71) and *AF*, December 1896, 207–8.

61. *CN*, November 23 and November 30, 1895, *RT*, April 15, 1895, 1 and 6 (the contributor was himself a Methodist clergyman), and *AF*, June 1894, 79 (see also July 1894, 106).

62. For the oath, see Kinzer (1964, 49). For Debs, see *LFM*, March 1894, 280–2. See also *LFM*, April 1894, 396, and *RT*, March 1, 1894, September 2, 1895, and October 1, 1895. For the SLP, see the editorial in *Chicago Labor*, May 12, 1894.

63. Boston *Labor Leader*, December 23, 1893, cited in Montgomery (1993, 147). McCraith held various positions in the International Typographical Union and was Secretary of the AFL in 1894 and 1895.

64. George Black (1926–29, No. 1, 9–10), who later became a Labor member of parliament, thought that many unionists had opposed the formation of a labor party when he—then a single taxer—suggested it in 1886, because they thought it was a device to obstruct the adoption of protectionism.

65. See Labor Council of NSW, General Meetings Minutes, June 27, 1890, and the appended proposal for "A Workman's Newspaper," ML A3829–A3831.

66. Trades and Labour Council of NSW, Parliamentary Committee Minute Book, 1884–1894, June 2, 1891, ML A2761. See also the letter to the *Trades and Labour Advocate*, December 21, 1889, 5, which argued against proposals for labor representation in parliament: "The sooner the matter is allowed to drop the better . . . I fear that too much devotion to one or the other of our two great political parties will tend to seduce our men from their allegiance to the cause of labour."

67. *AW*, May 2, 1891, 4. For the party's official position, see its election flyer "Sinking the Fiscal Issue" in Harris (1970, 122). For the difficulties in agreeing on a platform, see *AW*, March 21, 1891, 3, March 28, 1891, 3, April 25, 1891, 3, and May 2, 1891, 4.

68. Murphy (1975, 25–29), Markey (1988, 179), Nairn (1989, 72–86), and J.D. Fitzgerald in NSW TLC, Parliamentary Committee Minute Book, 1884–1894, September 12, 1892, ML A2761.

69. ICTUC (1886, 32), ICTUC (1888, 65). On a Victorian attempt in 1886, see Coghlan (1918, III: 1489), Serle (1971, 120), and Bongiorno (1996, 25–6).

70. *Hummer*, January 30, 1892, 2–3.

71. *AW*, April 18, 1891, 3, and Nairn (1989, 70).

72. *Bulletin*, June 13, 1891, 6–7.

73. *Bulletin*, December 26, 1891, 6. According to the *Bulletin*, this attempt to set sectarian passions afire "fizzled drearily and went out."

74. NSW TLC, Parliamentary Committee Minute Book, 1884–1894, April 6, 1891, ML A2761. For other examples, see *AW*, January 17, 1891, 3, and *Hummer*, January 30, 1892, 5, and February 15, 1892, 3. Overall, Protestant and Temperance Halls seemed to be more frequently used than Catholic ones. Pubs or saloons are often called hotels in Australia.

75. Brennan and Fitzgerald.

76. *AW*, May 16, 1891, 1.

77. *AW*, September 26, 1891, 2. Emphasis added. However temperance issues were not ignored by the labor press. A number of prominent unionists and Labor MPs were temperance advocates. See the *Hummer*, May 28, 1892, and June 18, 1892 for Spence's support for abstinence, and Nairn (1989, 70) for teetotallers among the parliamentarians. Both the *AW* (September 26, 1891) and the *Hummer* (January 16, 1892) supported a moderate critique of excess drinking, and the *AW* (April 18, May 2, May 9, and June 27, 1891) provided a forum for all sides of the debate with a series of articles on "Poverty and Drink." How all this was received by ordinary workers is a different question. One temperance advocate wrote in the *AW* (April 18, 1891) that at most labor meetings "the teetotaller is listened to with ill-disguised impatience, if not with open derision."

78. *Bulletin*, January 13, 1894, 4.

79. See the bootmakers' insistence on protectionism in Labor Council of NSW, General Meetings Minutes, May 8, 1890, ML A3829–A3831.

80. Gompers thought that Henry George's free-trade commitments would undermine the prospects for the United Labor party established after his 1886 mayoral campaign in New York (Kaufman, 1987, 47). See also Pearce's welcoming comments to the 1886 FOTLU conference (Kaufman, 1986, 454). The iron and steel workers' union had withdrawn from FOTLU for four years after the latter shifted away from supporting protection in 1882 (Taft, 1957, 14, and Couvares, 1984, 66).

81. Jensen (1971, 86–7) treats these respondents as having no preference. But it is more likely that most did not want to answer: often on Protestant theological grounds. Data on ethnicity might provide a proxy, but it also has limitations. Many discussions of Chicago, for example, rely on a ward-by-ward breakdown of the nationality of registered voters in 1892. For this data, see *Chicago Daily News Almanac for 1894*, 318 and Tarr (1971, 317, 34–5). However, this does not help with the 50 percent of voters who were born in the United States. For additional data, see Hirsch (1990, 36, 98–103, and 125–6). On the ethnic composition of labor organizations in 1886, see Bogart and Thompson (1920, 454 and 458) and Keil (1983, 158 and 162–3).

82. Couvares (1984, 67–9), Kleppner (1979, 273–97), Staley (1930, 81–2), Jensen (1971, 265–7), and Schneirov (1998, 317–8 and 227–9).

83. In Spring Valley, the labor-populists won 54 percent. This was their best result in any precinct in Illinois. In Illinois coal towns as a whole, they won an average of about 18 percent (Nash, 1982, 54, Jensen, 1971, 245 and 257). For similar support in the coal mining areas of Ohio and Pennsylvania, see (Kleppner, 1970, 248–9, and Nash,

1982, 52–5 and 171–3). For the persistence of religious and partisan divisions among Pennsylvania steel workers, see Nash (1982, 20–1 and 174). Even in Homestead, the populists secured no more than 28 percent in 1894 (Marcus, 1987, 71–2).

84. For the collapse and later recovery of the UMW, see Schneirov et al. (1999, 187–8), Laslett (1970, 198), Wolman (1924, 45 and 110), and Marks (1989, 166 and 170). For union membership in Chicago, see Schneirov (1998, 306–7 and 344).

85. Coal miners in Spring Valley, Illinois organized the largest APA chapter in the country in 1893 (Jensen, 1971, 235). In Homestead, Pennsylvania, anti-Catholic nativist organizations had more than 300 members by 1892, and their leader, who was also prominent in the steel workers' union, was elected President of the School Board (Krause, 1992, 215–6).

86. *LFM*, March 1894, 280–2, and April 1894, 396. See also the letter defending the APA in *RT*, October 1, 1895, 4, in response to Debs's criticism in *RT*, September 2, 1895.

87. *LFM*, April 1894, 396. For similar observations from Gompers' supporters, see Pomeroy in AFL (1895a, 46), and Lennon in AFL (1895, 66).

88. *AF*, July 1894, 105.

89. He also emphasized patriotism, law and order, and the threat of anarchy.

90. *CSJ*, November 14, 1894, 6.

91. But was Gompers' alternative strategy viable? Gompers emphasized the problems party loyalty created for any strategy of partisan political action. But party loyalty also created problems for his own preferred strategy of pressure-group politics. If involvement in partisan politics could not wean workers from their loyalty to the dominant parties, how could pressure-group politics do so? And if pressure-group politics could not do this, how could its strategy of rewarding labor's friends and punishing its enemies be effective? If a Republican worker would not vote for an independent labor party, it is surely even less likely that he would vote for a Democrat, as this strategy supposes he might. And if independent labor politics would antagonize party loyalists, surely this strategy would do so even more. As the failure of the AFL's strategy in the 1906 and 1908 elections showed, their earlier failure to challenge party loyalties made it difficult for the unions to effectively pursue *any* political strategy.

CHAPTER 8

SOCIALISM

1. For McCraith, see AFL (1895, 21–22) and *AF*, August 1896, 109. For the *CSJ*, see November 30, 1892, 4–5; June 21, 1893, 8; January 10, 1894, 8; May 23, 1894, 6; and December 5, 1894, 6. For Foster, see *AF*, March 1894, 5.

2. Bell (1996), Foner (1955, 278–299), Laslett and Lipset (1984, 3–51 and 118–69), Marks (1989, 225–32), and the next note. Bell's well-known argument is concerned with the failure of the socialist movement rather than the formation of a labor party.

3. Moore (1970, 205–8), Lipset (1996, 60–67 and 79–80), Lipset and Marks (2000, 33–34, 167–173, and 195–202).

4. Metin (1977, 180–1, and 50–55, 178).

5. Churchward (1952, 258). See also Gollan (1960, 105–6 and 119–24), Scates (1997), and Churchward (1979, 114–7).

6. The *Hummer* (see "Knowledge Is Power," January 9, 1892 and subsequent issues) sold works by Gronlund, Donnelly, and Bellamy, and three works by George. The *Worker* sold Bellamy, Gronlund, George, and Olive Schreiner's *Story of an African Farm* (Gollan, 1962, 128–9). Cf *RT* ("What to Read," February 15, 1894), which recommended Bellamy, Donnelly, and the Chicago populist Lester C. Hubbard.

7. Gollan (1960, 121–4, and 1962, 119–36), Docker (1982, 64–66), and Markey (1988, 243).

8. See also Fitzgerald (1915, 17) on the "happily blended mixture of socialism . . . and individual freedom," and Lane, who saw a system of equality in which "individualism finds unlimited scope" (Wilding, 1980, 37).

9. *Hummer*, March 12, 1892, 3. See also Reeves (1969 [1902], 1: 68), Ebbels (1983, 55), and Fitzgerald (1915, 18).

10. Churchward (1952, 259–63), Gollan (1960, 105 and 119–21), and Markey (1988, 298–301).

11. See also Gollan (1960, 121), Reeves (1969 [1902], 1: 69), and Ebbels (1983, 52).

12. "The Effects of the Strike," *Centennial Magazine*, September 1890 (Ebbels, 1983, 55).

13. The first name he mentioned was Karl Marx, but when pressed for an exposition of his position, the first book he mentioned was the *Co-operative Commonwealth*.

14. *AW*, August 1, 1891, 2; August 22, 1891, 2; and August 29, 1891, 1 and 4.

15. Docker (1982, 66 and 83–86). See also "'Ceasar's Column'—Will It Be Built," *Hummer*, March 12, 1892, 3, and Spence (1892, 9).

16. According to George Black, the Knights' activities in the United States encouraged some activists to consider the potential for establishing a labor party. See "Labor in Politics" at ML Q 329.31/P.

17. These included a number of shearers' leaders such as W.G. Spence, the editor of the Queensland *Worker*, William Lane, the editor of the *Hummer*, W.W. Head, and the sometime editor of the *AW* and subeditor of the *Bulletin*, George Black. See Churchward (1952, 263–6), Harris (1970, 61–2), and the few holdings on the Knights of Labor at ML Q 330.9901/110–113.

18. Ebbels (1983, 119–21); NSW Royal Commission on Strikes (1891, 362); Black, *History of the NSW Political Labor Party*, manuscript p. 45 in ML A2562; *AW*, August 15, 1891, 1, and September 5, 1891, 2; Burgmann (1985); Scates (1997); and Murphy (1975, 136).

19. For example, William Morris's *News from Nowhere* was a direct response to, and a libertarian socialist critique of, Bellamy's *Looking Backward*, and exchanges between British and American activists helped precipitate the formation of the Fabian Society (Clark, 1894, xxii–xxiii).

20. AFL (1894, 14) and AFL (1895a, 4–14 and passim). John Burns himself attended the 1894 convention as a representative of the British Trades Union Congress. See also the role of British developments in the following year's debate (AFL, 1895), in the AFL's 1890 debate (Kaufman and Albert, 1989, 77–78), and in the Cigar Makers' union in the early 1880s (Kaufman, 1973, 131–3).

21. TLC (1891, 9–12), Labour Defence Committee (1890, 18–19), the report of the Intercolonial Labour Conference in Spence (1909, 126–32), and ICTUC (1891, 90–104).

22. On Australia, see Scates (1997, 13–14, 21–23, 66, and 119–22), Avrich (1988, 260–68), Gollan (1960, 124–5), Burgmann (1985, 39–43, 53, 62–67, and 107–11). On the U.S., see Hirsch (1990), Nelson (1988), and the series on anarchism in *CSJ*, March, April, and May 1894.

23. Higgs in NSW Royal Commission on Strikes (1891, 362) refers to a recently published account by the English journalist W.H. Dawson (1890). On Dawson's influence in England, see Rogers (1998, 61–62). See also O'Farrell (1958, 157).

24. "Political Labor League—Handbills, etc.," folio 120, in ML Q 329.31/P.

25. Reeves (1969, 74), Harris (1966, 16), and Flynn in ICTUC (1891, 94). For correspondence with Liebknecht, see *AW*, February 14, 1891, March 28, 1891, and December 12, 1891.

26. Queensland *Worker*, July 1, 1890 (Wilding, 1980, 41–43), NSW Royal Commission on Strikes (1891, 362), and *AW*, May 9, 1891, 2. A few individuals also had personal connections to Marx and Engels. These included the President of the South Australian TLC in 1891, G.H. Buttery, who had sat on the Council of the International Workingmen's Association before he had emigrated (Burgmann, 1985, 159), as well as some German '48ers who had come to Australia (Mayer, 1964, 148).

27. On Lane, see his brother's recollections in Harris (1966, 28). On the *AW*, see "The Socialist's Bible," January 23, 1892. On the *Manifesto*, see Harris (1966, 27–28) and Mayer (1964, 147). On Holman, see Evatt (1942, 39–44) and his 1893 ASL pamphlet, *Karl Marx*. On discussing *Capital*, see O'Farrell (1958, 157).

28. Kaufman (1973), Dick (1972, 9–51), and Messer-Kruse (1998, 228–30, 245, and 255–56).

29. Metin (1977, 54), Lloyd (1902, 376), Clark (1906, 118), Reeves (1969, 68), and Coghlan in McQueen (1986, 20).

30. See also the *AW* series on labor reform ideologies from January 23, 1892 to June 24, 1893 covering socialism, communism, nihilism, individualism, trades-unionism, single-taxism, land-nationalization, Malthusianism, and anarchism.

31. *AW*, January 9, 1892, 4, and *CSJ*, November 30, 1892, 4–5.

32. Foner (1955, 119–28 and 145–54), and Kaufman (1986, 429–30, and 1987, 45).

33. Fink (1983, 26–30), Foner (1955, 128–30 and 155–56), and Oestreicher (1986, 172–87).

34. On Chicago, see Bogart and Thompson (1920, 466–70), Staley (1930, 71–83), Foner (1955, 130–31 and 154–55) and Schneirov (1998, 211–35).

35. On labor-populism in Illinois, see Staley (1930, 84–139) and Destler (1946, 162–254). See also Bogart and Thompson (1920, 160–67), Foner (1955, 311–35), and Schneirov (1998, 343–48).

36. Labor Council of NSW, General Meetings Minutes, February 20 and 27, 1890 at ML A3829–A3831. See also Executive Committee Minutes from February 11 and 24, and March 4, 1890 regarding complaints by single taxers against a council member. On wariness of socialists and single taxers, see Markey (1988, 240) and Ebbles (1983, 56). But note that in 1888 the ICTUC (1888, 83–86) had unamimously passed a single tax resolution with little or no debate.

37. See NSW TLC General Meetings Minutes, Special Meetings, March 17, 24, and 31; *SMH*, March 25, 1891, 8; and *AW*, March 21, 1891, 3, and March 28, 1891, 3. See also Scates (1997, 84), Loveday (1975, 22), and Nairn (1989, 48).

38. "Forewarned is Forearmed. No schism of that sort for Australians!" urged Lane (Picard, 1953, 52). On the ULP, see *AW*, February 21, 1891, 3, February 28, 1891, supplement, and March 7, 1891, 3. On George, see Watson (Ebbels, 1983, 176, and Markey, 1988, 299) and O'Sullivan (Picard, 1953, 58).

39. Picard (1953, 45–63) and Scates (1984, 1986, and 1997, 74–116). See also Gollan (1960, 135–39), Loveday (1975, 22–42 and 62–70), and Markey (1988, 176–89, 232–35, and 239–42).

40. Even before the labor party had been established, the single taxer, Frank Cotton, had been privately relaying the union movement's decisions to the Premier and Free Trade leader, Henry Parkes (Picard, 1953, 51–52). The *AW*, December 26, 1891, 2, argued for an affinity between socialism and protectionism, but recognized there were some "Freetrade Socialists."

41. *Hummer*, April 30, 1; May 21, 1; May 14, 3; June 4, 3; June 11, 2; June 18, 3; July 2, 3; July 9, 2; July 16, 2 and 3; August 6, 2; and August 13, 3. All in 1892. Cf the similar debate in the *RT*, March 15, April 16, May 15, and June 1, 1894. As in the shearers' union, single taxers were prominent in the ARU (Salvatori, 1982, 374, n7, Markey, 1988, 300–1, and Scates, 1997, 78–80).

42. Up to 11 of the 22 LEL branch delegates may have been single taxers (Picard, 1953, 62). Loveday (1975, 29) puts the number at seven. In addition to the 22 LEL delegates, there were 11 TLC delegates.

43. See his correspondence with Tom Mann in May and September 1894 (Kaufman and Albert, 1989, 504 and 588). Similarly, the seamen's union suggested that in principle you could have both unionism and labor politics, but that American socialists made it impossible in practice. See *CSJ*, November 30, 1892, 4 and 5, June 7, 1893, 8, May 23, 1894, 6, and September 26, 1894, 6.

44. For the personal experience of some of Gompers's allies, see Gitelman (1965, 74–82) on Strasser of the cigar makers' union, Galenson (1983, 67–73) on McGuire of the carpenters' union, Kaufman (1986, 23–29) on Weissman of the bakers' union, and Weintraub (1959, 16–19 and 45–51) on Furuseth of the seamen's union.

45. Ferdinand Lassalle had argued that trade unions could do little good until workers had acquired electoral rights and used them to gain control of the state.

46. On the cigar makers' union, see Kaufman (1986, 247–9, 272–3, and 365–7); on conflict with the Knights, see Kaufman (1986, 159–63 and 468); and on conflict with the SLP, see Kaufman (1987, 191ff, 386–409, and 1989, 16–17).

47. See also Gompers's comments to the SLP's New York *Volkszeitung* following the convention (Kaufman, 1987, 425–27), and the similar sentiments of the veteran labor leader George E. McNeil (AFL, 1891a, 14).

48. In September 1893, he claimed "there is not one demand of the socialists that is not also put forward by the trade unionists and by me" (Kaufman and Albert, 1989, 398). For similar sentiments, see *CSJ*, June 28, 1893, 9, and May 23, 1894, 6.

49. Publically, Engels kept clear of the dispute, but privately he seems to have sympathized with Gompers's position (Foner, 1955, 284–5, and Kaufman and Albert, 1989, 7–11 and 120–1).

50. *AF*, December 1894, 225–6.

51. This delegate, Patrick McBryde, should not be confused with John McBride, who replaced Gompers as President. Both were officials of the miners' union.

52. Morgan was even more prone to get distracted into arguing about his personal integrity and reputation.

53. For editorials, see *AF*, March 1894, 10–11, April 1894, 30–31, October 1894, 172–3, and the similar argument in *AF*, July 1894, 101. For the 1894 debate, see the comments of delegates Gompers and Sullivan (AFL, 1895a, 10 and 56–57). For earlier examples, see (Kaufman and Albert, 1989, 16, and AFL, 1891a, 36). By 1896, Gompers was suggesting that the leader of the SLP may be "a paid hireling of Pinkerton's Detective Agency." See *AF*, April 1896, 52.

54. AFL (1891a, 35–36). For similar sentiments in a private letter, see Kaufman (1987, 428–9).

55. "A Parting Word," *AF*, January 1895, 257, and Kaufman and Albert (1989, 606).

56. For quotes, see the *People*, December 24, 1893, and March 18, 1894, and Foner (1955, 286–7). De Leon became editor of the *People* in 1892 and sharply increased its level of invective. From August 1893, he began calling on SLP members to withdraw from the AFL. For the cartoon, see *People*, November 26, 1893 (also in Kaufman and Albert, 1989, 418–9), and the similar cartoon on February 11, 1894. On De Leon's rival union center, see Foner (1955, 296–9), Seretan (1979, 149–152), and Kaufman *et al.* (1991, 102–6). Dismayed by this kind of disruption, John McBride concluded at the end of 1895 that disagreements "over different isms" made it a "useless waste of time and effort" to establish an independent party "at this time" (AFL, 1895, 16).

57. Hoerder and Keil (1988, 146 and 150–4), Keil (1988, 5–14), Kaufman (1973, 102, 128, and 134), Bell (1996, 32), and Hillquit (1903, 258).

58. Kazin in Bell (1996, xxxiv), Lipset (1996, 79–80), Lipset and Marks (2000, 34), Salvatore (1982, 62–5 and 311–2), Bowman (1958, 27–36 and 255–68) and Destler (1963, 192–8). Debs was still largely uninfluenced by Marxism in the early 1890s.

59. For similar metaphors, see *NLT*, February 1, 1890, and *CSJ*, December 7, 1892.

60. Weismann had his own anarchist factional axe to grind. But others made similar contributions. See delegates Lennon, Gompers, Strasser, Pomeroy, Daley, Macarthur, and O'Sullivan (AFL, 1895a, 8 and 20, 10, 35–6, 47, 49, 55, and 56).

61. For a similar position, see *UMWJ*, December 20, 1894.

62. See his letter to Lloyd on September 6, 1895 (Salvatore, 1982, 375, n32), and his minority report to the Illinois State Federation of Labor on July 4, 1894 (Staley, 1930, 117).

63. *AF*, March 1894, 7.

64. Ibid.

65. NSW TLC, General Meetings Minutes, March 12, 1891.

66. *AW*, August 22, 1891, 2.

67. In the early 1890s, the ASL had no paper of its own, and the *AW* reported in some detail on socialist as well as TLC and union events.

68. See Minutes of the Victorian Trades Hall Council Meetings, July 17, 1891, held at the University of Melbourne Archives, and Burgmann (1985, 112, 115, 145–9, and 173–7).

69. ICTUC (1891). Nor was it mentioned in TLC (1890 and 1891), Labour Defence Committee (1890), or Spence (1909, 126–132).

70. The issues were similar but not identical. Lucian Sanial was claiming credentials as the SLP's representative on the New York Central Labor Federation, which accepted

the SLP as an affiliate, while W.D. Flynn in Australia was claiming credentials directly as a delegate of the Social Democratic League.

71. ICTUC (1891, 14 and 93–94) and Sutcliffe (1967, 108–9).

72. *AW*, August 22, 1891, 2. Italics in original.

73. The Labour Defence Committee (1890, 18) did foresee a time when "Trades-unionism has fulfilled its mission," but, it went on, "we are not there yet; and in the meantime there is ample work on the old lines." Its basic message was that "whilst we must go on ever increasing our capacity for fighting as we have fought before, the time has come when Trades-unionists must use the Parliamentary machinery."

74. For this estimate, see Scates (1997, 14). The League itself claimed 8,000. See also Ford (1966, 140), O'Farrell (1958, 153 and 156), and Nairn (1989, 37).

75. On ideological fluidity, see Scates (1997, 72 and 94). For ASL lectures, see Burgmann (1985, 53–55) and Scates (1997, 26–27). For quote, see Fitzhardinge (1964, 33). For the similar openness of ASL lectures in the late 1880s, see O'Farrell (1958, 153) and Burgmann (1985, 39 and 43). On Hughes, who later became Prime Minister, see Fitzhardinge (1964, 30–33). For Black's series on reform ideologies, see *AW* from January 23, 1892 to June 24, 1893. In early 1890, Black found no difficulty in speaking at the banquet to welcome Henry George, even though he then thought of himself as a Fabian socialist. See folio 45 of his manuscript *History of the New South Wales Labor Party* at ML A2562. On ASL MPs, see Burgmann (1985, 82–83). For members' support, see O'Farrell (1958, 162–4) and Markey (1988, 241–2).

76. On conflicts over a socialist objective, see Ford (1966, 191–231), Murphy (1975, 62–68), Burgmann (1985, 81–90), Markey (1988, 248–55), and Scates (1997, 111–16). On earlier internal conflicts, see O'Farrell (1958, 154–6 and 163), Burgmann (1985, 39–43 and 162–7), and Markey (1988, 246–8). During one such conflict, members almost came to blows over accusations that S.A. Rosa had betrayed the Haymarket Martyrs in the United States. See *AW*, November 14, 1891, 2, and November 21, 1891, 3.

77. Brennan and Houghton represented the TLC on the NSW Labour Defence Committee, and Brennan and Spence were respectively Chairman and Secretary of the Intercolonial Labour Conference that was formed during the strike.

78. See "Brennan" in *Australian Dictionary of Biography*, vol 3, 225, and NSW Royal Commission on Strikes (1891, 92).

79. Ford (1966, 103). On Brennan, see Nairn (1989, 31–35, 38–39, 41, and 43), "Brennan" in *Australian Dictionary of Biography*, vol 3, 224–6, and the biographical sketch in *Australian Star*, October 6, 1890.

80. *Worker*, March 31, 1894, and Spence (1892, 8–9).

81. On Houghton, see Nairn (1989, 33–34 and 45–46), "Houghton" in the *Australian Dictionary of Biography*, vol 9, 374, and the biographical sketch in *Australian Star*, October 6, 1890. On Spence, see Merritt (1986, 104–8), Markey (1988, 244–46), Burgmann (1985, 54–55 and 70–72), and Lansbury (1967, 3–10).

82. For Gompers's and Strasser's testimony, see U.S. Senate Committee on Education and Labor (1885, 374–5 and 460).

83. Spence, in particular, was influenced by Bellamy, George, Morris, and other English socialists (Serle, 1971, 114, and Markey, 1988, 244).

84. Markey (1988, 244–55), Burgmann (1985, 87–100), Ford (1966, 208–18), and Nairn (1989, 166–94).

CONCLUSION

1. See the private correspondence of AFL officials in Destler (1946, 183), Foner (1955, 290), Kaufman (1987, 364), and Kaufman and Albert (1989, 585).

2. For example: for 1892, see AFL (1892, 13) and Kaufman and Albert (1989, 202–4); for 1894, see AFL (1894, 14) and the following paragraph; and for 1896, see AFL (1896, 22). The same fear was also voiced when the AFL took the exceptional step of endorsing independent labor politics in 1886 (AFL, 1886, 16, and Kaufman, 1986, 453–4).

3. AFL (1894, 14).

4. AFL (1895a, 6–8, 12, 36, 44, 46, 49, 51, and 56).

Bibliography

NOTE ON PRIMARY SOURCES:

Full references to unpublished primary sources, and to items in newspapers and periodicals, are included in the notes. All other published primary sources are included in the bibliography that follows.

Aaron, Daniel (1951), *Men of Good Hope*, New York: Oxford University Press.

Abbott, Ernest Hamlin (1903), *Religious Life in America*, New York: The Outlook Company.

Abell, Aaron I. (1945), "The Reception of Leo XIII's Labor Encyclical in America, 1891–1919," *Review of Politics*, vol VII.

Abell, Aaron I. (1960), *American Catholicism and Social Action: A Search for Social Justice, 1865–1950*, New York: Hanover House.

Abell, Aaron I. (1962), *The Urban Impact of American Protestantism, 1865–1900*, Hamden, Connecticut: Archon.

Abramson, Harold J. (1971), "Inter-ethnic Marriage among Catholic Americans and Changes in Religious Behavior," *Sociological Analysis*, vol 32, no 1, Spring.

Adams, Francis (1893), *The Australians: A Social Sketch*, London: T. Fisher Unwin.

Adams, Jane (1997), "Quiescence Despite Privation: Explaining the Absence of a Farm Laborers' Movement in Southern Illinois," *Comparative Studies in Society and History*, vol 39, no 3, July.

AFL (1886), *Report of the Sixth Annual Convention of the Federation of Organized Trades and Labor Unions of the U.S. and Canada* and *Report of Proceedings of the First Annual Convention of the American Federation of Labor* held at Columbus, Ohio, December 8 to 12, in AFL (1905).

AFL (1887), *Report of Proceedings of the Second Annual Convention of the American Federation of Labor* held at Baltimore, Maryland, December 13 to 17, in AFL (1905).

AFL (1888), *Report of Proceedings of the Third Annual Convention of the American Federation of Labor* held at St. Louis, Missouri, December 11 to 15, in AFL (1905).

AFL (1889), *Report of Proceedings of the Ninth Annual Convention of the American Federation of Labor* held at Boston, Massachusetts, December 10 to 14, in AFL (1906).

AFL (1890), *Report of Proceedings of the Tenth Annual Convention of the American Federation of Labor* held at Detroit, Michigan, December 8 to 13, in AFL (1906).

AFL (1891), *Report of Proceedings of the Eleventh Annual Convention of the American Federation of Labor* held at Birmingham, Alabama, December 14 to 19, in AFL (1906).

AFL (1891a), *An Interesting Discussion at the [1890] Convention of the American Federation of Labor*, New York: American Federation of Labor.

AFL (1891b), *Official Book of the American Federation of Labor*, New York: AFL.

AFL (1892), *Report of Proceedings of the Twelfth Annual Convention of the American Federation of Labor* held at Philadelphia, Pennsylvania, December 12 to 17, in AFL (1906).

AFL (1892a), *Official Book of the American Federation of Labor*, New York: AFL.

AFL (1893), *Report of Proceedings of the Thirteenth Annual Convention of the American Federation of Labor* held at Chicago, Illinois, December 11 to 19, in AFL (1905a).

AFL (1894), *Report of Proceedings of the Fourteenth Annual Convention of the American Federation of Labor* held at Denver, Colorado, December 10 to 18, in AFL (1905a).

AFL (1895), *Report of Proceedings of the Fifteenth Annual Convention of the American Federation of Labor* held at New York, New York, December 9 to 17, in AFL (1905a).

AFL (1895a), *An Interesting Discussion on a Political Programme at the [1894] Denver Convention of the American Federation of Labor*, American Federation of Labor.

AFL (1896), *Report of Proceedings of the Sixteenth Annual Convention of the American Federation of Labor* held at Cincinnati, Ohio, December 14 to 21, in AFL (1905a).

AFL (1897), *Report of Proceedings of the Seventeenth Annual Convention of the American Federation of Labor* held at Nashville, Tennessee, December 13 to 21, in AFL (1905b).

AFL (1905), *Proceedings of the American Federation of Labor 1881, 1882, 1883, 1884, 1885, 1886, 1887, and 1888*, Bloomington, Illinois: Pantagraph Printing and Stationery Company.

AFL (1905a), *Proceedings of the American Federation of Labor 1893, 1894, 1895, 1896*, Bloomington, Illinois: Pantagraph Printing and Stationery Company.

AFL (1905b), *Proceedings of the American Federation of Labor 1897, 1898*, Bloomington, Illinois: Pantagraph Printing and Stationery Company.

AFL (1906), *Proceedings of the American Federation of Labor 1889, 1890, 1891, 1892*, Bloomington, Illinois: Pantagraph Printing and Stationery Company.

Allen, Howard W., and Vincent A. Lacey (1992), *Illinois Elections, 1818–1990*, Carbondale, Illinois: Southern Illinois University Press.

Allen, Robert C. (1994), "Real Incomes in the English Speaking World, 1879–1913" in George Grantham and Mary MacKinnon, eds., *Labour Market Evolution*, London: Routledge.

Ahlstrom, Sydney E. (1972), *A Religious History of the American People*, New Haven, Connecticut: Yale University Press.

Akenson, Donald Harman (1988), *Small Differences: Irish Catholics and Irish Protestants, 1815–1922: An International Perspective*, Montreal: McGill-Queens University Press.

American Railway Union (1893), *Declaration of Principles*, Chicago: American Railway Union.

Anderson, David M., and David Killingray (1991), *Policing the Empire: Government, Authority and Control, 1830–1940*, Manchester, England: Manchester University Press.

Ansell, Christopher K., and Arthur L. Burris (1997), "Bosses of the City Unite! Labor Politics and Political Machine Consolidation, 1870–1910," *Studies in American Political Development*, vol 11, no 1, Spring.

Archer, Robin (1997), "Why Is There No Labor Party? Class and Race in the United States and Australia," in Rick Halpern and Jonathan Morris, eds. (1997).

Archer, Robin (1998), "Unions, Courts and Parties: Judicial Repression and Labor Politics in Late Nineteenth-Century America," *Politics and Society*, vol 26, no 3, September.

Archer, Robin (2001), "Does Repression Help to Create Labor Parties? The Effect of Police and Military Intervention on Unions in the United States and Australia," *Studies in American Political Development*, vol 15, no 2, Fall.

Argersinger, Peter H. (1980), "'A Place on the Ballot': Fusion Politics and Antifusion Laws," *American Historical Review*, vol 85, no 2, April.

Argersinger, Peter H. (1989), "The Value of the Vote: Political Representation in the Gilded Age," *Journal of American History*, vol 76, no 1, June.

Atchinson, Rena Michaels (1894), *Un-American Immigration: Its Present Effects and Future Perils. A Study from the Census of 1890*, Chicago: Charles H. Kerr and Company.

Austin, A.G. (1961), *Australian Education 1788–1900: Church State and Public Education in Colonial Australia*, Melbourne: Sir Isaac Pitman and Sons.

Austin, A.G., ed. (1965), *The Webbs' Australian Diary 1898*, Melbourne: Sir Isaac Pitman and Sons.

Avrich, Paul (1984), *The Haymarket Tragedy*, Princeton, New Jersey: Princeton University Press.

Avrich, Paul (1988), *Anarchist Portraits*, Princeton, New Jersey: Princeton University Press.

Bain, George S., and Farouk Elsheikh (1976), *Union Growth and the Business Cycle*, Oxford: Blackwell.

Bain, George S., and Robert Price (1980), *Profiles of Union Growth*, Oxford: Blackwell.

Baldwin, Peter (1990), *The Politics of Social Solidarity*, Cambridge: Cambridge University Press.

Baltzell, E. Digby (1958), *Philadelphia Gentlemen: The Making of a National Upper Class*, New York: Free Press.

Bartolini, Stephano (2000), *The Political Mobilization of the European Left, 1860–1980*, Cambridge: Cambridge University Press.

Bebbington, D.W. (1989), *Evangelicalism in Modern Britain: A History from the 1730s to the 1980s*, London: Unwin Hyman.

Bebbington, David (1993), "Evangelicalism in Modern Britain and America: A Comparison," in Rawlyk and Noll, eds., *Amazing Grace*.

Beckert, Sven (2001), *The Monied Metropolis: New York City and Consolidation of the American Bourgeoisie, 1850–1896*, Cambridge: Cambridge University Press.

Beckner, Earl R. (1929), *A History of Labor Legislation in Illinois*. Chicago: University of Chicago Press.

Beever, Margot, and F.B. Smith, eds. (1967), *Historical Studies: Selected Articles: Second Series*, Melbourne: Melbourne University Press.

Bell, Daniel (1996), *Marxian Socialism in the United States*, Ithaca, New York: Cornell University Press.

Bell, Philip, and Roger Bell (1993), *Implicated: The United States in Australia*, Melbourne: Oxford University Press.

Bellamy, Edward (1894), "Introduction to this American Edition" in G. Bernard Shaw, ed., *Socialism: The Fabian Essays*, Boston: Charles E. Brown and Co.

Bellamy, Edward (1897), *Equality*, New York: D. Appleton and Company.

Bellamy, Edward (1938), *Edward Bellamy Speaks Again!*, Chicago: The Peerage Press.

Bellamy, Richard (1990), "T.H. Green and the Morality of Victorian Liberalism," in Richard Bellamy, ed. (1990).

Bellamy, Richard, ed. (1990), *Victorian Liberalism*, London: Routledge.

Bennett, David H. (1988), *The Party of Fear*, Chapel Hill, North Carolina: University of North Carolina Press.

Bennett, Laura (1994), *Making Labour Law in Australia*, Sydney: Law Book Co.

Bensel, Richard Franklin (2000), *The Political Economy of American Industrialization, 1877–1900*, Cambridge: Cambridge University Press.

Bickel, Alexander M. (1962), *The Least Dangerous Branch: The Supreme Court at the Bar of Politics*, Indianapolis, Indiana: Bobbs-Merrill.

Black, George (1926–29), *A History of the NSW Labor Party from Its Conception until 1917*, published in parts, Sydney: George A. Jones.

Blair, George S. (1960), *Cumulative Voting*, Urbana, Illinois: University of Illinois Press.

Bogart, Ernest Ludlow, and John Mabry Mathews (1920), *The Modern Commonwealth, 1893–1918*, The Centennial History of Illinois, Volume Five, Springfield, Illinois: Illinois Centennial Commission.

Bogart, Ernest Ludlow, and Charles Manfred Thompson (1920), *The Industrial State, 1870–1893*, The Centennial History of Illinois, Volume Four, Springfield, Illinois: Illinois Centennial Commission.

Bogue, Donald J. (1985), *The Population of the United States: Historical Trends and Future Predictions*, New York: Free Press.

Boix, Carles (1999), "Setting the Rules of the Game: The Choice of Electoral Systems in Advanced Democracies," *American Political Science Review*, vol 93, no 3, September.

Bollen, J.D. (1972), *Protestantism and Social Reform in New South Wales 1890–1910*, Melbourne: Melbourne University Press.

Bolton, G.C. (1973), "Louis Hartz," *Australian Economic History Review*, vol XIII, no 2, September.

Bolton, Geoffrey, and Helen Gregory (1992), "The 1891 Shearers Strike Leaders: Railroaded?," *Labour History*, no 62, May.

Bongiorno, Frank (1994), "Class, Populism and Labour Politics in Victoria, 1890–1914," *Labour History*, no 66, May.

Bongiorno, Frank (1996), *The People's Party: Victorian Labor and the Radical Tradition 1875–1914*, Melbourne: Melbourne University Press.

Bourke, Paul F. (1967), "Some Recent Essays in Australian Intellectual History," *Historical Studies*, vol 13, no 49, October.

Bowman, Sylvia E. (1958), *The Year 2000: A Critical Biography of Edward Bellamy*, New York: Bookman Associates.

Bowman, Sylvia E. *et al.* (1962), *Edward Bellamy Abroad: An American Prophet's Influence*, New York: Twayne Publishers.

Bowman, Sylvia E. (1986), *Edward Bellamy*, Boston: Twayne Publishers.

Brady, David W. (1988), *Critical Elections and Congressional Policy Making*, Stanford, California: Stanford University Press.

Brandon, Ruth (1980), *The Dollar Princesses: Sagas of Upward Nobility, 1870–1914*, New York: Alfred A Knopf.

Brecher, Jeremy (1997), *Strike!*, Boston: South End Press.

Breuilly, John (1990), "Comparative Labour History," *Labour History Review*, vol 55, no 3, Winter.

Breuilly, John (1992), *Labor and Liberalism in Nineteenth Century Europe*, Manchester, England: Manchester University Press.

Bridges, Amy (1986), "Becoming American: The Working Classes in the United States before the Civil War," in Katznelson and Zolberg, eds. (1986).

Brinkley, Alan (1998), *Liberalism and Its Discontents*, Cambridge, Massachusetts: Harvard University Press.

Brody, David (1983), "On the Failure of U.S. Radical Politics: A Farmer–Labor Analysis," *Industrial Relations*, vol 22, no 2, Spring.

Brody, David (1993), *In Labor's Cause*, New York: Oxford University Press.

Brown, E.H. Phelps, with Margaret H. Browne (1968), *A Century of Pay*, London: Macmillan.

Bryce, James (1921), *Modern Democracies, Volume II*, London: Macmillan.

Buckley, Ken, and Ted Wheelwright (1988), *No Paradise for Workers*, Melbourne: Oxford University Press.

Buhle, Mari Jo, Paul Buhle, and Dan Georgakas, eds. (1998), *Encyclopedia of the American Left*, second edition, New York: Oxford University Press.

Buhle, Paul (1987), *Marxism in the United States*, London: Verso.

Burch, Philip H. (1981), *Elites in American History*, New York: Holmes and Meier.

Bureau of the Census (1975), *Historical Statistics of the United States: Colonial Times to 1970*, Part I, Washington, D.C.: United States Department of Commerce, Bureau of the Census.

Burgmann, Verity (1978), "Capital and Labour: Responses to Immigration in the Nineteenth Century," in Curthoys and Markus, eds. (1978).

Burgmann, Verity (1985), *'In Our Time': Socialism and the Rise of Labor, 1885–1905*, Sydney: George Allen and Unwin.

Burgmann, Verity (1992), "Premature Labour: the Maritime Strike and the Parliamentary Strategy," in Hagan and Wells (1992).

Burgoyne, Arthur G. (1979 [1893]), *Homestead*, Pittsburgh: University of Pittsburgh Press.

Burrow, Edwin G., and Mike Wallace (1999), *Gotham: A History of New York City to 1898*, New York: Oxford University Press.

Butlin, N.G. (1959), "Colonial Socialism in Australia, 1860–1900," in Hugh G.J. Aitken, ed., *The State and Economic Growth*, New York: Social Science Research Council.

Byrd, Robert C. (1988), *The Senate 1788–1988*, Addresses on the History of the United States Senate, Vol 1, Washington, D.C.: U.S. Government Printing Office.

Cahill, A.E. (1960), "Catholicism and Socialism–The 1905 Controversy in Australia," *Journal of Religious History*, vol 1, no 2, December.

Cahill, A.E. (1966), "Catholics and Politics in New South Wales," *Journal of Religious History*, vol 4, no 1, June.

Cahill, A.E. (1989), "Cardinal Moran's Politics," *Journal of Religious History*, vol 15, no 4, December.

Calder, Winty (1985), *Heros and Gentlemen: Colonel Tom Price and the Victorian Mounted Rifles*, Melbourne: Jimaringle Publications.

Calhoun, Craig (1988), "The Radicalism of Tradition and the Question of Class Struggle" in Michael Taylor, ed., *Rationality and Revolution*, Cambridge: Cambridge University Press.

Camm, J.C.R., and R. Sumner (1982), "Counting People in Queensland—A Survey of the Queensland Censuses, 1861–1901," *Australian Historical Statistics*, no 5, May.

Campbell, Craig (1976), "Liberalism in Australian History: 1880–1920," in Jill Roe, ed., *Social Policy in Australia*, Stanmore, NSW: Cassell Australia.

Campbell, Peter (1958), *French Electoral Systems and Elections*, London: Faber.

Carroll, Henry K. (1893), *The Religious Forces of the United States*, New York: Christian Literature Co.

Carroll, Henry K. (1894), *Report on Statistics of Churches in the United States at the Eleventh Census: 1890*, Washington D.C.: Government Printing Office.

Carstairs, Andrew McLaren (1980), *A Short History of Electoral Systems in Western Europe*, London: George Allen and Unwin.

Carwardine, William H. (1894), *The Pullman Strike*, Chicago: Charles H. Kerr and Company.

Castles, Alex C. (1982), *An Australian Legal History*, Sydney: Law Book Company.

Chandler, Alfred D. (1977), *The Visible Hand: The Managerial Revolution in American Business*, Cambridge, Massachusetts: Belknap Press.

Chandler, Alfred D. (1980), "The United States: Seedbed of Managerial Capitalism," in Alfred D. Chandler and Herman Daems, eds., *Managerial Hierarchies*, Cambridge, Massachusetts: Harvard University Press.

Chicago Daily News Company (1894), *The Daily News Almanac and Political Register for 1894*, Chicago: Chicago Daily News Co.

Chicago Daily News Company (1895), *The Daily News Almanac and Political Register for 1895*, Chicago: Chicago Daily News Co.

Chicago Daily News Company (1896), *The Daily News Almanac and Political Register for 1896*, Chicago: Chicago Daily News Co.

Choper, Jesse H. (1980), *Judicial Review and the National Political Process*, Chicago: University of Chicago Press.

Christiano, Kevin J. (1987), *Religious Diversity and Social Change: American Cities, 1890–1906*, Cambridge: Cambridge University Press.

Churchill, Allen (1970), *The Upper Crust: An Informal History of New York's Highest Society*, Englewood Cliffs, New Jersey: Prentice Hall.

Churchward, L.G. (1952), "The American Influence on the Australian Labour Movement," *Historical Studies*, vol 5, no 19, November.

Churchward, L.G. (1953), "Trade Unionism in the United States and Australia: A Study in Contrasts," *Science and Society*, vol 17, Spring.

Churchward, L.G. (1979), *Australia and America 1788–1972: An Alternative History*, Sydney: Alternative Publishing Cooperative.

Clanton, Gene (1984), "'Hayseed Socialism' on the Hill: Congressional Populism, 1891–1895," *Western Historical Quarterly*, vol XV, no 2, April.

Clark, Manning (1955), *Select Documents in Australian History, 1851–1900*, Sydney: Angus and Robertson.

Clark, Victor S. (1906), *The Labour Movement in Australasia*, Westminster [London]: Archibald Constable and Co.

Clark, William (1894), "The Fabian Society and Its Work," in G.B. Shaw *et al.*, eds., *Socialism: The Fabian Essays*, Boston: C.E. Brown.

Clyne, Robert (1987), *Colonial Blue: A History of the South Australian Police Force, 1836–1916*, Adelaide: Wakefield Press.

Coffman, Edward M. (1986), *The Old Army: A Portrait of the American Army in Peacetime, 1784–1898*, New York: Oxford University Press.

Coghlan, T.A. (1891), *New South Wales Statistical Register for 1890*, Sydney: George Stephan Chapman, Acting Government Printer.

Coghlan, T.A. (1891b), *Wealth and Progress of New South Wales, 1890–91*, Sydney: George Stephan Chapman, Acting Government Printer.

Coghlan, T.A. (1892), *New South Wales Statistical Register for 1891*, Sydney: Charles Potter, Government Printer.

Coghlan, T.A. (1893a), *Wealth and Progress of New South Wales, 1892*, Sydney: Government Printer.

Coghlan, T.A. (1893b), *Wealth and Progress of New South Wales, 1893*, Sydney: Charles Potter, Government Printer.

Coghlan, T.A. (1894a), *General Report on the Eleventh Census of New South Wales [taken in 1891]*, Sydney: Charles Potter, Government Printer.

Coghlan, T.A. (1894b), *Results of a Census of New South Wales . . . 1891*, Sydney: Charles Potter, Government Printer.

Coghlan, T.A. (1894c), *New South Wales Statistical Register for 1893*, Sydney: Charles Potter, Government Printer.

Coghlan, T.A. (1895), *Wealth and Progress of New South Wales, 1894*, Sydney: Charles Potter, Government Printer.

Coghlan, T.A. (1898), *New South Wales Statistical Register for 1897*, Sydney: William Applegate Gullick, Government Printer.

Coghlan, T.A. (1898b), *A Statistical Account of the Seven Colonies of Australasia, 1897–8*, Sydney: William Applegate Gullick, Government Printer.

Coghlan, T.A. (1902), *Wealth and Progress of New South Wales, 1900–01*, Sydney: Government Printer.

Coghlan, T.A. (1902b), *A Statistical Account of the Seven Colonies of Australasia, 1901–1902*, Sydney: William Applegate Gullick, Government Printer.

Coghlan, T.A. (1903), *New South Wales Statistical Register for 1901*, Sydney: William Applegate Gullick, Government Printer.

Coghlan, T.A. (1918), *Labour and Industry in Australia*, Oxford: Oxford University Press.

Cohen, William (1991), *At Freedom's Edge: Black Mobility and the Southern White Quest for Racial Control, 1861–1915*, Baton Rouge, Louisiana: Louisiana State University Press.

Collier, David (1991), "The Comparative Method: Two Decades of Change," in Dankwart A. Rustow and Kenneth Paul Erickson, eds., *Comparative Political Dynamics*, New York: Harper Collins.

Collins, Hugh (1985), "Political Ideology in Australia: The Distinctiveness of a Benthamite Society," in Stephen R. Graubard, ed., *Australia: The Daedalus Symposium*, Sydney: Angus and Robertson.

Colvin, D. Leigh (1926), *Prohibition in the United States*, London: Hodder and Stoughton.

Commissioner of Labor (1890), *Fifth Annual Report of the Commissioner of Labor. 1889. Railroad Labor*. Washington, D.C.: Government Printing Office.

Commissioner of Labor (1896), *Tenth Annual Report of the Commissioner of Labor. 1894. Strikes and Lockouts*. Washington, D.C.: Government Printing Office.

Commissioner of Labor (1901), *Sixteenth Annual Report of the Commissioner of Labor. 1901. Strikes and Lockouts*. Washington, D.C.: Government Printing Office.

Commons, John R., *et al.* (1918), *History of Labour in the United States: Volume II*, New York: MacMillan.

Constantine, J. Robert (1995), *Gentle Rebel: Letters of Eugene V. Debs*, Urbana, Illinois: University of Illinois Press.

Cooke, Edward F., and Edward G. Janosik (1965), *Pennsylvania Politics*, New York: Holt, Rinehart, and Winston.

Cooper, Jerry M. (1977), "The Army as Strikebreaker—The Railroad Strikes of 1877 and 1894," *Labor History*, vol 18, no 2, Spring.

Cooper, Jerry M. (1980), *The Army and Civil Disorder: Federal Military Intervention in Labor Disputes, 1877–1900*, Westport, Connecticut: Greenwood Press.

Cooper, Rachel C. (1996), "Making the New South Wales Union Movement?," UNSW Studies in Australian Industrial Relations, no 39.

Coulthard-Clark, Chris (1981), "The Military as Strikebreakers," *Pacific Defence Reporter*, May.

Couvares, Francis G. (1984), *The Remaking of Pittsburgh: Class and Culture in an Industrializing City, 1877–1919*, Albany, New York: State University of New York Press.

Crisp, L.F. (1979), "'Remember the Literature, Comrades!' Labour Party Reading Then and Now," *Labour History*, no 36, May.

Crisp, L.F. (1984), *C.C. Kingston: Radical Federationist*, Canberra: Australian National University Press.

Crowley, F.K., ed. (1974), *A New History of Australia*, Melbourne: Heinemann.

Curthoys, Ann (1978), "The Seamen's Strike of 1878," in Curthoys and Markus, eds. (1978).

Curthoys, Ann, and Andrew Markus, eds. (1978), *Who Are Our Enemies? Racism and the Working Class in Australia*, Sydney: Hale and Iremonger.

Dale, George (1918), *The Industrial History of Broken Hill*, Melbourne: Fraser and Jenkinson.

David, Henry (1952), "Upheaval at Homestead," in Daniel Aaron, ed., *America in Crisis*, New York: Alfred Knopf.

Davison, Graeme (1978), "Sydney and the Bush: An Urban Context for the Australian Legend," *Historical Studies*, vol 18, no 71, October.

Davison, Graeme (1979), "The Mobility Theme," *Australia 1888*, no 1, February.

Davison, Graeme (1979b), "The Dimensions of Mobility in Nineteenth Century Australia," *Australia 1888*, no 2, August.

Davis, Mike (1986), *Prisoners of the American Dream*, London: Verso.

Dawson, William Harbutt (1890), *Bismarck and State Socialism*, London: Swan Sonnenschein and Co.

Dealey, James Quayle (1907), *Our State Constitutions*, Philadelphia: American Academy of Political and Social Science.

Debs, Eugene V. (1894), *Address of Eugene V. Debs at the Convention of the American Railway Union at Chicago, Illinois, June 12, 1894*, Terre Haute, Indiana: Moore and Langen.

Debs, Eugene V. (1895), "Liberty: A Speech by Eugene V. Debs," Terre Haute, Indiana: E.V. Debs and Co.

Debs, Eugene V. (1895a), "Labor Omnia Vincit," in Debs (1948).

Debs, Eugene V. (1948), *Writings and Speeches of Eugene V. Debs*, New York: Hermitage Press.

Della Porta, Donatella (1996), "Social Movements and the State: Thoughts on the Policing of Protest," in Doug McAdam *et al.* (1996).

Dennis, Peter *et al.* (1995), *The Oxford Companion to Australian Military History*, Melbourne: Oxford University Press.

Destler, Chester McArthur (1946), *American Radicalism 1865–1901*, Chicago: Quadrangle Books.

Destler, Chester McArthur (1963), *Henry Demarest Lloyd and the Empire of Reform*, Philadelphia: University of Pennsylvania Press.

Dick, William M. (1972), *Labor and Socialism in America: The Gompers Era*, Port Washington, New York: Kennikat Press.

Dickey, Brian (1966), "The Broken Hill Strike, 1892," *Labour History*, no 11, November.

Dickey, Brian (1969), *Politics in New South Wales 1856–1900*, Melbourne: Cassell.

Dickey, Brian (1974), "'Colonial Bourgeois'—Marx in Australia? Aspects of a Social History of NSW, 1856–1900," *Australian Economic History Review*, vol XIV, no 1, March.

Dickey, Brian (1993), "Evangelical Anglicans Compared," in Rawlyk and Noll, eds. (1993).

Dilke, Charles Wentworth (1890), *Problems of Greater Britain*, London: Macmillan.

Docherty, J.C. (1973), "The Rise of Railway Unionism," MA thesis, ANU.

Docherty, J.C. (1982), *Selected Social Statistics of New South Wales 1861–1976*, Sydney: History Project Incorporated, University of New South Wales.

Docker, John (1982), "Can the Centre Hold: Conceptions of the State, 1890–1925," in Sydney Labour History Group, eds., *What Rough Beast: The State and Social Order in Australian History*, Sydney: George Allen and Unwin.

Docker, John (1991), *The Nervous Nineties: Australian Cultural Life in the 1890s*, Melbourne: Oxford University Press.

Dodd, Lawrence C., and Calvin Jillson, eds. (1994), *The Dynamics of American Politics*, Boulder, Colorado: Westview Press.

Dole, Robert J. (1989), *Historical Almanac of the United States Senate*, Washington, D.C.: Government Printing Office.

Donovan, P.F. (1972), "Australia and the Great London Dock Strike: 1889," *Labour History*, no 23, November.

Dowling, Edward (1893), *Australia and America in 1892*, Sydney: NSW Commissioners for the World's Columbian Exposition, Chicago.

Drury, E.R. (1891), "Special Service by Corps of the Queensland Defence Force," in Queensland, *Votes and Proceedings*, 1891, 2, pp. 335–51.

Dubofsky, Melvyn (1966), "The Origins of Western Working-Class Radicalism, 1890–1905," *Labor History*, 7, Spring.

Dubofsky, Melvyn (1994), *The State and Labor in Modern America*, Chapel Hill, North Carolina: University of North Carolina Press.

Dubofsky, Melvyn, and Warren Van Tine, eds. (1987), *Labor Leaders in America*, Urbana, Illinois: University of Illinois Press.

Duncan, Bruce (1991), *The Church's Social Teaching: From Rerum Novarum to 1931*, Melbourne: Collins Dove.

Dunstan, Keith (1968), *Wowsers*, Sydney: Angus and Robertson.

Duverger, Maurice (1954), *Political Parties*, London: Methuen.

Easson, Michael, ed. (1990), *The Foundation of Labor*, Sydney: Pluto Press.

Ebbels, Noel (1983), *The Australian Labor Movement 1850–1907: Historical Documents*, Sydney: Hale and Iremonger.

Edwards, P.K. (1981), *Strikes in the United States, 1881–1974*, Oxford: Basil Blackwell.

Ellem, B., J. Hagan, and K. Turner (1988), "The Origins of the Labor Party in the Southern Wheatbelt of New South Wales, 1891–1913," *Labour History*, 55, November.

Ellis, John Tracy (1952), *The Life of James Cardinal Gibbons: Archbishop of Baltimore, 1834–1921, Volume 1*, Milwaukee, Wisconsin: The Bruce Publishing Co.

Ellis, John Tracy, ed. (1962), *Documents in American Catholic History*, Milwaukee, Wisconsin: The Bruce Publishing Co.

Ellis, John Tracy (1979), "Australian Catholicism: An American Perspective," *Journal of Religious History*, vol 10, no 3, June.

Ellis, Richard J. (1993), *American Political Cultures*, New York: Oxford University Press.

Elster, Jon (1989), *Nuts and Bolts for the Social Sciences*, Cambridge: Cambridge University Press.

Elster, Jon (1998), "A Plea for Mechanisms," in Hedstrom and Swedberg, eds. (1998).

Ely, Richard (1981), "Secularisation and the Sacred in Australian History," *Historical Studies*, vol 19, no 77, October.

Emsley, Clive (1983), *Policing and Its Context, 1750–1870*, London: Macmillan.

Emsley, Clive (1984), *Essays in Comparative History*, Milton Keynes, England: Open University Press.

Engerman, Stanley, and Claudia Goldin (1994), "Seasonality in Nineteenth-Century Labor Markets," in Thomas Weiss and Donald Schaefer, eds. (1994), *American Economic Development in Historical Perspective*, Stanford, California: Stanford University Press.

Engstrom, Richard L., and Michael D. McDonald (1981), "The Election of Blacks to City Councils," *American Political Science Review*, vol 75, no 2, June.

Epstein, Leon D. (1986), *Political Parties in the American Mold*, Madison, Wisconsin: The University of Wisconsin Press.

Ericson, David F., and Louisa Bertch Green, eds. (1999), *The Liberal Tradition in American Politics*, New York: Routledge.

Ernst, Daniel R. (1995), *Lawyers Against Labor*, Urbana, Illinois: University of Illinois Press.

Esping-Andersen, Gosta (1990), *The Three Worlds of Welfare Capitalism*, Cambridge: Polity.

Evans, Eldon Cobb (1917), *A History of the Australian Ballot System in the United States*, Chicago: University of Chicago Press.

Evans, Peter (1995), "Peter Evans," in Atul Kohli *et al.*, "The Role of Theory in Comparative Politics," *World Politics*, vol 48, October.

Evatt, H.V. (1918), *Liberalism in Australia*, Sydney: The Law Book Co. of Australasia Ltd.

Evatt, H.V. (1942), *Australian Labour Leader: The Story of W.A. Holman and the Labour Movement*, Sydney: Angus and Robertson.

Fahey, Charles (1993), "'Abusing Horses and Exploiting the Labourer': The Victorian Agricultural and Pastoral Labourer, 1871–1911," *Labour History*, no 65, November.

Fanshaw, E.L. (1893), *Liquor Legislation in the United States and Canada*, London: Cassell and Co.

Finegold, Kenneth, and Theda Skocpol (1984), "State, Party, and Industry: From Business Recovery to the Wagner Act in America's New Deal," in Charles Bright and Susan Harding, eds., *Statemaking and Social Movements*, Ann Arbor, Michigan: University of Michigan Press.

Fink, Gary M. (1984), *Biographical Dictionary of American Labor Leaders*, Westport, Connecticut: Greenwood Press.

Fink, Leon (1983), *Workingmen's Democracy: The Knights of Labor and American Politics*, Urbana, Illinois: University of Illinois Press.

Fink, Leon (1987), "Labor, Liberty, and the Law: Trade Unionism and the Problem of Constitutional Order," *Journal of American History*, vol 24, no 3, December.

Finke, Roger, and Rodney Stark (1992), *The Churching of America, 1776–1990*, New Brunswick, New Jersey: Rutgers University Press.

Finn, J.F. (1973), "AF of L Leaders and the Question of Politics in the Early 1890s," *Journal of American Studies*, vol 7, no 3, December.

Finnane, Mark (1991), "The Varieties of Policing: Colonial Queensland, 1860–1900," in Anderson, David M. and David Killingray (1991).

Finnane, Mark (1994), *Police and Government: Histories of Policing in Australia*, Melbourne: Oxford University Press.

Finnane, Mark and Stephen Garton (1992), "The Work of Policing: Social Relations and the Criminal Justice System in Queensland, 1880–1914," Part I, *Labour History*, no 62, May, Part II, *Labour History*, no 63, November.

Fischer, Lewis R. (1988), "International Maritime Labour, 1863–1900: World Wages and Trends," *The Great Circle: Journal of the Australian Association for Maritime History*, vol 10, no 1, April.

Fisher, Shirley (1979), "The Mobility Myth: Some Sydney Evidence," *Australia 1888*, no 2, August.

Fitzgerald, John D. (1915), *The Rise of the New South Wales Political Labor Party*, Sydney.

Fitzgerald, Ross (1999), *Seven Days to Remember: The World's First Labor Government*, St Lucia: University of Queensland Press.

Fitzgerald, S. (1987), *Rising Damp: Sydney 1870–90*, Melbourne: Oxford University Press.

Fitzhardinge, L.F. (1964), *William Morris Hughes. Vol I: That Fiery Particle 1862–1914*, Sydney: Angus and Robertson.

Flora, Peter (1983), *State, Economy, and Society in Western Europe 1815–1975*, London: Macmillan.

Fogarty, Robert S. (1990), *All Things New: American Communes and Utopian Movements, 1860–1914*, Chicago: University of Chicago Press.

Fogelson, Robert F. (1989), *America's Armories*, Cambridge, Massachusetts: Harvard University Press.

Foner, Eric (1984), "Why Is There No Socialism in the United States?," *History Workshop Journal*.

Foner, Philip S. (1955), *History of the Labor Movement in the United States: Volume II*, New York: International Publishers.

Forbath, William E. (1991), *Law and the Shaping of the American Labor Movement*, Cambridge, Massachusetts: Harvard University Press.

Forbath, William E. (1991a), "Courts, Constitutions, and Labor Politics in England and America," *Law and Social Inquiry*, vol 16, no 1, Winter.

Ford, Patrick (1966), *Cardinal Moran and the A.L.P.: A Study of the Encounter between Moran and Socialism 1890–1907*, Melbourne: Melbourne University Press.

Forstall, Richard L., ed. (1996), *Population of the States and Counties of the United States: 1790–1990*, Washington D.C.: Department of Commerce, U.S. Bureau of the Census.

Fosbery, Edmund (1890), "Report of the Inspector-General of Police on . . . the Late Strike," *Votes and Proceedings of the Legislative Assembly, New South Wales, During* the Session of 1890, vol VII, pp. 627–36, Sydney: Charles Potter, Government Printer.

FOTLU (1881), *Report of the First Annual Session of the Federation of Organized Trades and Labor Unions of the United States and Canada* held in Pittsburgh, Pennsylvania, November 15 to 18, 1881.

FOTLU (1882), *Report of the Second Annual Session of the Federation of Organized Trades and Labor Unions of the United States and Canada* held in Cleveland, Ohio, November 21 to 24, 1882.

Frankfurter, Felix, and Nathan Greene (1930), *The Labor Injunction*, New York: Macmillan.

Fredman, L.E. (1967), "The Introduction of the Australian Ballot in the United States," *Australian Journal of Politics and History*, vol XIII, no 2, August.

Fredman, L.E. (1968), *The Australian Ballot*, East Lansing, Michigan: Michigan State University Press.

Fredrickson, George M. (1981), *White Supremacy: A Comparative Study of American and South African History*, New York: Oxford University Press.

Fredrickson, George M. (1997), *The Comparative Imagination*, Berkeley, California: University of California Press.

Freeden, Michael (1978), *The New Liberalism*, Oxford: Oxford University Press.

Freeden, Michael (1986), *Liberalism Divided*, Oxford: Oxford University Press.

Freeden, Michael (1990), "The New Liberalism and Its Aftermath," in Richard Bellamy, ed. (1990).

Freudenberg, Graham (1990), "The Great Strike," in Michael Easson, ed. (1990).

Friedman, Gerald (1991), "Worker Militancy and Its Consequences: Political Responses to Labor Unrest in the United States, 1877–1914," *International Labor and Working-Class History*, no 40, Fall.

Friedman, Lawrence M. (1973), *A History of American Law*, New York: Simon and Schuster.

Friedman, Lawrence M. (1984), *American Law*, New York: W.W. Norton and Co.

Fry, Eric (1956), "The Condition of the Urban Wage-Earning Class in Australia in the 1880s," PhD thesis, Australian National University.

Gaboury, William J. (1967), "From Statehouse to Bull Pen: Idaho Populism and the Coeur d'Alene Troubles of the 1890s," *Pacific Northwest Quarterly*, vol 58, no 1, January.

Gaboury, William J. (1988), *Dissension in the Rockies: A History of Idaho Populism*, New York: Garland Publishing.

Galambos, Louis (1975), *The Public Image of Big Business in America, 1880–1940*, Baltimore: Johns Hopkins University Press.

Galenson, Walter (1983), *The United Brotherhood of Carpenters*, Cambridge, Massachusetts: Harvard University Press.

Ganoe, William Addleman (1924), *The History of the United States Army*, New York: D. Appleton and Co.

Garraty, John A. (1968), *The Transformation of American Society, 1870–1890*, Columbia, South Carolina: University of South Carolina Press.

Garrett, Geoffrey (1998), *Partisan Politics in the Global Economy*, Cambridge: Cambridge University Press.

Gates, John B. and Charles A. Johnson, eds. (1991), *The American Courts: A Critical Assessment*, Washington, D.C.: Congressional Quarterly Press.

Gates, P.W. (1975), "Public Land Disposal in California," *Agricultural History*, January.

Geary, Dick (1981), *European Labour Protest, 1848–1939*, London: Methuen.

Geisst, Charles R. (2000), *Monopolies in America*, New York: Oxford University Press.

George, Alexander L., and Andrew Bennett (2005), *Case Studies and Theory Development in the Social Sciences*, Cambridge, Massachusetts: MIT Press.

George, Henry (1883), *Progress and Poverty*, fifth edition, London: Kegan Paul, Trench and Co.

Gerring, John (1997), "Party Ideology in America: The National Republican Chapter, 1824–1924," *Studies in American Political Development*, vol 11, no 1, Spring.

Gerring, John (1998), *Party Ideologies in America 1828–1996*, Cambridge: Cambridge University Press.

Gerstle, Gary (1994), "The Protean Character of American Liberalism," *American Historical Review*, vol 99, no 4, October.

Gibbney, H.J. (1978), "Charles Lilley: An Uncertain Democrat," in Murphy and Joyce, eds. (1978).

Gibson, N.R. (1994), "The Role of the Military in Industrial Disputes: Australia and New Zealand, 1879–1921," MA (Hons) thesis, University of Canterbury.

Gilbert, Alan D. (1976), *Religion and Society in Industrial England*, London: Longman.

Gilbert, Alan D. (1980), *The Making of Post-Christian Britain*, London: Longman.

Gilbert, Alan D. (1980a), "Religion and Society," *Australia 1888*, no 6, November.

Gilbert, Alan D. (1988), "Religion and the Bicentenary," *Journal of Religious History*, vol 15, no 1, July.

Gilmore, Glenda Elizabeth (1996), *Gender and Jim Crow*, Chapel Hill, North Carolina: University of North Carolina Press.

Ginger, Ray (1949), *The Bending Cross: A Biography of Eugene Victor Debs*, New Brunswick, New Jersey: Rutgers University Press.

Ginger, Ray (1958), *Altgeld's America: 1890–1905*, Chicago: Quadrangle Paperbacks.

Gitelman, H.M. (1965), "Adolph Strasser and the Origins of Pure and Simple Unionism," *Labor History*, vol 6, Winter.

Gladden, Washington (1886), *Applied Christianity: Moral Aspects of Social Questions*, Boston: Houghton, Mifflin and Company.

Glazier, Michael and Thomas J. Shelley, eds. (1997), *The Encyclopedia of American Catholic History*, Collegeville, Minnesota: The Liturgical Press.

Godkin, E.L. (1895), *Reflections and Comments 1865–1895*, New York: Charles Scribner's Sons.

Goldstein, Robert Justin (1978), *Political Repression in Modern America*, Cambridge, Massachusetts: Schenkmen Publishing Co.

Gollan, Robin (1960), *Radical and Working Class Politics: A Study of Eastern Australia, 1850–1910*, Melbourne: Melbourne University Press.

Gollan, Robin (1962), "The Australian Impact," in Sylvia E. Bowman *et al.* (1962).

Gollan, Robin (1963), *The Coalminers of New South Wales*, Melbourne: Melbourne University Press.

Gollan, Robin (1965), "American Populism and Australian Utopianism," *Labour History*, no 9, November.

Gompers, Samuel (1892), "Organized Labor in the Campaign," *North American Review*, vol 155, no 1, July.

Gompers, Samuel (1925), *Seventy Years of Life and Labor, Volume 1*, New York: E.P. Dutton.

Gompers, Samuel, and Herman Guttstadt (1902), *Meat vs. Rice: American Manhood vs. Asiatic Coolieism: Which Shall Survive?*, American Federation of Labor.

Goodin, Robert E., *et al.* (1999), *The Real Worlds of Welfare Capitalism*, Cambridge: Cambridge University Press.

Goodrich, Carter (1928), "The Australian and American Labour Movements," *Economic Record*, vol IV, no 7, November.

Goodwyn, Lawrence (1976), *Democratic Promise: The Populist Moment in America*, New York: Oxford University Press.

Graham, Hugh Davis, and Ted Robert Gurr, eds. (1969), *The History of Violence in America: Historical and Comparative Perspectives*, New York: Frederick A. Praeger.

Green, James R. (1980), *The World of the Worker*, New York: Hill and Wang.

Green, T.H. (1881), *Liberal Legislation and Freedom of Contract*, Oxford: Slater and Rose.

Greene, Victor R. (1968), *The Slavic Community on Strike: Immigrant Labor in Pennsylvania Anthracite*, Notre Dame, Indiana: University of Notre Dame Press.

Greene, Julie (1998), *Pure and Simple Politics*, Cambridge: Cambridge University Press.

Greenstone, J. David (1986), "Political Culture and American Political Development: Liberty, Union, and the Liberal Bipolarity," *Studies in American Political Development*, vol 1.

Greenstone, J. David (1993), *The Lincoln Persuasion: Remaking American Liberalism*, Princeton, New Jersey: Princeton University Press.

Greenwood, Gordon, ed. (1955), *Australia: A Social and Political History*, Sydney: Angus and Robertson.

Gregory, J.S. (1973), *Church and State: Changing Government Policies towards Religion in Australia*, Melbourne: Cassell Australia.

Grey, Jeffrey (1990), *A Military History of Australia*, Cambridge: Cambridge University Press.

Griffith, S.W. (1889), "The Distribution of Wealth," *The Centennial Magazine*, vol I, no 12, July.

Grob, Gerald N. (1958), "The Knights of Labor, Politics, and Populism," *Mid-America*, vol 40, no 1, January.

Grob, G.N. (1961), *Workers and Utopia*, New York: Quadrangle.

Gronlund, Laurence (1884), *The Cooperative Commonwealth*, Boston: Lee and Shepard.

Grumm, John G. (1958), "Theories of Electoral Systems," *Midwest Journal of Political Science*, vol 2.

Gutman, Herbert G. (1966), "Protestantism and the American Labor Movement: The Christian Spirit in the Gilded Age," *American Historical Review*, vol LXXII, no 1, October.

Hacker, Barton C. (1969), "The United States Army as a National Police Force: The Federal Policing of Labor Disputes, 1877–1898," *Military Affairs*, 33, April.

Hagan, Jim (1966), *Printers and Politics: A History of the Australian Printing Unions, 1850–1950*, Canberra: Australian National University Press.

Hagan, Jim and Ken Turner (1991), *A History of the Labor Party in New South Wales, 1891–1991*, Melbourne: Longman Cheshire.

Hagan, Jim, and Andrew Wells (1992), *The Maritime Strike: A Centennial Retrospective*, Wollongong, NSW: Five Islands Press.

Haig, Bryan (1989), "International Comparisons of Australian GDP in the 19th Century," *Review of Income and Wealth*, series 35, no 2, June.

Haldane, Robert (1995), *The People's Force: A History of the Victorian Police*, Melbourne: Melbourne University Press.

Hall, Kermit L. (1980), "Children of the Cabins: The Lower Federal Judiciary, Modernisation, and the Political Culture, 1789–1899," *Northwestern University Law Review*, vol 75, no 3.

Hall, Kermit L. (1984), "Progressive Reform and the Decline of Democratic Accountability: the Popular Election of State Supreme Court Judges, 1850–1920," *American Bar Foundation Research Journal*, no 2, Spring.

Hall, Kermit L. ed. (1992), *The Oxford Companion to the Supreme Court of the United States*, New York: Oxford University Press.

Hall, Kermit L. *et al.*, eds. (1996), *American Legal History*, New York: Oxford University Press.

Hall, Thomas Cuming (1930), *The Religious Background of American Culture*, Boston: Little Brown and Co.

Halpern, Rick and Jonathan Morris, eds. (1997), *American Exceptionalism? U.S. Working-Class Formation in an International Context*, London: Macmillan.

Hamilton, Celia (1958), "Irish-Catholics of New South Wales and the Labor Party, 1890–1910," *Historical Studies*, vol 8, no 31, November.

Hamilton, Howard D. (1967), "Legislative Constituencies: Single-Member Districts, Multi-Member Districts, and Floterial Districts," *Western Political Quarterly*, vol 20.

Hammack, David C. (1987), *Power and Society: Greater New York at the Turn of the Century*, New York: Columbia University Press.

Handy, Robert T. (1976), *A History of the Churches in the United States and Canada*, Oxford: Clarendon Press.

Handy, Robert T. (1991), *Undermined Establishment: Church-State Relations in America, 1880–1920*, Princeton, New Jersey: Princeton University Press.

Harrington, Michael (1972), *Socialism*, New York: Saturday Review Press.

Harris, Joe (1970), *The Bitter Fight*, Brisbane: Queensland University Press.

Harris, Joseph P. (1929), *Registration of Voters in the United States*, Washington D.C.: Brookings Institute.

Harris, W.J.H. (1966), *First Steps: Queensland Workers' Moves towards Political Expression, 1857–1893*, Canberra: Australian Society for the Study of Labour History.

Hartz, Louis (1955), *The Liberal Tradition in America*, New York: Harcourt Brace.

Hartz, Louis (1964), *The Founding of New Societies*, New York: Harcourt Brace.

Hatch, Nathan O. (1990), "The Democratization of Christianity," in Noll, ed. (1990).

Hattam, Victoria C. (1992), "Institutions and Political Change: Working Class Formation in England and the United States, 1820–1896," in Sven Steinmo *et al.*, eds., *Structuring Politics*, Cambridge: Cambridge University Press.

Hattam, Victoria C. (1993), *Labor Visions and State Power: The Origins of Business Unionism in the United States*, Princeton, New Jersey: Princeton University Press.

Hawkins, Richard (1991), "The 'Irish Model' and the Empire," in Anderson, David M., and David Killingray (1991).

Hayes, George H. (1900a), "Representation in State Legislatures," *Annals of the American Academy of Political and Social Science*, vol XV, no 2, March.

Hayes, George H. (1900b), "Representation in the Legislatures of the North Central States," *Annals of the American Academy of Political and Social Science*, vol XV, no 3, May.

Haynes, Evan (1944), *The Selection and Tenure of Judges*, Newark, New Jersey: National Conference of Judicial Councils.

Hearn, Mark, and Harry Knowles (1996), *One Big Union: A History of the Australian Workers Union, 1886–1994*, Melbourne: Cambridge University Press.

Hedstrom, Peter, and Richard Swedberg, eds. (1998), *Social Mechanisms*, Cambridge: Cambridge University Press.

Higham, John (1992 [1955]), *Strangers in the Land: Patterns of American Nativism, 1860–1925*, New Brunswick, New Jersey: Rutgers University Press.

Hilliard, David (1988), "Anglicanism," in S.L. Goldberg and F.B. Smith, eds., *Australian Cultural History*, Cambridge: Cambridge University Press.

Hillquit, Morris (1903), *History of Socialism in the United States*, New York: Funk and Wagnalls Company.

Hirsch, Eric L. (1990), *Urban Revolt: Ethnic Politics in the Nineteenth-Century Chicago Labor Movement*, Berkeley, California: University of California Press.

Hirsch, Susan E. (1999), "The Search for Unity among Railroad Workers: The Pullman Strike in Perspective," in Schneirov, Stromquist, and Salvatore, eds. (1999).

Hirst, John (1988), "Egalitarianism," in S.L. Goldberg and F.B. Smith, eds., *Australian Cultural History*, Cambridge: Cambridge University Press.

Hirst, J.B. (1988a), *The Strange Birth of Colonial Democracy: New South Wales, 1848–1884*, Sydney: Allen and Unwin.

Hobhouse, L.T. (1893), *The Labour Movement*, London: T. Fischer Unwin.

Hobhouse, L.T. (1911), *Liberalism*, Oxford: Oxford University Press.

Hobson, J.A. (1909), *The Crisis of Liberalism*, London: P.S. King and Son.

Hoerder, Dirk, ed. (1983), *American Labor and Immigration History, 1877–1920s*, Urbana, Illinois: University of Illinois Press.

Hoerder, Dirk, and Hartmut Keil (1988), "The American Case and German Social Democracy at the Turn of the 20th Century, 1878–1907," in Jean Heffer and Jeanine Rovert, eds., *Why Is There No Socialism in the United States*, Paris: Ecole des Hautes Etudes en Sciences Sociales.

Hofstadter, Richard, and Seymour Martin Lipset, eds. (1968), *Turner and the Sociology of the Frontier*, New York: Basic Books.

Hogan, Michael (1987), *The Sectarian Strand: Religion in Australian History*, Melbourne: Penguin.

Holmes, George K., and John S. Lord (1896), *Report on Farms and Homes, 11th Census 1890*, Washington, D.C.: Government Printing Office.

Holt, James (1977), "Trade Unionism in the British and U.S. Steel Industries, 1880–1914," *Labor History*, vol 18, no 1, Winter, also in Clive Emsley (1984).

Hooker, Richard J. (1981), *Food and Drink in America*, Indianapolis, Indiana: The Bobbs-Merrill Company.

Hopkins, Charles Howard (1940), *The Rise of the Social Gospel in American Protestantism 1865–1915*, New Haven, Connecticut: Yale University Press.

Hovenkamp, Herbert (1991), *Enterprise and American Law, 1836–1937*, Cambridge, Massachusetts: Harvard University Press.

Hughes, Colin A. (1970), "Labour in the Electorates" in D.J. Murphy *et al.*, eds. (1970).

Hughes, Colin A., and B.D. Graham (1968), *A Handbook of Australian Government and Politics 1890–1964*, Canberra: Australian National University Press.

Hughes, Colin A., and B.D. Graham (1975), *Voting for the New South Wales Legislative Assembly 1890–1964*, Canberra: Department of Political Science, Research School of Social Sciences, Australian National University.

Hughes, William Morris (1910), *The Case for Labor*, Sydney: The Worker Trustees.

Hunt, Doug (1978), "Exclusivism and Unionism: Europeans in the Queensland Sugar Industry, 1900–10," in Curthoys and Markus, eds. (1978).

Huntington, Samuel P. (1957), *The Soldier and the State*, Cambridge, Massachusetts: Belknap Press.

Huntington, Samuel P. (1981), *American Politics: The Promise of Disharmony*, Cambridge, Massachusetts: Belknap Press.

Hurst, James Willard (1950), *The Growth of American Law*, Boston: Little, Brown and Co.

Husbands, C.T. (1976), "Editor's Introductory Essay," in Werner Sombart (1976 [1906]).

Illinois Adjutant General's Office (1895), *Biennial Report of the Adjutant General of Illinois . . . 1893 and 1894*, Springfield, Illinois: Ed. F. Hartman.

Illinois Bureau of Labor Statistics (1894), *Thirteenth Annual Coal Report*, Springfield, Illinois: State Printers.

Illinois Bureau of Labor Statistics (1899), *Eighteenth Annual Coal Report*, Springfield, Illinois: State Printers.

Illinois Bureau of Labor Statistics (1904), *Twelfth Biennial Report, 1902*, Springfield, Illinois: State Printers.

Illinois Secretary of State (1894), *Official Vote of the State of Illinois Cast at the General Election held November 6, 1894*, Springfield, Illinois: State Printers.

Ingham, John N. (1978), *The Iron Barons: A Social Analysis of an American Urban Elite, 1874–1965*, Westport, Connecticut: Greenwood Press.

Ingham, John N. (1991), *Making Iron and Steel: Independent Mills in Pittsburgh, 1820–1920*, Columbus, Ohio: Ohio University Press.

Ingham, John N. (1993), "'Fort Frick' and the Amalgamated: The Homestead Lockout of 1892 in Historical Perspective," *Labour/Le Travail*, no 31, Spring.

Inglis, K.S. (1958), "Catholic Historiography in Australia," *Historical Studies*, vol 8, no 31, November.

Inglis, K.S. (1963), *Churches and the Working Classes in Victorian England*, London: Routledge and Kegan Paul.

Inglis, K.S. (1967), "Australia Day," *Historical Studies*, vol 13, no 49, October.

ICTUC (1879), *The First Intercolonial Trades Union Congress: Report of Proceedings . . . commencing on October 6th, 1879*, Sydney: Trades & Labour Council of NSW.

ICTUC (1884), *The Second Intercolonial Trades Union Congress: An Official Report of the Debates . . . During the 22nd, 23rd, 24th, and 25th April, 1884*, Melbourne: Walker, May and Co.

ICTUC (1885), *Official Report of the Third Intercolonial Trades Union Congress Held in Sydney on the 4th, 5th, 6th, and 7th of October, 1885*, Sydney: Batson & Co.

ICTUC (1886), *Official Report of the Fourth Intercolonial Trades Union Congress Held in Adelaide on the 2nd, 3rd, 6th, and 7th of September, 1886*, Adelaide: Burden and Bonython.

ICTUC (1888), *Official Report of the Fifth Intercolonial Trades Union Congress Held in Brisbane on the 2nd, 5th, 6th, and 7th of March, 1888*, Brisbane: Warwick and Sapsford.

ICTUC (1889), *Official Report of the Sixth Intercolonial Trades and Labor Union Congress Held in Hobart on the 5th, 6th, 7th, and 8th February, 1889*, Hobart: "Tasmanian News" Steam Printing Office.

ICTUC (1891), *Official Report of the Seventh Intercolonial Trades and Labor Union Congress of Australasia Held at Ballarat on the 22nd, 23rd, 24th, 25th, 27th, 28th, and 29th April, 1891*, Ballarat, Victoria: J. Anderson and Co.

Jackson, H.R. (1987), *Churches and People in Australia and New Zealand, 1860–1930*, Wellington: Allen and Unwin.

Jackson, Hugh (1988), "'White Man Got No Dreaming': Religious Feeling in Australian History," *Journal of Religious History*, vol 15, no 1, 1988.

Jackson, R.V., and Mark Thomas (1995), "Height, Weight and Wellbeing: Sydney Schoolchildren in the Early Twentieth Century," *Australian Economic History Review*, vol XXXV, no 2, September.

Jacobi, Sanford M. (1991), "American Exceptionalism Revisited: The Importance of Management," in Sanford M. Jacobi, ed. (1991).

Jacobi, Sanford M., ed. (1991), *Masters to Managers: Historical and Comparative Perspectives on American Employers*, New York: Columbia University Press.

Jacobson, Matthew Frye (1998), *Whiteness of a Different Color: European Immigrants and the Alchemy of Race*, Cambridge, Massachusetts: Harvard University Press.

Jaher, Frederic Cople (1973), *The Rich, the Well Born, and the Powerful*, Urbana, Illinois: University of Illinois Press.

Jaher, Frederic Cople (1982), *The Urban Establishment: Upper Strata in Boston, New York, Charleston, Chicago, and Los Angeles*, Urbana, Illinois: University of Illinois Press.

James, E.J. (1899), "The Growth of Great Cities in Area and Population," *Annals of the American Academy of Political and Social Science*, vol XIII, no 1, January.

Jensen, Joan M. (1991), *Army Surveillance in America, 1775–1980*, New Haven, Connecticut: Yale University Press.

Jensen, Vernon H. (1950), *Heritage of Conflict: Labor Relations in the Nonferrous Metals Industry up to 1930*, Ithaca, New York: Cornell University Press.

Jensen, Richard J. (1971), *Winning the Midwest: Social and Political Conflict, 1888–1896*, Chicago: University of Chicago Press.

Jensen, Richard (1972), "The Religious and Occupational Roots of Party Identification: Illinois and Indiana in the 1870s," in Joel L. Silbey and Samuel T. McSeveney, eds., *Voters, Parties, and Elections*, Lexington, Massachusetts: Xerox College Publishing.

Johnson, Bruce (1976), "Taking Care of Labor: The Police in American Politics," *Theory and Society*, vol 3, no 1, Spring.

Johnson, D.H. (1975), *Volunteers at Heart: The Queensland Defence Forces, 1860–1901*, St Lucia: University of Queensland Press.

Jorgenson, Lloyd P. (1987), *The States and the Non-Public School, 1825–1925*, Columbia, Missouri: University Press of Missouri.

Josephy, Alvin M. (1975), *The Congress of the United States*, New York: American Heritage Publishing Co.

Joyce, R.B. (1978), "Samuel Walker Griffith: A Liberal Lawyer," in Murphy and Joyce, eds. (1978).

Judd, Stephen, and Kenneth Cable (1987), *Sydney Anglicans: A History of the Diocese*, Sydney: Anglican Information Office.

Jupp, James (1991), *Immigration*, Sydney: Sydney University Press.

Jupp, James, ed. (2001), *The Australian People*, Cambridge: Cambridge University Press.

Karson, Marc (1958), *American Labor Unions and Politics, 1900–1918*, Carbondale, Illinois: Southern Illinois University Press.

Karson, Marc (1984), "Catholic Anti-Socialism," in Laslett and Lipset, eds. (1984).

Katznelson, Ira (1981), *City Trenches: Urban Politics and the Patterning of Class in the United States*, New York: Pantheon.

Katznelson, Ira, and Aristide R. Zolberg, eds. (1986), *Working-Class Formation: Nineteenth-Century Patterns in Western Europe and the United States*, Princeton, New Jersey: Princeton University Press.

Katznelson, Ira (1997), "Working-Class Formation and American Exceptionalism, Yet Again," in Halpern and Morris, eds. (1997).

Kaufman, Stuart Bruce (1973), *Samuel Gompers and the Origins of the American Federation of Labor: 1848–1896*, Westport, Connecticut: Greenwood Press.

Kaufman, Stuart B., ed. (1986), *The Samuel Gompers Papers. Volume 1: The Making of a Union Leader, 1850–86*, Urbana, Illinois: University of Illinois Press.

Kaufman, Stuart B., ed. (1987), *The Samuel Gompers Papers. Volume 2: The Early Years of the American Federation of Labor, 1887–90*, Urbana, Illinois: University of Illinois Press.

Kaufman, Stuart B., and Peter J. Albert, eds. (1989), *The Samuel Gompers Papers. Volume 3: Unrest and Depression, 1891–94*, Urbana, Illinois: University of Illinois Press.

Kaufman, Stuart B., Peter J. Albert, and Grace Palladino, eds. (1991), *The Samuel Gompers Papers. Volume 4: A National Labor Movement Takes Shape, 1895–98*, Urbana, Illinois: University of Illinois Press.

Kazin, Michael (1986), "The Great Exception Revisited: Organized Labor and Politics in San Francisco and Los Angeles, 1870–1940," *Pacific Historical Review*, vol LV, no 3, August.

Kazin, Michael (1995), "The Agony and Romance of the American Left," *American Historical Review*, vol 100, no 5, December.

Kehl, James A. (1981), *Boss Rule in the Gilded Age*, Pittsburgh: University of Pittsburgh Press.

Keil, Hartmut (1983), "The German Immigrant Working Class in Chicago, 1875–1890," in Dirk Hoerder, ed. (1983).

Keil, Hartmut (1988), "German Working-Class Immigration and the Social Democratic Tradition of Germany," in Keil, ed., *German Workers' Culture in the United States 1850 to 1920*, Washington, D.C.: Smithsonian Institution Press.

Keil, Hartmut and John B. Jentz, eds. (1983), *German Workers in Industrial Chicago, 1850–1910*, DeKalb, Illinois: Northern Illinois University Press.

Keiser, John H. (1972), "Black Strikebreakers and Racism in Illinois, 1865–1900," *Journal of the Illinois State Historical Society*, vol LXV, no 3, Autumn.

Kennedy, Brian (1978), *Silver, Sin, and Sixpenny Ale: A Social History of Broken Hill, 1883–1921*, Melbourne: Melbourne University Press.

Kenway, H. (1970), "The Pastoral Strikes of 1891 and 1894," in D.J. Murphy *et al.*, eds. (1970).

Kerr, K. Austin (1985), *Organized for Prohibition*, New Haven, Connecticut: Yale University Press.

Keyssar, Alexander (2000), *The Right to Vote*, New York: Basic Books.

King, Gary, Robert O. Keohane, and Sidney Verba (1994), *Designing Social Inquiry*, Princeton, New Jersey: Princeton University Press.

Kingston, Beverley (1988), *The Oxford History of Australia, Vol 3, 1860–1900*, Melbourne: Oxford University Press.

Kinzer, Donald L. (1964), *An Episode in Anti-Catholicism: The American Protective Association*, Seattle: University of Washington Press.

Kipnis, Ira (1952), *The American Socialist Movement, 1897–1912*, New York: Columbia University Press.

Klain, Maurice (1955), "A New Look at the Constituencies," *American Political Science Review*, vol XLIX, no 4, December.

Klandermans, Bert (1988), "The Formation and Mobilization of Consensus," in Klandermans *et al.*, eds. (1988), *International Social Movement Research*, vol 1, Greenwich, Connecticut: JAI Press.

Kleinberg, S.J. (1989), *The Shadow of the Mills: Working Class Families in Pittsburgh, 1870–1907*, Pittsburgh: University of Pittsburgh Press.

Kleppner, Paul (1970), *The Cross of Culture: A Social Analysis of Midwestern Politics, 1850–1900*, New York: Free Press.

Kleppner, Paul (1978), "From Ethnoreligious Conflict to 'Social Harmony': Coalitional and Party Transformations in the 1890s," in Seymour Martin Lipset, eds., *Emerging Coalitions in American Politics*, San Francisco: Institute for Contemporary Studies.

Kleppner, Paul (1979), *The Third Electoral System: 1853–1892*, Chapel Hill, North Carolina: University of North Carolina Press.

Kleppner, Paul (1981), "Partisanship and Ethnoreligious Conflict: The Third Electoral System, 1853–1892," in Paul Kleppner *et al.*, eds., *The Evolution of American Electoral Systems*, Westport, Connecticut: Greenwood Press.

Knibbs, G.H. (1912), *Official Year Book of the Commonwealth of Australia, 1901–11*, no 5, Commonwealth Bureau of Census and Statistics.

Korpi, Walter (1983), *The Democratic Class Struggle*, London: Routledge and Kegan Paul.

Krause, Paul (1992), *The Battle for Homestead, 1880–1892*, Pittsburgh: University of Pittsburgh Press.

Labour Defence Committee (1890), *Official Report and Balance Sheet of the New South Wales Labour Defence Committee . . . August to November 1890*, Sydney: Higgs and Townsend.

Lakeman, Enid (1974), *How Democracies Vote*, fourth edition, London: Faber.

La Nauze, J.A. (1965), *Alfred Deakin*, Melbourne: Melbourne University Press.

Lane, A.T. (1987), *Solidarity or Survival? American Labor and European Immigrants, 1830–1924*, New York: Greenwood Press.

Lane, William [John Miller] (1892), *The Workingman's Paradise*, Sydney: Edwards, Dunlop and Co.

Lansbury, Coral (1967), "William Guthrie Spence," *Labour History*, no 13, November.

Laslett, John (1970), *Labor and the Left: A Study of Socialist and Radical Influences in the American Labor Movement, 1881–1924*, New York: Basic Books.

Laslett, John H.M. (1996), "British Immigrant Colliers and the Origins and Early Development of the UMWA, 1870–1917," in Laslett, ed., *The United Mine Workers of America*, Pennsylvania State University Press.

Laslett, John H.M., and Seymour Martin Lipset, eds. (1974), *Failure of a Dream? Essays in the History of American Socialism*, first edition, Berkeley, California: University of California Press.

Laslett, John H.M., and Seymour Martin Lipset, eds. (1984), *Failure of a Dream? Essays in the History of American Socialism*, revised edition, Berkeley, California: University of California Press.

Laslett, John H.M. (2000), *Colliers across the Sea: A Comparative Study of Class Formation in Scotland and the American Midwest, 1830–1924*, Urbana, Illinois: University of Illinois Press.

Lasser, William (1988), *The Limits of Judicial Power*, Chapel Hill, North Carolina: University of North Carolina Press.

Lawson, Sylvia (1987), *The Archibald Paradox*, Melbourne: Penguin.

Lawton, William James (1990), *The Better Time to Be: Utopian Attitudes to Society among Sydney Anglicans 1885–1914*, Sydney: New South Wales University Press.

Lee, Jenny and Charles Fahey (1986), "A Boom for Whom? Some Developments in the Australian Labour Market, 1870–1891," *Labour History*, no 50, May.

Lee, Matthew C. (1991), "Onward Christian Soldiers: The Social Gospel and the Pullman Strike," *Chicago History*, vol XX, nos 1 and 2, Spring and Summer.

Leinenweber, Charles (1984), "Socialism and Ethnicity," in Laslett and Lipset, eds. (1984).

Leuchtenburg, William E. (1963), *Franklin D. Roosevelt and the New Deal, 1932–1940*, New York: Harper and Row.

LeWarne, Charles P. (1968), "Equality Colony," *Pacific Northwest Quarterly*, vol 59, no 3, July.

Lewis, Ronald L. (1987), *Black Coal Miners in America*, Lexington, Kentucky: University Press of Kentucky.

Lichtenstein. Nelson (1989), "From Corporatism to Collective Bargaining," in Steve Fraser and Gary Gerstle, eds., *The Rise and Fall of the New Deal Order*, Princeton, New Jersey: Princeton University Press.

Lichtenstein, Nelson and Howell John Harris (1993), *Industrial Democracy in America*, Cambridge: Cambridge University Press.

Lieberson, Stanley (1963), *Ethnic Patterns in American Cities*, New York: The Free Press of Glencoe.

Lightfoot, Gerald and J.T. Sutcliffe (1915), "The Historical Development of Trade Unionism in Australia," in Meredith Atkinson, ed., *Trade Unionism in Australia*, Sydney: Burrows and Co.

Lijphart, Arend (1971), "Comparative Politics and the Comparative Method," *American Political Science Review*, vol 65.

Lijphart, Arend (1994), *Electoral Systems and Party Systems*, Oxford: Oxford University Press.

Lindsey, Almont (1942), *The Pullman Strike: The Story of a Unique Experiment and of a Great Labor Upheaval*, Chicago: University of Chicago Press.

Lipset, Seymour Martin (1950), *Agrarian Socialism*, Berkeley, California: University of California Press.

Lipset, Seymour Martin (1963), *The First New Nation: The United States in Historical and Comparative Perspective*, London: Heinemann.

Lipset, Seymour Martin (1977), "Why No Socialism in the United States?" in Seweryn Bialer and Sophia Sluzar, eds., *Sources of Contemporary Radicalism*, Boulder, Colorado: Westview Press.

Lipset, Seymour Martin (1985), "Radicalism or Reformism: The Sources of Working-Class Politics," in *Consensus and Conflict*, New Brunswick, New Jersey: Transaction Books.

Lipset, Seymour Martin (1990), *Continental Divide*, New York: Routledge.

Lipset, Seymour Martin (1996), *American Exceptionalism: A Double-Edged Sword*, New York: W.W. Norton.

Lipset, Seymour Martin, and Gary Marks (2000), *It Didn't Happen Here: Why Socialism Failed in the United States*, New York: W.W. Norton.

Lipset, Seymour Martin, and Earl Raab (1971), *The Politics of Unreason*, London: Heinemann.

Lipset, Seymour Martin, and Stein Rokkan (1967), *Party Systems and Voter Alignments*, New York: Free Press.

Little, Daniel (1991), *Varieties of Social Explanation*, Boulder, Colorado: Westview Press.

Lloyd, Caro (1912), *Henry Demarest Lloyd 1847–1903*, New York: G.P. Putnam's Sons.

Lloyd, Henry Demarest (1893), *The Safety of the Future Lies in Organized Labor*, Washington D.C.: American Federation of Labor.

Lloyd, Henry Demarest (1900), *A Country Without Strikes*, New York: Doubleday, Page and Co.

Lloyd, Henry Demarest (1902), *Newest England*, New York: Doubleday, Page and Co.

Lloyd, Henry Demarest (1910), *Lords of Industry*, New York: G.P. Putnam's Sons.

Lodge, Henry Cabot (1891), "The Restriction of Immigration," *North American Review*, vol 152.

Lopez, David E. (1977), "Cowboy Strikes and Unions," *Labor History*, vol 18, no 3, Summer.

Love, Peter (1984), *Labour and the Money Power: Australian Labour Populism 1890–1950*, Melbourne: Melbourne University Press.

Loveday, Peter (1975), "New South Wales," in D.J. Murphy, ed. (1975).

Loveday, Peter, and A.W. Martin (1966), *Parliament Factions and Parties*, Melbourne: Melbourne University Press.

Loveday, Peter, *et al.* (1977), *The Emergence of the Australian Party System*, Sydney: Hale and Iremonger.

Lowi, Theodore J. (1984), "Why Is There No Socialism in the United States? A Federal Analysis," in Robert T. Golembiewski and Aaron Wildavsky, eds., *The Costs of Federalism*, New Brunswick, New Jersey: Transaction Books.

Lucy, Richard (1990), "The Division of Powers Between the British Empire and its Australian Self-Governing Colonies, 1855–1900," *Australian Journal of Law and Society*, vol 6.

Lum, Dyer (1892), *Philosophy of Trade Unions*, New York: American Federation of Labor.

Lumb, R.D. (1983), *Australian Constitutionalism*, Sydney: Butterworths.

Lumb, R.D. (1991), *Constitutions of the Australian States*, fifth edition, St Lucia: Queensland University Press.

McAdam, Doug (1982), *Political Process and the Development of Black Insurgency, 1930–1970*, Chicago: University of Chicago Press.

McAdam, Doug, John D. McCarthy, and Mayer N. Zald (1996), *Comparative Perspectives on Social Movements*, Cambridge: Cambridge University Press.

Macarthy, P.G. (1967), "Labor and the Living Wage: 1890–1910," *Australian Journal of Politics and History*, vol XIII, no 1, May.

Macarthy, P.G. (1970), "Victorian Trade Union Statistics, 1889–1914," *Labour History*, no 18, May.

McCloskey, Robert G. (1960), *The American Supreme Court*, Chicago: the University of Chicago Press.

MacColl, Gail, and Carol McD. Wallace (1989), *To Marry an English Lord*, New York: Workman Publishing.

McConville, Chris (1979), "Catholics and Mobility in Melbourne and Sydney," *Australia 1888*, no 2, August.

McConville, Chris (1985), "The Victorian Irish: Emigrants and Families, 1851–91," in Patricia Grimshaw *et al.*, eds., *Families in Colonial Australia*, Sydney: George, Allen and Unwin.

McCormick, Richard L. (1981), *From Realignment to Reform: Political Change in New York State, 1893–1910*, Ithaca, New York: Cornell University Press.

Macintyre, Stuart (1991), *A Colonial Liberalism*, Melbourne: Oxford University Press.

Macintyre, Stuart (1992), "'The Blessed Reign of Mobocracy': George Higinbotham and the Maritime Strike," in Hagan and Wells (1992).

Macintyre, Stuart, and Richard Mitchell, eds. (1989), *Foundations of Arbitration: The Origins and Effects of State Compulsory Arbitration, 1890–1914*, Melbourne: Oxford University Press.

Mackie, Thomas T., and Richard Rose (1991), *International Almanac of Electoral History*, Basingstoke, England: Macmillan.

McLean, Ian W. (1999), "Consumer Prices and Expenditure Patterns in Australia 1850–1914," *Australian Economic History Review*, vol 39, no 1, March.

McLoughlin, William G. (1959), *Modern Revivalism*, New York: Ronald Press.

McLoughlin, William G. (1978), *Revivals, Awakenings, and Reform*, Chicago: University of Chicago Press.

McMath, Robert C. (1993), *American Populism: A Social History 1877–1898*, New York: Hill and Wang.

McNaughton, I.D. (1955), "Colonial Liberalism, 1851–92," in Gordon Greenwood, ed. (1955).

McQueen, Humphrey (1986), *A New Britannia*, third edition, Melbourne: Penguin.

McQueen, Rob (1987), "Master and Servants Legislation in the 19th Century Australian Colonies," in Diane Kirkby, ed., *Law and History in Australia*, vol IV, Melbourne: Legal Studies Department, La Trobe University.

McSeveney, Samuel T. (1972), *The Politics of Depression: Political Behavior in the Northeast, 1893–1896*, New York.

Maddison, Angus (1991), *Dynamic Forces in Capitalist Development*, Oxford: Oxford University Press.

Maddox, G. (1998), "The Australian Settlement and Australian Political Thought," in Paul Smyth and Bettina Cass, eds., *Contesting the Australian Way*.

Mahoney, James and Dietrich Rueschemeyer, eds. (2003), *Comparative Historical Analysis in the Social Sciences*, Cambridge: Cambridge University Press.

Mandel, Bernard (1955), "Samuel Gompers and the Negro Workers, 1886–1914," *Journal of Negro History*, vol 40, no 1, January.

Mann, Michael (1993), *The Sources of Social Power: Volume II: The Rise of Classes and Nation-States, 1760–1914*, Cambridge: Cambridge University Press.

Marcus, Irwin M., *et al.* (1987), "Change and Continuity: Steel Workers in Homestead, Pennsylvania, 1889–1895," *Pennsylvania Magazine of History and Biography*, vol CXI, no 1, January.

Markey, Raymond (1978), "Populist Politics: Racism and Labor in NSW, 1880–1900," in Curthoys and Markus, eds. (1978).

Markey, Ray (1985), "New Unionism in Australia, 1880–1900," *Labour History*, no 48, May.

Markey, Raymond (1988), *The Making of the Labor Party in New South Wales, 1880–1900*, Kensington: New South Wales University Press.

Markey, Raymond (1994), *In Case of Oppression: The Life and Times of the Labor Council of New South Wales*, Sydney: Pluto Press.

Markey, Ray (1996), "Colonial Forms of Labour Organisation in Nineteenth Century Australia," Department of Economics, University of Wollongong, Working Paper Series WP 96–7.

Marks, Gary (1989), *Unions in Politics: Britain, Germany, and the United States in the Nineteenth and Early Twentieth Centuries*, Princeton, New Jersey: Princeton University Press.

Markus, Andrew (1974), "Divided We Fall: The Chinese and the Melbourne Furniture Trade Union, 1870–1900," *Labour History*, no 26, May.

Markus, Andrew (1978), "Talka Longa Mouth: Aborigines and the Labour Movement, 1890–1970," in Curthoys and Markus, eds. (1978).

Markus, Andrew (1979), *Fear and Hatred: Purifying Australia and California, 1850–1901*, Sydney: Hale and Iremonger.

Markus, Andrew (1994), *Australian Race Relations, 1788–1993*, Sydney: Allen and Unwin.

Marsden, George (1977), "Fundamentalism as an American Phenomenon, A Comparison with English Evangelicalism," *Church History*, vol 46.

Marsden, George M. (1991), *Understanding Fundamentalism and Evangelicalism*, Grand Rapids, Michigan: William B. Eerdmans.

Marsden, K. Gerald (1958), "Patriotic Societies and American Labor: The American Protective Association in Wisconsin," *Wisconsin Magazine of History*, vol 41, no 4, Summer.

Martin, A.W. (1956), "The Legislative Assembly of New South Wales, 1856–1900," *Australian Journal of Politics and History*, vol II, no 1, November.

Martin, A.W. (1967), "Henry Parkes and Electoral Manipulation, 1872–1882," in Beever and Smith, eds. (1967).

Martin, A.W. (1973), "Australia and the Hartz 'Fragment' Thesis," *Australian Economic History Review*, vol XIII, no 2, September.

Marty, Martin E. (1970), *Righteous Empire: The Protestant Experience in America*, New York: The Dial Press.

Mawby, R.I. (1990), *Comparative Policing Issues: The British and American Experience in International Perspective*, London: Unwin Hyman.

May, Henry F. (1949), *Protestant Churches and Industrial America*, New York: Harper and Brothers.

Mayer, Henry (1964), *Marx, Engels and Australia*, Melbourne: F.W. Cheshire.

Mazmanian, Daniel A. (1974), *Third Parties in Presidential Elections*, Washington, D.C.: The Brookings Institution.

Melleuish, Gregory (1995), *Cultural Liberalism in Australia*, Cambridge: Cambridge University Press.

Merritt, Adrian Suzanne (1981), "The Development and Application of Masters and Servants Legislation in New South Wales—1845 to 1930," PhD thesis, Australian National University.

Merritt, J.A. (1973), "W.G. Spence and the 1890 Maritime Strike," *Historical Studies*, vol 15, no 60, April.

Merritt, John (1986), *The Making of the AWU*, Melbourne: Oxford University Press.

Messer-Kruse, Timothy (1998), *The Yankee International: Marxism and the American Reform Tradition, 1848–1876*, Chapel Hill, North Carolina: University of North Carolina Press.

Metin, Albert (1977 [1901]), *Socialism Without Doctrine*, Sydney: Alternative Publishing Co-operative.

Miles, Nelson A. (1894), "The Lesson of the Recent Strike," *North American Review*, vol 159, no 2, August.

Miller, John [William Lane] (1980 [1892]), *The Workingman's Paradise*, Sydney: Sydney University Press.

Miller, Perry (1956), *Errand into the Wilderness*, Cambridge, Massachusetts: Harvard University Press.

Miller, Sally (1984), "Socialism and Race," in Laslett and Lipset, eds. (1984).

Miller, Stuart Creigton (1969), *The Unwelcome Immigrant: The American Image of the Chinese, 1785–1882*, Berkeley, California: University of California Press.

Miller, Wilbur, R. (1975), "Police Authority in London and New York, 1830–1870," in Clive Emsley (1984).

Miller, Wilbur R. (1977), *Cops and Bobbies: Police Authority in New York and London, 1830–1970*, Chicago: University of Chicago Press.

Mink, Gwendolyn (1986), *Old Labor and New Immigrants in American Political Development: Union, Party and State, 1875–1920*, Ithaca, New York: Cornell University Press.

Mittelman, Edward B. (1920), "Chicago Labor in Politics 1877–96," *Journal of Political Economy*, vol 28.

Mol, Hans (1971), *Religion in Australia*, Melbourne: Thomas Nelson.

Monkkonen, Eric H. (1981), *Police in Urban America, 1860–1920*, Cambridge: Cambridge University Press.

Montgomery, David (1967), *Beyond Equality*, New York: Knopf.

Montgomery, David (1987), *The Fall of the House of Labor: The Workplace, the State and American Labor Activism, 1865–1925*, Cambridge: Cambridge University Press.

Montgomery, David (1993), *Citizen Worker*, Cambridge: Cambridge University Press.

Montgomery, E.G. and C.H. Kardell (1930), *Apparent Per Capita Consumption of Principle Foodstuffs in the United States*, United States Department of Commerce, Domestic Commerce Series—No. 38, Washington D.C.: Government Printing Office.

Montgomery, Maureen E. (1989), *"Gilded Prostitution" Status, Money, and Transatlantic Marriages, 1870–1914*, London: Routledge.

Moore, Blaine Free (1909), *History of Cumulative Voting*, Urbana, Illinois: University of Illinois Press.

Moore, John Hammond (1977), *Australians in America, 1876–1976*, St Lucia: University of Queensland Press.

Moore, R. Laurence (1970), *European Socialists and the American Promised Land*, New York: Oxford University Press.

Moorhead, James H. (1984), "Between Progress and Apocalypse: A Reassessment of Millennialism in American Religious Thought, 1800–1880," *Journal of American History*, vol 71, no 3, December.

Morgan, Kenneth O. (1976), "The Future of Work: Anglo-American Progressivism 1890–1917," in H.C. Allen and Roger Thompson, eds., *Bicentennial Essays in Anglo-American History*, London: G. Bell and Sons.

Morris, Aldon D. and Carol McClurg Mueller (1992), *Frontiers in Social Movement Theory*, New Haven, Connecticut: Yale University Press.

Mosely Industrial Commission (1903), *Reports of the Delegates*, Manchester, England: Co-operative Printing Society.

Moses, John A. (1982), *Trade Unionism in Germany from Bismarck to Hitler 1869–1933: Volume One 1869–1918*, London: George Prior.

Moss, Jim (1985), *Sound the Trumpets: History of the Labour Movement in South Australia*, Adelaide: Wakefield Press.

Moss, Jim (1992), "The Maritime Strike at Port Adelaide, 1890," in Hagan and Wells (1992).

Muccigrosso, Robert (1994), "New York Has a Ball: The Bradley Martin Extravaganza," *New York History*, vol 75, April.

Mulhall, Michael George (1892), *Dictionary of Statistics*, London: G. Routledge and Sons.

Mullin, Debbie (1993), "The Porous Umbrella of the AFL: Evidence from Nineteenth-Century Labor Bureau Reports on the Establishment of American Unions," PhD dissertation, University of Virginia.

Murphy, D.J. (1975), *Labor in Politics: The State Labor Parties in Australia, 1880–1920*, St Lucia: Queensland University Press.

Murphy, D.J., R.B. Joyce, and Colin A. Hughes, eds. (1970), *Prelude to Power: The Rise of the Labour Party in Queensland, 1885–1915*, Brisbane: The Jacaranda Press.

Murphy, D.J., and R.B. Joyce, eds. (1978), *Queensland Political Portraits 1859–1952*, St Lucia: University of Queensland Press.

Murphy, D.J., ed. (1983), *The Big Strikes: Queensland 1889–1965*, St Lucia: University of Queensland Press.

Murphy, Walter (1962), *Congress and the Courts*, Chicago: University of Chicago Press.

Murrin, John M. (1990), "Religion and Politics in America from the First Settlements to the Civil War," in Noll, ed. (1990).

Nagel, Stuart S. (1965), "Court-Curbing Periods in American History," *Vanderbilt Law Review*, vol 18, no 3, June.

Nairn, Bede (1967), "A Note on a Colonial Treasurer's Resignation," *Historical Studies*, vol 13, no 49, October.

Nairn, N.B. (1967), "The Role of the Trades and Labour Council in New South Wales, 1871–1891," in Margot Beever and F.B. Smith, eds. (1967).

Nairn, Bede (1969), "Brennan, Peter Joseph," in *Australian Dictionary of Biography*, vol 3, 1851–1890, A–C, Melbourne: Melbourne University Press.

Nairn, Bede (1989), *Civilising Capitalism: The Beginnings of the Australian Labor Party*, Melbourne: Melbourne University Press.

Nash, Michael (1982), *Conflict and Accommodation: Coal Miners, Steel Workers, and Socialism, 1890–1920*, Westport, Connecticut: Greenwood Press.

Nelson, Bruce C. (1988), *Beyond the Martyrs*, New Brunswick, New Jersey: Rutgers University Press.

Nelson, Daniel (1995), *Managers and Workers: Origins of the Twentieth-Century Factory System in the United States 1880–1920*, second edition, Madison, Wisconsin: University of Wisconsin Press.

Neto, Octavio Amorim (1997), "Electoral Institutions, Cleavage Structures, and the Number of Parties," *American Journal of Political Science*, vol 41, no 1, January.

Nicholls, Bob (1988), *Colonial Volunteers: The Defence Forces of the Australian Colonies, 1836–1901*, Sydney: Allen and Unwin.

Niles, Russell D. (1966), "The Popular Election of Judges in Historical Perspective," *The Record of the Association of the City of New York*, vol 21, no 8, November.

Noll, Mark A., ed. (1990), *Religion and American Politics*, New York: Oxford University Press.

Noll, Mark A. (1992), *A History of Christianity in the United States and Canada*, Grand Rapids, Michigan: Eerdmans Publishing Co.

Noll, Mark A., et al., eds. (1994), *Evangelicalism: Comparative Studies of Popular Protestantism in North America, the British Isles, and Beyond, 1700–1990*, Oxford: Oxford University Press.

Norst, Marlene J. and Johanna McBride (1988), *Austrians and Australians*, Sydney: Athena Press.

NSW Legislative Assembly (1890), "Police Department (Report for 1889)," *Votes and Proceedings of the NSW Legislative Assembly . . . 1890*, vol VII, pp. 617–19.

NSW Legislative Assembly (1890), "The Late Strike (Report of the Inspector-General of Police)," *Votes and Proceedings of the NSW Legislative Assembly . . . 1890*, vol VII, pp. 627–636.

NSW Legislative Assembly (1892–3), "Broken Hill Strike," *Votes and Proceedings of the NSW Legislative Assembly*, vol 3, 1892–3, pp. 283–309.

NSW Royal Commission on Strikes (1891), *Report of the Royal Commission on Strikes*, Sydney: George Stephen Chapman, Acting Government Printer.

O'Brien, G.M. (1960), *The Australian Police Forces*, Melbourne: Oxford University Press.

O'Connor, Jean E. (1967), "1890-A Turning Point in Labour History: A Reply to Mrs Philipp," in Margot Beever and F.B. Smith, eds. (1967).

O'Farrell, P.J. (1958), "The Australian Socialist League and the Labour Movement, 1887–1891," *Historical Studies*, vol 8, no 30, May.

O'Farrell, P.J. (1962), "The History of the New South Wales Labour Movement, 1880–1910. A Religious Interpretation," *Journal of Religious History*, vol 2, no 2, December.

O'Farrell, Patrick (1969a), *The Catholic Church in Australia: A Short History: 1788–1967*, London: Geoffrey Chapman.

O'Farrell, Patrick, ed. (1969b), *Documents in Australian Catholic History. Vol II: 1884–1968*, London: Geoffrey Chapman.

O'Farrell, Patrick (1976), "Writing the General History of Australian Religion," *Journal of Religious History*, vol 9, no 1, June.

O'Farrell, Patrick (1988), "The Cultural Ambivalence of Australian Religion," in S.L. Goldberg and F.B. Smith, eds., *Australia Cultural History*, Cambridge: Cambridge University Press.

O'Farrell, Patrick (1992), *The Catholic Church and Community: An Australian History*, third revised edition, Sydney: New South Wales University Press.

O'Farrell, Patrick (1993), *The Irish in Australia*, Sydney: University of New South Wales Press.

Oestreicher, Richard (1986), *Solidarity and Fragmentation: Working People and Class Conscience in Detroit, 1875–1900*, Urbana, Illinois: University of Illinois Press.

Oestreicher, Richard (1988), "Urban Working-Class Political Behavior and Theories of American Electoral Politics, 1870–1940," *The Journal of American History*, vol 74, no 4, March.

Orloff, Ann Shola, and Theda Skocpol (1984), "Why Not Equal Protection? Explaining the Politics of Public Social Spending in Britain and the United States, 1880s–1920," *American Sociological Review*, vol 49, December.

Orren, Karen (1987), "Organized Labor and the Invention of Modern Liberalism in the United States," *Studies in American Political Development*, vol 2.

Orren, Karen (1991), *Belated Feudalism: Labor, Law, and Liberal Development in the United States*, Cambridge: Cambridge University Press.

O'Sullivan, E.W. (1890), "Labor in Australasia and Its Relation to Labor in Great Britain," *The Centennial Magazine*, vol 2, no 8, February.

O'Sullivan, E.W. (1892), *Social, Industrial, Political, and Co-operative Associations, etc.*, Sydney: NSW Commission for the World's Columbian Exhibition, Chicago.

Parkes, Henry (1892), *Fifty Years in the Making of Australian History*, vol II, London: Longmans, Green and Co.

Parmet, Robert D. (1981), *Labor and Immigration in Industrial America*, Boston: Twayne Publishers.

Patmore, Greg (1991), *Australian Labour History*, Melbourne: Longman Cheshire.

Pearson, Charles (1892), *National Life and Character*, London: Macmillan.

Peetz, David (1998), *Unions in a Contrary World*, Cambridge: Cambridge University Press.

Pelling, Henry (1965), *Origins of the Labour Party*, second edition, Oxford: Oxford University Press.

Pelling, Henry (1992), *A History of British Trade Unionism*, fifth edition, London: Penguin Books.

Pennsylvania Bureau of Industrial Statistics (1893), *Annual Report of the Secretary of Internal Affairs, Part III, Industrial Statistics*, vol XX, 1892, Harrisburg, Pennsylvania: Edwin K. Meyers, State Printer.

Pennsylvania Bureau of Industrial Statistics (1895), *Annual Report of the Secretary of Internal Affairs, Part III, Industrial Statistics*, vol XXII, 1894, Harrisburg, Pennsylvania: Clarence M. Busch, State Printer.

Perlman, Selig (1923), *A History of Trade Unionism in the United States*, New York: Macmillan.

Perlman, Selig (1928), *A Theory of the Labor Movement*, New York: Kelley.

Pernica, Joseph (1958), "Electoral Systems in New South Wales to 1926: with Special Reference to Proportional Representation," thesis submitted for the degree of Master of Economics, University of Sydney.

Perry, H. Francis (1898), "The Workingman's Alienation from the Church," *American Journal of Sociology*, vol IV.

Phelen, Craig (1994), *Divided Loyalties: The Public and Private Life of Labor Leader John Mitchell*, SUNY Press.

Phelps Brown, E.H., and Margaret H. Browne (1968), *A Century of Pay*, London: Macmillan.

Philipp, June (1967), "1890-The Turning Point in Labour History?" in Margot Beever and F.B. Smith, eds. (1967).

Phillips, W.W. (1969), "Christianity and its Defence in New South Wales circa 1880 to 1890," PhD thesis, Australian National University.

Phillips, Walter (1970), "The Churches and the Sunday Question in Sydney in the 1880s," *Journal of Religious History*, vol 6, no 1.

Phillips, Walter (1972), "Religious Profession and Practice in New South Wales, 1850–1901: The Statistical Evidence," *Historical Studies*, vol 15, no 59, October.

Phillips, Walter (1981), *Defending "A Christian Country": Churchmen and Society in New South Wales in the 1880s and after*, St Lucia: University of Queensland Press.

Phillips, Walter (1982), "Statistics on Churchgoing and Sunday School Attendance in Victoria, 1851–1901," *Australian Historical Statistics*, no 5, May.

Phillips, Walter (1985), "The Social Composition of the Religious Denominations in late Nineteenth Century Australia," *Church Heritage*, vol 4, no 2, September.

Picard, F. (1953), "Henry George and the Labour Split of 1891," *Historical Studies*, vol 6, no 21, November.

Pierce, Bessie Louise (1957), *A History of Chicago: Volume III, The Rise of a Modern City, 1871–1893*, New York: Alfred A. Knopf.

Pierce, Michael (2000), "The Populist President of the American Federation of Labor: The Career of John McBride, 1880–1895," *Labor History*, vol 41, no 1.

Piggin, Stuart (1994), "The American and British Contributions to Evangelicalism in Australia," in Noll *et al.*, eds. (1994).

Piggin, Stuart (1996), *Evangelical Christianity in Australia*, Melbourne: Oxford University Press.

Pike, Douglas (1967), *Paradise of Dissent*, Melbourne: Melbourne University Press.

Plotke, David (1996), *Building a Democratic Political Order*, Cambridge: Cambridge University Press.

Pole, J.R. (1993), *The Pursuit of Equality in American History*, revised edition, Berkeley, California: University of California Press.

Pollack, Norman, ed. (1967), *The Populist Mind*, Indianapolis, Indiana: The Bobbs-Merrill Company.

Pope, David, and Glenn Withers (1994), "Wage Effects of Immigration in Late-Nineteenth Century Australia," in Timothy J. Hatton and Jeffrey G. Williamson, eds., *Migration and the International Labor Market, 1850–1939*, London: Routledge.

Porter, Kirk H. (1918), *A History of Suffrage in the United States*, Chicago: Chicago University Press.

Portus, J.H. (1958), *The Development of Australian Trade Union Law*, Melbourne: Melbourne University Press.

Price, Charles (1963), *Southern Europeans in Australia*, Melbourne: Oxford University Press.

Przeworski, Adam and John Sprague (1986), *Paper Stones: A History of Electoral Socialism*, Chicago: University of Chicago Press.

Queensland Registrar-General (1892), *Census of Queensland, 1891: Report of the Registrar-General*, Brisbane: James C. Beal, Government Printer.

Quinlan, Michael (1989), "'Pre-Arbitral' Labour Legislation in Australia and Its Implications for the Introduction of Compulsory Arbitration," in Macintyre and Mitchell (1989).

Quinlan, Michael (1996), "Regulating Employment in a 'Working Man's Paradise'? The Rise and Slow Decline of Master and Servant Laws in Australia, 1828–1962," unpublished manuscript.

Quinlan, Michael, and Margaret Gardner (1994), "Researching Industrial Relations History: The Development of a Database on Australian Trade Unions, 1825–1900," *Labour History*, no 66, May.

Quinlan, Michael, Margaret Gardner, and Peter Akers (2003), "Reconsidering the Collective Impulse," *Labour/Le Travail*, no 52, Fall.

Quint, Howard H. (1953), *The Forging of American Socialism*, Indianapolis, Indiana: Bobbs-Merrill Company.

Rae, Douglas W. (1971), *The Political Consequences of Electoral Laws*, New Haven, Connecticut: Yale University Press.

Ragin, Charles (1987), *The Comparative Method*, Berkeley, California: University of California Press.

Rawlyk, George A., and Mark A. Noll, eds. (1993), *Amazing Grace*, Grand Rapids, Michigan: Baker Books.

Rayback, Joseph G. (1966), *A History of American Labor*, expanded and updated, New York: The Free Press.

Reeves, W. Pember (1969 [1902]), *State Experiments in Australia and New Zealand*, Melbourne: Macmillan.

Reinders, Robert (1977), "Militia and Public Order in Nineteenth-Century America," *Journal of American Studies*, vol 11, no 1, April.

Reynolds, John F., and Richard L. McCormick (1986), "Outlawing 'Treachery': Split Tickets and Ballot Laws in New York and New Jersey, 1880–1910," *Journal of American History*, vol 72, no 4, March.

Rich, Bennett Milton (1941), *The Presidents and Civil Disorder*, Washington D.C.: Brookings Institution.

Rickard, John (1976), *Class and Politics: New South Wales, Victoria and the Early Commonwealth, 1890–1910*, Canberra: Australian National University Press.

Rickard, John (1984), *H.B. Higgins: The Rebel as Judge*, Sydney: George Allen and Unwin.

Rickard, John (1988), *Australia: A Cultural History*, London: Longman.

Ridge, Martin (1962), *Ignatius Donnelly*, Chicago: University of Chicago Press.

Ritchie, D.G. (1887), *The Moral Function of the State*, London: Women's Printing Society.

Ritchie, David G. (1891), *The Principles of State Interference*, London: Swan Sonnenschein and Co.

Rodgers, Daniel T. (1998), *Atlantic Crossings: Social Politics in a Progressive Age*, Cambridge, Massachusetts: Harvard University Press.

Roediger, David R. (1991), *The Wages of Whiteness: Race and the Making of the American Working Class*, revised edition, London: Verso.

Rogin, Michael (1962), "Voluntarism: The Political Functions of an Antipolitical Doctrine," *Industrial and Labor Relations Review*, vol 15, no 4, July.

Rokkan, Stein (1970), "Electoral Systems" in *Citizens, Elections and Parties*, Oslo: Universitetsforlaget.

Roohan, James Edmund (1976), *American Catholics and the Social Question, 1865–1900*, New York: Arno Press.

Rose, Richard (1974), *Electoral Behavior: A Comparative Handbook*, New York: Free Press.

Rosenbloom, Joshua L. (1998), "Strikebreaking and the Labor Market in the United States, 1881–1894," *The Journal of Economic History*, vol 58, no 1, March.

Rosenstone, Steven J., Roy L. Behr, and Edward H. Lazarus (1984), *Third Parties in America*, Princeton, New Jersey: Princeton University Press.

Ross, Dorothy (1977), "Socialism and American Liberalism: Academic Social Thought in the 1880s," *Perspectives in American History*, vol XI.

Rowse, Tim (1978), *Australian Liberalism and National Character*, Melbourne: Kibble Books.

Roydhouse, Thos. R., and H.J. Taperell (1892), *The Labour Party in New South Wales: A History of its Formation and Legislative Career*, Sydney: Edward, Dunlop and Co.

Ruck, Jerrold G. (1970), "The Effect of the Australian Ballot Reform on Split Ticket Voting: 1876–1908," *American Political Science Review*, vol LXIV, no 4, December.

Salvatore, Nick (1982), *Eugene V. Debs: Citizen and Socialist*, Urbana, Illinois: University of Illinois Press.

Sandeen, Ernest R. (1970), *The Roots of Fundamentalism: British and American Millenarianism 1800–1930*, Chicago: University of Chicago Press.

Sanders, Elizabeth (1999), *Roots of Reform: Farmers, Workers, and the American State 1877–1917*, Chicago: University of Chicago Press.

Saposs, David J. (1933), "The Catholic Church and the Labor Movement," *Modern Monthly*, vol VII, no 4, May.

Sarasohn, David (1989), *The Party of Reform*, Jackson, Mississippi: University Press of Mississippi.

Sartori, Giovanni (1970), "Concept Misformation in Comparative Politics," *American Political Science Review*, vol LXIV, no 4, December.

Sartori, Giovanni (1976), *Parties and Party Systems*, Cambridge: Cambridge University Press.

Sartori, Giovanni (1994), "Compare Why and How: Comparing, Miscomparing, and the Comparative Method," in Mattei Dogan and Ali Kazancigil, eds., *Comparing Nations*, Oxford: Blackwell.

Sassoon, Donald (1996), *One Hundred Years of Socialism*, London: Fontana.

Saunders, Kay (1978), "Masters and Servants: The Queensland Sugar Workers Strike 1911," in Curthoys and Markus, eds. (1978).

Sawer, Marian (2000), "The Ethical State: Social Liberalism and the Critique of Contract," *Australian Historical Studies*, vol 31, no 114, April.

Saxton, Alexander (1971), *The Indispensable Enemy: Labor and the Anti-Chinese Movement in California*, Berkeley, California: University of California Press.

Saxton, Alexander (1990), *The Rise and Fall of the White Republic: Class Politics in Nineteenth-Century America*, London: Verso.

Scates, Bruce (1984), "'Wobblers': Single Taxers in the Labour Movement, Melbourne 1889–1899," *Historical Studies*, vol 21, no 83, October.

Scates, Bruce (1986), "'Millennium or Pandemonium?': Radicalism in the Labour Movement, Sydney, 1889–1899," *Labour History*, no 50, May.

Scates, Bruce (1992), "Gender Household and Community Politics: The 1890 Maritime Strike in Australia and New Zealand," in Hagan and Wells, eds. (1992).

Scates, Bruce (1997), *A New Australia: Citizenship, Radicalism, and the First Republic*, Cambridge: Cambridge University Press.

Scharnau, Ralph William (1973), "Thomas J. Morgan and the United Labor Party of Chicago," *Journal of the Illinois State Historical Society*, vol LXVI, no 1, Spring.

Schattschneider, E.E. (1942), *Party Government*, Westport, Connecticut: Greenwood Press.

Scheinberg, Stephen J. (1963), "Theodore Roosevelt and the A.F. of L.'s Entry into Politics, 1906–1908," *Labor History*, 3.

Schlesinger, Arthur M. (1932), "A Critical Period in American Religion, 1875–1900," *Proceedings of the Massachusetts Historical Society*, vol LXIV, June.

Schlesinger, Arthur M. (1947), *Learning How to Behave: A Historical Study of American Etiquette Books*, New York: Macmillan.

Schneider, Linda Goldstein (1975), *American Nationality and Workers' Consciousness in Industrial Conflict: 1870–1920*, PhD thesis, Columbia University, New York.

Schneirov, Richard (1994), "Rethinking the Relation of Labor to the Politics of Urban Social Reform in Late Nineteenth-Century America: The Case of Chicago," *International Labor and Working-Class History*, no 46, Fall.

Schneirov, Richard (1998), *Labor and Urban Politics: Class Conflict and the Origins of Modern Liberalism in Chicago, 1864–97*, Urbana, Illinois: University of Illinois Press.

Schneirov, Richard, Shelton Stromquist, and Nick Salvatore, eds. (1999), *The Pullman Strike and the Crisis of the 1890s*, Urbana, Illinois: University of Illinois Press.

Schwantes, Carlos A. (1996), *In Mountain Shadows: A History of Idaho*, Lincoln, Nebraska: University of Nebraska Press.

Serle, Geoffrey (1971), *The Rush to be Rich: A History of the Colony of Victoria 1883–1889*, Melbourne: Melbourne University Press.

Seretan, L. Glen (1979), *Daniel DeLeon: The Odyssey of an American Marxist*, Cambridge, Massachusetts: Harvard University Press.

Sexton, Patricia Cayo (1991), *The War on Labor and the Left*, Boulder, Colorado: Westview Press.

Shafer, Byron E. (1991), *Is America Different? A New Look at American Exceptionalism*, Oxford: Clarendon Press.

Shalloo, J.P. (1933), *Private Police: With Special Reference to Pennsylvania*, Philadelphia: The American Academy of Political and Social Science.

Shannon, Fred A. (1936), "The Homestead Act and the Labor Surplus," *American Historical Review*, vol XLI, no 4, July.

Shannon, Fred A. (1966), *The Farmer's Last Frontier: Agriculture, 1860–1897*, New York: Holt, Rinehart and Winston.

Shaw, Wm. Harlan (1982), *American Men's Wear 1861–1982*, Baton Rouge, Louisiana: Oracle Press.

Shefter, Martin (1986), "Trade Unions and Political Machines: The Organization and Disorganization of the American Working-Class in the Late Nineteenth Century," in Ira Katznelson and Aristide R. Zolberg, eds. (1986).

Sheldon, Peter (1989), "In Division Is Strength: Unionism among Sydney Labourers, 1890–1910," *Labour History*, no 56, May.

Shergold, Peter R. (1982), *Working-Class Life: The "American Standard" in Comparative Perspective, 1899–1913*, Pittsburgh: University of Pittsburgh Press.

Shorter, Edward and Charles Tilly (1974), *Strikes in France, 1830–1968*, Cambridge: Cambridge University Press.

Shugart, Matthew Soberg and John M. Carey (1992), *Presidents and Assemblies*, Cambridge: Cambridge University Press.

Silbey, Joel H. (1991), *The American Political Nation, 1838–1893*, Stanford, California: Stanford University Press.

Silva, Ruth C. (1964), "Compared Values of the Single- and the Multi-Member Legislative District," *Western Political Quarterly*, vol 17, September.

Skocpol, Theda (1979), *States and Social Revolutions*, Cambridge: Cambridge University Press.

Skocpol, Theda (1992), *Protecting Soldiers and Mothers: The Political Origins of Social Policy in the United States*, Cambridge, Massachusetts: Belknap Press.

Skocpol, Theda, and Margaret Somers (1980), "The Uses of Comparative History in Macrosocial Inquiry," *Comparative Studies in Society and History*, vol 22.

Skowronek, Stephen (1982), *Building a New American State: The Expansion of National Administrative Capacities, 1877–1920*, Cambridge: Cambridge University Press.

Skowronek, Stephen (1993), *The Politics Presidents Make*, Cambridge, Massachusetts: Belknap Press.

Smith, Bruce (1969 [1925]), *The State Police*, Montclair, New Jersey: Patterson Smith.

Smith, R.W. (1961), *The Coeur d'Alene Mining War of 1892*, Corvallis, Oregon: Oregon State College.

Smith, Rogers M. (1993), "Beyond Tocqueville, Myrdal, and Hartz: The Multiple Traditions in America," *American Political Science Review*, vol 87.

Smith, Rogers M. (1999), "Liberalism and Racism" in Ericson and Green, eds. (1999).

Smith, Timothy L. (1957), *Revivalism and Social Reform*, New York: Abingdon Press.

Snooks, G.D. (1995), "Wealth and Well-Being in Australasia in the Early Twentieth Century," *Australian Economic History Review*, vol XXXV, no 2, September.

Snow, David A., *et al.* (1986), "Frame Alignment Processes, Micromobilization, and Movement Participation," *American Sociological Review*, vol 51.

Snow, David A., and Robert D. Benford (1988), "Ideology, Frame Resonance, and Participant Mobilization," in Bert Klandermans *et al.*, eds. (1988), *International Social Movement Research*, vol 1, Greenwich, Connecticut: JAI Press.

Solomon, R.J. (1988), *The Richest Lode: Broken Hill, 1883–1988*, Sydney: Hale and Iremonger.

Sombart, Werner (1976 [1906]), *Why is there no Socialism in the United States?*, London: Macmillan.

Sombart, Werner (1909), *Socialism and the Social Movement*, London: J.M. Dent and Co.

Somers, Margaret (1989), "Workers of the World, Compare!," *Contemporary Sociology*, vol 18, no 3, May.

Souter, Gavin (1981), *A Peculiar People: William Lane's Australian Utopians in Paraguay*, St Lucia: University of Queensland Press.

Spence, C.H. (1894), "An Australian's Impressions of America," *Harper's New Monthly Magazine*, July.

Spence, W.G. (1892), *The Ethics of New Unionism*, Creswick, Victoria: Martin and Grose.

Spence, W.G. (1909), *Australia's Awakening: Thirty Years in the Life of an Australian Agitator*, Sydney: The Worker Trustees.

Spence, W.G. (1961 [1911]), *History of the A.W.U.*, Sydney: The Worker Trustees.

Spiers, Edward M. (1992), *The Late Victorian Army, 1868–1902*, Manchester, England: Manchester University Press.

Spillman, Lyn (1997), *Nation and Commemoration: Creating National Identities in the United States and Australia*, Cambridge: Cambridge University Press.

Staley, Eugene (1930), *History of the Illinois State Federation of Labor*, Chicago: University of Chicago Press.

Stanley, Peter (1988), "'Soldiers and Fellow-Countrymen' in Colonial Australia," in M. McKernan and M. Browne, eds., *Australia: Two Centuries of War and Peace*, Canberra: Australian War Memorial.

Stanley, Harold W., and Richard G. Niemi (1998), *Vital Statistics on American Politics*, Washington, D.C.: Congressional Quarterly Inc.

Steinmo, Sven H. (1994), "American Exceptionalism Reconsidered: Culture or Institutions?" in Dodd and Jillson, eds. (1994).

Stephens, John D. (1979), *The Transition from Capitalism to Socialism*, London: Macmillan.

Sterns, Peter N., and Daniel J. Walkowitz, eds. (1974), *Workers in the Industrial Revolution: Recent Studies of Labor in the United States and Europe*, New Brunswick, New Jersey: Transaction Books.

Stinchcombe, Arthur L. (1991), "The Conditions of Fruitfulness of Theorizing about Mechanisms in Social Science," *Philosophy of the Social Sciences*, vol 21, no 3, September.

Stromquist, Shelton (1987), *A Generation of Boomers: The Pattern of Railroad Labor Conflict in Nineteenth-Century America*, Urbana, Illinois: University of Illinois Press.

Sumner, William Graham (1883), *What Social Classes Owe to Each Other*, New York: Harper and Brothers.

Sundquist, James L. (1983), *Dynamics of the Party System*, revised edition, Washington D.C.: The Brookings Institution.

Sutcliffe, J.T. (1967 [1921]), *A History of Trade Unionism in Australia*, Melbourne: Macmillan.

Svensen, Stuart (1989), *The Shearers' War: The Story of the 1891 Shearers' Strike*, St Lucia: University of Queensland Press.

Svensen, Stuart (1995), *The Sinews of War: Hard Cash and the 1890 Maritime Strike*, Sydney: University of New South Wales Press.

Swierenga, Robert P. (1990), "Ethnoreligious Political Behaviour in the Mid-Nineteenth Century," in Noll, ed. (1990).

Swinton, John (1892), *Address before the American Federation of Labor Convention*, Washington D.C.: AFL.

Swinton, John (1894), *Striking for Life*, American Manufacturing and Publishing Co.

Taft, Philip (1957), *The A.F. of L. in the Time of Gompers*, New York: Harper and Brothers.

Taft, Philip, and Philip Ross (1969), "American Labor Violence," in Graham and Gurr, eds. (1969).

Tampke, Jurgen (1979), "Pace Setter or Quiet Backwater? German Literature on Australia's Labour Movement and Social Policies, 1890–1914," *Labour History*, no 36, May.

Tampke, Jurgen (1982), *Wunderbar Country: Germans Look at Australia, 1850–1914*, Sydney: Hale and Iremonger.

Tanner, Lindsay (1982), "A Protracted Evolution: Labor in Victorian Politics 1889–1903," *Labour History*, no 42, May.

Tarr, G. Alan, and Mary Cornelia Porter (1988), *State Supreme Courts in State and Nation*, New Haven, Connecticut: Yale University Press.

Tarr, Joel Arthur (1971), *A Study in Boss Politics: William Lorimer of Chicago*, Urbana, Illinois: University of Illinois Press.

Tarrow, Sidney (1994), *Power in Movement*, Cambridge: Cambridge University Press.

Taylor, Alan M. (1994), "Mass Migration to Distant Southern Shores," in Timothy J. Hatton and Jeffrey G. Williamson, eds., *Migration and the International Labor Market, 1850–1939*, London: Routledge.

Thernstrom, Stephan (1964), *Poverty and Progress: Social Mobility in a Nineteenth-Century City*, Cambridge, Massachusetts: Harvard University Press.

Thernstrom, Stephen (1974), "Working-Class Social Mobility in Industrial America," in Stearns and Walkowitz, eds. (1974).

Thernstrom, Stephen (1974), "Socialism and Social Mobility" in Laslett and Lipset, eds. (1974).

Thomas, John L. (1983), *Alternative America: Henry George, Edward Bellamy, Henry Demarest Lloyd, and the Adversary Tradition*, Cambridge, Massachusetts: Belknap Press.

Thomas, Mark (1995), "'A Substantial Australian Superiority?' Anglo-Australian Comparisons of Consumption and Income in the Late Nineteenth Century," *Australian Economic History Review*, vol XXXV, no 2, September.

Thompson, Elaine (1994), *Fair Enough: Egalitarianism in Australia*, Sydney: University of New South Wales Press.

Thompson, Roger C. (1994), *Religion in Australia: A History*, Melbourne: Oxford University Press.

Thorelli, Hans B. (1954), *The Federal Antitrust Policy*, Stockholm: Kungl. Boktryckeriet P.A. Norstedt and Soner.

Thorpe, F.N., ed. (1909), *The Federal and State Constitutions, Colonial Charters, and Other Organic Laws*.

Tichenor, Daniel J. (2002), *Dividing Lines: The Politics of Immigration Control in America*, Princeton, New Jersey: Princeton University Press.

Tilly, Charles, Louise Tilly, and Richard Tilly (1975), *The Rebellious Century: 1830–1930*, London: J.M. Dent and Sons.

Tiryakian, Edward A. (1993), "American Religious Exceptionalism," *Annals of the American Academy of Political and Social Science*, vol 527, May.

TLC (1890), *Report and Balance Sheet of the Trades and Labour Council of New South Wales . . . for the Half-Year ending 30th June, 1890*, Sydney: Higgs and Townsend.

TLC (1891), *Report and Balance Sheet of the Trades and Labour Council of New South Wales . . . for the Half-Year ending 31st December, 1890*, Sydney: Higgs and Townsend.

Tocqueville, Alexis de (1990), *Democracy in America*, New York: Vintage Books.

Todd, Alpheus (1894), *Parliamentary Government in the British Colonies*, London: Longmans, Green and Co.

Tomlins, Christopher L. (1985), *The State and the Unions: Labor Relations, Law, and the Organized Labor Movement in America, 1880–1960*, Cambridge: Cambridge University Press.

Tomlins, Christopher L. (1993), *Law, Labor, and Ideology in the Early American Republic*, Cambridge: Cambridge University Press.

Tregenza, John (1968), *Professor of Democracy: The Life of Charles Henry Pearson, 1830–1894*, Melbourne: Melbourne University Press.

Trivett, J.B. (1912), *The Official Year Book of New South Wales, 1911*, Sydney: NSW Government Printer.

Trivett, J.B. (1913), *The Official Year Book of New South Wales, 1912*, Sydney: NSW Government Printer.

Trivett, J.B. (1914), *The Official Year Book of New South Wales, 1913*, Sydney: NSW Government Printer.

Turner, Fredrick Jackson (1920), *The Frontier in American History*, New York: H. Holt.

Turner, Ian (1965), *Industrial Labour and Politics*, Canberra: ANU Press.

Twain, Mark (1897), *Following the Equator: A Journey Around the World*, Vol 1, New York: Arper and Brothers.

Twopeny, R.E.N. (1883), *Town Life in Australia*, London: Elliot Stock.

United States Bureau of the Census (1975), *Historical Statistics of the United States: Colonial Times to 1970*, Part I, Washington, D.C.: United States Department of Commerce, Bureau of the Census.

United States Census Office (1894a), *Report on Statistics of Churches in the United States at the Eleventh Census: 1890*, Washington, D.C.: Government Printing Office.

United States Census Office (1894b), *Report on Population of the United States at the Eleventh Census: 1890. Part I*, Washington, D.C.: Government Printing Office.

United States Census Office (1897), *Report on Population of the United States at the Eleventh Census: 1890. Part II*, Washington, D.C.: Government Printing Office.

United States Census Office (1902), *Census Reports Vol VII, Twelfth Census of the United States Taken in the Year 1900, Manufactures, Part I*, Washington, D.C.: U.S. Census Office.

United States Census Office (1904), *Special Reports: Occupations at the Twelfth Census*, Washington, D.C.: Government Printing Office.

United States Commissioner of Labor (1896), *Tenth Annual Report of the Commissioner of Labor, 1894*, Washington, D.C.: Government Printing Office.

United States Commissioner of Labor (1901), *Sixteenth Annual Report of the Commissioner of Labor, 1901*, Washington, D.C.: Government Printing Office.

United States Commissioner of Labor (1904), *Eighteenth Annual Report of the Commissioner of Labor, 1903*, Washington, D.C.: Government Printing Office.

United States Industrial Commission (1901), *Reports of the Industrial Commission on Immigration . . . and on Education . . . , Volume XV*, Washington, D.C.: Government Printing Office.

United States Senate Committee on Education and Labor (1885), *Report . . . upon the Relations between Labor and Capital*, Volume I, Washington, D.C.: Government Printing Office.

United States Strike Commission (1895), *Report on the Chicago Strike of June-July 1894*, in Executive Documents of the Senate of the United States for the 3rd Session of the 53rd Congress 1894–95, vol 2, no 7 (Washington, D.C.: Government Printing Office, 1895).

Vamplew, Wray, ed. (1987), *Australians: Historical Statistics*, Sydney: Fairfax, Syme and Weldon Associates.

Van Tine, W. (1973), *The Making of the Labor Bureaucrat: Union Leadership in the United States, 1879–1920*, Amherst, Massachusetts: University of Massachusetts Press.

Verba, Sidney (1967), "Some Dilemmas in Comparative Research," *World Politics*, Vol XX, No 1, October.

Voss, Kim (1993), *The Making of American Exceptionalism: The Knights of Labor and Class Formation in the Nineteenth Century*, Ithaca, New York: Cornell University Press.

Voss, Kim (1996), "The Collapse of a Social Movement: The Interplay of Mobilizing Structures, Framing, and Political Opportunities in the Knights of Labor," in Doug McAdam *et al.* (1996).

Walker, Robin (1968), "The Maritime Strikes in South Australia, 1887 and 1890," *Labour History*, no 14, May.

Walker, Robin (1984), "The New South Wales Police Force, 1862–1900," *Journal of Australian Studies*, no 15, November.

Walker, R.B. (1964), "Presbyterian Church and People in the Colony of New South Wales in the Late Nineteenth Century," *Journal of Religious History*, vol 2, no 1, June.

Walker, R.B. (1969), "Methodism in the 'Paradise of Dissent,' 1837–1900," *Journal of Religious History*, vol 5, no 4, December.

Walker, R.B. (1970), "The Ambiguous Experiment: Agricultural Co-operatives in New South Wales, 1893–1896," *Labour History*, no 18, May.

Walker, R.B. (1986), "Violence in Industrial Conflicts in New South Wales in the Late Nineteenth Century," *Historical Studies*, vol 22, no 86, April.

Wanna, John (1981), *Defence Not Defiance: The Development of Organised Labour in South Australia*, Adelaide: Adelaide College of the Arts and Education.

Wanna, John (1987), "A Paradigm of Consent: Explanations of Working Class Moderation in South Australia," *Labour History*, no 53, November.

Ward, David (1971), *Cities and Immigrants*, New York: Oxford University Press.

Ward, John M. (1973), "Introduction" to R.E.N. Twopeny, *Town Life in Australia*, facsimile edition, Sydney: Sydney University Press.

Ward, Russel (1958), *The Australian Legend*, Melbourne: Oxford University Press.

Ward, Russel (1978), "The Australian Legend Revisited," *Historical Studies*, vol 18, no 71, October.

Ware, Alan (2000), "Anti-Partism and Party Control of Political Reform in the United States: The Case of the Australian Ballot," *British Journal of Political Science*, vol 30, no 1, January.

Webb, Sidney, and Beatrice (1920), *The History of Trade Unionism*, revised edition, New York: Longmans, Green and Co.

Weintraub, Hyman (1959), *Andrew Furuseth*, Berkeley, California: University of California Press.

Whatley, Warren C. (1993), "African-American Strikebreaking from the Civil War to the New Deal," *Social Science History*, vol 17, no 4, October.

White, Richard (1981), *Inventing Australia*, Sydney: Allen and Unwin.

Wiener, Jonathan M. (1979), "Class Structure and Economic Development in the American South, 1865–1955," *American Historical Review*, vol 84, no 4, October.

Wigmore, John H. (1889), *The Australian Ballot System*, second edition, Boston: Boston Book Company.

Wilcox, Craig (1998), *For Hearths and Homes: Citizen Soldiering in Australia, 1854–1945*, Sydney: Allen and Unwin.

Wilding, Michael (1980), "Introduction" in Miller [Lane] (1980), *The Workingman's Paradise*, Sydney: Sydney University Press.

Wilentz, Sean (1984), "Against Exceptionalism: Class Consciousness and the American Labor Movement, 1790–1920," *International Labor and Working-Class History*, no 26, Fall.

Will, Allen Sinclair (1922), *Life of Cardinal Gibbons: Archbishop of Baltimore*, Volume I, New York: E.P. Dutton and Co.

Williamson, Chilton (1960), *American Suffrage: From Property to Democracy, 1760–1860*, Princeton, New Jersey: Princeton University Press.

Williamson, Jeffrey (1995), "The Evolution of Global Labor Markets since 1830," *Explorations in Economic History*, vol 32, no 2, April.

Williamson, Joel (1986), *A Rage for Order: Black/White Relations in the American South since Emancipation*, New York: Oxford University Press.

Wise, B.R. (1892), *Industrial Freedom: A Study in Politics*, London: Cassell and Co.

Wish, Harvey (1939), "The Pullman Strike: A Study in Industrial Warfare," *Journal of the Illinois State Historical Society*, vol XXXII, no 3, September.

Wolman, Leo (1924), *Growth of American Trade Unions, 1880–1923*, New York: National Bureau of Economic Research.

Woodman, Harold D. (1979), "Comments," *American Historical Review*, vol 84, no 4, October.

Woodward, C. Vann (1951), *The Origins of the New South, 1877–1913*, Baton Rouge, Louisiana: Louisiana State University Press.

Wooster, Robert (1993), *Nelson A. Miles and the Twilight of the Frontier Army*, Lincoln, Nebraska: University of Nebraska Press.

Wright, Don, and Eric Clancy (1993), *The Methodists: A History of Methodism in New South Wales*, Sydney: Allen and Unwin.

Wright, J.F.H. (1980), *Mirror of the Nation's Mind*, Sydney: Hale and Iremonger.

Yellen, Samuel (1974 [1936]), *American Labor Struggles, 1877–1934*, New York: Monad Press.

Zamagni, V. (1989), "An International Comparison of Real Industrial Wages, 1890–1913: Methodological Issues and Results," in Peter Scholliers, ed., *Real Wages in 19th and 20th Century Europe: Historical and Comparative Perspectives*, New York: Berg.

Index

PRINCETON STUDIES IN AMERICAN POLITICS

HISTORICAL, INTERNATIONAL, AND COMPARATIVE PERSPECTIVES

Series Editors

Ira Katznelson, Martin Shefter, and Theda Skocpol

Why Is There No Labor Party in the United States? by Robin Archer

Political Foundations of Judicial Supremacy: The Presidency, the Supreme Court, and Constitutional Leadership in U.S. History by Keith E. Whittington

Governing the American State: Congress and the New Federalism by Kimberley S. Johnson

What a Mighty Power We Can Be: African-American Fraternal Groups and the Struggle for Racial Equality by Theda Skocpol, Ariane Liazos, and Marshall Ganz

Filibuster: Obstruction and Lawmaking in the U.S. Senate by Gregory Wawro and Eric Schickler

When Movements Matter: The Townsend Plan and the Rise of Social Security by Edwin Amenta

Disarmed: The Missing Movement for Gun Control in America by Kristin A. Goss

Shaping Race Policy: The United States in Comparative Perspective by Robert C. Lieberman

How Policies Make Citizens: Senior Political Activism and the American Welfare State by Andrea Louise Campbell

Managing the President's Program: Presidential Leadership and Legislative Policy Formulation by Andrew Rudalevige

Shaped by War and Trade: International Influences on American Political Development edited by Ira Katznelson and Martin Shefter

Dividing Lines: The Politics of Immigration Control in America by Daniel J. Tichenor

Dry Bones Rattling: Community Building to Revitalize American Democracy by Mark R. Warren

The Forging of Bureaucratic Autonomy: Reputations, Networks, and Policy Innovations in Executive Agencies, 1862-1928 by Daniel P. Carpenter

Disjointed Pluralism: Institutional Innovation and the Development of the U.S. Congress by Eric Schickler

The Rise of the Agriculture Welfare State: Institutions and Interest Group Power in the United States, France, and Japan by Adam D. Sheingate

In the Shadow of the Garrison State: America's Anti-Statism and Its Cold War Grand Strategy by Aaron L.Friedberg

Stuck in Neutral: Business and the Politics of Human Capital Investment Policy by Cathie Jo Martin

Uneasy Alliances: Race and Party Competition in America by Paul Frymer
Faithful and Fearless: Moving Feminist Protest inside the Church and Military
by Mary Fainsod Katzenstein
Forged Consensus: Science, Technology, and Economic Policy in the United States,
1921-1953 by David M. Hart
Parting at the Crossroads: The Emergence of Health Insurance in the United States
and Canada by Antonia Maion
Bold Relief: Institutional Politics and the Origins of Modern American Social Policy
by Edwin Amenta
The Hidden Welfare State: Tax Expenditures and Social Policy in the United States
by Christopher Howard
Morning Glories: Municipal Reform in the Southwest by Amy Bridges
Imperiled Innocents: Anthony Comstock and Family Reproduction in Victorian
America by Nicola Beisel
The Road to Nowhere: The Genesis of President Clinton's Plan for Health Security
by Jacob Hacker
The Origins of the Urban Crisis: Race and Inequality in Postwar Detroit
by Thomas J. Sugrue
Party Decline in America: Policy, Politics, and the Fiscal State by John J. Coleman
The Power of Separation: American Constitutionalism and the Myth of the Legislative
Veto by Jessica Korn
Why Movements Succeed or Fail: Opportunity, Culture, and the Struggle for Woman
Suffrage by Lee Ann Banaszak
Kindred Strangers: The Uneasy Relationship between Politics and Business in America
by David Vogel
From the Outside In: World War II and the American State
by Bartholomew H. Sparrow
Classifying by Race edited by Paul E. Peterson
Facing Up to the American Dream: Race, Class, and the Soul of the Nation
by Jennifer L. Hochschild
Political Organizations by James Q. Wilson
Social Policy in the United States: Future Possibilities in Historical Perspective
by Theda Skocpol
Experts and Politicians: Reform Challenges to Machine Politics in New York,
Cleveland, and Chicago by Kenneth Finegold
Bound by Our Constitution: Women, Workers, and the Minimum Wage
by Vivien Hart
Prisoners of Myth: The Leadership of the Tennessee Valley Authority, 1933–1990
by Erwin C. Hargrove
Political Parties and the State: The American Historical Experience by Martin Shefter
Politics and Industrialization: Early Railroads in the United States and Prussia
by Colleen A. Dunlavy
The Lincoln Persuasion: Remarking American Liberalism by J. David Greenstone
Labor Visions and State Power: The Origins of Business Unionism in the United States
by Victoria C. Hattam